W9-AFL-161

The Modern German Novel

By the same author

Realism Today: Aspects of the Contemporary West German Novel

The Modern German Novel

Edited by

KEITH BULLIVANT

OSWALD WOLFF BOOKS
BERG PUBLISHERS
Leamington Spa / Hamburg / New York
Distributed exclusively in the US and Canada by
St. Martin's Press, New York

Published in 1987 by
Berg Publishers Limited
24 Binswood Avenue, Leamington Spa, CV32 5SQ, UK
Schenefelder Landstr. 14K, 2000 Hamburg 55, W.-Germany
175 Fifth Avenue/Room 400, New York, NY 10010, USA

British Library Cataloguing in Publication Data

The Modern German novel.—(Oswald Wolff books)
1. German fiction—20th century—History and criticism
I. Bullivant, Keith
833′.914′09 PT1334

ISBN 0–85496–522–X

Library of Congress Cataloging-in-Publication Data

The Modern German novel.

"Oswald Wolff books."
Bibliography: p.
Includes index.
1. German fiction—20th century—History and criticism. I. Bullivant, Keith.
PT772.M593 1987 833′.914 86–32683
ISBN 0–85496–522–X

Printed in Great Britain by Billings of Worcester

Contents

Introduction

In shaping this volume, the editor was faced with two immediate problems of definition: what do we understand by 'modern' and by 'German'? The former, exceedingly elastic, term has been taken to mean, within the context of this volume, the period after 1945, proceeding from what has become a by now natural historical hiatus; it is the novel of this period, too, which has not received in the English-speaking world the attention it merits. 'German' has been interpreted as applying to works written in German and, therefore, the volume concerns itself with four German literatures: West and East German, Austrian and Swiss. It is, however, clearly not possible to do justice to the full range of these literatures and in this respect, as elsewhere, the volume represents a compromise: the selection of individual authors comprises those authors who, in the opinion of the editor, belong to the major novelists of the West German literary scene of recent years, no matter what their provenance, while a number of 'survey' essays attempt to introduce the reader to the range of German literatures.

The period since 1945, now stretching over forty years, has been a very rich one for the German novel, with particularly strong surges being identifiable at the end of the 1950s and in the 1970s. The selection presented here is but the tip of the iceberg, with a whole host of important writers being mentioned only by name, and yet the modern German novel is not well known in the English-speaking world. Böll, Grass and Siegfried Lenz are the names that are probably best known abroad, with Peter Handke and Christa Wolf coming to join them more recently. Others, even Martin Walser, whose highly successful novella *Ein fliehendes Pferd* was quickly remaindered (at a price of 25p!) in England, are hardly known. While certain American publishers are to be congratulated for their efforts to promote the German novel in translation, very little in the way of studies of it and of the major novelists has appeared. English publishers are particularly hesitant, claiming that there is little interest in the German novel amongst the reading public. This chicken-and-egg situation has meant that the great wealth of recent German novel writing has gone unnoticed — and this at a time when the English novel, with certain significant exceptions, has tended to stagnate. It is difficult to know why this is so: the expense of translating is one excuse frequently heard, but Latin American and French literature, for example, do not suffer the same fate; cultural prejudice would also not seem to be a factor, judging by the interest in the New German Cinema and the public fascination with Edgar Reitz's film *Heimat.* It is tempting to suspect that the situation has to do with the difference in the novel traditions, but the critical response to Latin American authors, as well as the relative success of such very different German authors as those named earlier, would go against this notion. There is undoubtedly no single reason as to why the rich seam of recent German novels has been so unfairly neglected, but Germanists clearly have a duty here to proselytise: to this end, quotations throughout this volume have been given in English, as well as in German, and it is hoped that, thereby, general interest in this fascinating body of literature might be stimulated. To make the essays as readable as possible, footnotes have been reduced to a minimum, although the material is in some cases such as to militate against this principle.

Without losing sight of the aim of introducing the modern German novel to a general readership, the contributors to this volume also hope to play some part in the ongoing debates amongst students of German on the state of the novel. The authors dealt with here are, as has been stated, but a selection, and there will undoubtedly be those who would have made a different choice. The volume should be seen, however, in conjunction with other publications in this imprint which attempt to address the rich body of recent German writing, including my own *Realism Today* and the forthcoming *German Literature of the Seventies: Writers and Themes* (ed. K. Bullivant). This latter volume, like the collection of essays presented here, also marks an attempt to bring to together colleagues from across the English-speaking world of German Studies and to help bring about a wider international debate amongst scholars of German literature. I am grateful to those colleagues from North America and Australasia who have supported me in this venture.

Keith Bullivant
Warwick, February 1987

DENNIS TATE

The Novel in the German Democratic Republic

The novel in the GDR is a remarkably homogeneous entity compared to its counterparts in the other German-speaking states. Its emergence, as a distinctive body of fiction displaying originality of narrative structure and critical concern for individual well-being in a far from perfect socialist society, is largely the achievement of the generation of authors who rose to prominence in the early 1960s, notably Christa Wolf, Günter de Bruyn, Brigitte Reimann, Franz Fühmann, Hermann Kant and Irmtraud Morgner. Their overriding preoccupation with the issue of identity derives from the unique complexity of their experience as children of the Third Reich, disorientated further by the repressive operation of Stalinist bureaucracy in the years after the creation of the GDR in 1949, who nevertheless believed that, in this new German socialist state, they could attain the goal of personal wholeness anticipated in the Weimar Classicism of Goethe and Schiller. What is to many fellow-writers in the West an antiquated or illusory notion of identity has been for them a fundamental element in their original, and continuing, commitment to the GDR. This has proved a virtually inexhaustible theme, as the need to take stock, after each critical phase in their own lives, of factors hindering their progress towards ultimate self-realisation has remained imperative, and they have come to employ increasingly subtle narrative methods in fulfilling this acute analytical task which they see themselves undertaking as representative citizens of the Republic. A literature which began with the rather schematic adaptation of the pattern of their early experience to fit the traditional structures of the *Entwicklungsroman* now maturely deploys quite unexpected historical and mythical perspectives to illuminate the gulf still separating them from their utopian projections of the quality of life attainable under socialism.

This definition of the East German novel in qualitative and specific thematic terms excludes virtually everything written before 1960, but there is no real disagreement today, least of all inside the GDR,[1] that the early 1960s mark a cultural watershed, separating

1. See I. Münz-Koenen (ed.), *Literarisches Leben in der DDR (1945–1960)* (Berlin,

this body of fiction from the clichés of the Socialist Realist industrial novel and revealing a new determination to evolve creative priorities outside the framework of SED (Socialist Unity Party) cultural policy. Its authors have come to see themselves as a generation of late developers, deprived of any breadth of literary awareness by the historical circumstances of the 1940s and 1950s and all too willing initially to conform to a cultural policy based on the delusion that the depiction of exemplary socialist personalities — especially in the most widely accessible of genres, the novel — would have a decisive educational impact on a people emerging from the material and psychological chaos left by Hitler's Germany. Literary quality had remained fairly low on the priorities of cultural spokesmen like Alexander Abusch, who, in 1948, had instigated the call for rapidly produced novels on the economic issues of the hour, content that their anticipated inspirational effect would amply compensate for any lack of enduring value.[2] Only gradually did the authors of Christa Wolf's generation realise that they had gone too far in simplifying their portrayal of personality growth and in depicting a state fighting for its economic and political survival as a harmonious community. Looking back at her first novel, *Das Signal steht auf Fahrt* (1959), Irmtraud Morgner acknowledged 'ein naives Streben . . ., alle damals akuten politischen Probleme aufgreifen und lösen zu wollen' ('a naïve endeavour to tackle and solve all the acute political problems of the time'). As early as 1957, Brigitte Reimann admitted privately that she felt repelled by the two stories she had just been encouraged to publish, commenting: 'ich habe sie verstoßen wie mißratene Kinder' ('I have disowned them like wayward children').[3]

There were few works of fiction published in the early years of the GDR which might have helped them to avoid the pitfalls of creative immaturity and political wishful-thinking. Anna Seghers had opted to abandon the montage techniques which made *Das siebte Kreuz* (1942) one of the outstanding novels of the exile years, and until the late 1960s devoted her main energies to producing a Tolstoyan epic chronicling what she saw as the decisive period between 1947 and 1953. The first part, *Die Entscheidung* (1959), may well be 'the most ambitious and effective socialist novel of the Fifties', but it is also a

---

1979), and D. Schlenstedt, *Wirkungsästhetische Analysen: Poetologie und Prosa in der neueren DDR-Literatur* (Berlin, 1979).

2. E. Schubbe (ed.), *Dokumente zur Kunst-, Literatur- und Kulturpolitik der SED*, vol. 1, (Stuttgart, 1972), p. 105.

3. G. Schneider (ed.), *Eröffnungen: Schriftsteller über ihr Erstlingswerk* (Berlin, 1974), p. 208; E. Elten-Krause and W. Lewerenz (eds.), *Brigitte Reimann in ihren Briefen und Tagebüchern* (Berlin, 1983), p. 44.

memorial to the impossibility of containing the complexities of the division of Germany within the framework of the panoramic nineteenth-century novel. As Seghers's biographer, Kurt Batt, pointed out, she is forced to rely on an anachronistic conception of German capitalism in her striving for epic totality, and the work as a whole becomes rather abstract and colourless.[4] Other developments which could have provided a real stimulus were stifled, if only temporarily. Uwe Johnson's *Mutmaßungen über Jakob* (1959), for example, a novel intended for an East German readership but still not published there, presents an obvious contrast to *Die Entscheidung* in its rejection of narratorial omniscience, its presentation of personality as elusive and ultimately unknowable (in the modernist style of a William Faulkner) and in its focus on the division of Germany at a period of intense crisis, the autumn of 1956. Only now, after Johnson's death, is the extent of his eventual influence on works like Christa Wolf's *Nachdenken über Christa T.* (1968) being acknowledged in the GDR, together with a hint of the loss to the East German novel represented by his departure at this stage.[5]

In this situation of reduced awareness of alternative means of introducing greater authenticity into fiction, Wolf's recognition that 'Vergangenheitslosigkeit' (the lack of a sense of the past) was a cardinal weakness of the GDR's officially fostered literature pointed a cautious way forward.[6] The structure of the *Entwicklungsroman* — advocated by Georg Lukács as early as the mid-1930s as a more appropriate vehicle than the Soviet stereotype of Socialist Realism for a distinctive German socialist fiction[7] — seemed initially to offer the best opportunity to use personal experience as a basis for the exemplary portrayal of contemporary equivalents of Goethe's Wilhelm Meister. Günter de Bruyn, for example, attempted to strike an ideologically acceptable compromise in *Der Hohlweg* (1963), taking his protagonist from an identity crisis as a young soldier on the Eastern front to integration as a newly qualified teacher in a village in the Mark Brandenburg. Although he took greater pains than most of his contemporaries not to over-simplify matters, emphasising Wolfgang Weichmantel's intellectual resistance, amidst the ruins of post-war Berlin, to socialist rhetoric, alongside his moral commitment to work for a better world, de Bruyn was later scath-

4. G. Bartram and A. Waine (eds.), *Culture and Society in the GDR* (Dundee, 1984), p. 11; K. Batt, *Anna Seghers* (Leipzig, 1973), pp. 247–73.

5. J. Grambow, 'Heimat in Vergangenen', *Sinn und Form* (Jan. 1986), pp. 136–7.

6. *Neue Deutsche Literatur* (Nov. 1955), p. 159.

7. See the introduction to my book *The East German Novel: Identity, Community, Continuity* (Bath & New York, 1984), pp. 1–11.

ingly self-critical of *Der Hohlweg* as a capitulation to a preconceived patterning of experience.[8] In the same way, Franz Fühmann, who had produced a more autobiographical cycle of stories honestly focusing on his misguided support for Hitler's objectives, was nevertheless soon to find it intolerable that he had ended *Das Judenauto* (1962) on an artificial note of absolute harmonisation of personal and political development, coinciding with the establishment of the GDR in 1949.[9]

The major breakthrough in the East German novel comes when critical presentation of the inadequacies of the new state begins to outweigh the pedagogic enthusiasm to accentuate the symbolic importance of its creation. It was brought about by the crisis of 1961, which culminated in the erection of the Berlin Wall. This act of desperation, needed to create a degree of economic and political stability in a state threatened with disintegration through the draining away of its population to the Federal Republic, generated a mood of determination amongst authors such as Christa Wolf and Brigitte Reimann to introduce 'Lebenswirklichkeit' ('the reality of life') into their portrayal of the GDR.[10] This also meant a decisive change in the communicative function of the novel, in the direction of dialogue with a readership now assumed to be mature enough to think for itself. Wolf's *Der geteilte Himmel* (1963) culminates in a rhetorical declaration by the sympathetic college tutor Schwarzenbach that attitudes must change decisively from this point onwards — a statement with unmistakable literary implications: 'Zum erstenmal sind wir reif, der Wahrheit ins Gesicht zu sehen. Das Schwere nicht in Leicht umdeuten, das Dunkle nicht in Hell . . . Sozialismus, das ist doch keine magische Zauberformel. . . . Die reine nackte Wahrheit, und nur sie, ist auf die Dauer der Schlüssel zum Menschen' ('For the first time we are mature enough to look truth in the eye. To stop making difficult things look easy and the darkness bright . . . socialism really isn't a magic formula. . . . The pure naked truth, and that alone, is in the long term the key to man').

Ironically, from the SED's point of view, a whole group of novels originally conceived in the affirmative terms of the 'Bitterfelder Weg' campaign of 1959 (which brought about an exodus of young writers to the building sites, factories and collective farms of the GDR), but published after 1961, initiated a modest cultural revolution of the

8. Schneider, *Eröffnungen*, pp. 138–43.
9. See Fühmann's afterword to the 1968 (Zurich) edn., p. 221.
10. *Neue Deutsche Literatur* (Oct. 1961), pp. 129–33.

kind the Party had never envisaged. Brigitte Reimann's *Die Geschwister* (1963) and Hermann Kant's *Die Aula* (1965) (where the context of socialist upheaval is educational rather than industrial) are, like *Der geteilte Himmel*, marked by a new quality of subjectivity indicated by the close relationship between their narrators and their protagonists — narrators also prepared to act as mediators between the experience of representative East German citizens and the SED's ideological understanding of events. In the spirit of open investigation proclaimed in *Der geteilte Himmel*, these novels represent a first attempt to assess the self-inflicted damage of the Stalinist 1950s, in terms of the alienation of productive individuals within an inflexible hierarchy of power. (This has remained an acutely sensitive area for further fictional analysis. Some of the most controversial novels of the 1980s — Christoph Hein's *Der fremde Freund* (1982) and *Horns Ende* (1985), or Günter de Bruyn's *Neue Herrlichkeit* (1984) — are those intent on depicting the effects of this intolerance of reasoned dissent, now seen as having had dubiously *petit bourgeois* ramifications, on the children of the 1950s, whose self-protective conformist attitudes now seriously threaten the GDR's long-term socialist aspirations.)

Some of the clichés of Socialist Realism persist in this 'Bitterfelder Weg' fiction, as if to counterbalance the critical force of the portrayal of disaffected citizens like Wolf's Manfred Herrfurth or Reimann's Ulrich Arendt: the idea that the deep-rooted identity problems of the generation brought up in Hitler's Germany would not affect children growing up with the GDR (Rita Seidel in *Der geteilte Himmel*), or the organic sense of community uniting substantial sectors of the working class. These weaknesses do not, however, seriously detract from the fundamental recognition, conveyed through Reimann's Elisabeth Arendt and Kant's Robert Iswall, that self-realisation presupposes a fulfilling private life as well as career achievements. That the superhuman dedication to work displayed by the 'positive heroes' of earlier *Betriebsromane* can actually threaten identity is as much a revelation here as the recognition that the emancipation of women, in terms of career opportunities, compels a radical reconsideration of roles within personal relationships.

The unprecedentedly open, if often bitter, cultural debate which novels like these generated in the GDR between 1963 and 1965 provided ample confirmation of the correctness of their authors' decision to make the contradictions of contemporary socialism the focus of a fiction aspiring to be convincingly realistic. Franz Fühmann's well-publicised letter of March 1964 to the Minister of Culture marks the resultant determination to go the decisive step further, beyond the limits defined even by a more permissive SED cultural policy, by ending the pretence that this aspiration could in future still somehow be reconciled with the conventions of affirmative genres like the *Betriebsroman*.[11] But in a culture governed by a narrowly classical conception of its literary heritage, there was still a paucity of ideas as to how the authenticity of personal experience might be translated into a more attractive plurality of fictional forms.

In this situation Johannes Bobrowski's *Levins Mühle* (1964) proved extraordinarily inspiring, as one of the first East German novels to transcend the parochial horizons of a literature which had hitherto lacked any wider historical perspective on the achievements of the GDR than that of the worst excesses of the Nazi era. Bobrowski's account of communal conflict in a West Prussian village of the 1870s, in which 'ordinary' German settlers assert their ascendancy over their Polish, Jewish and gypsy neighbours, appears deceptively parochial itself, until its continuing significance as a model of ethnic relations — 'ein Modellfall für das Verhalten der Nationalitäten untereinander' — is underlined. The thought that ordinary Germans might still be so pettily vindictive, that the German past cannot be as rapidly overcome ('bewältigt') as the authorities in the GDR might wish to pretend, is left challengingly hanging. Equally importantly, *Levins Mühle* marks the rediscovery of the oral tradition of the narrator, a figure entirely open about his self-doubts in this role, who makes his uncertainties about his own identity — 'wo befinde ich mich?' — into the central motif of his narrative framework, and who has no compunctions about introducing the dimension of fantasy (the 'ghostly apparitions' experienced by grandfather Johann) as a comic *Verfremdungseffekt* into a literature otherwise preoccupied with surface realism.

Bobrowski's innovations, in a widening context of creative experimentation and self-confident openness to West German influences, could have helped to generate an unexpected harvest of East German fiction in the mid-1960s. The ambitious plans of a whole range of authors were seriously disrupted, however, by the most repressive administrative intervention into cultural affairs since the watershed of 1961, at the December 1965 plenum of the SED's Central Committee, when they were reprimanded for undermining public morale by 'popularising' the difficulties of the hour and by raising utopian expectations. Among the significant works of fiction prevented from reaching their East German readership (either

11. *Essays, Gespräche, Aufsätze*, (Rostock, 1983), pp. 7–16.

entirely or for some considerable time) were picaresque novels such as Fritz Rudolf Fries's *Der Weg nach Oobliadooh* and Günter Kunert's *Im Namen der Hüte*, and others seeking to challenge taboos of the Stalinist 1950s; Werner Bräunig's *Der eiserne Vorhang* (which was never completed) and Stefan Heym's first version of what was to become *Fünf Tage im Juni*.

Another group of novels conceived at this stage and published gradually thereafter take up the theme of identity in a less overtly confrontational manner, although they are unmistakably concerned with the threat to personal development represented by a society still failing, in the 1960s, to develop its socialist potential — Wolf's *Nachdenken über Christa T.*, de Bruyn's *Buridans Esel* (1968), Reimann's posthumous *Franziska Linkerhand* (1974), and, to a lesser extent, Kant's *Das Impressum* (1972). Although still broadly concerned with the structure of personality growth in the tradition of the *Entwicklungsroman*, the schematism of works like *Der Hohlweg* has now almost entirely disappeared. The dimension of the reflective narrator is markedly extended, and the complex interplay between narrator and protagonist involves a profound degree of identification, even when, as in *Christa T.*, the protagonist is explicitly not an autobiographical figure. Wolf's novel and *Franziska Linkerhand* in particular achieve through this interplay the quality that Wolf was later to define as 'subjektive Authentizität'.[12] The identity problems of their generation are now seen as being rooted in the belief that an emotional conversion to socialism would allow them somehow to excise their previous 'fascist' self — an idea nurtured by the predilection of older East German authors like J.R. Becher for the concept of a dramatic *Anderswerden*. Only later does the obvious question occur to Wolf's narrator: 'Wie aber trennt man sich von sich selbst?' ('But how do you separate yourself from your own self?'). The long-term effect of this attempt to deny the past on Reimann's Franziska is her sense of being organically divided into two warring personalities, even when she is fully involved in her demanding career as an architect planning the development of her representative Neustadt. Her personal problems are, of course, compounded by her anonymous and chaotic surroundings, which seem to be turning the populace into mindless television addicts — in a total reversal of the image of socialist *Gemeinschaft* Reimann had helped to create in earlier novels like *Ankunft im Alltag* (1961). In the face of recurring frustration at work, difficult personal relation-

12. Interview of 1973 with Hans Kaufmann in C. Wolf, *Fortgesetzter Versuch: Aufsätze, Gespräche, Essays* (Leipzig, 1979), p. 83.

ships and the bleakness of her environment, the positive element now amounts to little more than her refusal to abandon her moral conviction that she will nevertheless someday succeed in reuniting her divided self.

It was Reimann's long fight against cancer rather than the continuing obstructiveness of cultural policy in the years after 1965 which delayed the publication of *Franziska Linkerhand* so considerably, but her grim portrait of life in the GDR's new towns would scarcely have caused less controversy than Wolf's *Christa T.* if it had been completed before 1971, when Erich Honecker replaced Walter Ulbricht as First Secretary of the SED. By the time it was published, in 1974, the cultural climate had changed decisively and there were many no less challenging novels to compare it with. Honecker's famous statement of December 1971 that there would henceforth be no taboos for East German writers firmly rooted in socialism did not, however, in itself stimulate the cultural renaissance of the 1970s. The plurality of narrative styles and the new depth of social analysis associated with the prose writing of this decade could, as already indicated, have been flourishing since the mid-1960s, but had been largely forced underground in the final years of the Ulbricht era. What Honecker did was to license this literature and allow it to rekindle the public debate broken off in 1965.[13] A lot of ground was made up rapidly, but although East German fiction had by now changed out of all recognition since the late 1950s, it remained in some respects curiously dated to its Western readership.

To take the obvious example: Ulrich Plenzdorf's *Die neuen Leiden des jungen W.* (1972), the work which made the most powerful public impact over the decade and was, in turn, imitated by several other East German authors, was essentially a local variant on Salinger's *Catcher in the Rye*, which had been available in a West German translation since 1954.[14] The colloquial freshness of the language of Edgar Wibeau and his fully justified rebelliousness, in the face of insensitive authority at home and at work, were undoubtedly the elements which contributed most to its popular success, but it is disappointing in its simplified presentation of the resulting identity conflict. Despite the apparent modernity of the narrative structure — the quest of those closest to the recently deceased Wibeau to solve the enigma of his personality, in an echo of *Mutmaßungen über Jakob* — Plenzdorf ensures, with the help of Wibeau's posthumous monologues, that the reader knows considerably more. The implication

13. See W. Emmerich, *Kleine Literaturgeschichte der DDR* (Darmstadt, 1981), p. 180.

14. See G. Shaw, 'Escape and Acquiescence: Edgar Wibeau and his followers' in I. Wallace (ed.), *The Adolescent Hero* (Dundee, 1984), pp. 5–17.

is that Wibeau rapidly discovers his 'true' self by isolating himself from the adult world, and is only prevented by a fatal accident from making a productive contribution to society. (It was this simplification of Wibeau's conflict which impelled Volker Braun to write his excellent, and politically more provocative, *Unvollendete Geschichte* (1975).)

Die neuen Leiden is nevertheless one of the few important prose works of the 1970s to focus on the contemporary experience of a range of ordinary citizens with something of the directness and popular accessibility which Socialist Realism was originally intended to have. Many of Plenzdorf's colleagues had, by now, come to share the scepticism expressed by Günter Kunert about any attempt to portray objective social reality in fictional form. In an interview of 1972 he argued that nothing other than the author's perspective on reality ('Bezug zur Wirklichkeit') can legitimately be described, concluding bluntly: 'Jedes Buch, das heute versucht, die Wirklichkeit darzustellen, wäre von vornherein eine Lüge. Die Wirklichkeit ist in ihrer ungeheuren Aufsplitterung, Vielfalt und Interpretationsmöglichkeit gar nicht mehr darstellbar' ('Any book attempting today to portray reality would be, from the outset, a lie. Reality, in its enormous fragmentation, many-sidedness and openness to interpretation, is now totally unportrayable').[15]

Among the authors who, despite these strictures, showed little inclination during the 1970s to accept this judgement were two who had learnt their literary skills well before the GDR's cultural revolution — Stefan Heym and Erich Loest. In the Federal Republic, Heym's *Fünf Tage im Juni* (1974) and *Collin* (1979) enjoyed the political notoriety of banned works demonstrating that there were indeed still taboo subjects in the GDR, although they are — with their predictable characterisation and contrived plots — essentially *Unterhaltungsliteratur* (light fiction) with a static, and at times fatalistic, view of human relations under socialism.[16] Loest's *Es geht seinen Gang* (1978), especially now that the author has provided an account of his battle to have it published,[17] is a more interesting case-study of the dilemma of the SED's cultural apparatus in this relatively liberal decade in the face of conventional realism. Loest explicitly set out 'wie Gottvater' ('like God the Father') to invent the typical young

15. J. Walther (ed.), *Meinetwegen Schmetterlinge: Gespräche mit Schriftstellern* (Berlin, 1973), p. 92.
16. See M. Pender, 'Stefan Heym', in I. Wallace (ed.), *The Writer and Society in the GDR* (Tayport, 1984), pp. 34–51.
17. *Der vierte Zensor: Vom Entstehen und Sterben eines Romans in der DDR* (Cologne, 1984).

East German of the mid-1970s — born like the state itself late in 1949, a son of the Leipzig proletariat now risen to the social respectability of a career as an engineer, living in a standard high-rise apartment with wife and young child, his premature marriage now disintegrating. What is controversial is Wolfgang Wülff's alienation from authority, his lack of career ambition, his striving for the uncomplicated contentment that a stable relationship, modest job satisfaction and leisure time close to nature might bring. For the first-person narrator of this well-crafted novel there are no long-term expectations of self-realisation under socialism: he is simply a cooperative citizen who expects to be allowed to live his own life. The eventual publication of *Es geht seinen Gang*, in the aftermath of the 'Biermann crisis' of 1976–7 (when the decision to expel the GDR's most flamboyant dissident poet provoked a writers' protest unprecedented in its scale and openness), is a reminder that Honecker's cultural policy has retained something of its earlier credibility. The conflict Loest's novel provoked, however, leading as it did to his departure to the Federal Republic in 1981, underlines the paradox that authors whose fiction has many structural features in common with Socialist Realism became more vulnerable to censorship in the 1970s than those whose rejection of conventional forms was a political as well as an aesthetic decision.

The middle generation of East German novelists was, in contrast, able with relative freedom to explore the possibilities of 'subjective authenticity' on a more ambitious scale than the 1960s had permitted. This led them in two quite different, but complementary, directions. Firstly, in works such as Wolf's *Kindheitsmuster* (1976) and Kant's *Der Aufenthalt* (1977) the cyclical process of confronting the contradictions in their own experience is taken a decisive stage further, more deeply into the past, towards a directly autobiographical recollection of childhood, the war years and their immediate aftermath. Although this threatens to explode the formal limits of the novel, neither author adopted the overtly autobiographical approach used by Fühmann in his *22 Tage oder die Hälfte des Lebens* (1973) — and even the latter only regarded the rigorous self-analysis he began in his diary of a visit to Budapest as the groundwork for a massive novel, his *Bergwerkroman*, in which he hoped to interweave his philosophical deliberations with a cycle of mythical and contemporary stories.[18] Kant presented his account of his time as a prisoner

18. Fühmann's plans for this abandoned project are described in the afterword to the posthumous collection of his stories, *Das Ohr des Dionysios* (Rostock, 1985), pp. 151–60.

of war in Poland in the form of a traditional third-person novel, using an autobiographical persona, Mark Niebuhr, rather as he had in *Die Aula*, but now rigorously excluding points of comparison with the present day to ensure intensity and precision in his narrative. Wolf, too, found it essential to invent a persona, Nelly Jordan, to convey her childhood experiences, but within a complex framework in which she separates off other aspects of her self, a second-person voice mediating between past and present, and the reflective first person of the contemporary narrator/author. This open structure was, for Wolf, a personal necessity, since she had in the course of writing *Kindheitsmuster* no sense of a continuous identity, feeling herself physically separated from her childhood self.[19] This makes her novel a compelling investigation into the possibility of reuniting these three parts of her personality and thus achieving, at least momentarily, on this aesthetic plane, at the climax of *Kindheitsmuster*, the reassurance of identity which contemporary life does not otherwise provide.

Reading these two novels in conjunction with the autobiographical fragments of Fühmann's *22 Tage* (or his equally illuminating *Vor Feuerschlünden : Erfahrung mit Trakls Gedicht* of 1982), it becomes clear that these formal differences are less significant than they might appear, and have little bearing on the perception of essential personal issues. There is now a persuasive consensus that there is no date at which the fascist past can be deemed to be 'overcome', that the behaviour patterns established in childhood persist tenaciously, that there were few of the wise educators or moments of spectacular revelation beloved of the *Entwicklungsroman* available to facilitate the transition to socialism (even the aura of death in the rubble of Warsaw, searingly described in *Der Aufenthalt*, makes little immediate impact on a Mark Niebuhr) and that the notion of a pseudo-religious conversion to socialism was a dangerous delusion, encouraging attitudes of guilty subservience rather than moral responsibility. If a point has to be marked at which the East German novel's central theme of identity is being treated with the unblinkered integrity and formal sophistication needed to command international respect, then few would disagree that it has been reached with the publication of *Kindheitsmuster* and *Der Aufenthalt*.

The second major achievement of the 1970s was the elaboration of a historical perspective, from within the cultural heritage of German socialism, which would further expose the falsity of the ideological

19. Wolf, *Fortgesetzter Versuch*, p. 112.

presupposition that the establishment of the GDR in itself marked the dawning of a new era, and point a warning about individual commitment turning to self-destructive despair in a society losing its revolutionary impetus. Johannes Bobrowski had again, with his story *Boehlendorff* (1965), provided an important stimulus, which Christa Wolf developed into a theory of 'epic prose' in her crucial essay of 1968, *Lesen und Schreiben.*[20] Bobrowski had consciously echoed Georg Büchner's *Lenz* — which conveys its theme of personal crisis and psychological breakdown with startling narrative immediacy — in an apparently historical study of an experience which contradicts the complacent assumptions about individual development to which an East German readership nourished on updated *Entwicklungsromane* had become accustomed. Wolf, in turn, not only acknowledged the special force of an intense narrator–protagonist identification transcending historical barriers; she also underlined the specific historical circumstances in which such an identification had achieved unique poignancy — where revolutionary hopes had been crushed in a period of political restoration hostile to individual sensitivities. It was no accident thereafter that a succession of prose works — biographical novels overlapping productively with biographical and critical essays — followed Bobrowski's example in portraying German intellectuals of the French Revolutionary era, such as Hölderlin, Kleist, Jean Paul and Karoline von Günderrode, facing the bleak realisation that their dreams of a new quality of human experience had been shattered by the failure of the Revolution. Some of these works, novels like Gerhard Wolf's *Der arme Hölderlin* (1972) and Christa Wolf's *Kein Ort. Nirgends* (1979), develop the stylistic link with *Lenz*; others, exemplified by Günter de Bruyn's biography, *Das Leben des Jean Paul Friedrich Richter* (1975), ensure that historical consciousness is heightened by explicit narrative commentary. The 'epic' dimension of the prose narratives means that the unsolved conflicts of the period around 1800 re-emerge as a challenge to today's GDR. Bobrowski's 'Wie muß eine Welt für ein moralisches Wesen beschaffen sein?' ('How must a world be constituted for a moral being?') acts as the leitmotif around which the alienation and torment of these victims of history is vividly described, in works persistently questioning the GDR's capacity to become, as the decade's most quoted phrase from *The Communist Manifesto* puts it, a state 'worin die freie Entwicklung eines jeden die Bedingung für die freie Entwicklung aller ist' ('in which the free development of each is the condition for the free develop-

20. *Lesen und Schreiben: Aufsätze* (Berlin, 1972), pp. 204–10.

ment of all').

Illuminating though this historical focus on the GDR has been, it also has evident limitations. It views the stagnation of East German socialism from a perspective which is exclusively German and cultural, presupposing that the reader is as intimately aware of the literary heritage of the Goethe era as the authors themselves. Even where the focus is shifted — to an early eighteenth-century feudal context, for example, in Martin Stade's *Der König und sein Narr* (1975) and Joachim Walther's *Bewerbung bei Hofe* (1982) — the nature of the warning is only marginally modified. With the notable exception of Wolf's portrayal of Karoline von Günderrode in *Kein Ort. Nirgends*, it is male intellectuals who come to grief in a militaristic and increasingly industrialised society dominated by other men, and no way beyond this hegemony of 'male' values is indicated. It has taken a women's literature exploring means of reducing this repressively male society to surmountable proportions, and armed with the weapons of fantasy and myth, to point a more hopeful way forward into the 1980s. Irmtraud Morgner's *Trobadora Beatriz* (1974) exposed the narrowness of the frame of reference of the mainstream GDR novel in the Honecker era, as dramatically as Bobrowski had done with his *Levins Mühle* in the previous decade.[21] Rather than revitalising neglected narrative techniques such as Büchner's free indirect speech in the pursuit of 'subjective authenticity', Morgner created her own species of montage-novel: a heterogeneous collection of short prose offering a variety of perspectives on her main theme. Her feminine aesthetic is intended to reflect the socially determined life-rhythm of ordinary women ('dem gesellschaftlich, nicht biologisch bedingten Lebensrhythmus einer gewöhnlichen Frau'), which obliges Morgner as an author and mother to write in short concentrated bursts. Through her 'fairy-tale' restoration to life of the medieval French *trobadora* Beatriz de Die, who in her twelfth-century lyrics was already anticipating the age when women would become the subjects rather than the objects of history, Morgner created a catalyst for radical change in a society failing to live up to its constitutional promise of sexual equality. Beatriz's experiences in the GDR, the 'promised land' to which she has been attracted as a new domicile, allow Morgner to take what were for East German literature unaccustomed satirical liberties with a variety of manifestations of male dominance, from sexual chauvinism to cultural bureaucracy. Her close friendship with

21. It originated in another novel suppressed in the mid-1960s, *Rumba auf einen Herbst*, excerpts from which form one strand of narrative within the montage.

Laura Salman, a partly autobiographical single parent, offers fresh hope to a personality divided and overburdened by her dual role as tram-driver and mother. Morgner adds an important element to the fictional presentation of the barriers to self-realisation in showing, through the lives of both her protagonists, that women need to be able to enjoy and retain control over their 'Produktivkraft Sexualität' if they wish to achieve identity. She also demonstrates forcefully that there can be no expectation of a genuine socialist revolution until the exploitation of women is brought to an end.

The most striking feature of the East German novel, the way in which established authors have, at each significant stage in its development, adopted broadly similar narrative structures to mark their diminishing confidence in the prospects for self-realisation within the GDR, has again been evident, if in a less clear-cut way, in the early 1980s. Morgner's *Amanda* and Wolf's *Kassandra*, both published in 1983, developed Morgner's feminist thesis from *Trobadora Beatriz* against the rapidly mounting threat of global destruction represented by the renewed arms race and the ecological crisis, which have, as they see it, been inflicted on the world by the insane logic of the confrontation of male-dominated political systems in East and West.[22] Both authors, quite independently, have now turned to mythic themes as the only evidence of how a society governed by feminine values might have functioned, before the rise of patriarchy and the recourse to war to assert political supremacy. Whereas Morgner was attracted to Pandora as the original incarnation of feminist hope, Wolf seized upon Cassandra as an essentially tragic figure at the tail-end of the matriarchal era, warning in vain against the consequences of the new intensity of male militaristic aggression — the carnage of the Greek–Trojan war, as recorded in our oldest surviving work of literature, Homer's *Iliad.*

In this case, however, the narrative treatment of what is jointly perceived as the only remaining source of utopian inspiration for an overwhelmingly threatened world has differed substantially. Morgner's *Amanda* has an extensive framework in which the superpower confrontations and the destruction of natural resources in the course of 1980 is documented by the unconventional narrator-team of Beatriz (reincarnated as a siren after dying at the end of the previous novel) and the well-travelled winged serpent Arke. The

22. For a detailed analysis of these novels, see J.H. Reid, 'Woman, Myth and Magic' in D. Childs (ed.), *Honecker's Germany* (London, 1985), pp. 97–117; for the wider context, see my essay 'Beyond Kulturpolitik: The GDR's established authors and the challenge of the 1980s' in I. Wallace (ed.), *The GDR in the 1980s* (Dundee, 1984), pp. 15–29.

narrative focus is still on the progress, however turbulent, being achieved by Laura Salman through the GDR of the later 1970s, amplified again on a variety of less mundane levels through Morgner's uninhibited flights of fantasy. Defining the structure of *Kassandra* is more problematic, since the four lectures accompanying the fiction, the *Voraussetzungen einer Erzählung*, serve the framework function of providing the personal and political context of the early 1980s, yet are not integrated into the text in any aesthetically satisfactory manner.[23] Cassandra's retrospective inner monologue offers a much bleaker perspective than Morgner's, with the warnings of impending disaster being ignored, as is preordained in the myth, and the demise of what appears to be the only narrative voice imminent. On closer inspection, of course, *Kassandra* relates as intimately to today's GDR as *Amanda*, in its function as what Wolf herself called a 'Schlüsselerzählung', a *roman à clef*.[24] Cassandra's apparently hermetic monologue is actually endowed with more extensive, and urgent, 'epic' significance than the open narrative structure of her earlier *Kein Ort. Nirgends* permitted, with the alienation from 'Trojan' authority of a strikingly autobiographical protagonist underlined through a wealth of deliberate anachronisms in her choice of language and unmistakable echoes of the GDR's cultural-political controversies.

The obvious structural contrasts between *Kassandra* and *Amanda* do not, therefore, imply that the two authors' current assessment of the socialist potential of the GDR (now inescapably judged in its wider international context) differs dramatically — even though Morgner has permitted her readers the morale-boosting relief of a continuing future for Laura and her son Wesselin, with her promise that *Amanda* is only the second part of a trilogy. In both novels male authority appears, behind a transparent allegorical veil, in a more brutal, cynical light than before, directly responsible for the split personality suffered by Laura (her creative *alter ego*, Amanda, is literally severed from her body by the diabolic Kolbuk as she approaches adulthood), and exploiting Cassandra's youthful willingness to serve Troy's propagandist purposes to the extent that she becomes inwardly divided ('gespalten in mir selbst') to an almost fatal degree. Cassandra later loses the entire basis of her earlier sense of identity, when Troy's new security-obsessed regime becomes morally indistinguishable from its Greek counterpart; Laura

23. See A. Stephens, '"Die Verführung der Worte" von *Kindheitsmuster* zu *Kassandra*' in M. Jurgensen (ed.), *Wolf: Darstellung, Deutung, Diskussion* (Berne, 1984), pp. 127–47.

24. *Voraussetzungen einer Erzählung: Kassandra* (Darmstadt, 1983), p. 119.

is gradually persuaded to assist Amanda and her faction of socialist witches in their guerilla campaign against the self-perpetuating rivalry of Kolbuk and his divine mirror-image Zacharias. Cassandra, in the utopian interlude with an 'alternative' community outside the gates of Troy, actually succeeds in achieving her personal ideal of wholeness ('das Glück, ich selbst zu werden'); Laura's reunification with Amanda is a realistic expectation for the sequel to Morgner's novel. The shared hope for a socialist future lies in the moderate feminism which can absorb creative, peace-loving men like Wolf's Anchises and Aeneas, and which, by ending socialist authority's exploitation of women as a class, will find an eventual solution to today's sterile international confrontationism.

In both *Amanda* and *Kassandra* this way forward can only be sketched out, in an allegorical or fantastic remoteness from contemporary realities which strains credibility to the utmost, and yet the ultimate trust in what Morgner can still refer to as 'die Weisheit unserer Weimarer Klassik' ('the wisdom of our Weimar Classicism') somehow survives as an article of socialist faith. This has proven to be the moral source of the continuity of the East German novel over the years since the GDR's watershed of 1961, tenaciously preserved against increasing political odds: the belief that its function must remain that of 'klassische Aufhebung (im Sinne von Bewahrung) des Idealprogramms von der Persönlichkeitsentfaltung im Sozialismus' ('classical preservation of the ideal conception of the unfolding of personality under socialism').[25]

25. Interview with Eva Kaufmann, *Weimarer Beiträge* (Sep. 1984), p. 1499.

MALCOLM PENDER

The German-Swiss Novel Since 1945

Adolf Muschg, speaking to writers and critics in the Federal Republic in 1980, was concerned to correct misconceptions about the contemporary literature of German-speaking Switzerland.[1] Firstly, he dismissed the traditional view that German-Swiss literature is characterised by certain distinct qualities, since that has failed to account for German-Swiss writers, ranging from Robert Walser (1878–1956) to Hermann Burger (born 1942), who possess other qualities. Secondly, the 'problem of Switzerland' — its composition and its political role in Western Europe — is no longer a concern of the younger German-Swiss generation; if these writers address themselves to the immediate environment in their work, it is not to highlight what they find there as being peculiarly Swiss, but, like writers the world over, to examine critically the particular manifestations of general problems. Thirdly, the writer in Zurich does not necessarily have to make a greater adjustment from the spoken to the written language than his colleagues in Ulm or Graz. In short, Muschg concluded that the platitudes long in currency about German-Swiss literature no longer have validity. Whilst Muschg stressed the personal nature of his views, it is legitimate to infer that he did not consider them so eccentric that they could not be delivered to a representative audience outside Switzerland. It is worthwhile tracing in outline the antecedents to the general situation described by Muschg, since the contemporary German-Swiss novel has developed as one of its constituent features.

For Switzerland, without direct experience of fascism or invasion and spared the social upheaval consequent on war, 1945 does not mark such a dramatic turning-point as was the case with most of her European neighbours. None the less, 1945 acts as a suitable point for measuring change in Switzerland for two reasons. Firstly, outside Switzerland, Europe was undergoing radical political and social changes in the wake of the Second World War which were bound to have repercussions on Switzerland. Secondly, 1945 marks the begin-

1. Adolf Muschg, 'Gibt es eine schweizerische Nationalliteratur?', Deutsche Akademie für Sprache und Dichtung, *Jahrbuch 1980* (Heidelberg, 1980), pp. 59–68.

ning of a period of internal assessment.[2] The cessation of hostilities ended the years of isolation during which Switzerland had been thrown back on her own resources, and the fact that the country had emerged intact was seen as a vindication of the values propagated during its encirclement. This powerful impetus imparted to conservative forces in society ensured their supremacy and led to an uninterrupted continuity of political structure and social fabric throughout the 1940s and 1950s. Yet 1945 also represents the point at which the very celebration of these values gave rise to a process of enquiry as to what they represented. It was a process which was very gradually to gather force over a quarter of a century and to which prose literature contributed, initially through a small number of texts published in the 1950s, then more widely through the work of those publishing for the first time in the 1960s. For those publishing for the first time in the 1970s, however, — many of whom had been born after 1945 — the historical conditions affecting their predecessors obtained to a significantly lesser degree, so that the themes of their work are different.

It is generally accepted that *Stiller* (1954) by Max Frisch (b. 1911) is the most important German-Swiss novel since 1945. Not only in its impact on a conservative society, but also thematically and formally, the novel marks a turning-point. It was a contemporary counterpart to the last great statement of the conservative imagination, *Schweizerspiegel* (1938) by Meinrad Inglin (1893–1971). The earlier novel depicts the tensions and difficulties created in *bürgerlich* Switzerland by the First World War, and finds a resolution to these problems by subsuming them under the idea of Switzerland, exhorting thus to a similar act of national faith as political dangers for Switzerland multiplied on the eve of the Second World War. The later novel, on the other hand, finds, in the Swiss society of the cold war, that the past acts as a ballast to forward movement. The hero's anger with Switzerland stems from his involvement with his country and from his perception of what it might be. But just as Swiss society does not wish to hear what the artist of moderate talent has to say and so forces him into an inappropriate role, so his strictures on Switzerland hold no lesson for his listeners. The statement in the epilogue to the novel: 'Er (Stiller) nahm es an, Schweizer zu sein'

2. Hugo Loetscher has discussed this view in several essays, most notably: 'Die intellektuelle Situation der Schweiz von heute', *Deutsche Beiträge zur geistigen Überlieferung*, VII (1972), 260–77; for a more recent statement in English, see 'The Situation of the Swiss Writer after 1945' in John L. Flood (ed.), *Modern Swiss Literature: Unity and Diversity* (London, 1985), pp. 25–38.

('Stiller accepted being Swiss') (III, 757)[3] is thus an ironically negative reversal of the traditional affirmative statement. Thematically, the novel represents the end of a tradition, in that no subsequent novel treated the 'problem of Switzerland' so radically in such a wide framework. Formally, its innovatory role in the German-Swiss novel lies not simply in the shifting perspectives from which an attempt is made to establish the elusive nature of reality, but in its questioning of the medium of language. *Stiller* was to influence subsequent key novels such as *Der Stumme* (1959) by O.F. Walter (b. 1927), *Die Hinterlassenschaft* (1965) by Walter Matthias Diggelmann (1927–79), *Albissers Grund* (1974) by Adolf Muschg (b. 1934) and *Die Rückfahrt* (1977) by E.Y. Meyer (b. 1946).

The influence of Friedrich Dürrenmatt (b. 1921) on the prose writing of his country is less well-known. Dürrenmatt, who was to establish his world reputation with his play *Der Besuch der alten Dame* in 1956, published in 1952 a collection of prose pieces entitled *Die Stadt.* In them, the predominant motifs of caves and labyrinths point forward not only to Dürrenmatt's reworking of these same themes in *Stoffe I–III* (1981), but also to *Abwässer* (1963) by Hugo Loetscher (b. 1929), *Der Kiosk* (1978) by Hans Boesch (b. 1926), *Die verborgenen Gärten* (1982) by Martin R. Dean (b. 1955) and Hermann Burger's *Die künstliche Mutter* (1982).[4] In Dürrenmatt's first use of these motifs in the early 1950s, the powerful apocalyptic visions in which they occur contrast with the outward appearance of a prosperous and well-ordered Switzerland of the time. This work, and Frisch's novel, were isolated phenomena in the 1950s, however. Kurt Guggenheim was publishing his affirmatory four-volume novel on the history of Zurich, *Alles in allem* (1952–5), and a year after *Stiller* appeared, Inglin published a revised version of *Schweizerspiegel* (1955). It is understandable that the writer Urs Widmer (b. 1938) should recall the Switzerland of the 1950s in which he grew up as 'damals ein Land, in dem es keine Alternativen zu geben schien' ('at that time a country in whch there appeared to be no alternatives).[5] Yet Frisch and Dürrenmatt, with their links to the outside world and their growing status there, had demonstrated that they could treat themes relating to Switzerland without being provincial.

The arrival of the so-called 'second generation', writers born in

3. Quotations from Frisch's work refer to Max Frisch, *Gesammelte Werke in zeitlicher Folge*, 6 vols. (Frankfurt, 1976).

4. See Anton Krättli, 'Labyrinthe und Höhlen. Beobachtungen an der deutsch–schweizerischen Gegenwartsliteratur', *Neue Rundschau*, 95 (1984), 71–87.

5. Urs Widmer, '1968' in W.M. Lüdke (ed.), *Nach dem Protest. Literatur im Umbruch* (Frankfurt, 1979), pp. 14–27 (p. 15).

the late 1920s and 1930s and publishing at the beginning of the 1960s, is heralded by the appearance of Walter's *Der Stumme* (1959). The novel takes up the themes of identity and inadequacy of language which are so central to *Stiller*. The drama between father and son is played out against the symbol of change, the new road, on the construction of which they are both engaged. A difference from *Stiller*, which was to set a precedent for the novels of this 'generation', is the narrowing of focus to one locality: here the outskirts of the fictitious town of Jammers, a composite creation with features of other Swiss towns, set in the 'Jurasüdfuß', the area between Biel and Olten in which others such as Jörg Steiner (b. 1930) and Gerhard Meier (b. 1917) were later to set novels. *Der Stumme* is not concerned with the 'problem of Switzerland', but with the problems of life in a given area. A second difference from the almost exclusively *bürgerlich* world of *Stiller* is the setting in the world of work — the detailed depiction of the working and living conditions of the construction gang represent a new departure. Formally, the novel is a reconstruction of the past through memories of the members of the gang, culminating in the macabre mock court at which the son publicly takes upon himself the guilt of the father. Yet, at the moment of recognition and possible reconciliation between the two, the son accidentally brings about the father's death. The symbolism of the struggle between the generations in *Der Stumme* had wider implications in Swiss society at the end of the 1950s and the beginning of the 1960s.

Yet the awareness of wider problems manifested in *Der Stumme* is not widely present in the country itself. 1959 also saw the decisive rejection of female suffrage at Federal level. In the same year the *Zauberformel* (magic formula) was created, an arrangement whereby all major political parties participate in the Bundesrat, the Federal Cabinet. Still in existence today, this ensures that while personnel may change (the first woman member of the Cabinet was introduced in 1985), there is effectively no change of direction to the government, and this exerts a strong conservative influence on Swiss life. In 1962, Dürrenmatt's *Die Physiker* had its successful première, and a year later the electorate, ironically confirming the pessimistic import of the play, rejected the opportunity to ban Swiss use of nuclear weapons. And in respect of literature itself, the conservative influence continues to manifest itself. In 1961 Guggenheim published *Heimat oder Domizil?*, his exhortation to his younger colleagues to affirm Switzerland in their work, and in 1963 Karl Schmid's *Unbehagen im Kleinstaat* appeared, a consideration of a number of past and present literary figures as outsiders to Swiss life.

But if society remained obdurately conservative, a new trend in the German-Swiss novel continued to develop in the early 1960s in the direction taken by *Der Stumme*, confronting that society by evoking in a literary framework the problems of living in it. Jörg Steiner's *Strafarbeit* (1962) describes an attempt by an inmate of an approved school to reconstruct his perceptions of his life prior to his entry to the establishment. From his description it is not clear what is and what is not real in objective terms. Steiner's novel presents, against a firmly drawn local background, the difficulty of defining personal reality, and in the course of the novel it is society, and not the young man, which gradually stands accused. 1962 also saw the publication of Diggelmann's *Das Verhör des Harry Wind*, an examination of the manipulative power of advertising over public opinion, and of *Canto*, by Paul Nizon (b. 1929), a depiction of a potential drop-out from society. In both of Hugo Loetscher's novels, *Abwässer* (1963) and *Die Kranzflechterin* (1964), a central theme is the daily work which bulks so large in the average life.

The appearance of *Die Hinterlassenschaft* in 1965 is the first of three interrelated events in the mid-1960s which mark an important stage in the altering literary climate in German-speaking Switzerland and which therefore have a direct bearing on the development of the novel. *Die Hinterlassenschaft* seeks to come to terms with the immediate Swiss past by investigating the reality of official attitudes to the Nazis and to the Jews during the War and by demonstrating a close link between pro-Nazi attitudes then and virulent anti-Communism later, most notably in the literary reconstruction of an actual persecution in the mid-1950s of a well-known Swiss Communist. The impact of the book in a Switzerland which was beginning to sense change in other directions was sensational, for Diggelmann, despite the faults of the novel and despite his faults in defending it from attack, had breached an important taboo. The book preceded the publication in 1970 of the official, government-commissioned history of the war years, and so played a part in encouraging proper consideration of the genuine dilemma facing the country during the war years, a dilemma which, Frisch claims, finds literary expression in the dichotomy presented in Brecht's *Der gute Mensch von Sezuan* (V, 371).

The second and third events, a public discussion in 1966 on the direction which German-Swiss literature should take and the so-called 'Zürcher Literaturstreit' of the following year, are important because they help to articulate in comprehensive fashion much that had already found individual expression. The public discussion was set in train by Max Frisch enquiring of his younger colleagues if

Switzerland was no longer a theme in their work. Of the replies to Frisch's question that of O.F. Walter reflects the attitude of his generation. Firstly, Walter insists that it is in his own locality that he experiences the world, and that as a result his locality is more important to him than being Swiss: 'Schweizer bin ich in etwa dritter Linie' ('For me being Swiss takes about third place').[6] Secondly, his generation is suspicious of traditional realism because it doubts the ability of language to reflect reality. And thirdly, literature, although it has no direct political effect, is always a political matter and the higher its artistic quality, the greater its social relevance. It was possibly the increasing emergence of this last point which prompted Emil Staiger to launch his attack a few months later on what he perceived as the squalor of modern literature. The 'Zürcher Literaturstreit' to which his speech gave rise is important in the present context for two reasons. Firstly, the controversy marks a stage in the progress in Switzerland of the view that literature must not simply affirm society but, by depicting problems in society, can contribute towards a general discussion of their solution. Secondly, since the controversy spread well beyond Switzerland to the Federal Republic and to Austria, it showed Swiss participants that their views, since they were shared by others, were not peculiar to themselves and so furthered the erosion, set in train by the international reputations of Frisch and Dürrenmatt, of the Swiss inferiority complex in literary matters.

A third international reputation was created in the mid-1960s for Peter Bichsel (b. 1935) by the huge success of his volume of short prose pieces *Eigentlich möchte Frau Blum den Milchmann kennenlernen* (1964), but it is *Die Jahreszeiten* (1967) which is of interest in the present context, since it is the first of three novels published that year which relate in some way to Walter's statement. *Die Jahreszeiten* constitutes the most radical departure from the traditional realism which Walter had called in question. Bichsel's book demonstrates the precarious nature of writing — invented reality reveals itself as too insubstantial, so that, for example, the author comes to the conclusion that his attempts to create his character Kieninger through language show that Kieninger does not exist. Here the distrust of language, which arises in the Swiss writer from the distance between his spoken and written language, concludes that language is a medium which systematises according to its own structures. If the seasons to which the title refers govern the natural

6. O.F. Walter, 'Unbewältigte schweizerische Vergangenheit', *Die Weltwoche*, 11 March 1966.

limitations of human life, the language of the book exemplifies its artificial limitations. In one sense, Adolf Muschg's *Gegenzauber* represents an opposite pole to *Die Jahreszeiten*, since it is characterised by exuberant and virtuoso use of language. A society, in thrall to a belief in an undefined notion of progress which annihilates the environment and seeks to eradicate all manifestations of individuality, is depicted with a verve which it patently lacks. In a highly conformist consumer-orientated Switzerland, the fraud which the small group at the centre of the novel perpetrates underlines the insecurity of a society which basically has no true values. *Noah. Roman einer Konjunktur* by Hugo Loetscher is located in a fictionalised Mesopotamia, but the society he portrays has the same basic characteristics as that of *Gegenzauber*. The ark which Noah creates for his escape from materialist values becomes part of society, an object from which profit can be made. Noah, who had decreed that the world was fit only to be flooded, ruins himself financially. He comes to the realisation that it does not matter who is rescued, since each single individual is representative of the generality. In this representative capacity, the impoverished Noah finally takes over the ark which no-one else wants. It is a conclusion which offers the only spiritual freedom in this society because, ironically, no rains come. Thus, in their different ways, Bichsel, Muschg and Loetscher are commenting on aspects of contemporary society which are recognisable to their readers.

These three novels, all published before 1968, reflect the widening spectrum of the possibilities of contemporary literature discussed by Walter in 1966. Increasingly, a trend in the novel is emerging which is leaving the theme of Switzerland behind and turning towards themes which, while in most cases realised in Swiss locations and in all cases relating in some way to contemporary Swiss society, have a more general validity. Another part of the process of gradual emancipation from historically conditioned attitudes is manifested by the beginnings of a re-assessment of the more immediate German-Swiss literary past, a process which began in the early 1960s with the re-discovery of Robert Walser and Albin Zollinger (1897–1941). An awareness spread that there is a certain line of writers, either neglected during their lives or forgotten after 1945, the reading of whose works permits a revaluation of the tradition in which contemporary novelists are writing. Significantly, in the 1970s the theme of the necessity of re-appraising the past at a personal level, as a prelude to meaningful action in the present, is one which is addressed in several novels, such as *Vorabend* (1975) by Gertrud Leutenegger (b. 1948), *Die Rückfahrt* (1977) by E.Y. Meyer and

Zunehmendes Heimweh (1978) by Silvio Blatter (b. 1946).[7] In retrospect, the adjustments and changes which occurred in the 1960s can be seen as the necessary preparation for the great achievements of the novel in the 1970s.

Yet, if in 1958 Max Frisch could describe the background against which the Swiss writer works as 'eine ziemlich intakte Bürgerlichkeit' ('a fairly intact bourgeoisie') (IV, 250), the situation had not radically altered a decade later, so that, in contrast to the Federal Republic, where the influence of the student movement gave rise to the notion of the death of traditional literature and to a call for a more authentic, documentary literature, 1968 represented very much less of an upheaval, since the conditions for the eruption in West Germany simply were not present in Switzerland. The strength of continuity which had its drawbacks at this point of dramatic introduction of new impulses into German cultural life, later assumes a more positive aspect in that there is in German Switzerland in the 1970s virtually no *Tendenzwende* (change of direction) in literature as there was in the Federal Republic. Indeed, not only are the 1970s characterised by the emergence of a new 'generation' of writers, a word to be understood in terms of first publication rather than of date of birth, but the previous 'generation' continues to publish, as does the 'generation' before that, Frisch with *Montauk* (1975) and *Der Mensch erscheint im Holozän* (1979). The widening consciousness of a Swiss tradition also continues, in critical surveys of aspects of twentieth-century German-Swiss literature, in the publication of anthologies, and, most importantly, in the re-issue of texts long out of print — a process which reaches its culmination in the early 1980s with the publication, under the editorship of Charles Linsmayer, of some thirty volumes of novels and short stories from the period 1890 to 1950.[8] Complementary to this activity was an awakened academic interest in forgotten or neglected authors, the rise of small publishing houses and the advent of an important forum for the serious and committed discussion of literature in *Drehpunkt*, a periodical founded in the late 1960s by the novelists Werner Schmidli (b. 1939) and Christoph Geiser (b. 1949).

From the many distinguished novels which appeared in the 1970s, it is possible to identify certain similarities which point to trends and directions. In the first place, there are, after the anguish of *Stiller* in the 1950s and the very conscious regional commitment of the 1960s,

7. Compare Karl Wagner, 'Dunkelfelder der Ideologien. Anmerkungen zu Schweizer Romanen der Gegenwart', *Literatur und Kritik*, 173/4 (1983), pp. 117–35.

8. Charles Linsmayer (ed.), *Frühling der Gegenwart. Der Schweizer Roman 1890–1950*, 30 vols. (Zürich, 1981–3).

those novels which, much more dispassionately than their predecessors, present new perceptions of Switzerland. One of the first of these novels, E.Y. Meyer's *In Trubschachen* (1973), is set in the Emmental in the small town of the title. Initially, a feeling of well-being is created by the unnamed narrator's description of the solidity of the hotel in which he has put up, of its unflurried routine, and of the very precise geography of the town. Gradually, this feeling is dispelled by the knowledge which he acquires about the economic forces which ruthlessly determine possession of the farms in the surrounding valleys, of the alcoholism and incest there, and, in Trubschachen itself, of the familial tensions and social gradations. The discussions in the hotel on the relationship between a concept of duty and the ethos of a competitive capitalist society set the specifically Swiss situation in the wider context of Western Europe in the second half of the twentieth century. The very precision with which the town has been evoked has given rise to expectations of affirmation, so that the calm, evenly paced demolition of these expectations is at once shocking and convincing. The idyll of Switzerland is irrevocably destroyed: that which, seemingly, was known, is shown to be darkly treacherous and without real foundation. Franz Böni (b. 1952), in his evocations of Swiss countryside and towns, describes in sober language a Switzerland which his characters, constantly on the move and deeply suspicious of their environment, find inhospitable (for example in *Schlatt*, 1979, and *Die Wanderarbeiter*, 1981). The unreality of the literary landscapes is a reflection of increasing disorientation in the real world. With the novels of Christoph Geiser, it is a social aspect of Switzerland which is constructed only to have its hollowness exposed, namely, the life style of the moneyed 'Großbürgertum'. *Grünsee* (1978) and *Brachland* (1980) show, as they create the solid façade, the all-pervading personal impoverishment and insecurity behind it.

Two novels published in 1974, Adolf Muschg's *Albissers Grund* and Werner Schmidli's *Fundplätze*, offer parallels in terms of the relationship between literature and social reality, and present a second feature of novels in the 1970s.[9] Both books create reconstructions of the lives of two contemporaries, one from a *bürgerlich*, the other from a working-class background, who both attempt to break with a social system which they feel to be both repressive and inimical to their needs. Albisser, who has lost his commission in the army, has been discharged from his post as a secondary school teacher and

9. I have drawn on Christoph Geiser's excellent essay, 'Die Wirklichkeit als Mosaik', *Drehpunkt*, 23, (June 1974), pp. 35–43.

who has sought unsuccessfully to establish contact with groups on the fringe of *bürgerlich* society, shoots and wounds Zerutt, a foreign psychiatrist of dubious standing in Switzerland whom he has been attending for therapy. The official investigation into the incident reveals, as it is developed in the course of the novel, a social structure which tolerates only a limited range of approved behaviour in its members, and its gradual implication, not of Albisser, but of the foreigner Zerutt, is indicative of its belief that protest from one of its members can only be a matter of temporary aberration. Accordingly, Albisser is eventually re-integrated into an accepted niche in society. Schuck, the hero of *Fundplätze*, is a young worker who has vanished leaving behind on a rubbish-tip two suitcases of documents pertaining to his life up to that point. The narrator sets out to reconstruct the life of the young man, and gradually a picture of the social pressures which have determined him emerges. In this process, the home, with the figure of the mother who has completely internalised the values and expectations of society, is shown to play a key role. And, as is the case with Albisser, Schuck fails to break this conditioning, for it transpires that he is in fact living in Australia, doing the same kind of work and conducting the same kind of marriage as he would have done had he remained in Switzerland. Thus both novels trace the development of a central figure who returns to play a role in society, but who, in terms of his own inner fulfilment, has capitulated. Pointing back to *Stiller*, who had his designation in the social structure determined in a manner to which his own pusillanimity contributed — and anticipating *Rückfälle* (1978) by Otto Marchi (b. 1942) whose hero, having attempted to break with social patterns, returns to society to become a vehement defender of the status quo — *Albissers Grund* and *Fundplätze* go further in that the final standpoint of each rejects the behaviour of its central character and so seeks to create a dimension of personal responsibility from which the reader can confront reality.

A third feature of the novels of the 1970s is the exploration of life styles which offer alternatives to that of contemporary capitalist society. The best, and best known, of these novels is O.F. Walter's *Die Verwilderung* (1977), which moves on from his chilling description of the incipient breakdown of society as currently constituted in *Die ersten Unruhen* (1972) to consider the difficulties which would be encountered in attempting to set up an alternative life style within the existing framework of society. A young worker and a girl from a *bürgerlich* background who is in the process of abandoning her studies, establish a co-operative, with the somewhat cynical, but increasingly committed involvement of an older journalist. The novel takes the form of an examination of future possibilities and their implications, and is not an account of past activities. With great density of detail, the practicalities of life in such undertaking are envisaged. There are few immediate difficulties with the neighbouring community, but more sinister and unsettling than confrontation is the constant feeling that the experiment is under concealed hostile observation. The belief in the right of the individual to live as he chooses, which sustains the trio in their venture, leads to tensions within the group itself since the girl insists on her right to have a relationship with both men. The young worker is shown seeking to adjust to the operation of the principle of individual choice, which he fully supports in respect of the existence of the co-operative, in an area to which he had not imagined it applied. In this manner, Walter underlines the radical rethinking which a break with traditional attitudes would entail. The collage technique, which was also employed in *Die ersten Unruhen*, here stresses possibilities and not collapse. For example, as the co-operative establishes its feasibility and more members gradually join, a departure from the destructive social attitudes portrayed in Keller's *Romeo und Julia auf dem Dorfe* is suggested by the juxtaposition of the possibilities of the co-operative and sections from the text of Keller's story. The experimental nature of the novel is emphasised by its end, which envisages two possibilities: on the one hand, a hesitant acceptance by the neighbouring community of the co-operative, or, on the other, its violent destruction, despite goodwill from some, by right-wing elements. Hope, however, is contained in the last words of the novel: 'Wir machen doch weiter! ('But we'll carry on!'). This expression of resoluteness is echoed in *Das Ende der bloßen Vermutung* (1978) by Rolf Niederhauser (b. 1951) in which a group of young people set out to test better forms of living together. The novels of Walter and Niederhauser both seek to promote more realistic attitudes in respect of alternative life styles.

While Walter's *Der Stumme* had set its action at the place of work of the central figures, the novel was not primarily concerned with the effect of their working conditions on them. Werner Schmidli's first novels, *Meinetwegen soll es doch schneien* (1967) and *Das Schattenhaus* (1969), form a bridge to later novels in that they portray — with an exactness which derives from the author's own experience — the narrowness of working-class life in the conurbation of Basel. The shallowness and pettiness of the dreams and aspirations which seek to compensate for the constrictions of reality are called in question by the rejection by one character of the way of life to which he is expected to conform. The early work of Silvio Blatter is much more concerned with the deleterious effect on the individual of the experiences and conditions which he undergoes at the actual workplace. Blatter's influential collection of short stories on this theme, *Schaltfehler* (1972), was followed by his novel *Genormte Tage, verschüttete Zeit* (1976). Here is portrayed the last day at the factory of a man who has decided to give up the financial security of his job tending a machine to try to realise himself more fully in the time he will have as an unemployed man. The repetitiveness which characterises his life is shown, not simply in the actions required of him in the factory, but also in his life outside and in the depressing awareness that untold thousands are having the same inauthentic experiences. Emil Zopfi (b. 1943), in two novels, *Jede Minute kostet 33 Franken* (1977) and *Computer für tausendundeine Nächte* (1980), describes the restrictions of the world of computers. Zopfi, who was for a period a member of a 'Werkstatt schreibender Arbeiter' ('workshop of writing workers')[10], describes in the first novel, in a technique reminiscent of *Genormte Tage, verschüttete Zeit*, the experiences, reflections and memories of a computer operator as he works one night-shift. The second novel examines the international dimensions of the computer world and the political intrigues and promotional machinations surrounding the sale of gigantic computer systems. The hero of *Der Technokrat* (1977) by Urs Karpf (b. 1939), is a computer expert who, with his relationship to the countries of the Third World, recalls the hero of Frisch's *Homo Faber* (1957). Whereas with Faber the chief problem was one of personal guilt and identity, in the world of Karpf's novel the belief in the value of technology and progress, not fundamentally questioned in the earlier novel, is undermined by economic recession and by an increasing awareness that raw materials are in finite supply. At the close the hero leaves for the Third World in the hope that his expertise can help to create a better society there. Karpf's *Die Versteinerung* (1981) also deals with shrinking expectations, this time in the more local world of a small Swiss town where the stresses to which the central character, a factory worker, is exposed through the ever-present threat of redundancy as markets shrink, are forcefully drawn. Depictions of a proletarian world in *Schachtelträume* (1974) by Walther Kauer (b. 1935) and of the erosion of work as the basis of village life due to the economic pressure of rich outsiders in *Spätholz* (1976) by the same author can also be mentioned as part of the treatment of a theme which was not previously in the mainstream of German-Swiss novels.

10. See Emil Zopfi, 'Schreiben im Kollektiv', *Drehpunkt*, 40/1 (October 1978) pp. 54–7.

Finally, one of the most interesting features of several novels in the 1970s is the manner in which the individual personality is presented. In Meyer's *In Trubschachen*, the central figure is referred to by the indefinite pronoun 'man' (one). On the one hand, 'man', at odds with expectations of personal identity, represents an attempt to establish such an identity. On the other hand, it is precisely the doubt and ambiguity created by this device which both reflects the main experience of the central figure in Trubschachen and which subverts firmly contoured expectations associated with an idyll in the Swiss countryside. Two other novels which run contrary to expectation in the presentation of individual character are *Schilten* (1976) by Hermann Burger and *Der schnurgerade Kanal* (1977) by Gerhard Meier. Burger's novel, like Meyer's a fiction in an actual location, takes the form of a report to a school inspector by a country school teacher. But the addressee of the report is invoked in discontinuous and disconcerting fashion so that the reader's confidence in the solidity of the fictional reality is undermined, his insecurity in this respect akin to that besetting the school teacher in respect of his own personality. For it transpires that the narrator's name is a pseudonym, a way of trying to look at himself from the outside, but this objectified subject is almost as opaque to himself as if he were someone else. This resistance to definition of personal identity is paralleled by the lack of control over personal destiny manifested in the school teacher's incipient mental illness. Like the protagonist in Frisch's *Der Mensch erscheint im Holozän* (1979) who seeks to reassure himself against the fury of the timeless elements outside his house in the mountains by reminding himself of the sum of man's knowledge to date, the narrator seeks vainly to protect his personality by parading his knowledge on a variety of topics as a form of protection, ultimately as a protection against death itself. In *Der schurgerade Kanal*, the reader's expectations are upset by the diary, the most personal form of expression, which is written in the *man* form, written moreover, not as if the depicted events were being recollected, however soon after they occurred, but as if they were happening simultaneously with the committal to paper. As in *Schilten*, the narrative deals with the presentation of an incapacity, with a figure's failure to find a mode of expression for his own personality, a failure to establish contact with reality, which has blighted his life and led to his suicide. But the framework of the story in which the diary is set suggests that the actual narrator, the writer K, has invented the story as a means of writing out of his own system the failure of contact which led to the invented suicide of the 'man' of the diary. All three novels reflect attempts to come to terms with the inadequacy of traditional narrative means of portraying personality.[11]

The novels of the 1970s, in addition to being considered thematically, can be viewed in relation to the prose writing of the two men who first made a name for German-Swiss writing outside Switzerland after 1945, Frisch and Dürrenmatt.[12] On the one hand, there are those novelists — Muschg, Walter, Kauer, Schmidli and Geiser, for example — who can be associated with the outlook and manner of Frisch. They represent a socially critical psychological realism which in the 1970s is characterised by an increasing concern with the nature of individual subjectivity, and the diary provides the pattern for much of this writing. The extent to which this approach permits a link between the individual and his social and historical circumstances varies from *Albissers Grund*, *Fundplätze* or *Grünsee* which contain penetrating social analyses, to *Gouverneur* (1980) by Gertrud Leutenegger where, in contrast to her highly-acclaimed *Vorabend* (1975), there is little relationship to experienced reality. The stance of the writer to the reader in the work of these novelists emphasises the tentative, cautious nature of writing which is regarded primarily as exploration. On the other hand, there are those writers such as Burger, Walter Vogt (b. 1927) and to some extent E.Y. Meyer and Gerold Späth (b. 1939), who can be associated with the prose writings of Dürrenmatt already mentioned. In this writing, there is a grotesque element which either exaggerates reality or which penetrates behind it, a strong satirical note and an exuberant profusion of language. The writer's stance tends to be one of mockery towards the accepted conventions of literature and society. This view of the novelists of the 1970s in relation to Frisch and Dürrenmatt, together with an awareness of the thematic expansion of their work in the same decade, conveys the broadening of interests within a framework of continuity which set the German-Swiss novel on a course which it is still following in the 1980s.

As has already been seen, however, there are retarding factors in Swiss society which act as a brake on the inevitability of gradualism there which might arguably be stimulated by the impact of litera-

11. For a stimulating discussion of the presentation of the individual in the work of six German-Swiss novelists, see Gerda Zeltner, *Das Ich ohne Gewähr. Gegenwartsautoren aus der Schweiz* (Zurich/Frankfurt, 1980).

12. The following groupings are suggested by Klaus Pezold in 'Die deutschsprachige Literatur der Schweiz in den sechziger und siebziger Jahren. Probleme, Thesen und offene Fragen', *Entwicklungstendenzen der deutschsprachigen Literatur der Schweiz in den sechziger und siebziger Jahren* (Karl-Marx-Universität, Leipzig, 1984), pp. 7–40 (pp. 30–2).

ture. The 1980s opened with one such example. The demonstrations and protests which started at the Zürich opera house in the summer of 1980 and lasted well into 1981 had no success in changing structures permanently and every success in reinforcing narrow and intolerant attitudes. *Zürich, Anfang September* (1981) by Reto Hänny (b. 1947) describes the implications of these attitudes in terms of their translation into action by the authorities. A year before, Gerold Späth's great novel *Commedia* (1980) had appeared. Significantly omitting Paradise from the structure modelled on Dante's *Divine Comedy*, and reversing the order of the other two sections so that the novel depicts a descent from Purgatory into Hell, Späth presents a panorama of modern Switzerland. The structure of the novel emphasises individual isolation and at every turn the enormous pressure to achieve socially approved goals and to participate in the consumer society is highlighted. Emotion and thought, art and knowledge have all been corrupted in the service of this destructive society. The life force of sex is presented as repressed, perverted or commercialised, at no point as liberating, and death is rendered all the more pervasive by having been made the great taboo: 'Der Tumor sind wir' says a character ('We are the tumour'),[13] a *reprise* of the thesis offered in *Mars* (1977) by Fritz Zorn (1944–76) that his own terminal cancer was a direct result of life-denying social attitudes in his moneyed *bürgerlich* background.

The 1980s has seen, in respect of the novel, a continuation of the productivity of the 1970s. The 'classics' Frisch and Dürrenmatt have both published: the former, *Blaubart* (1982), while with *Stoffe I–III* (1981) Dürrenmatt has added a significant contribution to his *oeuvre*. The second generation has published: first, and notably, Jürg Federspiel (b. 1931), *Die Ballade von Typhoid Mary* (1982); Loetscher, *Herbst in der großen Orange* (1982); Walter, *Das Staunen der Schlafwandler am Ende der Nacht* (1983); and Muschg, *Das Licht und der Schlüssel* (1984). The third generation have been equally productive with, for example: Gerhard Meier, *Borodino* (1982) and *Die Ballade vom Schneien* (1986); Geiser, *Wüstenfahrt* (1984); and Schmidli, *Warum werden Bäume im Alter schöner* (1984) and *Der Mann am See* (1985). In addition, the women writers who had started to publish in the 1970s (for example, Margit Baur (b. 1937), Maja Beutler (b. 1936) and Margrit Schriber (b. 1939)) continued to publish as did the best known amongst them, Erica Pedretti (b. 1930, winner of the Ingeborg Bachmann prize in 1984) with *Valerie oder Das unerzogene Auge* (1986). The 1980s, moreover, appear to be following the pattern of

13. Gerold Späth, *Commedia* (Frankfurt, 1983), p.167.

previous decades in that the advent of another new generation (the fourth since 1945) has been hailed,[14] members of which are Jürg Amann (b. 1947), Martin R. Dean, Marcel Konrad (b. 1954) and Beat Sterchi (b. 1949) whose much acclaimed novel *Blösch* (1983) depicts far-reaching changes in the Swiss countryside.

The developments of the novel since 1945 substantiate the claim advanced by Adolf Muschg that German-Swiss literature has altered from traditional perceptions. Change is associated with the fact that the 'problem of Switzerland' has been left behind as a theme. This restrictive legacy of the 1930s, 1940s and 1950s, challenged in the 1960s, no longer holds sway.The fear of being provincial, which beset Zollinger up to his death at the beginning of the War and which characterised the concerns of Frisch in his middle years, has given way to a recognition that the concept of province is either everywhere or nowhere. Not only do the circumstances which gave rise to the inferiority complex no longer obtain, the political situation in German-speaking Europe since 1945 has been such that there is no acknowledged cultural centre which sets prescriptive standards. As a consequence, there is a greater acceptance of cultural differences, so that a large number of German-Swiss novels are now published in the Federal Republic without the authors having to make undue concessions in respect of characteristics which indicate their origin. Important too for the self-perception of writers in Switzerland has been the gradual re-discovery of a tradition of novel writing which was far from being affirmative of the social order in Switzerland, and this reinforced the increasing conviction that the novel should have social relevance. Certainly, the society in which novels are written is still in the mid-1980s a conservative one, which is not without a bearing on the relatively modest formal experiments in the German-Swiss novel. And the sheer vitality of the novel over the last fifteen years raises the question as to its effect on general attitudes in this society. Urs Widmer, returning to Switzerland in 1985 after living in the Federal Republic for almost twenty years, is struck by the manner in which his countrymen see themselves as having links to the land — each considers himself to be a 'Bauer' (farmer); although this self-image is no barrier to the creation of literature, it might constitute an impediment to its reception: 'Bauern! — können durchaus Schriftsteller werden: man kann beim Schreiben so schwitzen, daß es einer Arbeit gleicht. Aber wie soll ein Bauer ein *Leser* werden? Gedachtes mitdenken, Geträumtes

14. See Hans Wysling, 'Zum Deutschschweizer Roman von 1945 bis zur Gegenwart', *Schweizer Monatshefte*, 64 (1984), pp. 335–47.

nachträumen?' ('Farmers! It's alright for farmers to become writers: writing can make you sweat so that it's like work. But how is a farmer to become a *reader*? To think through thoughts, to dream through dreams?').[15] Widmer's ironic formulation of the nature of the resistance in Switzerland to the influence of literature contains a challenge for the German-Swiss novel.

15. Urs Widmer, 'Heimgekehrt ins Land der Kuh', *Merkur*, 19 (1985), pp. 1084–8 (p. 1085).

SIMON RYAN

New Directions in the Austrian Novel

Even a brief sampling of the novels produced by Austrian writers since 1960 reveals an extraordinary thematic and stylistic diversity. Recent critical studies have highlighted the importance of the contribution made by Austrian novelists to the overall development of the German novel in the past two decades.[1] It can be argued that a disproportionate number of the leading exponents of the novel form at the present time are Austrian citizens. Peter Handke still remains internationally the most widely known of these authors followed closely by Thomas Bernhard, but the recent history of the German novel would be much impoverished without the novels of Konrad Bayer, Oswalk Wiener, Andreas Okopenko, Ingeborg Bachmann, Alfred Kolleritsch, Barbara Frischmuth, Gert Jonke, Michael Scharang, Gerhard Roth, Helmut Eisendle, Franz Innerhofer, Elfriede Jelinek, Brigitte Schwaiger, and Klaus Hoffer, to name only some of those whose reputations are already well established outside Austria.

Towards the end of the 1950s this was far from being the case. Between 1945 and the emergence of a younger generation of Austrian writers in the mid-1960s, the novel form was dominated in Austria by the monumental epic constructions of Heimito von Doderer (*Die erleuchteten Fenster*, 1950; *Die Strudlhofstiege*, 1951; *Die Dämonen*, 1956); Albert Paris Gütersloh (*Sonne und Mond*, 1962); and George Saiko (*Auf dem Floß*, 1945; *Der Mann im Schilf*, 1955). In their work, much of which was already written or at least conceived in the 1930s, the preoccupations of classical Modernist fiction continue to guide and shape the narrative. The vast cultural sweep of these novels, the intensity with which they strive to become total works of art, and their effort to build a bridge between an often idealised

1. See, for example: Ulrich Greiner, *Der Tod des Nachsommers: Aufsätze, Porträts, Kritiken zur österreichischen Gegenwartsliteratur* (Munich, 1979); Peter Laemmle and Jörg Drews (eds.), *Wie die Grazer auszogen, die Literatur zu erobern: Texte, Porträts, Analysen und Dokumente junger österreichischer Autoren*, 2nd rev. edn. (Munich, 1979); Walter Weiß, 'Die Literatur der Gegenwart in Österreich' in Manfred Durzak (ed.), *Deutsche Gegenwartsliteratur — Ausgangspositionen und aktuelle Entwicklungen* (Stuttgart, 1981), pp. 602–19.

Habsburg past and the new, post-war Austria all serve to contrast them with novels which appear after 1960. In terms of the cultural realities of the emerging Second Republic and international tendencies in art, the aesthetic on which these novels were based was retrospective. Their literary achievement remains overshadowed by that of Musil and Broch although their work was little read in Austria at the time.

The cultural climate which prevailed during the early years of the Second Republic was oppressive. The gaze of Austria's cultural establishment, including the majority of authors and critics, was almost hypnotically fixed in contemplation of a fertile 'Habsburg myth'. Claudio Magris[2] has unmasked this persistence of the 'Austrian idea' in the 1950s as a form of cultural inertia arising from an inability to come to terms with the more mundane or disquieting realities of the present. A quasi-mystical absorption in the vision of Austria's rich cultural tradition — 'das Große Erbe' (the Great Heritage) — was believed to be capable of restoring the spiritual harmony shattered by the collapse of the First Republic and the subsequent National Socialist interregnum. A policy of 'Austrianism' was widely promulgated in the 1950s by such official cultural organs as *Forum* and *Wort in der Zeit.* It was an attempt to uncover a specifically Austrian literary tradition, primarily to dispel the guilt and anxiety caused by the nearly fatal recent merger with a more sinister 'Greater-German Tradition'. Authors and critics set out to promote the 'timeless and enduring qualities' of Austrian literature and to create a separate Austrian identity.

For Doderer, Gütersloh, and Saiko, all of whom were born before the turn of the century, there was no contradiction between their artistic aims and this concentration on a spiritual reconstruction of a greater past: they had experienced the final years of the Habsburg era at first hand and could now draw on it creatively. (Doderer and Gütersloh were in fact among the few artists who actively encouraged avant-garde literary experiments in the 1950s.) But for younger novelists of the middle generation the restaurative tendency of 'Austrianism' proved to be a fatal lure which stifled their own creativity and arrested the development of the Austrian novel at a time when other European literatures were engaged in productive experimentation.

The initial failure of the post-war Austrian novel to break with an

2. Claudio Magris, *Der hapsburgische Mythos in der österreichischen Literatur* (Salzburg 1966). See also his essay, 'Der unauffindbare Sinn. Zur österreichischen Literatur des 20. Jahrhunderts in *Klagenfurter Universitätsreden*, Heft 9, 1978.

oppressive past and confront the new, post-Habsburg world is clearly evident in the novels Herbert Eisenreich (b. 1925) and Gerhard Fritsch (1924–69) published in the 1950s. A sense of inertia predominates in Eisenreich's first novel, *Auch in ihrer Sünde* (1953). The narrative follows the progress of a revolutionary's widow through the harrowing years of the First Republic, the dictatorship and the war. The novel is only vaguely structured and top-heavy with flash-backs and passages of agonised reflection as the protagonist, Viktoria Baumann, struggles to establish a balance between individual and collective guilt for the tragic events of her life. Eisenreich's theoretical essays on the art of the novel (*Reaktionen: Essays zur Literatur*, 1964) reveal the influence of Doderer in their advocacy of the totality of art. The associated vision of the artist striving to create a personal order in a chaotic world places Eiseneich firmly in the idealist tradition of Austrian literature which looks back to Stifter and views the present in terms of cultural decline. As a leading member of Austria's conservative PEN Club Eisenreich has continued to take a conservative line, supporting the idea of an unbroken tradition in Austrian literary history from the time of Grillparzer onwards, a view with which many of the following generation have strongly disagreed.

Fritsch was a more contradictory proponent of the novel form. In the 1950s he remained faithful to the idealist version of the Great Austrian Tradition. In *Moos auf den Steinen* (1956) he produced the novel which Eisenreich greeted as the most representative work of his generation. More recently Hans Wolfschütz described the same novel as the 'Höhepunkt seiner emotionalen Regression in die Welt des Alten Österreichs . . .' ('the climax of his emotional regression into the world of old Austria . . .').[3] The stones of the title belong to a crumbling Baroque castle inhabited by a retired major of the imperial army and his daughter. The plot and the fate of the too obviously symbolic castle hinge on the daughter's pending decision as to which of two, equally symbolic, suitors she will agree to marry. One, who wants to turn the old castle into a modern cultural centre, she eventually rejects. But tragically, the other, who shares her reverence for the timeless traditions of the old world, is killed in an accident.

Viewed now with the hindsight of what was to become of the Austrian novel only a few years hence, *Moos auf den Steinen* reads almost as a self-parody of 'Austrianism'. Fritsch himself was soon to

3. Hans Wolfschütz, 'Gerhard Fritsch' in Heinz Ludwig Arnold (ed.), *Kritisches Lexikon zur deutschsprachigen Gegenwartsliteratur* (KLG) (Munich, 1979ff.), p. 5.

see through this negative attachment to the past and proceeded to reverse his earlier position. In 1963 he identified the essential components of this traditionalism as 'sentimentality, illusory escape into the past', 'pseudo-redemption', and 'fixation on death'.[4] In a later novel, *Fasching* (1967), Fritsch openly satirises the same Austrian tradition, describing it not as a repository of enduring values but as an insular and hypocritical form of escapism which was reducing Austrian culture to the level of a mean-spirited provincialism.

Anyone searching the 'New Releases' shelves of even the most progressive Viennese bookshop at the end of the 1950s might well have concluded that the Austrian novel was rapidly fossilising. Austria's small publishing industry was highly conservative. Publishers like the Otto Müller Verlag and Stiasny Bücherei who derived much of their income from a thriving trade in Austrian *Heimatliteratur* were positively discouraging to authors interested in experimentation. It is no accident that nearly all of Austria's leading contemporary novelists were first published across the border in West Germany. Until very recently the Second Republic has provided its authors with almost none of the opportunities afforded by the unique and not infrequently envied network of literary communications which constititutes the West German *Literaturbetrieb*. The risks which highly professional publishers like Suhrkamp and Rowohlt were prepared to take with the work of unknown young authors were anathema in Austria. Nor were Austrian literary critics prepared to bring to the attention of the reading public literary works which seriously challenged the status quo. This situation has been bitterly lamented by Austrian authors.

The indifference with which major post-war Austrian authors have been treated by Austrian publishers is not economic in origin. It is itself symptomatic of the 'geistige Provinzialismus' (Kolleritsch: 'intellectual provincialism') which was particularly rife in the early years of the Second Republic. Scharang ironically described his situation as that of a 'Gastarbeiter, der zwar sein Land nicht verlassen mußte, der aber nichtdestoweniger im Ausland sein Geld verdiente, um im eigenen Land leben zu können ('foreign worker who admittedly didn't have to leave his country, but was nevertheless earning his money abroad, to be able to live in his own

4. Walter Weiß, 'Die Literatur der Gegenwart in Österreich', p. 609. Full text of this translated extract (Weiß refers to Fritsch's poem 'Bilanz'): ' . . . Absage an die "traditionelle Gesinnung" als Sentimentalität, als illusionäre Flucht in die Vergangenheit, als Pseudoerlösung, als Fixierung auf den Tod'.

country').[5] The appearance on the scene of Salzburg's small but determined Rezidenz Verlag at the end of the 1960s and the founding of other small presses like the Verlag Droschl in Graz have only slightly lessened the dependence of Austrian novelists on income from West German publishers. In the 1950s the inevitable consequence was that those engaged in the search for the new were driven underground. The first signs that the Austrian novel would make a radical break with tradition appear in the experimental prose of that offshoot of the 'Wiener Artclub' which became known in the early 1950s as the 'Wiener Gruppe'. Before discussing this avant-garde branch of the recent Austrian novel, however, it is necessary to outline the general pattern of development after 1960.

At the beginning of the 1960s frustration with the parochial attitudes of the conservative old guard who controlled Austrian cultural affairs came to a head. The cultural history of the decade is marked by a series of bitter confrontations over the urgent need for change and renewal in the arts.[6] Within a few years the Austrian novel found itself in the hands of a much younger generation who were determined that it should become a vehicle, not only for charting the realities of life in the very different society of the Second Republic, but for genuine literary experiment as well. A key event which acted as a powerful catalyst for change in Austrian writing was the founding in Graz of the decidedly anti-traditionalist artists organisation Forum Stadtpark in November 1960. It was through readings and performances arranged by Forum Stadtpark and in the pages of its long-surviving publication *manuskripte* that novelists like Handke, Frischmuth, Scharang, Jonke, Roth, Kolleritsch, Eisendle, and Hoffer, along with members of the 'Wiener Gruppe' and other literary artists of note, reached their initial audience and attracted the attention of the West German publishers and critics on whom their livelihood depended. Austrian literature appears to have been destined, both historically and geographically, to experience its difficult rebirth in

5. Michael Scharang, 'Modellathlet Deutschland', *manuskripte*, 76 (1982), pp. 3–9. This quote p. 3.

6. Useful sources on the cultural politics of the period include: Manfred Mixner, 'Ausbruch aus der Provinz' in Laemmle and 'Drews (eds.), *Wie die Grazer auszogen, die Literatur zu erobern*, p. 13–28; Erika Weinzierl and Kurt Skalnik (eds.), *Das neue Österreich. Geschichte der Zweiten Republik* (Graz, 1975) (Wieland Schmied's essay 'Bildende Kunst' is particularly revealing on Austria's cultural malaise); Heinz Fischer (ed.), *Das politische System Österreichs*, 2nd edn. (Vienna, 1979); Elizabeth Wiesmayr, *Die Zeitschrift 'manuskripte' 1960–1970* (Dissertation) (Königstein, 1980).

that most reactionary of all cities, '. . . in Graz, das wirklich die "moderne Kunst" hysterisch ablehnt . . .' ('in Graz which hysterically rejects "modern art"').[7]

The arguments for a new literature written to oppose the 'Mystifikation einer Nationalliteratur' ('mystique of a national literature') and the dangers of a cultural-political situation 'in das immer mehr braune Luft einströmt'[8] ('into which more and more brown air is flowing') can be traced through Kolleritsch's editorial 'marginalien' in *manuskripte*. The specific targets of the polemic were the policy of 'Austrianism' and the resurgence of an unrepentant *Heimatliteratur* of the *Blut und Boden* variety — alongside the merely conservative novels of Peter Rosegger, Karl-Heinz Waggerl, and Paula Grogger, there flourished the more ideologically poisonous works of authors like Bruno Behm and Joseph Papesch. In 1961 under Fritsch's editorship — his new open-mindedness soon got him sacked — the relatively conservative *Wort in der Zeit* published Humbert Fink's essay 'Warm und zufrieden im Provinziellen?' ('Cosy and contented in your parochialism?') which accused practising novelists of neglecting the real problems of life in post-war Austria. The prose which began to appear in *manuskripte* represented a more radical response to the situation than Fink himself perhaps at first envisaged but left no doubt that younger authors were taking positive issue with Austria's cultural inertia.

By the end of the decade a sufficient number of new novels had been produced to enable a configuration of types to be discerned. Writers closely associated at the time with Forum Stadtpark and *manuskripte* — Kolleritch, Handke, Frischmuth, Hoffer, Eisendle, Roth, Jonke, and Scharang — tended to favour the formalist pole of the realist/formalist opposition. The early novels of these authors identified as the so-called 'Grazer Gruppe'[9] are all characterised by

7. Alfred Kolleritsch in a letter to Peter Hamm, 10 May 1963. This quotation from Wiesmayr, *Die Zeitschrift 'manuskripte' 1960–1970*, p. 35.

8. Alfred Kolleritsch in a letter to Hans Magnus Enzensberger in 1963. This quotation: Wiesmayr, p. 30.

9. The exact nature and criteria for 'membership' of the 'sogenannte Grazer Gruppe' is a matter of literary–historical dispute. In terms of Helmut Kreuzer's definition of 'formal' and 'informal' group formation amongst bohemian and avant-garde artists, the 'Grazer Gruppe' corresponds to the informal type. (Cf. Helmut Kreuzer, *Die Boheme: Analyse und Dokumentation der intellektuellen Subkultur vom 19. Jahrhundert bis zur Gegenwart*, Stuttgart 1971.) Taking into consideration both the pattern of association with Graz's 'Forum Stadtpark' and its publication *manuskripte*, and the distinctive group profile established through the critical reception of works by the 'Grazer', it is possible to distinguish a relatively closed 'inner circle' and a looser 'outer circle' of Graz authors. In the early 1970s this inner circle included: Kolleritsch, Handke, Bauer, Frischmuth, Falk, Hoffer, Hengstler, Gruber, Roth, and

a degree of linguistic experimentation aimed at probing and unmasking the unconscious tyranny of ordinary language over personal and social life. They were committed to an open, non-programmatic approach to matters of form and content: 'Literatur, heißt es für *manuskripte*, ist das, was wir Literatur nennen: Literatur nennen wir das, für das wir Grund haben (glauben Grund zu haben), es Literatur zu nennen' ('For *manuskripte* literature is what we call literature: What we call literature is that which we have reason (believe we have reason) to call literature').[10] This assertion by Kolleritsch in 1965 of the author's autonomous right to make aesthetic judgements is oppositional and deliberately circular. It should not be misconstrued as a neo-Romantic mystification of the creative process. Like Handke's later essays, 'Ich bin ein Bewohner des Elfenbeinturms' and 'Die Literatur ist romantisch' (in *Ich bin ein Bewohner des Elfenbeinturms*, 1972), it argues that the literature of the present cannot be defined in advance of its making and opposes subordination both to official Austrian cultural policy and the strong pressures to politicise literature being exerted by many of their West German contemporaries. The 'Grazer' insist that literature is something made (Handke: 'das Geschriebene als Gemachtes') refusing to concede that good writing can be produced to a formula (Handke: 'Automatismus' and 'angewöhnte Natürlichkeit').[11]

Although the editorial policy of *manuskripte* remained open, writers who favoured a more traditional, realist approach and wished to give overt fictional expression to socio-political concerns tended to distance themselves from the 'Grazer'. Scharang's confrontation with Kolleritsch (and Handke) over the editorial policy of *manuskripte* in 1969 highlighted the division between the formalists and the narrative realists over the role of language. Although by no means philosophically stringent, the novels of the 'Grazer Gruppe', along with those of Bernhard, imply a form of linguistic determinism. It is this which permits the work of the Graz authors to be seen as a continuation of an alternative Austrian tradition, that of the *Sprachkritik*, the ongoing Austrian preoccupation with the nature of language. It is this same factor which proved unacceptable to novelists like Scharang, Innerhofer, Jelinek, Peter Turrini, and Gernot Wolfgruber who argue that to equate a critique of language with a

---

Eisendle — Scharang and Jonke had already distanced themselves from the group's literary activities.

10. Alfred Kolleritsch with Günter Waldorf, in the 'marginalie' to *manuskripte*, 13 (1965).

11. Peter Handke, *Ich bin ein Bewohner des Elfenbeinturms* (Frankfurt, 1972), p. 204 and p. 205.

critique of society is mistaken. Again it is an irony of Austrian literary history that the realist opposition to the work of the 'Grazer' is largely centered in Vienna, that writers in the provinces should prove to be more experimental than those in the capital. By the early 1970s Graz was hailed in the jargon of reviewers as Austria's 'geheime Literaturhauptstadt' ('secret literary capital'), an index for a literature which was 'modern . . . jung, experimentell, avantgardistisch und progressiv'. In 1971 Scharang became one of the founder members of the left-wing 'Arbeitskreis der Literaturproduzenten' which comprised, amongst others, authors associated with the Vienna publication *Neues Forum*, Lutz Holzinger, Fredrich Geyerhofer, and Michael Springer. The Vienna-based publication *Wespennest*, edited by Helmut Zenker, also became a focal point for more Marxist-orientated authors. After his expulsion from *Wort in der Zeit*, Fritsch help to found *Literatur und Kritik*, a journal more receptive to new forms of writing. Only Bernhard remained scornfully independent of all such groups and alliances.

Some, although by no means all, of the initial interest of the 'Grazer' in exploring the links between language, consciousness, and the workings of power, whether at the level of the village (Jonke: *Geometrischer Heimatroman*, 1969), the state (Kolleritsch: *Die Pfirsichtöter. Ein seismographischer Roman*, 1972), the school system (Frischmuth: *Die Klosterschule*, 1968), or within the mind of the individual (Handke: *Die Angst des Tormanns beim Elfmeter*, 1970; Roth: *die autobiographie des albert einstein*, 1972), can be attributed to their contact with the work of the 'Wiener Gruppe' (Friedrich Achleitner, H.C. Artmann, Konrad Bayer, Gerhard Rühm, Oswald Wiener). Bayer, Rühm, and above all Wiener (in the 'novel', *Die Verbesserung von Mitteleuropa*, 1969) grappled with the aesthetic and critical potential of Wittgenstein's propositions about language and the world. Although Wiener's labyrinthine novel, for example, also includes passages from Mauthner, Kraus, Frege, and Carnap, Wittgenstein none the less functioned as a consistent *Begleitfigur* for the group's activities. When the Graz authors began their literary careers in the 1960s, amongst progressive-minded students, at least a superficial grasp of Wittgenstein's better-known propositions was mandatory. The notion that language constitutes a fundamental mode of human orientation in the world was very much in the air and rapidly established itself as a basic working hypothesis of progressive literary consciousness in Austria. To this effect Walter Weiß has observed:

> Wittgensteins oft zitierter Satz aus dem Tractatus: 'Die Grenzen meiner Sprache bedeuten die Grenzen meiner Welt', schlägt nicht nur den

> Grundton an, auf den die Philosophie unserer Zeit gestimmt ist, sondern ebenso einen Grundton der Gegenwartsliteratur. Es ist bezeichnend, daß sich fast alle der bisher erwähnten Gegenwartsautoren [Weiß here refers to West German authors like Mon and Heißenbüttel as well as those mentioned above], und nicht nur sie, auf diesen Satz und (oder) seinen Verfasser Wittgenstein beziehen.[12]
>
> (Wittgenstein's frequently quoted proposition from the *Tractatus*: 'The limits of my language mean the limits of my world', not only strikes the keynote to which the philosophy of our time is tuned, but it is equally the keynote of contemporary literature. It is characteristic that practically all the contemporary authors mentioned so far, and not only they, refer to this proposition and (or) its author, Wittgenstein.)

The influence of Wittgenstein's key propositions about language and the Austrian Modernist tradition of the *Sprachkrise/Sprachkritik* (crisis and critique of language) on the novel as it emerges from Graz is generally more indirect than direct. Amongst the 'Grazer' only Kolleritsch, Eisendle, and Hoffer (and the poet Gunter Falk) appear to have studied Wittgenstein in depth. By over-emphasising the link between the 'Wiener Gruppe' and the Graz authors, critics are apt to exaggerate the importance of Wittgenstein's ideas in their work. As a stock solution to problems in the intellectual history of recent Austrian literature it obscures more than it reveals. Handke, for example, is known to have read the *Tractatus Logico-Philosophicus* while he was working on his novel *Die Hornissen* in Graz. Yet publicly Handke has been curiously off-hand about the influence of Wittgenstein's ideas on his work. His interest appears to be of the most general kind and does not go beyond recognising the prime importance of ordinary language and the pervasive role of social convention in language behaviour: 'Was ich gar nicht will: eine eigene Sprache erfinden, das finde ich idiotisch, das ist immer noch dieses Auftreten als Dichter. Ich möchte mich vielmehr in der gegebenen Sprache ausdrücken, und das ist das, was ich immer noch von Wittgenstein gelernt habe, so wenig mich diese Philosophie interessiert: die Bedeutung eines Worts ist sein Gebrauch' ('What I really don't want is to invent a personal language. I find that idiotic — still this playing the part of the writer. I would much rather express myself in ordinary language and that's what I've

12. Walter Weiß, 'Zur Thematisierung der Sprache in der Literatur der Gegenwart', *Festschrift für Hans Eggers zum 65. Geburtstag: Beiträge zur Geschichte der deutschen Sprache und Literatur*, 94 (Sonderheft) (Tübingen, 1972), pp. 669–93. This quotation: pp. 673–4.

learned from Wittgenstein, in so far as this philosophy interests me at all: the meaning of a word is its use').[13]

As is the case with most other Graz authors, the sources of Handke's developing ideas on the relationship between language, consciousness, and social behaviour were in the main literary or the product of wide general reading. His early reading of the French *nouveau roman* brought him into contact with ideas on language derived ultimately from Husserlian phenomenology. He was also interested in Russian Formalist thinkers, including Boris Eichenbaum whose essays he reviewed on the radio in Graz in 1965. The model for the narrative strategy employed in *Die Angst des Tormanns beim Elfmeter* was derived from a clinical study of nascent schizophrenia. The Austrian psychiatrist Leo Navratil's widely received *Schizoprenie und Sprache* (1966) was similarly influential in the creation of Roth's *die autobiographie des albert einstein.* A more directly philosophical application of Wittgenstein's thought can be found in later novels by Kolleritsch, Eisendle, and Hoffer, but even here aesthetic considerations remain primary.

The range of ideas about language which inform the narrative and thematic structure of novels by the 'Grazer' is broader in scope than some previous literary-historical surveys have indicated. The period of the dictatorship and the Anschluss had violently interrupted the reception in Austria of the earlier Modernist experiments of Dada and Surrealism. In an effort to foster the growth of an alternative Austrian literary tradition, throughout the 1960s *manuskripte* not only published works by the 'Wiener Gruppe', who had been instrumental in reviving interest in such pre-war experiments, but encouraged direct links with the past by rediscovering, for example, the work of the forgotten Austrian Dadaist, Raoul Hausmann.

The most radically avant-garde examples of the new Austrian novel up to 1970 are those of Bayer, Wiener, and Okopenko. They present considerable difficulty to readers whose expectations of the novel are limited to the conventions of narrative realism. It is not profitable here to enter into the tortuous critical debate of the mid-1970s which attempted to oppose the 'genuinely experimental' work of these

13. Peter Handke, in an interview with Christian Lindner, 'Schreiben als Kommunikationsappell', *National-Zeitung*, Basel, 4 April 1974. (Reprinted as 'Die Ausbeutung des Bewußtseins. Gespräch mit Peter Handke' in Christian Lindner, *Schreiben und Leben* (Cologne, 1974), pp. 36ff.)

authors to the 'post-experimental compromises' supposedly struck between experiment and tradition by some of the 'Grazer'. There is some truth in the argument advanced by Reinhard Priessnitz and Mechthild Rausch[14], that members of the 'Wiener Gruppe' adopted a more rigorously neo-positivist stance towards language which links them closely with such West German proponents of *konkrete Literatur* such as Heißenbüttel and Mon. Opinions about the avant-garde 'purity' or otherwise of these novels must be offset against their ability to communicate with only a limited audience of what one of the Graz authors, Roth, refers to as 'literarische Fans'.

A clear indication that the Austrian novel would work to extend the limits of awareness is to be found in the more intriguing and aesthetically successful of Bayer's two experimental novels, *der kopf des vitus bering* (1965). Published shortly after Bayer's tragic suicide, this short novel, subtitled *Porträt in Prosa* ('Portrait in Prose'), is a complex narrative constructed as a montage around quotations from historical documents relating to the polar explorer, Vitus Bering (1680–1741). Studies of shamanism, the occult, cannibalism, navigation and medicine are interwoven with biographical detail. The result is a trance-like vision of Bering's arctic voyage and eventual death from scurvy after a shipwreck. By repeating and varying his montage units, centring them about the figure of Bering and a minimal plot, Bayer creates a unified text which succeeds in articulating shadowy and atavistic areas of the individual and collective unconscious. *der kopf des vitus bering* ranks amongst the finest prose works produced by members of the Wiener Gruppe and its particular fascination acted as a stimulus for a number of early works by the Graz authors, including Handke and Roth.

Bayer's second, uncompleted novel, *der sechste sinn* (1966), takes as its central figure the partly autobiographical Franz Goldenberg. As the title suggests, this work continues to explore the limits of human experience and the possibility of a deeper knowledge of reality. The narrative, constructed as a series of digressions, renders impossible the reader's desire to impose a linear pattern on events. Blurred glimpses of everyday society, of a love-affair, of historically 'recognisable' persons — Bayer includes tangential sketches of his 'Art-Club' friends — are rapidly eclipsed by a bewildering complex of memories and associations.

If the familiar outlines of our everyday 'consensus reality' are obscured by the narrative perspective of Bayer's second novel, in

14. Reinhard Priessnitz and Mechthild Rausch, 'tribut an die tradition. aspekte einer postexperimentellen literatur' in Laemmle and Drews, *Wie die Grazer auszogen*,pp. 126–52.

Oswald Wiener's *Die Verbesserung von Mitteleuropa* (1969) they disappear almost entirely. Wiener's labyrinthine assemblage of speculative essays, quotations, notes, observations, aphorisms, complete with its opening 'personen- und sachregister', three appendices, and a lengthy bibliography, is an anti-novel in the most literal sense. *Die Verbesserung von Mitteleuropa* is the most extreme assertion of linguistic determinism in recent Austrian literature. Wiener categorically denies that we can use language to comprehend a reality which is itself beyond language. Wittgenstein's views on the limits of language and his concept of the 'Sprachspiel' ('language game') are central to Wiener's 'argument'. He insists that 'die sprachliche Darstellung de Wirklichkeit nicht mehr mit der Wirklichkeit selbst verglichen werden kann, weil dies exklusiv in ihrer sprachlichen Darstellung gegeben ist' ('the linguistic representation of reality can no longer be compared with reality itself because reality is manifested exclusively in its linguistic representation').[15] In other words a sentence which we would normally think of as a 'description of reality' cannot be measured against reality itself but only against other sentences. If accepted, Wiener's proposition holds devastating consequences and not only for the mimetic theory of the novel. Applied consistently it unmasks 'die illusion deutlicher zu werden' ('the illusion of attaining clarity')[16] or, as Elizabeth Wiesmayr elaborates it: 'die Unsinnigkeit des Versuchs durch Beschreibung eines Gegenstands habhaft zu werden, wie in einer mehrzeitigen verwirrenden Deskription eines Bleistifts' ('The absurdity of the attempt to grasp [the reality of] an object by describing it, as in a many-sided, confusing description of a pencil').[17] Wiener echoes strongly Austria's turn-of-the-century *Sprachkrise* when he complains that 'die organisation der wirklichkeit durch die sprache ist unerträglich' ('the organisation of reality by language is unbearable').[18] His anarchic conclusion is to urge acts of sabotage and terror against prevailing conventions of language. Any hope of social or political improvement — the betterment of Central Europe referred to in the title — depends on the notion that 'ein Aufstand gegen die Sprache ist ein Aufstand gegen die Gesellschaft' ('a revolt against language is a revolt against society').

As much as he was admired by young Austrian novelists inclined

15. Friedrich Geyrhofer, 'Oswald Wiener', *Neues Forum*, 3 (1973), pp. 64–6. This quotation p. 65.

16. Oswald Wiener, *Die Verbesserung von Mitteleuropa. Roman* (Hamburg, 1969), p. XI (Vorwort).

17. Wiesmayr, *Die Zeitschrift 'manuskripte'*, p. 70.

18. Wiener, *Verbesserung*, p. LII.

towards linguistic experiment, none were prepared to follow Wiener into the exile from all mimetic conventions to which his reflections on language eventually lead. *Die Verbesserung von Mitteleuropa* remains as a monument to an intellect which in its consistency is both playful and terrifying.

A further experiment with the novel form which helps to indicate the variety of approaches to be found on the formalist side of this literary-critical division is Okopenko's *Lexikon-Roman* (1970). Okopenko's protest against the conventions of a sterilised, bureaucratic world is more personal and more bohemian in its anarchy than Wiener's. Okopenko rejects those neo-positivist elements in the work of the Wiener Gruppe which deny the possibility of an authentic subjectivity. Against their reductionism he posits a personal sphere of language within which the individual can find a genuine sense of identity: prevailing narrative and descriptive conventions, however, must first be scattered to the four winds. *Lexikon-Roman* is a montage of impressions, parodies, and reflections bearing on the 'sentimental journey' of the protagonist to an export conference in Druden (on the Danube).Chronological narration is rejected because Okopenko seeks to escape the causal necessity such a linear view of time imposes on events. No plot or story line is evident. Instead the reader is confronted with an alphabetically arranged collection of materials which can be browsed through at random or according to the 'Gebrauchsanweisung' included in the text. In these instructions Okopenko outlines various routes, shorter or longer according to the time available, which the reader may take through the text. As with Wiener's 'novel' this encyclopedic text defies the convention of linearity so completely that it is all but impossible to read the book from cover to cover. The active participation of the reader in selecting one or more of a vast number of perspectives on events is thus encouraged.

The principle of active participation on the part of the consumer of the product 'novel' as opposed to being passively entertained, no matter how elevated the level, is a distinguishing feature of a number of novels by the 'Grazer' as well. Although a rise in the demand for audience participation is an international feature in many art-forms from the mid-1960s onwards, the specific desire to heighten awareness of the subject–language–object relation appears in a remarkably concentrated form in recent Austrian literature. But in spite of the positive critical reception of these experiments in the novel form by Bayer, Wiener, and Okopenko, the actual breakthrough of the Austrian novel in terms of widespread critical reception — firstly in West Germany and not unexpectedly somewhat later at home in Austria — depended to a much greater extent on the high profile earned between 1966 and the early 1970s by members of the 'Grazer Gruppe'.

The year 1966 can be seen as a turning-point in the development of Austrian literature in the Second Republic. The leading representative of the pre-war generation, Heimito von Doderer, died and Peter Handke, who was destined to become the most prominent member of the post-war generation, made his extraordinary debut on the West German literary scene. It was Handke who became the most celebrated and the most vilified young author of the time. It was the public attention which this young Austrian writer attracted in West Germany and the continuing interest his work aroused which played an essential role in bringing to the attention of West German publishers and critics the work of other young Graz authors, an interest which rapidly extended to other young Austrian writers as well. Amongst West German publishers and critics the impression was reinforced that Austria was, as Heinz Ludwig Arnold later remarked, the source of most of the interesting advances in German literature.

At home the meteoric launching of Handke's literary career brought encouragement and a feeling of confidence to those with whom he had been associated in Graz, whether their interest at the time lay in drama like Wolfgang Bauer, or, like Frischmuth, Jonke, Kolleritsch, Roth, Eisendle and Hoffer, in the novel.

Although by no means conventional narrative, the experimental novels of the 'Grazer' are based on a narrative strategy which makes significant concessions to matters of chronology and linear organisation. It is because they are largely accessible to the 'ordinary reader' that these works provide a steep but navigable route to more extreme or abstract forms of experiment. They can be seen as the products of a period of apprenticeship to avant-garde literary technique with a heightened critical awareness of language at its centre. An account of the literary-historical situation of the Graz authors given by Roth, sees in the pioneering work of the 'Wiener Gruppe' and their associates a positive response to the changed historical circumstances of the Second Republic: 'Diese Beschäftigung mit der Sprache, die zu ästhetisch hochwertigen Arbeiten geführt hat, hat auch gleichzeitig zu einer Reinigung der Sprache von einigen durch die politischen Ereignisse geschädigten Begriffen geführt. Es wurde wieder eine Dimension erarbeitet, in der man schriftstellerisch tätig sein könnte' ('This preoccupation with language which has led to works of high aesthetic quality, has also led to a purging of a number of politically damaged concepts from the language. A dimension has again been established in which one can engage in literary activities').[19]

To view with Priessnitz and Rausch the work of the Graz authors as a backsliding into traditional narration obscures their largely positive reception of avant-garde linguistic experiments. Within the perspective of Austria's overall literary development since 1945 their work can be seen as the logical next step forwards. Roth's account of this process is representative of the situation of his fellow authors: 'Die Grazer Autoren sind nach der sogennanten Wiener Gruppe um einen Schritt weitergegangen. Sie haben im großen und ganzen das, was die Wiener Gruppe an Sprache erarbeitet haben — an brauchbarer Autorensprache — begonnen in eine neue Form des Erzählens umzusetzen' ('After the so-called "Wiener Gruppe" the Graz authors have gone one step further. By and large they have begun to turn what the "Wiener Gruppe" worked for in the way of language — a language writers can use — into a new form of narration').[20] How this worked in practice can be exemplified here in outline with reference to some early novels by the 'Grazer'.

Handke's first novel *Die Hornissen*, published more as a risk venture than as a certainty by Suhrkamp in March 1966, at first attracted scant critical attention. Its intricately embedded narrative point of view brings this work much closer to the type of the French *nouveau roman* than other novels published in German at the time. The difficulty for the reader lies in knowing which level of the narrative is the controlling one. The problem of interpretation is only partly solved in the ironic final section where we learn that what we have just struggled through are the confused recollections of one who has gone blind trying to recall the events of a Sunday in his childhood when his brother drowned. The text begins to make final sense when one realises that its central theme is actually the business of narration itself. The novel's complex narrative strategy is employed by Handke as an experimental model to demostrate how reality is mediated ('vermittelt') by language. Behind this is Handke's rejection of the (Sartrian) notion that language can be made to resemble glass through which things may be seen in their true form.[21]

Handke's next novel, *Der Hausierer* (1967), uses the language of the detective genre to demonstrate how the clichés and conventions of a popular form — he uses the term 'schemata' — were once the linguistic representations of real human fears and emotions. By

19. Gerhard Roth, in an unpublished interview with Simon Ryan, Obergreith, October, 1980.

20. Ibid.

21. Peter Handke, p. 41.

making himself and others aware of the genre's hidden game rules he hoped to be able to make conscious use of these 'schemata' to portray real experiences. In *Der Angst des Tormanns beim Elfmeter* (1970) and *Der kurze Brief zum langen Abschied* (1972) he succeeds in adapting the narrative strategies of the popular thriller to produce just that effect. In succeeding novels the unmasking of the habits of convention becomes more refined and greatly extended in its social and historical reach. Increasingly, as in *Wunschloses Unglück* (1972), which utilises the techniques of the *Frauenbiographie* to reflect on the reasons behind his mother's suicide, Handke is able to apply these deconstructed conventions to the narration of genuine experience.

The search for oneself and the preservation of individual identity amidst the mass of hidden conventions imposing on behaviour is central to Frischmuth's *Die Klosterschule* (1968). She offers an ironic portrayal of daily routine in a Catholic boarding school. With the aim of promoting liberation from the deadening restraint of such institutionalised language, Frischmuth employs a montage technique to offset against the rules the girls have learned by heart, the reality of their lives. She achieves this effect by allowing naíve 'misreadings' to intrude into the ordered world of the school's prescriptions for acceptable behaviour. In her later novels (e.g. the trilogy: *Die Mystifikation der Sophie Silber*, *Amy oder Die Metamorphose*, *Kai und die Liebe zu den Modellen*; 1976–9) Frischmuth shifts away from this structural approach to a less formal consideration of the role models controlling the relationships between woman, man, and child. Her presiding interest in conventions and the way language encapsulates and reinforces them remains central.

Jonke's highly successful first novel *Geometrischer Heimatroman* (1969) is the product of his transferrence of suspicions about the subject–language–object relation to suspicions about the nature of a society in which objects are allowed to determine the pattern of human existence. It is also one of a series of anti-*Heimatromane*, a characteristic form of the new Austrian novel from Bernhard's *Frost* (1963) through the work of Handke, Innerhofer, Jelinek, Scharang, Roth, and Wolfgruber to Reinhard Gruber's satirical *Aus dem Leben Hödlmosers* (1983). Here Jonke proceeds in the manner of a geometrician to set forth spatial and other formal relations governing the arrangement of the landscape and the placement of the village, along with its component objects and the human 'figures' it contains. In Chapter Four we learn that the village square is a structural pattern ('strukturales Muster'). The pattern of life it determines resembles that of Toytown. As the product of a limited set of functional sentences the village is a wholly artificial creation, a closed system intended by

Jonke as a satirical model of a correspondingly closed society.

In *Geometrischer Heimatroman*, Jonke attacks by implication the illusory nature of the 'narrative' controlling real and repressive social conventions. In later novels he adopts a less structural approach to narration and utilises other closed linguistic systems to great aesthetic advantage. Where Wiener puts the emphasis on tearing down present language conventions, Jonke prefers the idea of aesthetic play leavened by a measure of ironic humour. In *Schule der Geläufigkeit* (1977), for example, he dissolves the boundaries between past and present, reality and illusion. The story depicts the blurring of awareness which results when the photographer, Diabelli, succeeds in staging a perfect recreation of last year's garden party. The model of perception Jonke builds up in the novel again implies that what we habitually take for reality is in fact the illusion created by the language we use to represent it.

In his earliest novel *die autobiographie des albert einstein* (1972), Roth mounts an anarchic attack on the misplaced confidence of scientific man in his own rationality. Like Eisendle, Roth's background lies in the sciences rather than the arts and he brings to this scurrilous and playful text a wealth of scientific fact. The first person narrator is a schizophrenic who lives in the illusion that he is the great scientist of the title. Roth is not interested in fashioning a literary account of a schizophrenic's world. Rather he is concerned with probing the fictional nature of that consensus reality which, as members of a rational technological society, we employ to restrict the boundaries of 'normal' or 'sane' experience. In the novel the doors of experience are thrust open. Roth explores the bizarre and fascinating realms which become manifest when the rigid categories of logic and positivist science are exploded and the mind is laid open to the transforming effects of untrammelled acts of imagination. The schizophrenic 'Einstein' enters into a series of 'zerebrale Paradiese' ('cerebal paradises'): 'jedes wörtchen wird zu einem opiat, das ein flimmern von bildern, eine sturzflut von neuen worten auslöst. Das tapetenmuster aus violetten gasflämmchen wirkte wie ein narkotikum' ('Each little word becomes an opiate which releases a flickering of images, a torrent of new words. The wallpaper pattern of tiny violet gas flames had the effect of a narcotic').[22] The surrealistic impulse seen earlier in the work of the Wiener Gruppe manifests itself strongly in Roth's early work and resurfaces in the phantasmagoric passages of his most recent novel *Landläufiger Tod* (1984).

22. Gerhard Roth, *die autobiographie des albert einstein. Menschen, Bilder, Marionetten. Prosa, Kurzromane, Stücke* (Frankfurt, 1979), p. 204.

Roth produced a number of successful shorter experimental narratives along similar lines but in 1973 he found that in pursuing experimental techniques for their own sake he had written himself into a corner. His situation was typical of that experienced by most of the Graz authors as they reached the end of their early experimental phase: 'Ich bin mir vorgekommen wie in einer Blackbox, in einer schwarzen Schachtel mit einer winzigen Öffnung, durch die ich auf Gegenstände und meine Umwelt blicke, die ich ganz mikroskopisch betrachte, und ich habe einfach Sehnsucht gehabt, sozusagen die Fensterläden aufzumachen und größere Ausschnitte einzufangen' ('It struck me that it was like being in a blackbox, inside a black enclosure with a tiny opening through which I glimpsed objects and my surroundings which I contemplated in microscopic detail, and I simply had a longing to open the windows so to say and take in a wider perspective').[23]

The link between imagination and the ground of experience was stretching to breaking-point. Until now Roth's work had failed to connect in any vital way with his biographical self or with the social nexus. Like other 'Grazer' around this time, he felt the need for a type of narrative which, while preserving the experimental impulse, would make possible the inclusion of a central character with whom he and others could readily identify and facilitate 'die Beschreibung meines Lebens in meiner Zeit' ('the description of my life in my time').[24]

This was the period which West German critics refer to as the 'Tendenzwende' (shift of direction) and associate with the emergence of a 'neue Subjecktivität' (new subjectivity) or, disparaging its apparent introversion, a 'neue Innerlichkeit' (new inwardness).[25] One of its major characteristics is a demand for 'authenticity' which is reflected in an upsurge of autobiographical input into the novel and a sudden flourishing of the genre, autobiography. Certainly a great deal more of 'real life' enters into novels by Graz authors in the early 1970s. But the linguistic sophistication of the 'Grazer', the deliberate fictionality of much of their work necessitates a certain caution when applying the concepts of the 'Tendezwende' to the development of the Austrian novel in the early 1970s.

23. Gerhard Roth, in an interview with Sigrid Esslinger. 'Gerhard Roth: Ein neuer Morgen', Bayerischer Rundfunk (Fernsehen), broadcast 23 May 1976, transcript, pp. 4–5.

24. Gerhard Roth, interview with Simon Ryan, Obergreith (October, 1980).

25. Cf. Helmut Kreuzer, 'Neue Subjektivität. Zur Literatur der siebziger Jahre in der Bundesrepublik Deutschland' in Manfred Durzak (ed.), *Deutsche Gegenwartsliteratur*, pp. 76–106.

Roth's immediate response to the problem was *Der große Horizont* (1974), a novel based on a trip he made to the USA. Its central character, the 'hypochondriac' Viennese bookseller, Daniel Haid, is a memorable creation. The novel contains many penetrating psychological observations and an intriguing view of America. But it is not a conventional narrative: confidence in a stable reality is constantly undermined by Haid's uncertain sense of identity. Haid's personality is linked by Roth to other fictions, including Philip Marlowe, the hero of Raymond Chandler's urban detective novels. Very little of what we learn about Haid — the name contains a reference to the Hyde of Robert Louis Stevenson's famous tale of a haunted personality — can be taken for granted.

Similar observations can be made about other novels produced by the 'Grazer' up to the present time. These narratives readily trap readers who mistakenly assume they are dealing with realist fiction. Handke's later novels, Kolleritsch's *Die grüne Seite* (1974), Eisendle's dialogue novels *Jenseits der Vernunft oder Gespräche über den menschlichen Verstand* (1976), *Exil oder der braune Salon* (1977), and Hoffer's novel in two parts *Halbwegs. Bei den Bieresch 1* (1979)' and *Der große Potlatsch. Bei den Bieresch 2* (1983), all subvert the realist presupposition that there is a one-to-one correspondence between our experience, language, and the world. *Caveat lector*!

The presuppositions of the realist approach are generally better understood. It should by now be apparent, however, that a majority of contemporary Austrian novelists have elected to work in the formalist mode. Only those authors and critics whose loyalty to the realist camp is ideological decry this fact. For those like Innerhofer and Wolfgruber whose largely autobiographical novels stem from a strongly felt need to portray the often brutal hardships of growing up amongst Austria's rural poor, the urgency to express content displaces more subtle reflections on language. The strength of works like Innerhofer's trilogy: *Schöne Tage* (1974), *Schattseite* (1975), and *Die großen Wörter* (1977), lies in their passionate but carefully modulated use of traditional realist techniques. Along with other novels set in rural Austria like Wolfgruber's *Auf freiem Fuß* (1975) and *Herrenjahre* (1976), or the young Josef Winkler's *Menschenkind* (1979), they bring an often disturbing immediacy to a realisation of the semi-feudal deprivations faced by the families of thousands of *Landarbeiter* (rural workers) and *Knechte* (farmhands) in the Second Republic while town and city dwellers experieced relative prosperity.

A correspondingly realistic portrayal of life in a rural clothing factory, this time from the point of view of a Marxist feminist writer, emerges from Elfriede Jelinek's novel *Die Liebhaberinnen* (1975). Jelinek's earlier successes had been in the area of the pop-novel, *wir sind lockvögel baby!* (1970) and a satire on the values of the entertainment industry, *Michael.Ein Jugendbuch für die Infantilgesellschaft* (1972). In *Die Ausgesperrten* (1980), which portrays the murder by a young man of his parents and his sister, Jelinek utilises material from a real criminal case of the 1960s. She accurately depicts the way the repressive family structure of lower-middle-class existence contributes to the warping of an ambitious personality.

One of the aims of this survey has been to give a degree of prominence to some less well-publicised aspects of the Austrian novel since 1960. The novels of Bachmann and Bernhard, two distinctive and important figures in the history of recent Austrian literature, have received scant mention in this survey. Their work is, however, discussed in detail elsewhere in this volume. Like a number of her generation, including the poet Erich Fried, Bachmann lived outside Austria for much of her creative life. In the 1970s there was a revival of interest in her work and her novel *Malina* (1971) was well received. In matters of Austrian cultural politics in the 1960s and early 1970s Bachmann maintained a conservative stance. Over the split between authors supporting what was to become in 1973 the 'Grazer Autorenversammlung' and the official Austrian PEN Club, she sided with Eisenreich and the conservative faction against the 'progressives'. This, despite Walter Jen's comment in 1961 that her appearance together with Ilse Aichinger at the Niendorf conference of West Germany's 'Gruppe 47' in 1952 signalled the beginning of a move away from narrative realism in post-war German literature.

Bernhard, on the other hand, has taken delight in offending conservatives and progressives alike and has remained aloof from all factions, preferring to concentrate single-handedly on his own devastatingly barbed attacks on a moribund '*felix* Austria'. His novels well illustrate Magris's observation that: 'Die Kontinuität der österreichischen Tradition besteht in der Tat aus einer Reihe von Rebellionen gegen eben diese Tradition. ('The continuity of Austrian tradition in fact consists of a series of revolts against just this very tradition').[26] The tortuous linguistic knots and vicious circles in which the morbid protagonists of Bernhard's novels (cf. *Das Kalkwerk,* 1970) enmesh themselves signify a preoccupation with decay and death which in its unflinching irony is distinctly, if not uniquely,

26. Claudio Magris, 'Der unauffindbare Sinn. Zur österreichischen Literatur des 20. Jahrhunderts', *Klagenfurter Universitätsreden*, Heft 9, 1978, p. 10.

Austrian.

Inevitably in a survey of this kind novelists well worthy of mention have received no comment. Authors not dealt with here whose novels have met with favourable critical reception are Peter Turrini, Bernhard Hüttenegger, Alois Brandstetter, and Brigitte Schwaiger. In *Die Abtei* (1977) Brandstetter stages a masterly revival of Austria's forgotten rhetorical tradition. On the lighter side, *Der Fieberkopf: Roman in Briefen* (1966) by the Graz dramatist, Wolfgang Bauer, should not be overlooked.

There are many issues within this period of Austrian literary history which have still to be documented and explored, including the reasons behind the apparent absence of any positive reception of Musil's experimental ideas amongst younger Austrian writers. For those interested in the reception of Freud, Kafka, or Wittgenstein there is a wealth of material to explore, from Roth's *Winterreise* (1978) to Hoffer's 'Bieresch' novels.

In conclusion, it remains only to reiterate what Weiß refers to as the 'produktive Vielfalt' ('productive diversity') evident in the Austrian novel since it first began to free itself from the weight of a negatively orientated tradition in the early 1960s. The role played by authors associated with the Graz literary revival in placing Austria firmly on the map of contemporary German literature remains central.

RHYS WILLIAMS

Alfred Andersch

In an autobiographical sketch entitled 'Böse Träume', which first appeared in 1981, after his death, Andersch was moved to pose a crucial question about his career and to answer it: 'Warum habe ich, aus dem Krieg, aus dem Leben in einer Diktatur entlassen, nicht sofort *geschrieben*? . . . Anstatt mit Schreiben habe ich meine Zeit mit Journalismus vergeudet. Artikel, Reportagen, Redaktionen' ('When I was released from the war, from life under a dictatorship, why didn't I start *writing* straight away? Instead I frittered my time away on journalism. Articles, reporting, editing').[1] This last self-assessment highlights three significant features of Andersch's literary life: the first, and obvious, point is that he was, on his own admission, not strictly a novelist. Only four of his works can be described as novels and he was easily as well known for his essays, short stories, radio plays and features, travelogues and editorial activity. Secondly, it seems that Andersch, towards the end of his life, perceived aesthetic and political concerns as mutually exclusive. As we shall see, the tension between literature and politics, or between aesthetic detachment and socio-political involvement, is rehearsed in a variety of ways throughout Andersch's *oeuvre*. Finally, his statement is revealing in that here he restates a version of his literary career which he repeatedly emphasised but which is open to challenge: namely, that he began to write after the war, or at least after his desertion to the Americans on the Italian Front in June 1944. If a certain amount of space is devoted here to unravelling some of the tangled threads in Andersch's early career, it is because his literary and political beginnings had a major bearing on what he wrote. Both the subject matter and the form of his novels are shaped by his own preoccupation with the factors which conditioned his life. In this sense, Andersch's work is profoundly autobiographical.

Until 1977 Andersch's biography was derived almost exclusively from his own version in *Die Kirschen der Freiheit* (1952). Here we learn that he left school at the age of fourteen, worked in a bookshop, was unemployed from 1931 to 1933, a period during which he rose to

1. Published in *Tintenfaß*, 2 (1981), pp. 43–69 (here p. 68).

become Communist Youth Organiser for Southern Bavaria. After the Reichstag fire he was arrested and interned in Dachau, to be released on the intervention of his mother, who drew attention to her late husband's impressive record of service both in the army and in the cause of National Socialism. Andersch's release was conditional upon good behaviour. His routine re-arrest in the autumn 1933 seems to have convinced him of the futility of further opposition to National Socialism. Although he was released after a night in the police cells, he broke with his former Communist associates. Events over the next eleven years are passed over in very few pages in *Die Kirschen der Freiheit*, all the emphasis being placed on his desertion in 1944. Thereafter, Andersch's career is a matter of public record. He was shipped to the United States, picked cotton as a prisoner of war in Fort Ruston, Louisiana, was then moved to Fort Kearney and Fort Getty in Rhode Island, where he collaborated on the POW periodical *Der Ruf* and participated in the re-education programme in which the Americans trained for future administrative positions in Germany those Germans who had displayed anti-Nazi, democratic inclinations. Andersch recalled the 'Umerziehung in der Retorte', this imprisonment in a golden cage, as a thoroughly positive, intellectually stimulating experience. He returned to Munich late in 1945 and worked on the *Neue Zeitung*, before establishing with Hans Werner Richter the German version of *Der Ruf* in 1946. This periodical, while it was anti-Communist, was also opposed to American de-Nazification programmes; it argued for a Germany which was socialist, demilitarised and free to determine its own future. With the intensification of the cold war, the American licensing authorities threatened to withdraw the licence unless *Der Ruf* changed its editorial policy: Richter and Andersch refused and resigned, planning to produce a literary journal *Der Skorpion*. When that periodical was in turn refused a licence, the contributors met to read their manuscripts to one another and the 'Gruppe 47' came into existence. It was, incidentally, to its second meeting that Andersch read his critical essay *Deutsche Literatur in der Entscheidung*, the first and only attempt ever made by the group to define a theoretical position.

To judge by his own autobiography, Andersch had impeccable credentials as a writer of the young generation: early opposition to National Socialism, a literary career which began after 1945 and was therefore uncompromised, and experience of the war within Germany rather than from exile. It was not until 1977, when Andersch conceded in an autobiographical fragment entitled 'Der Seesack' that he had published a short story in the literary section of the *Kölnische Zeitung* on 25 April 1944, that Andersch's own image of himself, promulgated through *Die Kirschen der Freiheit*, was seriously called into question.[2] Since his death in 1980 Andersch's papers have been available at the Deutsches Literaturarchiv in Marbach. Recent research has explored in detail Andersch's early literary career and arrived at a more differentiated, more illuminating, picture of the pressures which operated on him both in the Third Reich and subsequently.

Andersch, it emerges, first embarked on a literary career in the mid-1930s as a direct response to his enforced abandonment of politics. Inspired by visits to Italy he wrote several poems, which he submitted to the criticism of his literary mentor, the Munich author Günther Herzfeld-Wüsthoff.[3] The titles: 'Aus Südtirol', 'Blick auf Umbrien', 'Innenhof des Palazzo Vecchio', together with the sometimes acerbic comments by Herzfeld-Wüsthoff in a letter dated 26 January 1937, give an impression of a neo-Romantic tone not untypical of what Hans Dieter Schäfer prefers to call the 'non-National Socialist literature of the young generation in the Third Reich'.[4] Andersch, while quoting extensively from his mentor's letter in *Die Kirschen der Freiheit*, blurs his identity by omitting to give his full name. With his move to Hamburg in 1937 and his first marriage Andersch appears to have lost touch with his Munich literary contacts. Late in 1939 he embarked on a series of short prose sketches — the earliest is dated 18 November 1939, the latest 30 August 1943.[5] These eleven passages are descriptions of scenes which, for the most part, rigorously exclude social concerns: human activity rarely impinges; where human beings are present, they partake of the static quality of the landscape. Characteristic products of the literature of *innere Emigration*, these sketches signal Andersch's predilection for landscapes devoid of people, a taste which remains with Andersch in his post-war travelogues. The intense heat of 'Heißer, sardischer Golf' (1961), the intense cold of *Hohe Breiten-*

2. 'Der Seesack' appeared in Nicolas Born and Jürgen Manthey (eds.), *Literaturmagazin, 7. Nachkriegsliteratur* (Reinbek, 1977), pp. 116–33.

3. The letter from Herzfeld-Wüsthoff to Andersch is preserved in the Deutsches Literaturarchiv, Marbach a.N. Extensive quotation from it is found in *Die Kirschen der Freiheit* (Zurich, 1971), pp. 50–1. I have opted to cite from the *Taschenbuch-Studienausgabe in Einzelbänden*, published by Diogenes, Zurich, on the grounds of its wider accessibility. All subsequent quotations are taken from this edition, unless otherwise indicated.

4. See Hans Dieter Schäfer, *Das gespaltene Bewußtsein. Deutsche Kultur und Lebenswirklichkeit 1933–1945* (Munich, 1981), pp. 7–54.

5. These prose sketches are preserved in the Andersch papers in Marbach under the title: 'Konvolut: Kurzprosa, die norddeutsche Landschaft beschreibend' (Zugangsnummer 80.583).

grade (1969) repeat a pattern laid down in the Third Reich.

In February 1942, Andersch submitted a longer prose work, 'Skizze zu einem jungen Mann' to the literary section of the *Frankfurter Zeitung*. The text, a curiously anachronistic study of aesthetic self-indulgence and decadence, is set in Munich in a period which more closely resembles the turn of the century than the 1930s.[6] Yet the narrator's self-confessed inability to offer more than an 'incomplete mosaic', the motif of flight from uncongenial social realities into the pure delights of mathematics ('die geheime Magie der abstrakten Formeln') or nature ('die Geheimnisse der Wiesen'), indicate the problems of writing in *innere Emigration*. The narrative strategy — a sympathetic outsider presenting a portrait of an admired figure's inner experience — is fraught with difficulty in a society in which the inner life must remain private, carefully preserved from the gaze of others. By February 1942, having taken part in the French campaign and having been stationed with the occupying forces in Northern France, Andersch was temporarily released from military duties. In March 1942 he moved to Frankfurt, where he continued to harbour literary ambitions. On 16 February 1943 Andersch made formal application to become a member of the Reichsschrifttumskammer.[7] In his application Andersch, not unnaturally, emphasised his military record in France and took pains to maximise his acceptability as a writer: 'Meine schriftstellerischen Bemühungen reichen schon einige Jahre zurück. Ernsthaft und in ausgebreitetem Umfang habe ich damit jedoch erst seit 1941 begonnen, eine Entwicklung zu der das Kriegserlebnis wohl entscheidend beitrug' ('My literary ambitions go back over a number of years. But I have only seriously begun to work since 1941, a development no doubt prompted by my war experience'). Significantly, Andersch replied to the question about which political parties he belonged to before 1933 with the laconic 'none'. Clearly, the idealised picture of Andersch as an opponent of the regime under Gestapo surveillance needs some correction. By 1933, at the age of nineteen, he had broken with the Communist Party. Intimidated, as hundreds of thousands were, by totalitarian terror, Andersch retreated completely from politics, blaming the Communist Party for its failure. By the time he had made his application to the Reichsschrifttumskammer he had been a model citizen for a decade; his Communist

6. The text is reproduced in full in Volker Wehdeking, *Alfred Andersch* (Stuttgart, 1983), pp. 166–77.

7. Andersch's application is to be found in the American Document Center in West Berlin.

sympathies could be dismissed as merely a youthful indiscretion. His application was duly accepted and he was officially freed from membership, the usual practice for those writers who had not published enough to be required to take up full membership. In February 1944, Andersch submitted three stories under the title *Erinnerte Gestalten* to Suhrkamp who declined to publish them as a volume but were impressed enough to ask him to send further work.[8] Thus, when 'Erste Ausfahrt' appeared in the *Kölnische Zeitung* in April 1944, Andersch had finally succeeded in fulfilling an ambition which he had harboured for many years. With that publication he became, if only just, an exponent of *innere Emigration.* It was his lack of success, rather than any conscious political choice, which limited the scope of his literary activities in the Third Reich. His silence about those activities, understandable given the atmosphere of the post-war years, helped to contribute to the myth of *Nullpunkt*, the theory that 1945 marked a decisive break, a radical new beginning in literature.

A knowledge of Andersch's own literary efforts under National Socialism helps to explain his defence of the literature of *innere Emigration* in his survey of the literary scene in *Deutsche Literatur in der Entscheidung*. His account is predicted upon the assumption that the literature of *innere Emigration* was one of resistance to National Socialism. All literature which was truly literature, he argues, was automatically opposed to National Socialism, for what was supportive of the regime was so inferior in quality as not to merit the name literature. Although he asserts the importance of political criteria in assessing literature, Andersch swiftly finds himself reintroducing the primacy of aesthetic criteria. Since Nazi literature is a contradiction in terms, he manages to save some rather dubious figures: Hans Grimm, Kolbenheyer, Schaefer, even Blunck. At the same time he applauds Stefan Andres, Horst Lange and Martin Raschke for having maintained their freedom from the Reichsschrifttumskammer and gives pride of place to Ernst Jünger on the grounds that the latter's symbolic mode is an ideal response to political tyranny. Andersch is generous to Thomas Mann but critical of the exponents of what he calls 'realistische Tendenzkunst' (Heintich Mann, Arnold Zweig, Döblin) because, he insists, true realism does not need to point up a political moral. Despite their progressive political allure,

8. The letter from Suhrkamp is reproduced in a letter written by Andersch to his mother on 21 May 1944. See Alfred Andersch, '. . . *einmal wirklich leben*'. *Ein Tagebuch in Briefen an Hedwig Andersch 1943–1975*, Winfried Stephan (ed.) (Zurich, 1986), pp. 37–8.

Andersch's views turn out to be profoundly conservative: art embodies freedom, the argument runs, and hence all art automatically opposes political power; if it fails to do so, then it is simply not art; if it jeopardises its essential freedom by being tendentious, then it is bad art. Viewed with hindsight, Andersch's argument seems considerably less radical than it appeared in 1948. It rehabilitates the writing of *innere Emigration* and is somewhat grudging to most of the literature written in exile. But, seen in context, it is an understandable work. Andersch reveals, as he did in his journalism, that he is wary of American de-Nazification programmes with their lists of good and bad Germans, but also firmly anti-Communist, uneasy about committed literature.

If *Deutsche Literatur in der Entscheidung* sought to isolate the literary *Nullpunkt, Die Kirschen der Freiheit* (1952) was Andersch's attempt to locate his personal *Nullpunkt* in the moment when he decided to desert to the Americans on 6 June 1944. His childhood experience of the post-revolutionary White Terror, his youthful Communism, the Dachau experience, his aesthetic escapism under National Socialism — all are recounted from the vantage-point of 1952 and set in an intellectual context typical of that time. Between an earlier fictionalised version of his desertion, serialised as 'Flucht in Etrurien' in the *Frankfurter Allgemeine Zeitung* (10–22 August 1950), and the finished version, Andersch decided to explain his actions in the light of a Sartrian existentialism which he enthusiastically adopted in the late 1940s. The work which influenced him most was Sartre's *L'existentialisme est un humanisme*, a work which, though not perhaps typical of Sartre's philosophical work as a whole, was, for compelling reasons, popular in Germany. At the risk of oversimplifying Sartre's argument, it could be outlined thus: existence precedes essence; it is through one's actions that one determines one's nature. It is not difficult to see the appeal of this theory in post-war Germany. The legacies, compromises and failures of the past can be cast aside through individual choice in an act akin, certainly in Andersch's portrayal of it, to religious conversion. This is how Andersch interprets freedom: it is the momentary sensation of limitless human potential in the moment which precedes choice; it embodies the absence of determinism and is, as such, located by Andersch outside society in the 'wilderness', or in 'no man's land'. Clearly, in the context of the cold war, a Marxist theory viewed as deterministic is the very antithesis of the freedom which Andersch extols.

Die Kirschen der Freiheit — the title itself betrays the problem of relating the world of moral freedom to a tangible, sensuous realm —

has a dual and conflicting intention. It seeks to explain how Andersch's early experience shaped the attitudes which made his desertion necessary, but at the same time it argues that the choice of desertion is free, that is, *not* determined, psychologically, historically, or otherwise. Put another way, he tries to present simultaneously an objective picture of himself as part of a historically, socially and psychologically determined reality and a sense of the moment of freedom from determinism, which is consequently outside society, outside history; private, individual, subjective. As an autobiographical work, *Die Kirschen der Freiheit* is problematic: Andersch ignores experiences which in the normal course of things we might expect him to regard as significant: his literary activities in the Third Reich are virtually ignored; his marriage and the birth of his daughter find no mention. Nor, it must be said, does the justification of his desertion appear entirely convincing. What is here presented as the casting off of a life of *mauvaise foi* in the Sartrian sense may well have appeared so to Andersch, but it is worth making the point that the desire not to be killed in a war which, by June 1944, Germany seemed certain to lose, seems a pre-eminently sensible reaction. But there are some uncomfortable ambiguities in Andersch's justification of his desertion, ambiguities which reveal a deeper-seated uncertainty.

While Andersch leans heavily on Sartre to explain his desertion on existential grounds, he also finds himself drawn into an assertion that his desertion was an act of rebellion, of resistance: 'Mein ganz kleiner privater 20. Juli fand bereits am 6. Juni statt' ('My very small, private 20 July took place on 6 June').[9] It is highly questionable, however, whether Andersch's action could be equated with the Stauffenberg bomb plot. The Stauffenberg conspirators were engaged on a political and military act and had to reckon from the outset with the possibility of failure and its consequences. Andersch's act, however sensible, was an act of self-preservation. It in no way altered the course of history. But while Andersch's post-war justification is historically inauthentic, it is psychologically revealing. It is the response of someone who, after the event, realised that he should have resisted. The failure to resist, the missed historical possibility, becomes a central theme in Andersch's writing. From the early story 'Heimatfront' (written in 1946, published posthumously) to the novel *Winterspelt* Andersch rehearses the possibilities of resistance. But within the Third Reich Andersch actually lived a life of outward conformity. When Hitler visits Munich he admits: 'da

9. *Die Kirschen der Freiheit*, p. 74.

öffnete auch ich meinen Mund und schrie: Heil!' ('I too opened my mouth and shouted: Heil!').[10] It never occurred to Andersch to go into exile, nor to fight in Spain, as he freely admits. While Andersch lived a life of *innere Emigration* under National Socialism, he seems to have spent the rest of his life exploring in his travelogues and fiction the other two possibilities open to non-Nazis of his generation: resistance and exile. His own desertion was neither, but he presents it retrospectively as both.

In *Die Kirschen der Freiheit* Andersch deliberately conflates existential and aesthetic freedom, indeed his evocation of moments of existential choice is invariably aesthetically satisfying. In his youth, he relates, he escaped the monotony of his bleak *petit bourgeois* childhood by entering the Munich art galleries, admiring the architecture of the city, enjoying the park at Schleißheim. By 1952, of course, he is fully aware of the dangers of aesthetic escapism, but when he comes to present his final act of escape from the determinism of history, the psychological mechanism of his experience under National Socialism reasserts itself and he presents his desertion as a fusion of aesthetic and existential freedom. The 'wilderness' — the setting for his act of freedom is significantly *outside* society — is, we are told 'very beautiful'. But Andersch has advanced to an awareness of the tension between social and historical determinism and escape into art. The very structure of *Die Kirschen der Freiheit* underlines the point: sober, factual accounts of early experiences, discursive sections on the nature of freedom, comradeship, cowardice and courage, historical reflections on Communism, but also, juxtaposed with these, purely sensuous moments in which time seems to stand still: 'Man ist überhaupt niemals frei außer in den Augenblicken, in denen man sich aus dem Schicksal herausfallen läßt' ('One is never free except in those moments when one allows oneself to drop out of one's fate').[11] Interestingly, when Andersch defines such moments, he extends his argument to equate freedom, existential freedom, with artistic modernism: Picasso and Apollinaire 'ließen sich . . . in die Freiheit fallen' ('dropped into freedom').[12] The existential leap of faith which constitutes Andersch's choice of political freedom is likened to a modernist rejection of representational art, a parallel which again becomes a leitmotif of Andersch's fiction. This might appear far-fetched, but here Andersch is more conditioned by German history than he would care to admit. The implication, if we

10. Ibid., p. 33
11. Ibid., p. 126.
12. Ibid., p. 127.

tease it out, is as follows: modernism in art and literature was repudiated by the Nazis as 'entartet', degenerate. Any art, however, which National Socialism rejects, must of necessity acquire a special value: therefore, Andersch's private act of revolt against National Socialism can be equated with the championing of modernism. Interestingly, Andersch's arguments in support of modernism are similar to those used in support of the literature of *innere Emigration*: namely, that all art which is not explicitly Nazi, is somehow positively subversive.

Andersch's championing of modernism is also reflected in his wide-ranging editorial activities which, in view of their importance, deserve brief mention. In 1949 he edited a series called *Europäische Avantgarde* with texts by Camus, Sartre, Simone de Beauvoir and Malraux; out of his work with Radio Frankfurt, later the Hessischer Rundfunk, came the 'studio frankfurt' series (1952–3) with texts by Böll, Arno Schmidt, Weyrauch, Hildesheimer, Bachmann; from 1955 to 1958 Andersch was simultaneously editor of the 'Radio Essay' programme of the Süddeutscher Rundfunk and editor of *Texte und Zeichen*, perhaps the single most progressive and influential periodical of the decade. On the radio Andersch introduced works by Ionesco and Beckett, excerpts from novels by Faulkner and Wilder, adapted by Martin Walser; he presented Grass's play *Hochwasser*, Hildesheimer's *Die Uhren* and the work of Nelly Sachs. In *Texte und Zeichen* he published selections of the radio material and also, for the first time in Germany in many cases, works by Beckett, Borges, Char, Dylan Thomas, Neruda, Vittorini, Pavese, Barthes. It is scarcely an exaggeration to claim that Andersch created the liberal, modernist, eclectic taste of West Germany in the 1950s. While in East Germany the tradition of Socialist Realism was being fostered, Andersch was shaping an alternative tradition which was distinctly West German: largely modernist, yet pluralist and undogmatic, fusing into a new canon the conservative writers of both exile and *innere Emigration* (Thomas Mann, Jünger, Benn) and the experimental (Arno Schmidt, Heißenbüttel, Bense), combining an older generation which had published before 1945 with a new group of writers who established themselves only after the war.

If Andersch's editorial activity in the 1950s brings a variety of different approaches to literature into a loose association, so too does his creative writing. In *Sansibar oder der letzte Grund* (1957) he returns to his preoccupation with existential freedom, once more seeking to fuse this freedom with both political and aesthetic freedom. Political freedom is given with the situation itself: the Nazi threat in 1937 to Communists, Jews, to the mentally ill, to 'entartete Kunst' is presented through Gregor, Judith, Knudsen's wife and the Barlach statue of the 'Klosterschüler' respectively. But, within the novel, the specific historical situation of Germany in 1937 is underplayed: the Nazis are simply 'die Anderen', and as Andersch knows from his reading of Sartre, 'l'enfer, c'est les Autres'. The existential dimension is central to the dilemma faced by each character, for each has been jolted out of a habitual pattern by a personal loss: Gregor has lost his girlfriend and his belief in the deterministic pattern of the historical process reflected in his earlier Communist commitment, Knudsen has lost his belief in the Communist Party and fears losing his wife to a euthanasia programme, Judith has lost her mother, the boy has lost his father, and Helander, the clergyman, has lost his God. Exposure to the extreme situation entails the necessity of choice. Through the boy and Helander, Andersch lifts the story out of its historical context to reveal what he prefers to regard as the existential implications. The boy's dissatisfaction is a function of his youth, of his sense of an unfulfilled life; Helander's crisis is a function of his age, of a sense that life has failed to vindicate his faith. Neither finds himself in direct conflict with the totalitarian state, for the crisis in each case is independent of the historical situation. Between these extremes, however, lies the adult world of practicality and action, but here too existential implications emerge. Gregor's crisis is not directly related to his immediate situation: he has come to reject the determinism of history as propounded by his Marxist teachers (an experience which Andersch himself had undergone in 1934, but which could be located in any setting). Gregor's crisis of faith, the Tarasovka experience, is aesthetic. On manoeuvres with the Red Army, he suddenly abandons a goal-directed, deterministic approach in which the ends justify the means, for a sensuous delight in objects for their own sake. In viewing the landscape aesthetically — the scene is presented as a painting with a painter's eye for colour — Gregor frees himself from utilitarian concerns and delights in things as they are. This is his betrayal: delight in the world as it is implies that the world does not need to be changed. Aesthetic contemplation replaces political activism, affirmation replaces criticism.

But if Andersch here seems to be rejecting politics in favour of art, he is also, after his experience of aesthetic escapism in the 1930s, more sensitive than most to the dangers of sheer aestheticism. For if aesthetic contemplation can free man from the determinism of history, such freedom is only momentary. Man cannot live by art alone. To prevent the reader of *Sansibar oder der letzte Grund* from jumping to the wrong conclusions, Andersch introduces not only the

'Klosterschüler' statue but also a model interpretation of it. The statue, as interpreted by Gregor, is intended to embody a tension between affirmative involvement and critical detachment, both submission to a deterministic world view and freedom from that determinism. Although on the surface *Sansibar* is about physical escape and political freedom, its more profound concern is with aesthetic freedom and the *dangers* of escapism (dangers which Andersch, from his experience in the 1930s knew so well). The aesthetic debate, the argument about the rival claims of political activism and aesthetic detachment is by no means congruent with the political subject matter. *Sansibar* turns out to be as much about the dilemma of left-wing intellectuals (both after Hitler's seizure of power and in the aftermath of the Hungarian uprising in 1956) as about escaping from Nazi Germany.

In *Die Rote* (1960) Andersch experiments with an existential act set in contemporary Italy. But despite the fashionable modernity of the trappings of the heroine's life, the burden of the German past weighs heavily on the action. The Gestapo interrogator, Kramer; Patrick, forced by Kramer to betray his contacts; Serafina, the Jewish orphan whose parents are the victims of Fascism; the Shylock figure of the jeweller; the setting in the Venetian ghetto — all point back to the theme of betrayal and the traumatic experience of the German past. Franziska, the heroine, fearing that she is pregnant, rejects a choice between her husband, Herbert, and her lover, Joachim, between pedantic aestheticism and power, and opts for escape. Incidentally, the choice of names, Herbert and Joachim, the theme of abortion and the importance of chance encounters, echo Max Frisch's novel *Homo faber*, which appeared in 1957. In *Die Rote* Franziska catches the first available train from Milan, a random choice, and finds herself in Venice in winter, a setting which enables Andersch to allude to two further works by two quite disparate authors, both of whom he admired: Thomas Mann's *Der Tod in Venedig* and Hemingway's *Across the River and into the Trees*. In Venice, Franziska is confronted with a further choice, again between power and escapism, this time in the guise of Kramer and Patrick. Once more she opts for a third possibility, embodied by Fabio Crepaz, ex-Communist and violinist for whom, like most of Andersch's heroes, aesthetic values have replaced political ones. Rejecting abortion as a possibility, Franziska chooses to remain in Mestre with Fabio's family and have her child. Death in Venice will become birth in Mestre, the industrial setting of contemporary Italian society replacing the cultural monuments of the past.

As in his earlier work, Andersch deliberately conflates existential choice and artistic sensibility. Franziska, like Fabio, is a product of her taste: like Andersch, she admires Faulkner, whose *The Wild Palms* supplies further motifs for *Die Rote*, and the Italian neo-realist cinema, while Fabio represents an older tradition exemplified by Giorgione's painting *Tempestà* and Monteverdi's opera *Orfeo*. It is another cultural artefact, Fra Mauro's *Mappa mundi*, the lines of which intersect on the Campanile in Venice, which prefigures the meeting of Fabio and Franziska. Not only does Andersch present art as embodying the resolution of the tension between freedom and determinisn, between escapism and power, but he smuggles into the text, through allusion and structural device, precisely the artistic and literary canon which he popularised through his editorial activities. Modernist stream of consciousness and elements of the popular crime story (which Andersch extolled) co-exist rather uneasily; arcane allusions to high culture are juxtaposed with practical observations on contemporary fashion and insights into Italian daily life. *Die Rote* is, amongst other things, a kind of superior tourist guide to Venice, offering full coverage of the cultural monuments of the city, but also practical tips on how to survive. Perhaps it is its rather self-conscious eclecticism which made the book, despite a largely negative critical reception, a popular success.

If Franziska's ambition in *Die Rote* is to penetrate the mysterious 'otherness' of Italian life, George Efraim, hero of Andersch's next novel *Efraim* (1967) is given a vantage-point outside Germany in order to explore its peculiar uniqueness. Efraim is the modern incarnation of the Wandering Jew: German by birth, English by adoption, resident in Rome. The trauma of his parents' death and his sense of rootlessness give him a detachment ideal for his job as a reporter for an English newspaper. But when his editor, Kier Horne, dispatches him to Berlin to report on the tensions following the Cuban crisis, he embarks on a journey of self-discovery, of the re-discovery of his German identity and with it of the profound inner ambivalence of the German Jew after National Socialism. His supplementary, private task of uncovering the fate of Horne's daughter, Esther, rekindles painful memories, but also exposes the inadequacies of his adult relationships. His marriage to Meg is undermined by her open affair with Horne, while his own relationship with Anna Krystek in Berlin proves fallible. Through Anna and her father Efraim flirts with the idea of regaining access to an unbroken German Communist tradition, but this hope is illusory. Anna's fiancé, the avant-garde composer Hornbostel (who is linked by name with Horne) serves to remind Efraim of unsuspected artistic possibilities and stimulates him to adopt for his own narrative a modernist approach, for the novel is Efraim's narration of events.

Efraim's vulnerability and sensitivity make him an ideal medium to register the uncomfortable social, political, even linguistic, realities of West Germany in the 1960s, in particular the legacy of anti-Semitism and the problematic relationship with the GDR. The visit to Berlin triggers Efraim's decision to abandon journalism for literature, a decision which is, of course, Andersch's own. Only literature, it is implied, can convey the essence of East–West tension, for it alone can convey not merely a perceived reality, but the processes of perception itself, in particular the structuring of that perception through memory and association. The novel itself both depicts and embodies Efraim's literary efforts. In order to be capable of addressing himself to the German past, Efraim develops a theory of chance, a conviction that it was pure chance that twenty years earlier Jews in Germany were exterminated. Only such a theory can offer him relief from the even more horrendous acceptance of human responsibility. While this theory is psychologically credible for someone of George Efraim's background, it is intellectually less satisfying and exposed Andersch to a considerable amount of criticism from reviewers.[13] Andersch's narrative strategy is a distinct advantage in the delineation from within of the subjective structuring of experience, but an equally clear disadvantage in its attempts to confront the social and historical reality of the treatment of Jews in Nazi Germany.

In Andersch's last novel *Winterspelt* (1974) he is drawn back once again to the issues of betrayal and desertion which have dominated his writing. Within the well-documented historical context of December 1944, when it is clear that the war has been lost, Andersch constructs a fictional alternative to history, centring on Major Dincklage's plan to hand over his entire batallion to the Americans and so to bring nearer the inevitable end of hostilities. Instrumental in transforming his speculation into a concrete, practical plan is Käthe Lenk, who enjoys a close relationship with a former Marxist, Hainstock, who in turn employs an art historian, Schefold, as a go-between. Schefold moves between the lines, conveying Dincklage's plan to Captain Kimborough, his American opposite number. The plan fails on several counts: the American command is suspicious of Kimborough's plans and refuses to sanction the action; Riedel, a homosexual NCO and Nazi, is impelled, for personal reasons, to shoot Schefold. Not only is each character conditioned by

13. Notably Marcel Reich-Ranicki, in his article 'Sentimentalität und Gewissensbisse'; *Lauter Verrisse* (Munich, 1970), pp. 47–56.

social, political and psychological motives, but the complexities of the operation are set within the context of the Ardennes offensive, which is about to be unleashed but of which all the participants are blissfully unaware. In *Winterspelt* Andersch speculates again on the interplay between freedom and determinism, between subjective perceptions and history. The distinction between historical event and fiction is central: the historical outcome stands; it is known to the reader. But fictional narrative can free man from what Andersch calls the 'dictatorship of the indicative' and allow him to speculate on alternative courses of action. Not only does Andersch's novel embody the interplay of determinism and free choice, but it employs a specific work of art to symbolise the idyll in the midst of war. Paul Klee's 'Polyphon umgrenztes Weiß' is rescued by Schefold and shares his no man's land with him; in point of fact Klee calls the original picture *Polyphon gefaßtes Weiß*, but Andersch alters the adjective to underline the fact that he is exploring a 'Grenze' here: the geographical border but also the borderline between determinism and freedom, between history and fiction. The setting of *Winterspelt* also makes it a personal love story, for it was this landscape in which Gisela Andersch spent the last years of the war and which inspired her early drawings.

It would be a disservice to Andersch's reputation if an account of his novels omitted all reference to his short stories. His fondness for this form, often exploiting material used elsewhere in radio plays or features, is reflected in three major collections: *Geister und Leute* (1958), *Ein Liebhaber des Halbschattens* (1963) and *Mein Verschwinden in Providence* (1971). To these may be added his last work, *Der Vater eines Mörders* (1980). Particularly impressive are the thinly-veiled autobiographical stories with the central character of Franz Kien. As Andersch concedes in the postscript to *Der Vater eines Mörders* the third person narrative 'allows the writer to be as honest as possible'. Like the earlier Franz Kien stories, *Der Vater eines Mörders* offers a subtle dual perspective: a personal and a wider socio-political one, though the latter is only implicit. Within a single Greek lesson, conducted by the headmaster of the Wittelsbacher Gymnasium and father of Heinrich Himmler, Andersch seeks to lay bare the mechanisms of an educational, indeed a whole social, system. He explores retrospectively the trauma of his own academic failure; the lesson explores, through its confrontations, the tension between bourgeois educational ideals and both aristocratic superiority (represented by Konrad Greiff) and *petit bourgeois* inferiority (embodied by Franz Kien). The narrower range of the short story forces Andersch to concentrate on the specific detail and allow it to speak for itself; it absolves him from the need to present explicit social and political perspectives. The result is subtler prose, in which the surface simplicity belies the complexities evoked.

Andersch's life and work were characterised by a tension between aesthetic and political concerns; he at once appears to advocate artistic autonomy and to imply political imperatives. In formal terms this tension is illustrated by his equal enthusiasm for the communicative virtues and straightforward narrative of popular fiction and for the most abstract and experimental of forms. Both these modes coincide in his work, to the consternation of critics, if not of readers. Nor surprisingly, perhaps, his reputation has suffered for this; his work has been the target, at various time, of both political and aesthetic purists. Yet it is precisely this tension which has fascinated his readers. Through his editorial activity he sought to make Sartre and Beckett accessible to a wider public; at the same time he tried to rehabilitate popular literature for an educated public. With the catholic taste and eclecticism of an autodidact, Andersch displayed a genuine openness to foreign literature, to the cinema, to the visual arts, to science and philosophy. In an essay on the English novel in 1968, Andersch praised its traditional virtues and in so doing offered a neat summing-up of his own achievement: the English novel, he argued, sought 'to portray relationships and conflicts between people, draw characters and emotional impulses, unfold an exciting plot, delineate clearly historical and social connections and beyond this to reflect the individuality of the author'.[14]

14. 'Auf der Suche nach dem englischen Roman', reprinted in *Die Blindheit des Kunstwerks* (Zurich, 1979), pp. 103–10 (here p. 104). The essay was first published in English in *The Times Literary Supplement*, 12 September 1968, pp. 981–2.

JULIET WIGMORE

Ingeborg Bachmann

When Ingeborg Bachmann died in 1973, she had published only one complete novel, *Malina*, which appeared in 1971, and it is on this work that her reputation as a novelist largely resides.[1] Prior to the publication of *Malina*, Bachmann had been admired as a poet and as the author of short stories, notably the collection *Das dreißigste Jahr* (1961). Although *Malina* remains her most significant contribution to extended prose narrative, there has recently been some critical interest in *Der Fall Franza*, a novel which was left incomplete on her death and whose subject matter reflects some of the issues evident in *Malina*. *Der Fall Franza* was conceived as the first of a series of novels and was partially complete by 1966 when Bachmann abandoned it to work on *Malina*. These two novels, together with the fragment 'Requiem für Fanny Goldmann',[2] have the collective title *Todesarten*, which was the working title of *Malina* until its publication.[3]

The three novels are linked not only by the overall idea of 'Todesarten' ('ways of death') which pervades their subject matter, but also by many allusions to characters and events, creating a particular social ambience. Some of the same characters recur in different roles, and Bachmann herself once stated that she intended a background figure in one novel to occupy a foreground position in another.[4] Recurrent motifs which emerge through a reading of Bachmann's fiction assume greater importance than individual characters, however, and this feature also applies to the short stories of *Das dreißigste Jahr* and *Simultan* (1972). In the novels, it is not a matter of piecing together the plot, in any naturalistic sense, but of viewing a constellation of ideas which, like some of the characters,

1. Except where stated, references are made to Ingeborg Bachmann, *Werke I–IV*, (Munich, 1978).

2. This work consists of approximately forty pages, *Werke III*, pp. 483–524.

3. Friedrich Heer, 'Eine Frau aus Österreich. In memoriam Ingeborg Bachmann', *Die Brücke*, I (1975), p. 95; Interview with Toni Kienlechner, Ingeborg Bachmann, *Wir müssen wahre Sätze finden* (Munich, 1983), p. 95. (References to this work are given henceforth as *WS*.)

4. See Kienlechner, *WS*, p. 96. As an example, Franziska Jordan, who is the central figure in *Der Fall Franza*, plays a major part in the short story 'Das Gebell' (*II*, 373–93) and is mentioned in *Malina*, (*III*, 21).

are issued in one work, only to be thrown into relief in another, a technique evident in *Malina* and *Der Fall Franza*, the works which will be discussed here.

Malina succeeded in achieving a large readership, yet critical attention was at first unsatisfactory, for it treated the novel at best with glowing praise, without much willingness to tackle the issues it raised.[5] The revival of interest in this work in particular came in the wake of feminist criticism in the late 1960s.[6] For while Bachmann's thought is to some extent pre-feminist, in the sense of the new German women's movement, the feminist critical angle has greatly contributed towards an understanding of the issues at stake in *Malina* and *Der Fall Franza*, both in terms of subject matter, the politics of oppression, and with respect to the narrative structure, an aspect of particular relevance to *Malina*, but also to the short stories. The approach of feminist critics has helped to elucidate the highly complex, multi-layered structure of *Malina*, which admits of various interpretations, but which cannot be satisfactorily read in exclusively 'naturalistic' terms.

Malina has the outer framework of a love story, in which the first-person narrator tells of the development and decline of her relationship with Ivan, and of the life she shares with a man called Malina. The demise of her relationship with Ivan brings about the annihilation of the narrator herself, because she is emotionally dependent upon him. She eventually disappears 'into the wall', in the apartment which she shares with Malina, whereupon he denies that she ever existed.

As the outline given above suggests, the motivation of the novel cannot be interpreted in the terms of a conventional love story, since even the basic framework of events demands explanation, especially the narrator's final disappearance. Nor is the mode of narration in any sense conventional. The novel consists of four main sections of varying length, the first of which is untitled and is a type of prelude, raising certain theoretical issues, such as notions of time, space and

5. See Elke Atzler, 'Ingeborg Bachmanns Roman "Malina" im Spiegel der literarischen Kritik', *Jahrbuch der Grillparzer-Gesellschaft*, 3.Folge, 15 (1983), pp. 155–71; Gabriele Bail, *Weibliche Identität. Ingeborg Bachmanns 'Malina'* (Göttingen, 1984) pp. 2–7.

6. Ellen Summerfield's work marks the beginning of this tendency. It may be seen at a sophisticated stage in the essays of Sigrid Weigel (ed.), *Ingeborg Bachmann* (Munich, 1984).

identity, whose importance becomes clear retrospectively. The three chapters which follow, entitled 'Glücklich mit Ivan', 'Der dritte Mann' and 'Von letzten Dingen' are disparate in many respects, most crucially in the fact that they occupy different dimensions of consciousness. The first chapter takes place in the outside world, the second is composed largely of dream sequences, interspersed with analytical dialogues between the narrator and Malina, while the third leaves the outside world almost entirely behind, concentrating only on the thoughts and perceptions of the narrator. Each of these levels corresponds to a different stage in the emotional life of the narrator, and the narrative mode varies correspondingly.

The structure of the novel has an experimental appearance, for it comprises many different formal styles of writing and alludes to various genres other than the epic: dramatic dialogue, a tale in the style of a *Märchen*, one end of telephone conversations, letters, an interview, musical motifs and a variety of forms of prose discourse, from philosophical meditation to dream sequences. This diversity is to be interpreted as part of the substance of the novel, for the narrator characterises herself as a writer by profession, and in narrating the outer novel, *Malina*, she seeks to give an account of her life, not as an autobiographical history, but as a depiction of her personality in the present, stage by stage. The role of the narrator as a creative artist partly explains why the greatest variety of form occurs in the first chapter, when Ivan's love acts as a stimulus to her and gives many facets to her life. Under his impetus, she narrates most of the tale of the 'Prinzessin von Kagran', the optimistic story of an ideal world of the past which is to be restored in the future, and in which she herself identifies with the person of the Princess. By the end of the novel, the narrative scope becomes more restricted, reflecting the deprived emotional life of the narrator, until, having lost Ivan, she loses her inspiration, and because she has no more to say, the narrator herself disappears.[7] Being deprived of love results in the artist's finding herself without language and so unable to maintain her identity, as an artist and as the narrator of the novel. Yet the problem of establishing and losing identity is also centred on the way the narrator relates to the other personae of the novel, particularly Ivan and Malina.

The characters of the novel occupy various levels of reality simulta-

7. In the short story *Undine geht* (*II*, 253–63) the female narrator disappears under similar circumstances.

neously and are delineated in terms of one another. On the one hand, the detailed descriptions of the place where they live, the Ungargasse in Vienna, gives them all a presence in the real world, and even the problematic figure of Malina is depicted as an individual person: 'Es gibt Leute, die meinen, Malina und ich seien verheiratet' ('Some people think that Malina and I are married') (*III*, 249). Yet the manner in which Malina and the narrator 'live together' is not that of a couple in the usual sense. They occupy different areas of the apartment and scarcely encroach upon one another, even though the narrator is dependent on Malina for many practical things. Most revealing is the fact that Malina pays little attention to the narrator's relationship with Ivan, suggesting that the two male characters do not represent rivals for her affections in any conventional sense and that the two relationships therefore operate in different dimensions.

Nevertheless, Malina and Ivan are directly contrasted in a way which helps to explain their roles in relation to the narrator: 'Ivan und ich: die konvergierende Welt. Malina und ich, weil wir eins sind: die divergierende Welt' ('Ivan and I: the converging world. Malina and I, because we are one: the diverging world' (*III*, 126). Both Ivan and Malina are thus defined in terms of the personality of the narrator, who is thereby portrayed in terms which are explicitly relative. As the passage quoted indicates, Malina and the narrator are in some sense aspects of one person, *Doppelgänger*, a relationship which, though problematic, helps to explain certain aspects of the text. In the material world, Malina and the narrator live side by side in an apartment on one side of the Ungargasse, while Ivan lives nearly opposite, and this spatial dimension suggests that Malina is closer to the narrator than Ivan is. Within the apartment, nevertheless, Malina and the narrator lead separate lives, and Malina's domain is in the depths, behind the narrator's: 'ich gehe ins Wohnzimmer, er geht weiter, nach hinten, denn das letzte Zimmer ist sein Zimmer' ('I go into the living room, he goes past, to the back of the flat, for the last room is his') (*III*, 23). This statement from the opening section of the novel is one of many in which spatial arrangements acquire psychological overtones: Malina and the narrator share the same space but also divide it between them, a pattern which anticipates in external terms the idea that they constitute an integral personality which at the same time is divided. Spatial relations are relative to the inner life of the perceiving subject, the narrator, and shed light on the way she relates to other people. In the same vein, she attaches importance to 'home', by which she means the part of the Ungargasse which is relevant to her emotional life: 'ich kann nicht sein, wo Ivan nicht ist, aber ebensowenig kann ich heimkommen, wenn Malina nicht da ist' ('I am unable to exist without Ivan's presence, but I am equally unable to return home without the presence of Malina') (*III*, 284). As this suggests, from the narrator's perspective Malina and Ivan are complementary figures. Her existence itself depends upon Ivan's 'being there' for her, yet if she retreats into her own sphere, Malina is necessarily present. She is unable to evade him, whereas she seeks to enter Ivan's domain with only limited success.

Malina's ambiguous status is indicated when the narrator insists, somewhat defensively, on her own logical priority, telling him in one of their dialogues: 'du bist überhaupt erst denkbar nach mir' ('it is only possible to conceive of you as consequent upon me') (*III*, 247). While he has a presence in the outer world, as a figure in the novel which she narrates, he also occupies a more abstract, psychological role as an aspect of her personality, which is ultimately the subject matter of the novel. In this capacity he represents some part which is younger than her physical existence, such as her adult self, or her *alter ego*, and it is his rational personality which she invokes to untangle awkward situations. One such occasion arises when she goes to stay with the Altenwyls and feels that she is wasting her time because she is separated from Ivan. It is then to Malina that she turns, asking him to send a telegram requesting her urgent return to Vienna. In another episode, she wonders how to behave towards the Bulgarian who is apparently suffering from leprosy and who begs money from her. Intellectually, she refers the situation to Malina: 'was täte Malina jetzt, was würde Malina tun?') ('If I were Malina, what would I do, what would Malina do?') (*III*, 114). Malina is thus her point of reference for rational behaviour, by contrast with which her own is susceptible to emotional blackmail. In the many dialogues in the latter part of the novel, Malina prompts her to analyse her feelings and her life, in a manner similar to that of a psychoanalyst, asking her, for example, brief questions about the dreams she describes to him, in order to elicit information about her responses to them: 'Warum kommt deine Schwester vor, wer ist deine Schwester?' ('Why does your sister appear in the dream? Who is your sister?') (*III*, 213). This analytical and therapeutic technique is used to make feelings conscious, and since Malina is at one level a part of the narrator's personality, the discussions are, in a sense, dialogues with the self. In them, the narrator attempts to come to terms with the unconscious fears which surface in her dreams, and which have far-reaching roots in both past and present. Thus, like the material of the dreams, the figures of Malina and the narrator themselves operate at various levels of consciousness.

Ivan's role is more limited and definable than is Malina's. Near the end of the novel, the narrator, lamenting the loss of Ivan's love, says: 'ich brauche mein Doppelleben, mein Ivanleben und mein Malinafeld' ('I need my double life, my Ivan-life and my Malina-field') (*III*, 284). Ivan is her lover, but also her opposite pole, for besides the locations where they live, their life styles contrast: the narrator's work keeps her at home, while Ivan frequently goes away for long periods, connected with his confidential work, and in this respect he lives in the outside world. This contrast between internal and external lifestyles is based partly on conventional characterisations of gender polarity, where they represent the lives of women and men respectively. Here, however, it also permeates the structure of the novel, for only in the first chapter, 'Glücklich mit Ivan', does the narrator have a life outside, including the reluctant trip to the Altenwyls and the encounter with the Bulgarian in the Café Landmann, for Ivan is said to offer the narrator 'Injektionen von Wirklichkeit' ('injections of reality') (*III*, 76). Once he has deserted her, she is abandoned entirely to her inner life, and into the hands of Malina, the detached intellectual side of her personality. In the division between active, external life and the intellect, represented by Ivan and Malina respectively, the artist is placed firmly in the scope of the intellect, yet paradoxically she cannot be an artist at all without the input of 'reality' embodied by Ivan. This aspect is very similar to the dichotomy between 'Leben' and 'Geist' in much of Thomas Mann's work, particularly with regard to the position of the artist.[8] Yet in *Malina* this is only one contributory factor in a schema which is also concerned with the position of the woman as artist in particular, and with her art as an aspect of her personality.

In different ways both Ivan and Malina contribute to the annihilation of the narrator: 'ich habe in Ivan gelebt und ich sterbe in Malina' ('Ivan was my life and Malina will be my death') (*III*, 335). The withdrawal of Ivan's affection is 'murderous', yet Malina also plays a fatal role, as when, representing the voice of reason, he urges her to stamp out her residual affection for Ivan and the children: 'ich möchte die Kinder nicht mehr sehen, vor allem die Kinder nicht, Ivan immer, aber nicht die Kinder, die er mir nehmen will. Ich kann Béla und András nicht mehr sehen . . . Malina flüstert in mir: Töte sie, töte sie' ('I don't want to see the children any more now, the

8. In *Malina* there are many allusions to Thomas Mann, particularly to *Doktor Faustus*, which in turn is associated with the motifs from Schoenberg which pervade *Malina*. See Karen Achberger 'Der Fall Schoenberg' in Weigel, *Bachmann*, pp. 120–31.

children above all, I'm always willing to see Ivan, but not the children who he is going to take away from me. I can't see Béla and András again . . . Malina whispers within me: kill them, kill them') (*III*, 315). The rational Malina destroys the part which has given her life and creativity, thereby denying her a meaningful existence. Hence, when she finally succumbs, it is Malina who remains triumphant and denies that she has ever existed. Only the intellectual side of her personality is left behind, without the emotional life in the real world which was to have restored her personality, her 'verschüttetes Ich' ('submerged ego') (*III*, 36) and make her a true artist.

At the same time as it presents the rival claims of reason and emotion in the person of the artist, *Malina* embodies the problems of a woman artist specifically, but also suggests that this aspect may be based in an inherent friction between the interests of men and women generally. In this context, the pattern of the external plot is a familiar one: a woman becomes dependent because of emotional ties, sacrifices her professional and creative life and eventually completely loses her identity. Yet the narrator in *Malina* is simultaneously seeking to establish her identity through her writing and to create an idealised persona in the person of the Prinzessin von Kagran, an attempt in which she ultimately fails. The paradoxical aspect lies in the fact that her creativity is inspired by Ivan, and the narrator comes to realise that it entirely depends upon him. She seeks to combine her inherent intellectualism, represented by the person of Malina, with an emotional, external life, which is at first alien to her but which she needs in order to give substance to her writing. While she makes an attempt to synthesise the two aspects within herself and to produce something creative, Ivan and Malina, seen as 'real' people, are oblivious of how one-dimensional they are. They have in common the fact that they destroy the female personality, even though they are diametrically opposed in other respects, and her demise can be seen as a consequence of the existence of warring factions, which at one level are based in male and female gender differences.

In conversation with Malina in the third chapter, the narrator castigates men in general: 'Die Männer sind nämlich verschieden voneinander, und eigentlich müsste man in jedem einzelnen einen unheilbaren klinischen Fall sehen' ('Men are different from one another, and indeed one might well see in every individual one of them an incurable clinical case') (*III*, 268). The psychosis frequently, but by no means always, occurs as cerebralism, a criticism directed at Malina: 'Tausendmal besser läßt sich das Zerebrale an einem Mann verstehen, für mich jedenfalls. Nur das, was allen gemeinsam sein soll, ist es ganz gewiß nicht. Was für ein Irrtum! Dieses Material, das eine Generalisierung zuließe, könnte man in Jahrhunderten nicht zusammentragen' ('Cerebralism is much easier to understand in a man, for me at least. Only it certainly isn't the thing they all have in common. What a delusion! That would be material for a generalisation, but it couldn't be substantiated in a hundred years') (*III*, 268). The narrator is groping for some such generalisation about what characterises men with regard to the way they relate to women and knows that it is not always intellectualism, but the generalisation which actually emerges from the novel as a whole is that men are destructive of women, as Ivan and Malina are in her own case, and this message is reinforced and generalised through the role of the father figure in the second chapter.

In the second chapter, entitled 'Der dritte Mann', the narrator dreams of her father in a variety of contexts, all of them characterised by violence done to her, and in some case to other people. The dreams are interspersed with dialogues between the narrator and Malina, in which Malina prompts her to analyse and interpret the fears which surface in her dreams. The dreams represent a highly personal inner world, of which Malina is a part, and yet it is suggested that they are also of more general significance and perhaps apply not only to the narrator's own life: 'Der Ort ist diesmal nicht Wien. Es ist ein Ort, der heißt Überall und Nirgends. Die Zeit ist nicht heute' ('This time the place is not Vienna. It is a place called Everywhere and Nowhere. The time is not the present') (*III*, 174). The dream is a means of bringing the past into the focus of the present.[9] As well as having an ambivalent time structure, the dreams are paradoxical in so far as they are individual experiences and yet they bring to light general issues.

A recurrent motif in the dreams is the 'Friedhof der ermordeten Töchter' ('cemetery of murdered daughters') (*III*, 175), suggesting that the narrator recognises that the fate which she suffers at the hands of her father is not an exclusively personal one. The brutal father figure appears in the dreams in various roles, but always characterised by the power and authority which he is able to exert

9. 'Da wird sozusagen das, was man sonst erzählen könnte als Vergangenheit, in diesen heutigen Träumen gebracht.' Interview with Otto Basil, 14 April 1971, *WS*, pp. 101–5 (p. 103).

over her. At the most intimate level, she dreams of an incestuous relationship with her father in childhood, which, it is implied, destroyed her mother and sister, suggesting that all the women in his sphere experience suffering. We do not know whether this dream episode has any foundation in reality, only that it is relevant to her present feelings. Later, her father appears with her mother's face:

> '*Ich*: Warum is mein Vater auch meine Mutter?
> *Malina*: Warum wohl? Wenn jemand alles ist für einen anderen, dann kann er viele Personen in einer Person sein'
>
> ('*Myself*: Why is my father also my mother?
> *Malina*: Why? When somebody is everything to another person, he can be many people in one') (*III*, 232).

By taking on the appearance of her mother, the father has usurped the woman's personality, denying her an independent existence, as well as having implications of androgyny which parallel the narrator's own dual personality. The absorption of the mother figure by the male counterpart in the dream foreshadows Malina's final denial that the narrator herself has ever existed, thereby suggesting that the dream sequence is a model for the way men relate to women. The dreams express the oppression which the narrator experiences with the knowledge that her relationship with Ivan is on the wane, and a parallel emerges between the brutality of various kinds practised by the father figure, seen in relation to the past, the programmatic anticipation of Malina's role at the end of the novel and Ivan's role relative to the present moment. Like the father in the dream, Ivan also to some extent plays the role of both father and mother to his children, with the result that the female narrator is made to feel excluded from his life: 'ich liebe niemand. Die Kinder selbstverständlich ja, aber sonst niemand' ('I don't love anybody. Except the children of course, but nobody else') (*III*, 58).

In the dreams, the daughter is violated by her father, not only in terms of the family, but also when he appears in powerful social and cultural positions, such as when she is forced to play a role in an opera which he is producing. As she is not equipped for the part, she is exposed and humiliated. The general significance of the dreams becomes more evident, however, when the narrator envisages her father as a Nazi murderer and herself as one of his victims in a concentration camp, and as a Jewish woman awaiting deportation (*III*, 175; *III*, 192–3). The patriarchal principle which oppresses women as individuals is presented as being also responsible for mass destruction. Because it appears in the style of a dream, the connection between these situations is not made explicit, but the reader must assume that the narrator has recognised, perhaps unconsciously, that the oppression she experiences is known to all oppressed peoples, and that women are one such category. Later, when awake, she mentions that she accidentally wrote 'Todesraten' ('death statistics') instead of 'Todesarten' ('ways of death') (*III*, 288), a Freudian slip which indicates that she is obsessed with death from a quantitative point of view, and not only with accounts of individual deaths, bizarre as they often are, such as that of the vagrant Marcel, who dies of shock when forced to take a shower (*III*, 282–3). In 'Der dritte Mann', the concentration camp scenario is in fact one of the first dreams to occur, and it seems that the narrator only later finds her way to the most fundamental form of oppression, in the family. Thus the series of dreams, with the father figure as central element and connecting link, implies that the oppression occurs initially at a personal level but has counterparts at the macro-political level and that they spring from the same source.

The father figure in the dreams is described as being the narrator's 'murderer', highlighting the implicit paradox that the source of her life should actively seek her extinction: 'Es ist nicht mein Vater. Es ist mein Mörder' ('It is not my father. It is my murderer') (*III*, 235). Similar terminology is later used to describe the narrator's disappearance: 'Es war Mord' ('It was murder') (*III*, 337). This murder is partly brought about by Ivan, but ultimately it is also the responsibility of Malina, the other part of herself. He becomes increasingly aloof, and their natures diverge continually. Ivan's departure from her life renders her susceptible to Malina, so that eventually she loses contact with 'life' which Ivan represented.

Before the narrator disappears into the wall, the 'murder', the wall has occurred as a motif with various connotations. While the relationship with Ivan was still happy, he asked: 'Warum gibt es nur eine Klagemauer, warum hat noch nie jemand eine Freudenmauer gebaut?' ('Why is there only a Wailing Wall? Why hasn't anybody yet built a Rejoicing Wall?') (*III*, 61). For the narrator, however, walls never have such optimistic connotations but are associated with acts of oppression, as when she is excluded from the house by her father (*III*, 219). The ending of the novel is only slightly more ambiguous, in so far as on that occasion the narrator is not restrained by the wall as a boundary but seems able to transcend it and to escape into another sphere. Yet there is no suggestion that this route leads anywhere positive, and the chapter heading 'Von letzten Dingen', which would normally imply a metaphysical dimension, is here ironical, since the narrator's existence is merely cancelled out.

The destruction of the narrator entails the destruction of art: 'Ein Tag wird kommen, und es wird nur die trockene heitere gute Stimme von Malina geben, aber kein schönes Wort mehr von mir' ('A day will come, and there will be only the dry, blithe, pleasant voice of Malina, but no beautiful words of mine') (*III*, 326). The optimistic tale of the Prinzessin von Kagran, which was inspired by Ivan's love, will never be completed. With it, the utopia of a golden age is also abandoned: 'Kein Tag wird kommen, es werden die Menschen niemals, es wird die Poesie niemals und sie werden niemals, die Menschen werden schwarze, finstere Augen haben, von ihren Händen wird die Zerstörung kommen, die Pest wird kommen' ('No day will come, people will never, poetry will never and they will never come, people will have dark, ominous eyes, destruction will come from their hands, there will be plague') (*III*, 303). The artist cannot survive the loss of Ivan, because she cannot continue to be an artist without his inspiration, and art itself is extinguished with her demise.

The vision of harmony which has been lost forever in the story of the Prinzessin von Kagran contrasts with the state of affairs in the present, as is echoed in the elegiac words from Schoenberg's *Pierrot Lunaire*, 'O alter Duft aus Märchenzeit' ('O ancient scent of fairy tale') (*III*, 15 etc.). In the tale, harmony between the lovers is set against the backdrop of a world in which there are no boundaries of national states, notably between Austria and Hungary in the Danube basin. Such spatial freedom contrasts with the restrictions imposed upon the narrator who constantly tries to make contact with Ivan, the Hungarian lover, often unsuccessfully. However, the contrast between the better world of the Prinzessin von Kagran and the imperfect world of the present, in which the narrator is writing, forms a parallel to the actual political divisions, the boundaries between Austria and the other states which were once a political unit. Something similar is implied too when the narrator refers to the matters important in her life as 'das Haus Österreich' ('the House of Austria) (*III*, 99). Again, Malina is said to originate from the border area of Yugoslavia, and the narrator appears to regard him almost as the mirror image of herself in geographical terms: 'die Stadt "Belgerad", deren Exotik und Bedeutung sich erst verflüchtigte, als sich herausstellte, daß Malina nicht aus Belgrad kommt, sondern nur von der jugoslavischen Grenze, wie ich selber' ('the city of "Belgerad" which only lost its exoticism and significance when it emerged that Malina does not come from Belgrade but only from the

Yugoslavian border, as I do myself') (*III*, 20). The boundaries, which in this context are political, are perceived primarily in personal terms, as is also the case when the narrator finally transcends the boundary of the wall. Yet the political metaphor of the Austrian frontiers, like that of the electric fence surrounding the concentration camp in her dream, helps to widen the context of the oppression which she experiences and to characterise it as something all-pervasive. It is probably for this reason that she emphasises at the outset that the novel is set in the present, suggesting that the problems treated are pertinent to the modern age (*III*, 12–13).

The links between the personal and the more general levels of the novel are in many cases established through exploiting the ambiguity of linguistic signs. For example, Ivan's name is of Slavonic origin and occurs frequently in the central European context, where it is the equivalent of 'Hans' in German, a suitably typical name for the male character in *Malina*.[10] Malina's name also has certain semantic reverberations, among them an allusion to French 'mâle' and English 'male', but also to the Romance root of 'malevolence'. Such an association is triggered by deliberate plays on words which make the reader conscious of the symbolic nature of language, as when the narrator says: 'Je suis tombée mal, je suis tombée bien' (*III*, 304), and also by the fact that a number of other characters in the novel have names which allude to Malina's, such as 'Melanie', the father's mistress, and 'Lina', the maid.

The relationship between Ivan and the narrator is partly characterised by the type of language they both use, to which explicit reference is made: 'Immerhin haben wir uns ein paar erste Gruppen von Sätzen erobert, törichten Satzanfängen, Halbsätzen, Satzenden, von der Gloriole gegenseitiger Nachsicht umgeben, und die meisten Sätze sind bisher unter den Telephonsätzen zu finden' ('All the same, we've mastered a few preliminary groups of sentences, silly sentence openings, half sentences, sentence endings, surrounded by the aura of consideration for one another, and up till now most of the sentences can be found among the telephone sentences') (*III*, 38). By the end of their relationship, silence comes

10. In *Undine geht*, the female narrator castigates all men on earth, and to her they are all called 'Hans': 'Ich habe einen Mann gekannt, der heiß Hans, und er war anders als alle anderen. Noch einen kannte ich, der war auch anders als alle anderen. Dann einen, der war ganz anders als alle anderen und er heiß Hans, ich liebte ihn!' (*II*, 258).

to prevail, but it is anticipated early on, when Ivan attempts to suppress aspects of the narrator's style, objecting to her use of the phrase 'zum Beispiel': 'um mir die Beispielsätze auszutreiben, verwendet er jetzt Beispielsätze' ('in order to banish my "for example" sentences, Ivan now uses "for example" sentences') (*III*, 40). At one point the narrator's use of this phrase implies that she herself is exemplary: 'ich, zum Beispiel, bin nicht neugierig' ('I, for example, am not curious') (*III*, 41). She ostensibly intends 'for example' as a sentence adverbial, yet the position of the adverb narrows its scope, so that it can also be understood as referring only to the subject of the sentence. In this way, language is sometimes used as a trap-door to her unconscious, or to another level of narrative, as in the dream sequence, when the father conceals the signs of brutality towards women collectively: 'Mein Vater läßt den See über die Ufer treten, damit nichts herauskommt, damit nichts zu sehen ist, damit die Frauen über Gräbern ertrinken, damit die Gräber ertrinken, mein Vater sagt: Es ist eine Vorstellung: WENN WIR TOTEN ERWACHEN' ('My father makes the lake flood the banks so that nothing emerges, nothing can be seen, so that the women drown over the graves, so that the graves themselves are drowned, my father says: it's a play, *When we dead awaken*') (III, 219). At this the narrator herself awakes, but the word 'Vorstellung' is the trigger for the dual level of the dream: it is an 'idea in the mind' which is embodied in the dream of a theatrical performance, and language is a means whereby various associations are established through the medium of the dream.

Malina is thus the story of an individual striving for perfection in her art, but whose vision of a better world is shattered by the failure of her emotional life to come to fruition. Eventually she is deprived of everything: the model for perfection, the inspiration and language. It is for this reason that she finally writes herself out of the story and disappears with the end of the novel. However, in spite of the subjective mode of narration, her experiences are not exclusively personal, for the patriarchal forces which subdue women are linked with the forces which gave rise to the collective nightmare of mass murder. There is no suggestion that the situation might change for the better, for the vision of an optimistic future, embodied in her art, is crushed, together with the artist herself. This pessimistic message is conveyed by the radical manner of narration, which suggests that the narrator's own oppression has many reverberations.

In an interview made for a film about her attitude to Austria,

Ingeborg Bachmann rejected the suggestion that *Malina* was primarily a political statement about fascism, but agreed that she had considered the nature of fascism, and, in a reference to 'Der dritte Mann', stated: 'Der Faschismus ist das erste in der Beziehung zwischen einem Mann und einer Frau, ich habe versucht zu sagen, in diesem Kapitel, hier in dieser Gesellschaft ist immer Krieg. Es gibt nicht Krieg und Frieden, es gibt nur den Krieg' ('Fascism is the first thing in the relationship between a man and a woman; in this chapter I have tried to say that, in this society, it is always war. It is not a matter of war and peace, there is only war').[11]

Whereas in *Malina* the political connotation is only one of the many aspects contributing to the characterisation of the relationship between the male characters and the female narrator, in *Der Fall Franza* the political and social context is wider and to a great extent more explicit and less intricate. In a draft introduction to the novel, Ingeborg Bachmann drew attention to a moral and political problem of modern time: 'Es ist mir, und wahrscheinlich Ihnen auch oft durch den Kopf gegangen, wohin das Virus Verbrechen gegangen ist — es kann doch nicht vor zwanzig Jahren (sc. 1946) plötzlich aus unserer Welt verschwunden sein, bloss weil hier Mord nicht mehr ausgezeichnet, verlangt, mit Orden bedacht und unterstützt wird' ('I have often wondered, as you probably have too, where the virus "crime" has gone — surely it cannot suddenly have disappeared completely twenty years ago just because murder is no longer something honoured, in demand, considered worthy of medals and actively promoted here') (*III*, 341).[12] In *Der Fall Franza* the crime is in the first instance a private one, as it is in *Malina*, perpetrated against Franza first by her husband and later by the stranger who rapes and violently assaults her. Nevertheless, the social and political parallels are more overt than they are in *Malina*, a result partly of the different narrative perspective. The most substantial extant parts of the novel, the first and third chapters, are mainly narrated from a point of view close to that of Franza's brother, Martin Ranner, but in the third person, with the result that the novel is less orientated towards the subjective narrator than *Malina* is and more weight accrues to events in the outside world.

In the second chapter, 'Jordanische Zeit', large portions of the very incomplete text are narrated in Franza's words. She describes to her brother the nature of her relationship with her husband, the

11. *WS*, p. 144.

12. The statement dates from 1966, when parts of the novel were read by Ingeborg Bachmann (*III*, 559).

psychiatrist Leo Jordan, from whom she has fled, and discusses the significance of the word 'fascism' in the private sphere: 'Du sagst Faschismus, das ist komisch, ich habe das noch nie gehört als ein Wort für ein privates Verhalten. . . . Aber das ist gut, denn irgendwo muß es ja anfangen, natürlich, warum redet man davon nur, wenn es um Ansichten und öffentliche Handlungen geht' ('You say fascism, that's odd. I've never heard that word used to describe a private attitude. . . . But that's right, for it must start somewhere after all, of course, why do people only talk about it when it's a matter of views and public activities') (*III*, 403). As in *Malina*, it is implied that the type of behaviour which is labelled 'fascism' should be treated in terms of individual psychology and social interaction, for it is not only or most fundamentally found in the wider political context. Franza herself is a victim of such 'fascism', a tyranny which has manifested itself in her husband's treating her as if she were a psychiatric 'case', a pattern which apparently bears the responsibility for inducing the paranoia to which she ultimately succumbs. Yet she is not alone in her suffering, for her husband was married twice previously: one wife would never leave the house and the second committed suicide, while Franza herself has suffered such violation that she aids and abets what is in effect murder.

That marriage itself may be responsible for the destruction of women is implied partly by the fact that Leo Jordan's three wives have suffered similarly, but also by the attention paid to the fact that Franza resumes her own name, which is that of her brother. She appears to believe that by giving up Jordan's name she has escaped her marriage: 'Jetzt bin ich die dritte, mit diesem Namen, die dritte gewesen, verbesserte sie sich' ('Now I'm the third to bear this name, was the third, she corrected herself') (*III*, 400). Paradoxically, the route which seems to offer an escape means regressing to childhood, something portrayed in social and geographical terms, rather than psychological ones. She returns to her home village, Galicien, to her brother, and resumes not only her maiden name but also her childhood forename 'Franza', instead of the more formal 'Franziska' by which she was known in Vienna. Yet, as in the case of the story of the 'Prinzessin von Kagran' in *Malina*, seeking refuge in a better world in the past is not sufficient to bring about a healing process.

The oppression exercised by patriarchal attitudes in *Der Fall Franza* is clearly shown as a parallel to what is normally understood by the term 'fascism'. During the archaeological expedition which Franza and her brother undertake to the Egyptian desert, with connotations of excavating a past which is at once collective and individual to Franza, she declares her solidarity with the most remote of oppressed peoples, as if she had discovered some fundamental principle: 'ich bin eine Papua' ('I am a Papuan woman') (*III*, 414). In the desert of 'die ägyptische Finsternis'[13] Franza is brutally raped by a white man, almost within sight of her brother who is unable to protect her. Franza then contributes to her own destruction by knocking her head against the stones of the pyramid, indicating how much she has internalised the violation of her personality and of her physical person, both of them forms of violence perpetrated in different ways by white men. Her last words to Martin suggest a connection between the personal level of violence, which is really the 'war' which goes on between the sexes, and the violence done to the desert itself by the imperialist mentality: 'Die Weißen, sie sollen. — Sie sollen verflucht sein' ('The Whites, may they be damned') (*III*, 469). That the European mentality is intrusive is suggested by references to Suez, for example, but also to intellectual imperialism: 'Wer fürchtet hier die von den Weißen katalogisierten Bakterien' ('Who is afraid here of the bacteria classified by white men') (*III*, 424).[14] Franza's death occurs just before the destruction of Wadi Halfa, which was drowned in the name of progress.

Both *Malina* and *Der Fall Franza* are thus primarily concerned with the internalised oppression of women by men, and yet it is suggested that there are parallels in political situations whose sinister nature is more generally acknowledged. There is, however, a difference in emphasis between the novels, which is related to the narrative technique and structure: in *Malina*, the wider political dimension is used largely as an image to clarify the nature of the way the narrator is oppressed and to extend her experience to women generally. In *Der Fall Franza*, by contrast, an attempt is made to place the theme of patriarchal oppression within the context of political oppression in contemporary time, and not only with reference to historical images of brutality. However, in extending the horizon in this way, *Der Fall Franza* loses much of the intensity which characterises *Malina*, where it derives to a great extent from the abandonment of traditional narrative modes along with established frameworks of thought.

13. Compare *Malina*, *III*, 54, where 'die ägyptische Finsternis' is part of the work *Todesarten* which the narrator is writing.

14. See Sara Lennox, 'Geschlecht, Rasse und Geschichte in "Der Fall Franza"', in Weigel, *Bachmann*, pp. 156–79.

Works by Ingeborg Bachmann

Bachmann, Ingeborg, *Werke* I–IV, (eds.) Christine Koschel, Inge von Weidenbaum and Clemens Münster (Munich and Zurich, 1978)

——, *Wir müssen wahre Sätze finden. Gespräche und Interviews*, (eds.) Christine Koschel and Inge von Weidenbaum (Munich and Zurich, 1983). References are to *WS*

GERALD FETZ

Thomas Bernhard and the 'Modern Novel'

> 'Das Furchtbarste ist für mich Prosa schreiben . . . überhaupt das Schwierigste. . . . Und von dem Augenblick an, in dem ich das bemerkt habe und gewußt hab', *habe ich mir geschworen*, nur noch Prosa zu schreiben . . .'
>
> Bernhard, 'Drei Tage'[1]
>
> ('The most dreadful thing for me is writing prose . . . it's absolutely the most difficult thing. . . . And from that moment on, in which I recognised it and knew it, I swore to myself that I would only write prose . . .'.)

Prior to the appearance of his first novel *Frost* in 1963, Thomas Bernhard had published three volumes of poetry and a variety of short prose pieces, but by and large he was virtually unknown outside the Austrian literary avant-garde. *Frost*, however, changed that, and it brought Bernhard accolades and wide recognition in the entire German-speaking realm. By the time he was awarded the prestigious Büchner Prize in 1970, he had published several additional works, including two novels, *Verstörung* (1967) and *Das Kalkwerk* (1970), and was no longer viewed merely as a promising, young literary talent, but had become a genuine literary phenomenon.[2]

It was quickly obvious to all who confronted Bernhard's work that his was a unique, provocative, and difficult literary voice. Not all critics or reviewers of these early prose works were whole-heartedly enthusiastic, however, particularly those who tried to measure and judge them with the expectations of representational prose or who

1. 'Drei Tage', text of a filmed interview. Printed as an appendix to T. Bernhard, *Der Italiener* (Munich, 1973), p. 85. I wish to acknowledge the generous support of grants from the American Philosophical Society and the University of Montana which have made possible much of the research for this essay and for ongoing work on Thomas Bernhard.

2. For the most up-to-date bibliography of both primary and secondary works by and on Bernhard, see the *Kritisches Lexikon*, vol. 1, published by C.H. Beck, Munich. The most recent Bernhard material therein was updated to 1.1.85.

insisted on traditional narration or a *story*. Several fellow writers though, as different as Zuckmayer, Handke, and Bachmann, were impressed by qualities in Bernhard's prose that made the expectations of traditional or representational narrative seem both irrelevant and inappropriate.[3] Numerous critics obviously agreed, for by 1975 Bernhard had received virtually every literary prize available to a German-language author.[4]

Since 1963 Bernhard has published at an incredibly prolific rate: at the beginning of 1986, his *oeuvre* counts eight novels, sixteen full-length plays, several volumes of shorter prose pieces, five autobiographical volumes, four volumes of poetry, short dramatic sketches, and a variety of non-fiction essays and commentaries. And his remarkable literary output has perhaps even been surpassed by that of critics and commentators who, both irritated and fascinated, continually try to grapple and come to terms with his dark, dense, and challenging writings. There is perhaps no other contemporary writer in German as controversial as Bernhard, who provokes and offends some readers to the point of total rejection, but who intrigues and attracts others to the point of hyperbolic praise. Not infrequently, it should be noted, he arouses contradictory responses in the same reader.

Regardless of where one is on that spectrum of Bernhard readers, one cannot deny that he has become one of the most important German-language authors of the century. As Peter Demetz recently suggested, Bernhard has unflinchingly written his way to a prominent place even in world literature.[5] With that in mind, then, it is only appropriate that Bernhard be discussed here together with the other contemporary German novelists who have attained such status.

As should be evident from the diverse discussions in this volume, no

3. Zuckmayer's review of *Frost* originally appeared in *Die Zeit*, but can also be found in Anneliese Botond (ed.), *Über Thomas Bernhard*, (Frankfurt, 1970); Handke's comments appeared in his essay, 'Als ich *Verstörung* von Thomas Bernhard las', also printed in Botond; Bachmann's 'Ein Versuch' is included in vol. 4, I. Bachmann, *Werke*, (Munich & Zurich, 1982).

4. To date, Bernhard has received the following prizes: Julius-Campe-Preis (1964); Literaturpreis der Freien und Hansestadt Bremen (1965); Literaturpreis der deutschen Industrie (1967); Österreichischer Staatspreis für Literatur (1968); Wildgans-Preis (1968); Georg-Büchner-Preis (1970); Franz-Theodor-Csokor-Preis (1972); Adolf-Grimme-Preis (1972); Grillparzer-Preis (1972); Hannoverscher Dramatikerpreis (1974); Prix Séguier (1974); Literaturpreis der österr. Bundeswirtschaftskammer (1976); Premio Mondello (1983).

5. Review of *Der Untergeher*, *Frankfurter Allgemeine Zeitung*, 17 September 1983.

general consensus exists, either among critics or the novelists themselves, about just what the modern novel is or what its central characteristics might be. Even though there are numerous similarities among many of the novelists presented here, there are undoubtedly more dissimilarities, even with regard to some of the most basic features of their works: themes or main concerns, philosophies of life and history, political viewpoints and ideologies, literary-political intentions, novelistic forms, perspectives of reality, narrative strategies, or in answer to the critical question of the possibility (or even desirability) of narrating or telling a story.

It is perhaps only to be expected that such diversity would prevail in a genre whose very existence has been called into question. For more than fifty years, at least, critics have not tired of announcing the 'crisis' of the novel or even declaring its 'death', underscoring thereby, at the minimum, the lack of any commonly held definitions or expectations for literary works which bear the designation *novel*. Yet, several excellent discussions of the 'modern novel' and its amazing vitality, even in the late twentieth century, have appeared: among the best in my mind are those by Gottfried Benn, Reinhold Grimm, Reinhard Baumgart, Bruno Hillebrand, Viktor Žmegač, and Wendelin Schmidt-Dengler.[6] From such clear-headed discussions it is evident that a 'crisis', and certainly the purported 'death', of the novel in our time can only be claimed by those who would attempt to impose outdated and normative expectations and definitions, both formal and thematic, on contemporary novels. Most such expectations derive, of course, from the tradition of the nineteenth-century bourgeois novel and reflect a view of reality and of the external world, as well as the writer's ability to re-create it, which is clearly at odds with the generally sceptical spirit of the late twentieth century. Such expectations, which only lead to disappointment and misunderstanding when applied to most contemporary novels, also assume that one can actually define the novel. But as Žmegač has correctly observed, the only real constant for the novel from the beginning has been its changeability, in other words, the *impossibility*

6. Gottfried Benn, 'Roman des Phänotyp', G.B. *Ges. Werke* II (Wiesbaden, 1958); R. Grimm, 'Romane des Phänotyp' (essay on Benn's work and beyond), H.L. Arnold & T. Buck (eds.) *Positionen des Erzählens* (Munich, 1976); R. Baumgart, *Ansichten des Romans oder hat Literatur Zukunft?* (Munich, 1970); B. Hillebrand, *Theorie des Romans von Hegel bis Handke*, 2. vols. (Munich, 1972); Viktor Žmegač, 'Zum Problem der Romantheorie' in P.M. Lützeler (ed.), *Deutsche Romane des 20. Jahrhunderts* (Königstein/Ts, 1983); W. Schmidt-Dengler, ''Schluß mit dem Erzählen': Die Polemik gegen das Prinzip des Erzählens in der österreichischen Literatur der Gegenwart' in F. Aspetsberger (ed.), *Traditionen in der neueren österreichischen Literatur*, (Vienna, 1980).

of defining it '*Den* modernen Roman gibt es nicht . . .' ('The modern novel does not exist') (Žmegač, 25). Considering all this, then, it would perhaps be more appropriate to speak of a 'crisis' of *novel criticism* than of a 'crisis' of the novel itself, and certainly we have not experienced the death of either.

If one takes as the point of departure the extent to which a story is told or narrated, as several of the commentators mentioned above have justifiably done, there appear to be two major tendencies in the post-war German-language novel. On the one hand, there are numerous novelists who have contributed both impressive individual works and general vitality to the contemporary novel by following the realistic or representational tradition of the nineteenth-century novel. These authors, even though they have sometimes had to make considerable concessions to our age's scepticism, tell a discernible story in which some type of visible chronology, character development, and external action are all present. Most of the novels of Grass, Böll, Siegfried Lenz, Hermann Kant, or certainly someone like Kempowski, fall into this category. On the other hand, though, a large number of novelists have contributed significant works and vitality to the modern novel by building on and extending the 'modernist' tradition in the genre; the tradition which has as a central trait a strong scepticism about the possibility of narrating in a logical, chronological, or linear fashion a forward-moving story. This scepticism about story-telling is often traced back to Rilke's *Aufzeichnungen des Malte Laurids Brigge*, in which the protagonist exclaims at one point: 'Daß man erzählte, wirklich erzählte, das muß vor meiner Zeit gewesen sein. Ich habe nie jemanden erzählen hören' ('That people told stories, really told stories, must have been before my time. I have never heard anyone tell a story').[7] It is in this 'modernist' tradition, formed by the novels of Kafka, Musil, Broch, Aichinger, and others, in which most of the prose works of such contemporary novelists as Uwe Johnson, Martin Walser, Christa Wolf, Peter Handke, Ingeborg Bachmann, Max Frisch, and Thomas Bernhard can best be understood.[8] In order to establish directly Bernhard's connection to this tradition, we need only recall that he has described himself as a 'Geschichtenzerstörer', ('a destroyer of stories') ('Drei Tage', 83). In the conclusion of

7. Rilke, *Aufzeichnungen des Malte Laurids Brigge*, vol. II (Leipzig, 1910) p. 23.

8. Not all of the prose works of these authors fit the description of this 'modernist' tendency to the same degree, and there are certainly 'modernist' features to the works of such writers as Böll and Grass. None the less, the writers in the one group tend to 'tell stories' in most of their works, those in the 'modernist' tendency do not.

this essay I will make some further assertions about this 'modernist' tendency in the contemporary German-language novel and Bernhard's place within that tendency, but first let us turn to his novels themselves.

Between 1963 and 1985, Bernhard published eight prose works which can be termed novels.[9] Contrary to the claim made by a few commentators that each Bernhard work is merely a repetition of the others, a close reading of the novels reveals, within the context of undeniable continuity and recurring themes and situations, significant variations and shifts in emphasis and tone. It is my contention, moreover, that a definite development occurs over the course of these eight novels during which a Bernhardian vision emerges which is not nearly so exclusively dark or apparently hopeless as that which prevails in the earliest ones.

With that said (and that claim will be substantiated as we proceed), it must also be admitted that many of the basic Bernhardian elements are already present in the first three novels which, because they display many similarities, both with regard to form and content, and can be seen as representing the first phase of Bernhard's novel writing, will be discussed together. In these first three novels, *Frost* (1963), *Verstörung* (1967), and *Das Kalkwerk* (1970), one finds an ever-increasing experimentation with and radicalisation of the role of the narrator. In *Frost*, for example, there is the rather traditional daily reporting, in semi-diarial form, of what the narrator has observed and heard that day. In *Das Kalkwerk*, however, the narration takes the form of a very complex attempt to splice together from several sources, given via indirect discourse sometimes several speakers removed, a plausible explanation of the motives and events upon which the novel focuses. It is an attempt, however, which ultimately fails miserably in that it results only in contradictions and leads inevitably to the conclusion that the narrator and his method are unreliable and not up to the task. That is not to say that the novel itself fails.

The narrators in both *Frost* and *Verstörung* are young students who, in the course of their transforming encounters with eccentric, misanthropic, old men who are prone to lengthy monologues, write down

9. The following editions of Bernhard's novels have been used and referred to here: *Frost*, (edition suhrkamp, 1972); *Verstörung* (Bibl. Suhrkamp, 1979); *Das Kalkwerk*, (suhrkamp taschenbuch, 1976); *Korrektur* (Suhrkamp, 1975); *Beton* (Suhrkamp, 1982); *Der Untergeher* (Suhrkamp, 1983); *Holzfällen* (Suhrkamp, 1984); *Alte Meister* (Suhrkamp, 1985).

their observations and, often verbatim, the monologues of these odd old protagonists. In *Frost* the narrator is a young medical houseman who has been sent by his supervising doctor to a very remote mountain village, Weng, in order to observe and report back on the actions, words, and behaviour of the doctor's estranged and allegedly insane brother, the painter Strauch, who had gone to the village some time earlier in an attempt to flee society. The houseman attaches himself to Strauch without revealing his purpose and becomes witness and auditor to the paradoxically disjointed, yet often compellingly incisive monologues given by the old man as the two walk and wander in and around this cold, isolated village. The novel consists of the twenty-six daily instalments of the narrator's report. In *Verstörung*, the young student-narrator has written a letter to his country-doctor father about their strained familial relationship and has been invited home for the weekend to discuss it. His father is called out on a medical emergency, however, and the father–son discussion never occurs, but the son accompanies his father on his rounds which lead them up a mountain valley, through an isolated and cold mountain landscape where the stories and visions of inhumanity, disease, decay, and death only increase as they move from one patient to the next, each worse off than the last. At day's end, the stunned and changed young student, unable to sleep, feels compelled to write. The results are the contents of the novel, approximately the last two-thirds of which consist of the monologue of the Prince of Saurau, the last patient visited.

As suggested above, the narrative situation of *Das Kalkwerk* is quite different. Here, the nameless life insurance agent-narrator recedes almost totally into the background, as it is his task to put together an *objective* report of statements provided by the three sources who saw, heard, and talked to Konrad, the novel's protagonist, in the months preceding his murdering his half-sister/wife. The narrator's attempts to determine any causality (to uncover a story!) are doomed, as the presence of diverse and competing versions of the same event or statement, of different and often contradictory perspectives, all offered in indirect discourse of varying complexity, serves to undermine completely all faith in the *apparently* objective protocol style and structure adhered to almost slavishly throughout. Bernhard is not only a destroyer of stories, but of narrative objectivity and reliability as well.

The main stylistic feature of each novel, often delivered in almost breathless and uninterrupted fashion by the protagonist and then reported by the narrator(s), is the monologue. One explanation for the use of the monologue is provided by the Prince: 'Wir sind in einem Zeitalter der Selbstgespräche. Die Kunst des Selbstgesprächs ist auch eine viel höhere Kunst als die Kunst des Gesprächs. . . . Aber Selbstgespräche sind genauso sinnlos wie Gespräche . . . wenn auch viel weniger sinnlos' ('We live in the age of monologues. The art of monologues is also a much higher art than the art of conversation. . . . But monologues are just as senseless as conversations . . . even if much less senseless') (*Verstörung*, 138). This passage is also useful in exemplifying the circularity of thought and language, the almost labyrinthian quality, and the paradoxical nature which characterises the monologues of all the protagonists. For Strauch, the Prince, and Konrad, thought, as the medium of absolute *subjectivity*, stubbornly refuses translation into and articulation in language, the inadequate means by which subjective thought is theoretically to be made *objective*, the inadequate means by which communication and connections between individuals are theoretically established.

Especially in the monologues of Strauch and the Prince, Bernhard sets up a basic constellation of concerns and themes as well as a level of hypercritical intensity which will (almost) remain trademarks of his writing. In a curious and intriguing mixture of realistic detail and overtly subjective exaggeration, of rational incisiveness and irrational tirade, Strauch and the Prince offer visions of rural brutality, animalistic sexuality, mental depravity, sickness, individual and societal decay, human isolation and estrangement, meaninglessness, and death. Not even nature, which darkly and threateningly surrounds them, provides any respite or exception to this dismal picture; but rather, nature is exposed as *the cause* of it all, as *the enemy* of human beings: nature's goal is not life, but death.

All three protagonists issue attacks on Austrian society which are clearly intended to be socially and politically critical in nature, for they are far too specific (at times) and there are far too many references to actual events, circumstances, and individuals for them to be merely allegorical. Yet, they are allegorical as well: Austria, its allegedly decaying society and institutions, as well as its other perceived ills, become representative, at least on one level, of the contemporary Western world and contemporary life in general. Bernhard is particularly radical in his attacks on dullness, superficiality, artificiality, deceit, and the lack of willingness to face up to the fact of death as a part of life wherever these reveal themselves. It is obviously false to claim that Bernhard is not concerned with Austria, his loved and hated homeland, or that his social and political criticism is merely a foil, but it is similarly wrong to overlook the fact that his concerns are also existential in nature and therefore transcend Austria's boundaries.

The characteristic style of the monologues is inimitably Bernhard and anticipates that of much of his later work. It can be described in sum as follows: a rather small vocabulary with certain words and phrases often repeated in almost leitmotif fashion; almost interminable, parenthetical sentences with a language that is convoluted, dense, and difficult to penetrate, but once penetrated, difficult to escape; an undeniable musical quality, especially in a syntax often reminiscent of the principles of (contrapuntal, atonal, and even twelve-tone!) composition; paradoxical and contradictory formulations; exaggeration and giant leaps in logic when sliding or jumping from specific assertions to broad generalisations of global and even cosmic proportions; and a rather insistent irony with some glimpses of (dark) humour. The style of these novels in general, but particularly of the monologues, is intended, in partnership with the content, to provoke, unsettle, agitate, and undermine certainty of any kind. It defiantly challenges the reader (and herein lies its didactic feature) to look beyond and beneath the clichés and artifices with which we all usually attempt to shield ourselves, our eyes, and our thoughts from the unpleasant, frightening, and often seemingly imponderable truth, facts, contradictions, and unanswerable questions of life and death.

At the beginning of *Frost*, as the narrator sits in the train on his way to Weng, he at least subconsciously anticipates the kind of experience with which he is about to be confronted. He muses that it will be his task '. . . etwas Unerforschliches zu erforschen . . .' ('. . . to research that which is unresearchable . . .') (*Frost*, 5). Essentially, that is the task of all of Bernhard's narrators and all of his readers. Initially, the young houseman attempts to comprehend and record what he sees and observes rather logically and almost mechanically, but gradually, and not primarily through any rational means of gaining insight, he begins to see things differently and becomes ensnarled in the simultaneously repulsive and entrancing, senseless and sensible web of Strauch's idiosyncratic thought and vision. The apparently simple assignment of observing and reporting another human being's actions and words becomes an enormous, frightening, and dangerous task: the young narrator finds himself peering into the abyss of human nature and, even though he 'escapes' and returns to the city and his studies, there is little doubt that he is transformed, marked by his experience in the dark village with Strauch. The same can be said for the young narrator in *Verstörung*, and, I would suggest, for innumerable readers of these novels as well.

The protagonists, Strauch, the Prince, and Konrad, share much in common: anti-heroes, they are in many ways the literary descendents of Büchner's Woyzeck and Lenz, Grillparzer's Jakob, or Canetti's Peter Kien. Bernhard has also claimed that they are modelled in part on his own grandfather, the Austrian writer Johannes Freumbichler. Each protagonist, but especially Strauch and the Prince, is already permeated by the 'frost' which accompanies (or immediately precedes) death, even though he is not yet physically dead. And each walks a very narrow line between incredible insight and insanity, and each displays qualities of (rather asocial) genius. Strauch and the Prince are estranged, embittered, and cynical to the point that their (suicidal) deaths, whether they actually occur in the novel (Strauch) or not (the Prince) seem virtually inevitable. Konrad, however, in spite of the noted similarities, is somewhat different in that, at least until the murder, he has an *activity*, a *project*, a *goal* which temporarily allows a hint of light and purpose into his life (and Bernhard's world).

Konrad, a self-made intellectual, has managed to achieve a long-term goal of gaining possession of an abandoned limeworks that had belonged to his family when he was young. After wandering for years rather aimlessly around the world, mostly at the insistence of his crippled half-sister/wife, he has settled there in search of the *right* place to complete (which means: write down) a complex study of *das Gehör* (hearing), and all-inclusive philosophical-scientific-musical-mathematical study which he has carried around in his head for years without, however, being able to write it down. In spite of withdrawing to the 'perfect' location to write the study, all attempts fail, because Konrad is pushed off track by the slightest distraction, real and imagined, and is unable to get beyond the bizarre and often tormenting experiments he undertakes on his sister–wife and her hearing or beyond the innumerable scraps of paper on which he has assiduously scribbled fragmentary notes. Finally, however, for somewhat obvious *and* impenetrable, inexplicable reasons, he snaps, shoots his sister/wife, and hides from the police. He is found, though, apparently completely insane, and taken away.

It is perhaps difficult to see much 'light' in Konrad, given the brutality of his crime and his ultimate insanity, but he is the first of Bernhard's protagonists who is not already totally dead, while still physically alive, the first who has not completely resigned simply to await that physical death, and the first who has set for himself a creative goal in an attempt to find enough meaning or sense in his life to avoid death before physical death. Whereas Strauch and the Prince have moved so far to the second end of the Schopenhauerian spectrum between *Wille* and *Vorstellung* to be able to connect with anyone or anything in the external world, Konrad does not fail primarily because of a lack of will. He fails in part, at least, because he has set an impossible task for himself: that of producing or creating a *perfect* study, a total work of art. But in Bernhard's world he deserves some (moral) credit for the attempt. The 'light' is dim, to be sure, but it is a light which shines less dimly in the novels to come.

Bernhard's fourth novel, *Korrektur* (1975), the only one published between 1970 and 1982, a period in which he wrote many plays and the autobiographical volumes, is in my mind his masterpiece to date. Because of its exceptional qualities and because it stands rather isolated in time *vis-à-vis* the other novels, I have chosen to discuss it separately. The radical narrative complexity in *Das Kalkwerk*, derived from the presence of multiple sources, yields in *Korrektur* to a complexity of content, derived partially from the existence of multiple protagonists. This complexity is heightened by a multiplication of themes and allusions (to Kafka, Wittgenstein, and Heidegger, for instance) as well as by the abandonment of the almost exclusive focus on a single isolated individual in an isolated location.

Drastically simplified, the contents of the novel (not to say: story or plot) can be described as follows: Roithamer, a professor in Cambridge, had commuted for years between England and his both loved and hated homeland, Austria. Most recently, for the time spent in Austria, he had set two major goals for himself: first, to design and build for his beloved sister an elaborate conical structure (*Kegel*) which he intended would be 'the perfect dwelling' for her, not only a house, but a 'perfect' *Kunstwerk* (work of art) as well: and second, to write a manuscript about the *Kegel*, its construction, and about his thoughts regarding both the *Kegel* and his home region, Altensam. Roithamer was also determined to liquidate his immense and burdensome inheritance, and the expensive project would do that as well. For the *Kegel* he had made elaborate mathematical and philosophical calculations, and for the all-inclusive manuscript, he made copious, fragmentary notes which he continually revised, *correcting* each version of the manuscript to be shorter, more condensed, and more precise than the last.

While in Austria, Roithamer always resided in the attic room of the extraordinary and unique house that his boyhood friend, a taxidermist by the name of Höller and the novel's second protagonist, had built against all logic and odds in the most precarious and dangerous location imaginable on the bank of a raging creek. Both the conical structure and the manuscript remain unfinished, however, even though Roithamer comes much closer to reaching his goal than had Konrad: shortly before Roithamer was able to finish the cone and begin concentrated work on the manuscript, his sister suddenly died, and Roithamer, submitting himself to what amounts to the final *correction*, subsequently hung himself in the woods.

That entire scenario is already history when the novel opens with the entry of the third protagonist, another boyhood friend and later companion of Roithamer's in Cambridge, who assumes the role of narrator. Just released from a lung sanatorium and still in a weakened state, he moves into Höller's attic room, in a sense replacing Roithamer, and sets himself the task of bringing order to Roithamer's fragmentary notes and manuscript versions. The extraordinarily dense novel which follows is related by this ailing and obviously neurotic friend. The contents are made up of his reflections, recollections, and restrospective observations about Roithamer's (as well as Höller's and his own) past; his anguished thoughts about his precarious, current situation and his rather absurd and at times comical efforts to organise Roithamer's papers; and many direct citations from Roithamer's fragmentary notes themselves.

As the reader is pushed and pulled through the thicket of the novel, familiar Bernhardian themes emerge: decay, disease, darkness, inhuman family relationships, the heavy burden of the (Austrian) past, the insidious and destructive power of nature, suicide, and death. Yet, the shift in tone hinted at in *Das Kalkwerk* is given considerable substance here, as the urge toward and process of creative activity become perhaps *the* central theme. Radically new in *Korrektur* is also the presence of both friendship and love, human dimensions almost totally lacking in the earlier novels.

The relationships between and among the three protagonists reveal themselves to be special and fascinating friendships that display, in the midst of their problematical and complex nature, mutual dependence and inspiration, as well as tremendous commitment. The lives (and thoughts) of these three friend-protagonists are so intertwined, in fact, that on one level they can be viewed as different aspects of the same person, aspects which are at once both complementary and contradictory.

Death and its dark shadow still loom large, but intellectual and artistic creation emerges in *Korrektur* as a theme which will remain central in the novels from this point on. All three protagonists *create* or at least attempt to: Höller, who is an interesting anomaly for Bernhard in that he is a rather silent, natural man, creates *artworks* in the form of stuffed birds, and has also succeeded in creating the remarkable house in its unique and dangerous location; Roithamer, a successful academic, has almost succeeded, inspired by Höller, in creating a 'perfect' home for his sister and has continually tried to create a more and more perfect manuscript; and the nameless narrator attempts to create order from chaos as he, inspired by Roithamer's genius, tries to organise and edit his friend's papers. And they all, inspite of enormous difficulties, find at least temporarily some kind of *meaning* and *sense* in their creative efforts. And that, in Bernhard's world, counts for a great deal. Ultimately though, in the framework of the novel, only Höller succeeds. Roithamer, it turns out, has miscalculated in his efforts to create the 'perfect' dwelling-as-work-of-art by failing to take into account both his sister's mortality and the possibility that perfection might be deadly for both of them. But undeniably, it is intellectual effort and artistic creativity, the attempt to transcend the boundaries of the possible, which provides here the means of avoiding dullness, complacency, and deadening cynicism, as well as the means of staying *alive* even in the face of the absurdity that is death.

It is also worth noting that the protagonists, although they possess some of the illnesses, neuroses, and ambivalences which their aged predecessors possessed, are considerably younger and vastly more active. The fact that this novel appeared simultaneously with Bernhard's first autobiographical volume is in this regard certainly not coincidental, and the autobiographical nature of the following novels only increases as he begins to use himself, one senses, more as the model for his protagonists rather than his grandfather.

Bernhard's final four novels, published one a year between 1982 and 1985, can also be discussed as a group. All four, for instance — *Beton* (1982), *Der Untergeher* (1983), *Holzfällen. Eine Erregung* (1984), and *Alte Meister* (1985) — are novels about artists, art, the artistic process, and the world of art and artists. Sickness, neuroses, hatred, hypercriticism, despair, death, and the other essential ingredients in Bernhard's undeniably dark view of the world are consistently in evidence for these younger, but still hypersensitive protagonists; yet virtually each one of them also displays the potential for friendship, compassion, love, and creativity. It must also be mentioned, even though space will not allow elaboration, that a great deal of humour, much of it dark and grotesque to be sure, also becomes a very important part of these later novels.

With only the final novel, *Alter Meister*, being technically an exception, these novels are all narrated in the first person by middle-aged *writers*, either of fiction or non-fiction. Each of these protagonist-narrators delivers a kind of monologue or a variation of one. Sometimes the monologue is interior, emanating from the head of the narrator (*Beton* and much of *Holzfällen*), and at other times it is indirect, originating in the mind of a second character (parts of *Holzfällen* and *Alte Meister*).

The structural complexity of these novels varies. *Beton*, a virtually uninterrupted first-person interior monologue, is perhaps more concentrated in both structure and content than any other Bernhard novel. There is no second person, even a protocol-providing narrator such as in *Frost* or *Verstörung*, whose occasional reflections offer another perspective. And with regard to content, *Beton* focuses almost to the last page very single-mindedly on the both pathetic and comical efforts of Rudolf, the deathly ill but perhaps even more neurotic protagonist-narrator, to find the *right* time and place to compose his ambitious study of Mendelssohn-Bartholdy. And in a very profound way, the novel even calls to mind the structure of a tightly composed musical score, played so that only one voice is heard.

Although not quite as simple and concentrated, the structures of both *Holzfällen* and *Alte Meister* are also not complex. In *Holzfällen*, for instance, the (heavily) autobiographical narrator delivers for the first part of the novel an interior monologue, consisting of his thoughts and recollections as he sits in a partially hidden chair in the corner of a Viennese apartment waiting for a late-evening dinner to begin, a dinner to which he has only begrudgingly accepted an invitation. In the second part, he relates the modified monologue, similar both in tone and content to his own, delivered at the table by the guest of honour, a retiring actor from the Burgtheater. In *Alte Meister*, even though there is a nominal narrator who has written down what one of the protagonists has told him, the real narrator is that protagonist whose interior monologue consists of his own recollections and observations about the major protagonist, the music critic Regler, as well as remembered fragments of monologues delivered to him in recent years by Regler. The occasion is provided for this set of observations about Regler and his views of art and the world when he invites the narrator, a younger friend and writer by the name of Atzbacher, to meet him in the Art History Museum in Vienna. The odd thing about the invitation is that Regler extends it not for one of the every-other-day visits to the museum which Regler has essentially made for thirty-six years (!), and in which Atzbacher has joined him in recent years, but on an *off-day*, a day *between* their strangely regular visits. Atzbacher arrives early in order to watch Regler without being seen himself and makes the observations which form the substance of his interior monologue at that time.

Only in *Der Untergeher*, among these late novels, do we find a more complex structure; one based on the presence of three protagonists. The impetus for the narrator to write the work is found in the suicide of his long-time friend Wertheimer, whom he has not, however, seen for some time. Stunned by the death, but also grieving and feeling somewhat guilty for neglecting him, the narrator has returned to the village where Wertheimer had spent most of his time in recent years, living a rather isolated and embittered existence. Here, he tries to come to terms with and understand Wertheimer's suicide. His attempts in this regard lead him to focus on the three-way friendship and competition among Wertheimer, himself, and the third friend, the famous Glenn Gould. All three, it is asserted, had been very gifted pianists who had met, become friends, and lived together while studying at the Mozarteum and participating in a master-class with Horowitz. Glenn Gould's talent showed itself to be obviously superior, however, and both Wertheimer and the narrator subsequently gave up the piano because being second-best was unacceptable to them. The narrator was able to find a suitable substitute profession as a writer, Wertheimer found none. It gradually emerges that, as incomprehensible as Wertheimer and his actions remain, it is only in the context of this friendship and this 'failure' to measure up to personal expectations, that the suicide of Wertheimer, the *Untergeher*, even begins to make sense for the narrator.

One can see a good illustration, ironically, in the change of tone in Bernhard's recent novels in the role which suicide plays. Suicide has been a constant part of Bernhard's dark world from the beginning, but in three of these recent novels *Beton*, *Der Untergeher*, and *Holzfällen*, suicide does not end the work, but provides the impetus for writing it. In each, someone's suicide shocks and moves the narrator to creative reflection, to re-assessments, to attempts to comprehend that individual, his or her life, and death, and even life and death in general. Ultimately, these suicides move the narrators to create the works which tell of those deaths, the lives before, and the lives and reflections after them. Perhaps the transforming power of those suicides to cause self-reflection and even a kind of renewal in the narrators is most evident in the case of Rudolf in *Beton*. Isolated, self-absorbed, hypochondriac, and misanthropic, he is close to being in the same 'frozen' situation as Strauch and the Prince, despite his alleged desire to create the musical study. It is only the *real entombment* of the young German woman he had met in Palma three years earlier and the shock of discovering that she had committed suicide which provide him the opportunity to escape the *figurative entombment*, the existential death into which he had withdrawn.

Bernhard's words and works have caused an amazing number of scandals and even frequent lawsuits. The stinging criticisms, virulent attacks, and sharp insults which he has regularly dished out in his fiction and non-fiction alike have been aimed at cultural and political institutions and personalities, from the Burgtheater to Kreisky; at virtually all of the -isms, from Communism and capitalism to Catholicism; at Austria, its allegedly dulled people, its provinces, its cities, and most of its 'national characteristics'; at other artists and thinkers, past and present, from Stifter to Handke, from Dürer to Heidegger. His attacks are highly subjective and exaggerated, often humorous and usually sharp, but at the core they are often irritatingly and uncomfortably justified and defensible. The outraged responses with which they are frequently met have more often than not indicated the extent to which these criticisms have struck home. Probably none of Bernhard's innumerable scandals has engendered as much public reaction as that caused by his appropriately subtitled novel, *Holzfällen. Eine Erregung*. The fact that Bernhard appeared to disregard the line between fiction and reality in this work more radically than in most of his other recent works with their tantalising mixture of autobiography and fiction, led several individuals to read the work as a *Schlüsselroman* of Austria's cultural establishment. One individual, the composer Gerhard Lampersberg, a one-time close friend of Bernhard, felt himself so slandered by the portrayal of one of the characters in the book, the host for the late-evening dinner, that he sued for libel, and the book was temporarily removed from all Austrian bookshops. Bernhard retaliated by issuing his own ban on the sale of all his books in Austria which was to have lasted for fifty years: a very dramatic public and media-promoted spectacle was created. The suit was subsequently withdrawn, however, Bernhard retracted his ban, and all of his books are back in the bookshops.

If one reads the novel as Lampersberg and numerous commentators did, who were outraged at what they viewed as Bernhard's totally unjustified and unveiled insults of specific individuals in Austria's cultural establishment, then the *real* novel, its fictional character, and its artistic exploration of significant themes and concerns are lost. *Holzfällen* is a novel in which Bernhard boldly investigates the grey, shady and ambiguous area between art and reality, between fiction and autobiography. It is a novel in which the author focuses on the nature of friendship, power, inspiration, dependence, disappointment, and betrayal. It is also a novel in which he explores, retrospectively, the promise of young talent and its later, all-too-frequent willingness to compromise and betray itself for conformity, security, and a piece of the establishment. It seems very apparent to me that Bernhard is taking a close and critical look at his own status as a very successful artist as well, a modern *Klassiker* even, and the compromises and betrayals he has made in the process of getting there. In this novel one sees not only the increase in the autobiographical element since *Korrektur*, but the increase in the self-critical aspect as well.

As stated earlier, at least since *Korrektur*, art has moved up alongside death as a central focus in Bernhard's novels, and that is perhaps nowhere as evident as in *Alte Meister*. As he has done on many occasions before, Bernhard launches here a radical attack on the cultural industry, the marketing of art, and artists who aid and abet that marketing, either directly or indirectly. Is it not obvious that there is also a good amount of self-incrimination intended? But Bernhard takes his art criticism even further than usual in *Alte Meister* by having his strange, yet rather sympathetic old protagonist Regler, an eighty-year-old music critic, call into question the ultimate value of art itself, of artworks, both great and not so great. Regler's attitudes to art are admittedly subjective, yet he asserts that no other attitudes to art are possible. His stated philosophy is that no such thing as a 'perfect' art work exists, '. . . daß es das Vollkommene, das Ganze, gar nicht gibt . . .' ('. . . that the Finished, the Complete, does not exist . . .') (*Alte Meister*, 42). His method is to study a work of art, even a masterpiece, until its weaknesses, even 'gravierende Fehler' emerge. Regler articulates here the key to Bernhard's vision of art and the world, the method of achieving that vision, and the reason for the fragmentary and *incomplete* nature of all his works. One also suspects that this is a description of Bernhard's method for banishing those artists and artworks and thinkers who have simultaneously inspired and intimidated him by their greatness and genius.

There is another reason, however, for Regler's suspicion of the ultimate value of art, and that is that he senses in most cases it is a means of compensating for that which is missing in life, a substitute for what really matters: love. Is this Thomas Bernhard? Regler asserts, for instance, that all of literature, works of art, musical compositions — all that which makes up the world which he loves and to which he has devoted his life, in spite of his criticism and ambivalence — are worth *nothing* compared to the love and companionship he shared with his wife before her recent death. This is a rather shocking statement to be made by an aged Bernhard protagonist who is in ways misanthropic, cynical, and hypercritical like those before him, but this statement and the view it represents have certainly been anticipated by some of the developments in the other recent works. None the less, it is remarkable that art is not 'ludicrous in the face of death', to quote Bernhard's often-cited phrase from a 1968 speech, but *in the face of love.*[10] Yet, the lure of art remains: the reason that Regler had invited Atzbacher to meet him was to suggest that they go that evening, despite Regler's long-standing refusal to do so, to see a play, Kleist's *Der zerbrochene Krug*, in the Burgtheater. The book ends, both humorously and almost predictably, with the assertion: 'the production was terrible'.

Before concluding this essay, there is one more component of Bernhard's writing that deserves to be mentioned. With the exception of some of the commentaries on his plays, critics have been very slow to recognise the extensive humour which has been present in Bernhard's works from the beginning, but which has become more extensive since the early 1970s. Bernhard's humor is theatrical: it is born of a sense of the absurd, of the grotesque, but also of play. His humour is a product of his mastery of word-play and of the ludicrous, of caricature and exaggeration, just as they, in turn, are a product of his (long overlooked) sense of humour. All of these types of humour are present and very important features of Bernhard's recent novels. Concerning those readers who cannot find a great deal to laugh at in Bernhard's incredible attacks on both Stifter and Vienna's 'toilet culture' in *Alte Meister*, for instance, I must agree with Schmidt-Dengler who suggested in a recent review of that novel: 'The sense of humour of those who cannot laugh when reading such a book as this is in very bad shape'.[11]

Is everything 'ludicrous' or 'laughable' *in the face of death*, as Bernhard pronounced in that 1968 speech, or *in the face of love*, as Regler seems to assert in *Alte Meister*? Is life a *comedy*? or a *tragedy* (to use the title of one of Bernhard's short prose pieces)?[12] Is art a *poor substitute for life*, as Regler asserts at one point, or can one see in art a *possibility for finding some sense or meaning in life*? These are some of the most critical and most repeated questions posed in an impressive number of ways in the novels (and other works) of this difficult, exasperating, and fascinating Austrian, Thomas Bernhard. They are also the

10. The statement — 'Alles ist lächerlich vor dem Tod' — was made in an acceptance speech in 1968. This speech was printed in *Neues Forum*, XV, no. 173 (May 1968).

11. Review of *Alte Meister*, *Kleine Zeitung* (Graz), 11 Oct. 1985.

12. 'Ist es eine Komödie? ist es eine Tragödie?' is included in the collection of prose pieces, *Prosa* (Frankfurt, 1967).

kinds of question asked both explicitly by the other writers in the 'modernist' tradition to which Bernhard both belongs and uniquely extends. The answers to these questions are anything but clear, either for Bernhard or, I suspect, for most of his readers. Bernhard's answers are paradoxical and contradictory, his vision, even in his most positive moments, is darkly ambivalent. He writes consistently against the grain, against us, his readers, and against himself. At one point of his autobiographical volumes, *Der Keller*, he calls himself a 'Störenfried', someone who destroys peace and tranquility. He also claims there that everything he writes, everything he does, is intended to disrupt and irritate.[13] The didactic aspect of such an intention is obvious, but it is certainly not didacticism of the usual Enlightenment variety.

Bernhard's scepticism toward clear answers and toward *telling stories* — shared with many writers and thinkers in our century — stems from a profound and consistent doubt that *reality* or *the meaning of life* can be comprehended or known in any rational, logical, or objective way. In fact, it is highly questionable whether they can be be comprehended or known by any means. Such doubt must lead, with writers who are consistent, to a rejection of linear narration and neatly developed portrayals of time and space, events and characters, portrayals which are artificial at best and, therefore, very misleading constructs. In its more radical expressions — such as we find with Bernhard — this doubt becomes a conviction that one cannot achieve anything which approximates an autonomous or objective overview of the world, of a society, of events, or of an individual. Even the notions of causality and plausibility, so crucial for most nineteenth-century fiction, fall victim, as they do in *Das Kalkwerk*, for instance, to such a conviction, as does any aspiration toward achieving psychological realism in character description. Bernhard's sceptical world view, shared with many other 'modernists', posits a critique of knowledge and cognition which is also accompanied — after Wittgenstein and Hofmannsthal's 'Lord Chandos Brief' — by a radical and consistent critique of language. With these writers, as Bruno Hillebrand contends: 'Die Wirklichkeit ist insgesamt fragwürdig geworden, erzählend läßt sie sich nicht mehr vermitteln' ('Reality has become questionable in its totality, and it no longer allows itself to be communicated by telling') (Hillebrand, 193).

That such a view proves to be extremely paradoxical and problematical for literature, which has traditionally lived through lan-

13. (Salzburg, 1976), p. 18.

guage and *telling*, has been aptly pointed out by Wendelin Schmidt-Dengler: 'Das Erzählen erweist sich in der Praxis als fragwürdig, zugleich aber als unumgehbar' ('*Telling* has proven itself to be questionable in practice, but at the same time to be unavoidable') (S-D, 'Schluß', 109). *Telling* and even writing in general are questionable enterprises, but these sceptics (note Bernhard's prolific publication record!) *tell* and *write* nevertheless. They no longer tell or write in the same way, however. For such writers as Bernhard, the old notion of *order* has been abandoned, whether that is with regard to a cosmic, world, or political order, or to an order in thought and language. If one of the goals of traditional nineteenth-century fiction was to make comprehensible the world, society, or individual human beings and possibilities, then the goal of novelists such as Bernhard (or Kafka, or Beckett, or Bachmann) is to confront their readers with the *incomprehensibility* of the world, society, and individual human lives.

One cannot find with such writers, therefore, a narrator who objectively and either sovereignly or omnisciently describes the world, its inhabitants, and events, but rather narrators like those described above in Bernhard's novels who are openly subjective and anything but omniscient, who are confused, often unreliable, and usually incapable of the narrative task they set before themselves. Such narrators no longer offer a unified perspective, but one which is fragmented, contradictory, and confusing. The characters they try to describe are hardly *heroic* in any traditional sense, but misfits, outsiders, failed individuals who appear as fragmented as the attempts to describe them. As Reinhard Baumgart has observed: 'Weder die Personen wollen sich zu Charakteren runden, noch die Vorgänge zur Handlung schließen' ('The persons refuse to round out into characters, and the occurrences refuse to become plot') (Baumgart, 84). If it exists at all, plot becomes very secondary in these novels, and there is often a drastic reduction or concentration of content. As we have observed with Bernhard, these novels move away from action and toward thought, away from dialogue and toward monologue, and away from any preoccupation with the external world and toward obsession with the internal. Because the narrators and protagonists are often exceedingly subjective in their views and assertions, in their perceptions and perspectives, the reader, who cannot trust either, must constantly be on guard and question and be sceptical of that which is claimed, reported, or merely said. Bernhard's novels, and those of the other 'modernists', are not 'easy reads', they do not invite the reader to enter a world of enticing of reassuring illusion, such as that into which Madame Bovary temporarily escaped in her reading of novels; rather, they provoke, challenge, and *estrange* the reader, forcing a confrontation with the same incomprehensibilities faced by narrator and protagonist alike.

Bernhard's novels, then, share a great deal in common with the works of the other 'modernist' writers, both the earlier ones such as Kafka and Broch, and the contemporary ones such as Johnson and Beckett. Yet, Bernhard's works are also unique: they possess a language, a vision, and a constellation of concerns not found with any other writer. It would perhaps be a bit exaggerated to agree with Walter Abish, who wrote in a recent review of Bernhard's autobiographical works that 'the memoir is a remarkable literary contribution to what, in the German-speaking world, at any rate, may soon come to be considered "the Age of Bernhard"'[14] — but there can be no doubt that Bernhard is one of the most important writers in the Western world today. His novels are well worth the confrontation they generate.

14. Abish, Review of *Gathering Evidence*, *New York Times Book Review*, 16 February 1985.

J.H. REID

Heinrich Böll: From Modernism to Post-Modernism and Beyond

Böll's early reading did not include the classics of the modern novel. National Socialist cultural policies banned most manifestations of modernism; in addition Böll's family were devout, if anti-clerical Catholics, and staunch Rhinelanders, who distrusted all 'Prussianism', including the literature of the 1920s, which they identified with Berlin.[1] 'Rein zufällig' ('purely by chance') Böll had read *Buddenbrooks*, but none of Mann's other novels (*I*, 245).[2] Rather it was the novelists of the *renouveau catholique* in France, Bloy, Bernanos, Mauriac, their English and German equivalents Chesterton, Reinhold Schneider, Gertrud von Le Fort, but also older foreign writers, notably Dickens and Dostoevsky, who inspired him in his youth. One exception to this list of relatively conventional writers is Marcel Proust, whom Böll read when he was about twenty (*I*, 591), and the influence of Proust's 'time remembered', the details of taste and smell which evoke a whole epoch, can clearly be traced in Böll's novels. After the liberation in 1945 Böll read voraciously everything he could get hold of. Joyce and Kafka were revelations, but there was also the great influx of American realists, Hemingway, Jones, Mailer, Steinbeck, together with Sartre, Camus, Graham Greene, and the new German writers, Andersch, Koeppen, Arno Schmidt. His appetite for reading does not, however, appear to have extended to the *émigré* writers, and Thomas Mann, Robert Musil, Hermann Broch are not major influences in Böll's writing.

Böll himself repudiated as 'terrorism' the notion that 'modernity' was in itself a guarantee of quality (*E*, *1*, 463–4). In an essay of 1960 he refused to accept that there was any one 'modern novel'

1. Heinrich Böll, *Was soll aus dem Jungen bloß werden? Oder: Irgendwas mit Büchern*, (Bornheim, 1981), p. 79.

2. References are to the following editions: Bernd Balzer (ed.), *Werke Romane und Erzählungen*, 5 vols. (Cologne, n.d., 1977), (*R*, *1–5*); Bernd Balzer (ed.) *Werke Essayistische Schriften und Reden*, 3 vols. (Cologne, n.d., 1978) (*E 1–3*); Bernd Balzer (ed.), *Werke Interviews I*, (Cologne, n.d., 1978) (*I*); *Fürsorgliche Belagerung. Roman* (Cologne, 1979) (*FB*); *Frauen vor Flußlandschaft. Roman in Dialogen und Selbstgesprächen* (Cologne, 1985) (*FF*).

form. Grass and Robbe-Grillet, Camus and Faulkner, Julien Green and Graham Greene were all writing the 'Roman der Gegenwart' (contemporary novel), yet each was worlds apart from the other. It was impossible to find agreement on what was 'gegenwärtig' (contemporary), let alone its novel. 'Verzweiflung' ('despair') could not in itself be a defining quality of modernity, for despair could too easily become merely modish; rather he regretted the absence of 'Humor' ('humour') in the contemporary novel, the humour which prevents the author from taking himself too seriously, as so many novelists did. He viewed with alarm the prospect of the 'automatischer Roman' ('automatic novel'), which would merely register the death-throes of mankind (*E*, *1*, 355–7). Similarly in 1975 he rejected 'Experimentieren nur um des Experimentierens willen' ('experimentation purely for its own sake') (*I*, 356). Böll believed he had responsibility not merely towards his art, but also towards the society in which he lived (*E*, *1*, 356). As a practising, if unorthodox Catholic, he could never subscribe to a definition of 'modernism' which depended on the assumption that, as Theodor W. Adorno put it in 1954, it was no longer possible to write like the nineteenth-century novelist Adalbert Stifter, because that presupposed 'daß die Welt sinnvoll ist' ('that the world is meaningful').[3] He believed passionately in the writer's duty to extract meaning, what in an early essay he called 'Wirklichkeit' ('reality'), from everyday, contemporary events (*E*, *1*, 71–5). But Böll also found it impossible to divorce form and content (*I*, 645). The writer had therefore also to be abreast of developments in his own craft, and Böll's writing reveals that he was acutely aware of literary as well as political and social developments. His writing was 'experimental' in the sense that he seldom repeated himself in the construction of his novels. But while adopting the successive literary models of his contemporaries he also adapted them in accordance with his conception of humour.

Böll regarded the novel form as 'indefinable'; as a rough guideline he suggested that a work which contained more than fifteen characters was a novel.[4] It could, however, never be merely a collection of short stories, the novel had a rhythm of its own which depended on the entry of the various characters (*I*, 642). This essay will concentrate on those works which Böll himself called 'novels', not therefore *Das Brot der frühen Jahre*, *Ende einer Dienstfahrt*, and *Die verlorene Ehre*

3. Adomo 'Standort des Erzählers im zeitgenössischen Roman', *Noten zur Literatur* (Frankfurt, 1958), p. 62.

4. '"Ich habe nichts über den Krieg aufgeschrieben". Ein Gespräch mit Heinrich Böll und Hermann Lenz', *Literaturmagazin 7, Nachkriegsliteratur* (Reinbek, 1977), pp. 72–3.

der Katharina Blum.

His early novels bear many of the external marks of modernism as the latter was perceived in West Germany in the 1950s. A number of aspects may be singled out. The first is the distrust of the external 'omniscient', commenting narrator-focaliser. In 1954 Wolfgang Kayser, for example, diagnosed the 'disappearance' of such a narrator as responsible for the 'crisis' of the contemporary novel, while in the same year Adorno saw the same phenomenon as the only possible response to the situation of the individual in a bureaucratised, absurd world.[5] A corollary was the disappearance of the 'narrator's audience', the 'gentle reader' invoked by the writers of earlier fiction. A further aspect is the reduction of plot to a minimum. In 1955 Böll attended a meeting with French colleagues, among them Robbe-Grillet, and reported that all, including therefore himself, had rejected both the plot novel and the psychological novel (*E*, *1*, 148). Related to this there is a tendency to 'spatialise' what had traditionally been a 'time form,' through montage, leitmotifs and the reduction of the narrated time.[6] Brecht regarded montage as central to his concept of 'epic', i.e. narrative theatre. Georg Lukács by contrast, in the famous 1930s controversy, rejected modernism in general and montage as a mere 'gimmick', urging socialist writers to adhere to the nineteenth-century conception of organic growth.[7] It is a nice irony and one which provides a clue to Böll's position with regard to modernism, that the collection of essays produced to celebrate his fiftieth birthday in 1967 opened with one by Adorno and closed with one by Lukács.[8] Leitmotifs are more closely associated with the novels of Thomas Mann. Rather than organically growing, Böll's novels from *Wo warst du, Adam?* to *Billard um halbzehn* are carefully constructed around a number of phrases, slogans, and other motifs.

Even before the war he had written several novels, none of which he even tried to have published, and after 1945 this was the genre he first explored, rather than that of the short story, although initially it was only the shorter works that were published (*I*, 14, 641). On

5. Wolfgang Kayser, 'Die Anfänge des modernen Romans im 18. Jahrhundert und seine heutige Krise', *DVLG* 28 (1954), pp. 417–46; Adorno, 'Standort', pp. 61–2.

6. See for example Joseph Frank, 'Spatial form in modern literature' in Mark Schorer, Josefine Miles and Gordon McKenzie (eds.), *Criticism. The Foundations of Modern Literary Judgment* (New York, 1958), pp. 379–92.

7. 'Es geht um den Realismus', in Hans Jürgen Schmitt (ed.), *Die Expressionismusdebatte. Materialien zu einer marxistischen Realismuskonzeption* (Frankfurt, 1973), especially pp. 210–12.

8. Marcel Reich-Ranicki (ed.), *In Sachen Böll Ansichten und Aussichten* (Cologne, 1968).

Böll's own account, *Wo warst du, Adam?* (1951) was a breakthrough not only because he found a publisher for it, but also because it was for this novel that he first devised a system of colours as an aid to composition, a graph with three layers, the one representing the present, the second the level of time remembered, the third the leitmotifs; each character and each leitmotif was allotted a different colour (*I*, 17). Böll continued to employ this technique for his later novels — reproductions of the graphs for *Haus ohne Hüter* and *Ende einer Dienstfahrt* have been published,[9] and he had a personal greetings card with a coloured reproduction of the graph for *Gruppenbild mit Dame*. Elsewhere he compared the novel to a painting (e.g. *I*, 642), to a spatial rather than a temporal construct, implying a conception of the novel which is more akin to montage than to the organic form of the Lukácsian model. While his utterances on the novel form are scanty, some further items are worth mentioning. His choice of first-person or third-person narration was always based on a conscious decision, and he insisted that his first-person narratives were never autobiographical — indeed he would be more likely to use the third person for an autobiography. Asked whether he always knew how the 'plot' of his novels would end, he replied that plot was not something that interested him particularly, rather it was 'Personen, Situationen, mehr innere Vorgänge' ('people, situations, more internal processes'), and that therefore the story line could take an unexpected turn.[10] And in 1975 he insisted that the characters of his novels were 'compositions', rather than psychological studies; he was not a 'psychological author' (*I*, 387).

Wo warst du, Adam? is an anti-war novel in two senses: it is against both war and conventional war novels. It is an intriguing mixture of modernist and pre-modernist styles. Most striking is the relative autonomy of the individual chapters, each of which is centred on a separate incident; few of these lead on to the chapter which follows. Critics suggested that it was not a novel at all, merely a collection of short stories;[11] their criticism ignores the nature of modernist writing. The montage effect is strengthened by the use of multiple internal focalisers, while the story is told by a largely covert extradiegetic narrator.[12] It is particularly obvious in the lack of any

9. Klaus Schröter, *Heinrich Böll mit Selbstzeugnissen und Bilddokumenten* (Reinbek 1982), pp. 64–5 and pp. 74–5.

10. Werner Koch, 'Ein paar Stichworte. Personen und Situationen. Ein Gespräch mit Heinrich Böll,' Werner Lengning (ed.), *Der Schriftsteller Heinrich Böll. Ein biographisch-bibliographischer Abriß*, 3rd edn. (Munich, 1972), pp. 102, 100.

11. Cf. Alfred Andersch's review in *Frankfurter Hefte* 6 (1951), pp. 939–41.

12. The terminology is that of Gérard Genette, outlined and modified by Shlomith

transition between, for example, the first and second chapters. In the first the focaliser is initially a collective one, the soldiers of the German army, observing with a mixture of 'Trauer, Mitleid, Angst und eine geheime Wut' (sadness, pity, fear and a secret rage) (*R*, *1*, 308) their various commanding officers, but gradually whittled down to the individual Feinhals, who becomes the centre of consciousness for the last part of the chapter. When the second chapter begins with 'Er hörte, daß eine Stimme "Bressen" sagte . . .' ('He could hear a voice say "Bressen" . . .'), we assume that the focaliser, the 'he', is still Feinhals, but eventually realise that it is Bressen himself; Feinhals arrives at the end of the chapter, but is not identified as such until addressed by name. More conventional fiction would have taken account of the requirements of the reader and would have avoided such confusion,[13] and indeed the beginning of the next chapter has a more overt narrator and therefore requires a more overt response. Otherwise, however, the lack of commenting narrator, such as one finds in Theodor Plievier's *Stalingrad*, emphasises the helplessness of the individual in war. There is no 'plot' as such which might provide the fiction that war can be conveyed according to traditional literary patterns. Feinhals is the most important figure; in the course of the novel he gains certain insights about life — the final chapter moves closer to the pattern of the *Entwicklungsroman*. But a man who is from time to time relegated to the status of a background figure in someone else's consciousness cannot be seen as a 'hero' in the traditional sense of the term. An underlying pattern is that of the collective hero, the 'group', which, as Böll pointed out, is to be found in many war novels, whether Werner Beumelburg's heroic *Gruppe Bosemüller* or Erich Maria Remarque's pacifist *Im Westen nichts Neues* (*E*, *1*, 460). But while we do on the whole follow a group composed of the General, the Colonel, Lieutnant Greck, and Feinhals, to each of whom we are introduced in turn in Chapter 1 and to whom, with the exception of Greck, who is dead, we return at the end, none of these seems aware of the others, and the myth of the group is thereby destroyed. In place of these traditional patterns Böll creates an autonomous aesthetic pattern based largely on the repetition of motifs: medals, and especially colours, red stars on the Soviet tanks, green cucumbers, the red and green furniture vans. And while Brecht's use of montage was designed to activate the reader or play-goer, Böll's tends more to

---

Rimmon-Kenan, *Narrative Fiction. Contemporary Poetics* (London, 1983).

13. Werner Koch criticised the beginning of *Das Brot der frühen Jahre* for its demanding opening sentence ('Ein paar Stichworte', p. 107).

contribute to this overall aestheticising effect. The words of Saint-Exupéry quoted at the beginning of the novel, that war is a 'eine Krankheit. Wie der Typhus' ('a disease. Like typhus') do not suggest that the individual has any influence on the course of events, even if the novel *were* to attempt to activate him.

Und sagte kein einziges Wort (1953), has more of a conventional story line. It describes a marital crisis which comes to a head during the weekend in which the story is set and which by the end of the novel seems about to be resolved. Attacking the Church for conniving in the restoration of the gap between rich and poor, it takes its literary models from Bloy, Bernanos, and Graham Greene. But there are also echoes of Joyce's ironic treatment of the *Odyssey* in the spatial patterns which Böll weaves around his two main characters, Fred and Käte Bogner: the former an Odysseus not long returned from a war which has intensified his conviction of the absurdity of human existence, wandering through the streets of an unidentified city, tempted by Circes and Nausicaas, looking for a hotel, for people he can borrow money from; while Penelope–Käte waits passively at home.

Böll employs the unusual narrative device of two first-person narrators, who relate the novel in alternate chapters. What is 'modernist' about Böll's technique is that there is no indication of why, when or for whom Fred and Käte are writing — or indeed that they are *writing* at all. They do not appear to be collaborating, for people and places they encounter independently are described anew as if the reader had not already met them or been there. There is no community of narrative, just as there is no community in their marriage. Nor are they looking back at past events in the autobiographical manner of an Oskar Matzerath or a Serenus Zeitblom. There are no prolepses implying for example that their marriage is now completely restored — by contrast, *Das Brot der frühen Jahre* is told from a temporal vantage-point which enables Fendrich to look back and wonder what might have happened had he not met Hedwig (*R*, *3*, 95).[14]

Haus ohne Hüter (1954) reverts to the technique of *Wo warst du, Adam?*. The story is narrated extra-diegetically, but the narrator is only rarely also the focaliser. Instead we have a complex montage of text narrated mainly from five separate internal points of view, those of the five major characters of the novel. There are significant

14. Rudolf Majut lists other examples of the technique in 'Der deutsche Roman vom Biedermeier bis zur Gegenwart' in Wolfgang Stammler (ed.), *Deutsche Philologie im Aufriß*, 2nd edn. (Berlin 1960), vol. 2, col. 1695.

exceptions. One of the few occasions when the narrator is more overt is when Martin's grandmother is showing him the archives of her late husband's jam-making business; the relation between capitalism and German militarism and the rise of fascism is here made fairly explicit. Another exception is the description of Heinrich's birth and early childhood, where an external narrator ironically contrasts the sheltered life which Albert's wealthy uncle Will has enjoyed, with the complete lack of protection that Heinrich has had to endure. Here the narrator is underlining one of the major themes of the novel, the existence of deep class divisions in post-war West German society. Usually, however; Böll is less direct in his criticism. As in *Wo warst du, Adam?* the openings of the individual chapters frequently leave the reader momentarily unsure of the identity of the focaliser, when the narrator temporarily witholds the name of the character involved and refers only to 'he' or 'she'. Again the technique underlines one of the themes of the novel, the lack of communication between the characters and especially between the adults and the children. It also creates difficulties of interpretation, as much of the overt criticism in the novel comes from characters whose 'reliability' is dubious. This is especially true of Nella, but to some extent it applies to all the adults. For the first time Böll tries to convey the thought processes of an adolescent, someone for whom the world appears as a strange, inexplicable place. Martin views the diners at Vohwinkels Weinstuben as monsters; he is baffled by the activities of Grebhake and Wolters, two older boys whom he glimpses in the bushes with red faces and open trouser flies. His slightly older friend Heinrich is coming to terms with the social difference between those who have money and those who lack it; he sees the world as a frozen pond whose ice may break at any moment. Paradoxically it is the adolescent focalisers whose view on society appears to the reader more reliable than that of the adults. Böll is anxious to show that adult behaviour is incomprehensible and indefensible. In this respect he is operating within a tradition which goes back at least to Grimmelshausen's *Simplicissimus*.

Haus ohne Hüter in many respects anticipates *Billard um halbzehn* (1959). Both novels introduce three generations of one family, a grandmother who wishes to assassinate a former Nazi, characters who are trapped in their own memories, unable to find a meaningful relationship to the present day. *Billard um halbzehn* too is a third-person narrative, whose narrator has disappeared even more completely behind no fewer than ten focalisers. Within individual chapters the focus alters between characters, and even there the narrative technique can shift from direct to indirect interior monologue to direct speech, as in the chapters in which Robert is telling Hugo or Heinrich Lenore about their respective pasts. Most confusing of all are the chapters centred on Johanna Fähmel, who has been confined to a mental hospital since the early part of the War. Although we are invited to regard her as saner than the others — she openly opposed the Nazis — the scene in which Robert is made to go upstairs to his dead wife Edith and Heinrich to climb a ladder to her room is especially confusing. *Billard um halbzehn* is modernist at least in the sense that, like *Ulysses* it 'cannot be read . . ., can only be re-read. A knowledge of the whole is essential to an understanding of any part'.[15]

Billard um halbzehn was widely regarded as the breakthrough to 'modernist' writing in Böll. Within a few years it had become the subject of three major articles.[16] Its modernism was itself, however, controversial. Walter Jens deplored the pressures which he believed had forced Böll into betraying his satirical vocation.[17] Karl August Horst, on the other hand, acclaimed the technique which, he claimed, Böll had learned from the French novelists of the *nouveau roman* and which had enabled him to create an aesthetic construct without parallel in post-war German literature.[18] What appeared radically new in *Billard um halbzehn* was Böll's treatment of time. Narrated time was reduced to about ten hours on Saturday, 6 September 1958 — by comparison 'Bloom's Day' in Joyce's *Ulysses* covers just under twenty-four hours from the morning of 16 June 1904 to the early hours of the next day. The past is refracted in the memories of the characters or in their accounts of it to others, but rarely in a straightforward linear manner. Again, montage is the governing principle, assisted by the extensive use of leitmotifs. In these years the 'problem of time' was widely regarded as a crucial feature of modern novel-writing,[19] and Böll told Horst Bienek in 1960 that precisely that was one of his own preoccupations (*I*, 13). He denied that there was any radical difference in this respect between *Billard um halbzehn* and his earlier works; the 'plot' of *Wo*

15. Frank, 'Spatial Form', p. 385.

16. Henri Plard, 'Böll le Constructeur. Remarques sur "Billard um halbzehn"', *Etudes germaniques*, 15 (1960), pp. 120–43; Fritz Martini, 'Heinrich Böll: "Billard um halbzehn"', *Moderna Sprak*, 55 (1961), no 1, pp. 27–38; Therese Poser, 'Heinrich Böll: Billard um halbzehn' in Rolf Geissler (ed.), *Möglichkeiten des modernen deutschen Romans. Analysen und Interpretationen*, (Frankfurt 1962), pp. 5–44.

17. *Deutsche Literatur der Gegenwart. Themen, Stile, Tendenzen* (Munich 1961), pp. 147–8.

18. 'Überwindung der Zeit', Lengning, Böll, pp. 67–71.

19. Cf. Walter Jens: 'Das Zeitproblem ist *das* Problem des modernen Romans, und es dürfte kaum einen Romancier von Rang geben, der sich nicht mit ihm auseinandergesetzt hätte', *Statt einer Literaturgeschichte*, 5th edn, (Pfullingen, 1962), p. 318.

warst du, Adam? was already minimal and covered only a few months, while in its successors the narrated time was reduced to a few days — 'Idealerweise . . . müßte ein Roman in einer Minute spielen können' ('Ideally . . . a novel ought to be able to take place in one minute') (*I*, 19). The element of time remembered is fundamental to *Billard um halbzehn*; *Haus ohne Hüter*, at least as far as the adult characters are concerned, is in this respect too most obviously a forerunner; but even in *Wo warst du, Adam?* we find chapters which mingle past and present in the consciousness of the protagonists, and in *Und sagte kein einziges Wort* the conversations of Fred and Käte revolve round the past.

The elimination both of the overt narrator and of the element of 'real time' are indications that the trend in Böll's novels up to this point is one in the direction of the autonomy of the aesthetic construct, itself perhaps the key characteristic of modernism altogether, and one whose most compelling expression in the German-speaking world of the post-war years is Gottfried Benn's *Probleme der Lyrik*. It is confirmed by other features of Böll's novels. None of the three novels of post-war Germany is given a specific geographical setting; one may assume that the city of *Und sagte kein einziges Wort* and *Billard um halbzehn* is Cologne, but it is never explicit. Although the dates of the novels' events can be determined down to the month, even day in the case of *Billard um halbzehn*, allusions to contemporary historical events are rare and usually covert: the officers' plot of 20 July 1944 in *Wo warst du, Adam?* (*R*, *1*, 332), in *Billard um halbzehn* the return of German nationals from the Soviet Union following the April 1958 agreements (*R*, *3*, 451). References to historical figures are similarly rare — Hindenburg in the latter novel is of mainly symbolic stature — and to contemporary figures lacking altogether.

By contrast, *Ansichten eines Clowns* (1961) is much more specific. Its opening words, 'Es war schon dunkel, als ich in Bonn ankam . . .' ('It was dark already when I arrived in Bonn . . .'), are brutally direct. Schnier has performed in Osnabrück, Hanover, Braunschweig, Celle, Cologne — even in the German Democratic Republic, and the description of his experiences there has meant that alone of Böll's major works *Ansichten eines Clowns* has never been published there; it also unleashed a storm of controversy in Böll's own country. At the end of *Billard um halbzehn* Johanna Fähmel shoots at an anonymous minister; in *Ansichten eines Clowns* Schnier inveighs against Strauss, Erhard and Adenauer, extols Alec Guinness and

Pope John XXIII, and distances himself from both CDU and SPD.

Ansichten eines Clowns may be regarded as a transitional work between Böll's modernist and post-modernist periods. For while its aesthetic autonomy is pierced by the topicality of these references, its narrative technique continues to adhere to the principles of modernism. It is a first-person narrative, like *Das Brot der frühen Jahre*. The latter is a conventional autobiography, in the sense that its narrative stance is retrospective — Fendrich is focalising his own past. *Ansichten eines Clowns*, however, is more akin to *Und sagte kein einziges Wort*; Schnier is narrating as he experiences. Like the Bogners he does not appear to be addressing any reader, his novel is monological. The ending is inconclusive. The reader knows no more than Schnier whether Marie will arrive and take pity on him as he busks outside the railway station. In its treatment of narrative time *Ansichten eines Clowns* also retains the modernist stance, restricting its story time to just over three hours.

In an essay of 1960 Böll claimed that whereas in socialist East Germany content was all, and direct politically critical statements therefore impossible, in West Germany anything was permissible provided it was put in an aesthetically acceptable manner (*E*, 1, 389f). Böll's critical stance was being submerged by the aesthetic patterns of his novels; while their content included an attack on contemporary West German society, their form implied a modernist aesthetic autonomy which allowed readers to ignore the former.[20] Böll was aware of the dilemma at least from *Haus ohne Hüter* onwards; the narcissistic stasis of the major part of both that novel and *Billard um halbzehn* is overcome by the endings, in which the principal characters, Nella, Albert, Robert, Heinrich are activated into giving their lives a new direction, when 'real time' is reintroduced.

The two stories *Entfernung von der Truppe* (1964) and *Ende einer Dienstfahrt* (1966) point to the new direction Böll was taking in his fiction. The former immediately breaks with the concept of the autonomous work of art: the narrator compares his text to a child's painting book, where dots have to be joined together and shapes filled with colour. He ironically comments on modernist changes in narrative time levels. And he introduces into his fictional narrative historical documents, newspaper cuttings, texts which are open to the reality of the reader. Where the earlier works set up the pretence that the narrative had neither a producer nor a recipient, *Entfernung von der Truppe* expressly attempts to activate the reader: '*Moral* Es

20. See Rainer Nägele, 'Aspects of the Reception of Heinrich Böll', *New German Critique*, 7 (1976), pp. 45–68.

wird dringend zur Entfernung von der Truppe geraten. ('*Moral* You are urgently advised to go AWOL') (*R*, *4*, 321). It foreshadows *Die verlorene Ehre der Katharina Blum* (1974), a further example of a directly polemical work, whose preface makes specific the parallel between the fictional 'Zeitung' and the real *Bild-Zeitung* and whose narrator continually draws attention to his own narrative technique — to the painting book of *Entfernung von der Truppe* corresponds the 'damming and draining' game of the later work.[21] *Ende einer Dienstfahrt* is a more conventional narrative — returning indeed to pre-modernist techniques, with an overt extra-diegetic narrator who serves to make the connection between the fiction of the text and the reader's reality. The post-modernism of *Ende einer Dienstfahrt* is more thematic: the central motif is a 'happening', and 'happenings' were one way in which artists in the 1960s attempted to breach the barriers between art and life which modernism had created. Böll himself was disappointed at his readers' failure to pick up the story's interventionist implication (*I*, 155). However, the motif of the 'happening' plays a role in all his later novels, not least in *Gruppenbild mit Dame* (1971), where Leni is saved from eviction when her friends the refuse-collectors block off a street with their lorries.

In *Gruppenbild mit Dame* Böll took up the techniques of *Entfernung von der Truppe*. By this time the literary situation had been radically changed by political developments. The student movement and the extra-parliamentary opposition to the government's Emergency Legislation and support for the Americans in Vietnam had led to a reappraisal of the function of literature. Hans Magnus Enzensberger, for example, who a few years previously had expressed the radically modernist view that literature could only have a political effect by being resolutely non-political, now condemned all post-war West German literature as elitist and declared that in the present political climate he could see no function for literature at all. Writers should either turn to direct action or to documenting the struggles of the oppressed, whether the workers, the Vietnamese or the Iranians.[22] Literary post-modernism in West Germany dates from around this time, although, as I have shown, it was anticipated by Böll four years previously. However, just as Böll could never accept the most radical manifestations of modernism, so he refused to

21. See Steve Giles, 'Narrative transmission in Böll's *Die verlorene Ehre der Katharina Blum*', *Modern Languages*, 65 (1984), pp. 157–63.

22. 'Poesie und Politik' (1962), *Einzelheiten II* (Frankfurt, n.d.), pp. 113–37; 'Gemeinplätze, die Neueste Literatur betreffend', *Kursbuch*, no. 15 (1968), pp. 187–97.

accept that the novel was 'dead',[23] and gave a spirited defence of imaginative literature on many occasions (*I*, 276ff.; *E*, *3*, 34ff.). *Gruppenbild mit Dame* is one of the most imaginative novels he wrote, abounding in invention both of characters and events; at the same time it deliberately breaks with the literariness of his earlier novels, to such an extent that it was dismissed by some critics as being badly written.[24]

A major feature of *Gruppenbild mit Dame* is the profusion of narrative levels it contains. There are two story levels, the inner one the biography of Leni Gruyten, the outer one the story of the writing of this biography. On the face of it this is a modernist technique, found in numerous twentieth-century novels. But whereas the modernist use of the technique is designed to stress the autonomy of the artistic process, to create the illusion of a self-reflecting work of art, Böll takes the opposite direction. His narrator's researches lead him to intervene in the story he is researching. The aesthetic stance is shown to be inadequate. To a certain extent this is repeated on the level of the various subsidiary narrators, the sources whom the 'Verf.', ('Author') consults for his researches, and at least some of whom join the action to help Leni. All these narrators have their corresponding 'audience', the 'Verf.', himself in the case of the intra-diegetic narrators, but he too explicitly addresses himself to his readers, the 'mehr oder weniger geduldige Leser' ('more or less patient reader') (*R*, *5*, 54) or even 'der geneigte Leser' ('the gentle reader') (229) of eighteenth- and nineteenth-century fiction.

It is this last, deliberately archaic phrase which gives an important clue to the status of the narrative of *Gruppenbild mit Dame*. Böll has abandoned the notion of the autonomy of the modernist literary artefact, the fiction that the novel simply 'is'. Direct references to the reader's contemporary world are numerous, frequently even trivial, as when the 'Verf.' has to pause in his researches to watch the Clay–Frazier boxing match. Like the post-modernist architect Böll has at his disposal the whole range of literary styles and techniques. His novel 'quotes' eighteenth-century narrative. It also 'quotes' the fashionable documentary novel of the late 1960s which eschewed fiction as politically inadequate. As in *Entfernung von der Truppe* a

23. Gerd Courts, 'Meine Heldin soll kein Image haben. Publik-Gespräch mit Heinrich Böll anläßlich seines neuen Romans "Gruppenbild mit Dame"', *Publik*, 13.8.71 (quoted by Manfred Durzak, see note 24, p. 177).

24. Especially by Marcel Reich-Ranicki, 'Nachdenken über Leni G.', *Die Zeit*, 6.8.1971, pp. 13–14; also by Manfred Durzak, 'Heinrich Bölls epische Summe? Zur Analyse und Wirkung seines Romans *Gruppenbild mit Dame*', *Basis 3* (1972), pp. 174–97.

number of 'documents' are reproduced: military regulations, accounts of life at the front, the report of a psychiatrist on the character of Leni's son Lev. Böll identified his sources to Manfred Durzak;[25] otherwise it is not obvious which of the documents are factual, which fictitious. By mingling document and fiction Böll is stressing both the fictionality of document and the factuality of fiction — as he put it in one of his earliest essays 'Das Wirkliche *ist* phantastisch' ('reality *is* fantastic') (*E*, *1*, 75). A comparable literary predecessor is Clemens Brentano's Romantic novel *Godwi*, subtitled 'ein verwilderter Roman' ('a novel run riot') — as Böll's might have been — and which similarly plays with narrative conventions, being an epistolary novel, in which the editor of these 'documents' himself becomes a character in a novel which has yet another author. The Brentano model and the documentary model are opposite extremes, the one proclaiming the supremacy of imagination, the other that of empirical reality; Böll's position is a synthesis of the two. The novel's ending is revealing. New developments begin — the relation between the 'Verf.' and Klementina, the story of Lev — but they are left incomplete, and the final pages simply present the reader with a further set of documents for his consideration. *Gruppenbild mit Dame* has been criticised as a 'Roman . . . im Rohzustand' ('rough version of a novel').[26] Böll himself admitted he could have gone on forever (*I*, 174). Its completion is deliberately left to the reader.

The collapse of the student movement, the upsurge in urban terrorism and the accompanying repressive measures taken by the state dashed the chiliastic hopes of left-wing West German intellectuals. Böll was particularly affected. Because of his intervention on behalf of the outlawed Ulrike Meinhof he became the object of unparalleled invective from the right-wing West German media. In 1977 three prominent public figures were assassinated, politicians made speeches from behind bullet-proof glass, a Lufthansa jet was hijacked, and the three most prominent members of the Baader-Meinhof group committed suicide in their Stammheim cells. All of this is reflected in *Fürsorgliche Belagerung* (1979), a novel which centres on the paradox of contemporary liberal democracies, that the methods used to preserve individual liberties may actually destroy these same liberties.

The novel is thus as topical as anything that Böll wrote. And yet, by comparison with *Ansichten eines Clowns*, for example, it is more indirect, more fictional in its treatment of West German political

25. See Durzak, 'Boll's epische Summe', pp. 179–80.
26. Ibid., p. 177.

realities. There are no references to contemporary political figures, other than obliquely to Holger Meins, who died in prison on hunger strike on 9 November 1974, and even more obliquely to Holger Börner, prime minister of the state of Hesse (*FB*, 118). SPD and CDU are mentioned only in passing. Geographical locations too are largely fictionalised, although identifiable as the area north-west of Cologne.

It is also much less interventionist than the works he had written from *Ende einer Dienstfahrt* onwards. The use of the 'happening' motif is revealing. Plans for an immense traffic jam, like that which saved Leni from eviction in *Gruppenbild mit Dame*, are called off, for fear that innocent people might be endangered if ambulances were unable to get through. Indeed it is the police who are planning something similar in order to combat terrorism (*FB*, 394f.). The characters of *Fürsorgliche Belagerung* have all withdrawn into a passivity similar to that of the characters of Böll's early works. And this retreat into earlier stances corresponds to Böll's return to the narrative techniques he employed in the 1950s. Once again the overt extradiegetic narrator is eschewed in favour of indirect interior monologue. Each chapter has its own separate focaliser — there are eleven of these in all — and again with each successive chapter opening Böll keeps the reader in suspense as to the identity of the focaliser. The technique is the formal equivalent of the isolation in which the characters live, each in his own armoured cell; the sense of community which was such an important aspect of *Gruppenbild mit Dame* has been lost once more. And in its treatment of time too *Fürsorgliche Belagerung* moves back in the direction of the autonomous, timeless work of art, restricting its story time to at most three days, possibly even forty-eight hours.[27]

Nevertheless, there is one way in which it can perhaps be placed in the post-modernist context. Böll himself called it a 'Krimi'.[28] It consciously parodies the 'thriller' of the variety exemplified in Frederick Forsyth's *Day of the Jackal*, in which the hired assassin comes closer and closer to his victim in spite of all the security precautions taken to frustrate him. Not until the final page of Böll's novel do we know whether Tolm will survive the threats on his life,

27. See my 'Back to the Billiards Table? — Heinrich Böll's *Fürsorgliche Belagerung*', *FMLS*, 19 (1983) pp. 135 and 140, note 25. Stephen Smith believes the duration of the novel is even shorter, see 'Schizos Vernissage und die Treue der Liebe. Von der Moral der Sprache in Heinrich Bölls Roman "Fürsorgliche Belagerung"' in Hanno Beth (ed.), *Heinrich Böll. Eine Einführung in das Gesamtwerk in Einzelinterpretationen*, 2nd edn. (Königstein 1980), pp. 101–2.

28. Quoted by Fritz J. Raddatz, 'Vom Überwachungs-Staat', *Die Zeit* 3.8 1979.

nor do we know who, if anyone, will be the assassin. Böll presents us with a series of red herrings. The reader's suspicion first falls on the butler, a traditional suspect in the genre, then on the latter's girlfriend, whose hobby is archery. A bicycle seems likely to be used — and promptly Erna Breuer resolves to cycle to Hubreichen. Tolm imagines that his grandson may have been trained to butt him in the chest, causing a heart attack; Holger eventually arrives from Beirut, butts his grandfather — but only in the stomach. And finally Veronica herself succeeds in evading the security forces — but having proved her point she gives herself up. Böll too is 'proving a point': total security is impossible, the attempt to fulfil it is counter-productive. The attack will always be from the quarter from which it is least expected. Nobody thought of arson — but that is what Holger has been trained to commit; Sabine is indeed 'abducted' — but she goes willingly, and with the policeman who was sent to guard her.

Fürsorgliche Belagerung was not the first time Böll had explored the thriller or detective story genre. *Ende einer Dienstfahrt* is a courtroom novel; in *Gruppenbild mit Dame* the 'Verf.' is a kind of private detective, investigating Leni Pfeiffer. *Katharina Blum* turns the murder story upside down, betraying the identity of the murderer at the outset. Böll even referred to his own autobiography as a 'Krimi' or detective story whose suspense lay in the question whether he would succeed in evading Himmler's 'bloodhounds'.[29] *Frauen vor Flußlandschaft*, Böll's last novel, exploits the genre once more. Its opening chapter confronts the reader with various puzzles. Who are the three people whose names must not be spoken aloud? Who is Bingerle and why has he been imprisoned? What are or were the 'Klossow documents', which were sent to the bottom of a lake fifteen years previously? Who is the mysterious person who has been breaking into the homes of bankers and carefully dismantling their grand pianos (the 'happening' theme once more)?

Most of these questions remain unanswered at the end of the novel. More important for Böll is the atmosphere of suspicion, intrigue, guilty secrets — the legacy of the West German political failure to come to terms with the Nazi past, Böll's oldest theme. As one of the characters puts it, 'Skandale hierzulande (werden) nie bis ins letzte aufgeklärt' ('scandals hereabouts are never fully cleared up') (*FF*, 92). The element of 'Kolportage' in the novel is thematised by another character, when he declares that 'das Wahre klingt

29. 'Brief an meine Söhne oder: Vier Fahrrader', *Die Zeit* 15.3.1985. Boll described a court trial for the *Frankfurter Allgemeine Zeitung* in 1955 (*E*, *1*, pp. 156ff.). See also *I*, 68.

immer unglaubhaft, das Wahre ist die wahre Kolportage' ('truth always sounds implausible, truth is true colportage') (*FF*, 184). *Frauen vor Flußlandschaft* was written during daily revelations of yet more corruption scandals in West Germany. It is set among the political establishment; ministers, bankers, senior civil servants, in their villas on the Rhine between Bonn and Bad Godesberg. It is a novel about the state, not about West German society as Böll's previous works were. And since once more there are no direct references to political figures, nor even to the names of specific political parties, one feels invited to see it as a coded allegory of actual events — Erftl-Blum as Adenauer, 'Number 1', whose life might have been saved, as Hanns-Martin Schleyer, for example. In this respect the most remarkable aspect of Böll's presentation of the political scene and its history is the radical exclusion of any reference to the SPD–FDP coalition which governed between 1969 and 1983. It is as if the 'Party' in power in 1984 — the CDU, but the parallel with East European one-party states cannot be fortuitous — had been governing uninterruptedly since 1949. The motif of the 'Klossow documents' thereby takes on political significance, for they were disposed of in 1969.

Frauen vor Flußlandschaft is written entirely in dialogue or monologue. Apart from its length it is outwardly indistinguishable from the text for a stage play. Long sections of dialogue are a feature of some of Böll's works. In *Fürsorgliche Belagerung* they are occasionally so extensive that Böll himself was not always sure who was speaking.[30] Nevertheless, *Frauen vor Flußlandschaft* is as radical an 'experiment' as anything Böll wrote. Since the characters know more than the reader but are not always allowed to say what they know, Böll's use of the dialogue form contributes to the atmosphere of suspense, even melodrama, which is his novel's key characteristic. Those characters such as Elisabeth Blaukrämer who do speak out are at once placed in an institution for the mentally ill — like Johanna Fähmel in 1943 in *Billard um halbzehn*. However, the radical dramatisation of the text through dialogue implies a return to the objectivity of the autonomous work of art in an even more extreme fashion than was the case with the quasi-narratorless novels of the 1950s. It was Henry James who enjoined novelists to 'Dramatise, dramatise', and in his wake the modernist novel aspired to mimesis, showing, rather then telling in the manner of Dickens or Thackeray.[31] In *Frauen vor Flußlandschaft* the 'narrator' confines himself to setting the

30. For examples see my 'Back to the Billiards Table?' (n.27), p. 138.
31. See Rimmon-Kenan, *Narrative Fiction*, p. 107.

scene, describing the appearance of the characters and their movements. It is possible to detect an attitude behind his remarks, in the very slight irony with which he describes Chundt and Kreyl for example. But otherwise Böll has to resort to monologue, as when Grobsch reveals the truth about Plukansi, the politician for whom he had to write a (dishonest) electoral pamphlet. *Hamlet* too is about the state (of Denmark), and the 'rottenness' of the state of Bonn is the target of this, Böll's final testament to his fellow-countrymen: 'Dies ist der einzige Staat, den wir haben, es gibt keinen anderen, auch keinen besseren. Er hat uns gemacht, und wir haben ihn gemacht?' ('This is the only state we have, there is no other, nor is there a better one. It has made us, and we have made it') (*FF*, 239).

While, as we have seen, Böll rejected experimentation for its own sake, he also regarded each successive work as an 'experiment' (*I*, 356). He had no 'theory' of the modern novel — too much theory could be fatal, he declared (*I*, 400). Rather, in Percy Lubbock's phrase, it was the 'craft of fiction' that he emphasised, writing was first and foremost 'eine handwerkliche Arbeit' (*I*, 355). And it is this willingness to experiment with his craft, one which *Frauen vor Flußlandschaft* illustrates in striking measure, that is not the least of his contributions to the genre.

ALFRED D. WHITE

Max Frisch

Frisch's first novel, *Jürg Reinhart* (1933), is derivative, pretentious, autobiographical and full of transparent symbols. The shy, gauche hero proves his manhood by helping an incurably ill girl to an easy death when no-one else dares to.[1] His next story was *Antwort aus der Stille* (1937), about a young man who performs one unique feat of mountaineering before settling to an ordinary life. In a third novel, *J'adore ce qui me brûle* (1943), influenced by his compatriot Albin Zollinger, he tries a wider canvas with more characters in continuing the story of Reinhart. Frisch's work so far is provincial and backward-looking. Bourgeois values and the self-image of society are accepted; the hero grows up and is integrated, in the traditional *Bildungsroman* mould, or else tragically fails to do so. Only when Frisch starts to question such values is his work freed into mature originality. Then, in his mid-thirties, he starts to write experimentally, though without a young writer's iconoclastic verve — not shocking for its own sake, nor destroying without knowing what he wishes to build, nor preaching a half-understood social revolution. The end of the Second World War seems to have awakened him to historical changes around him. New attitudes are seen first in a series of plays — largely on topical subjects, from the aftermath of Nazism to the atomic threat — written between 1944 and 1953. In the *Tagebuch 1946–1949* entries of factual, autobiographical and literary nature cover many important subjects and contemporary themes (time, nature, the writer's duty to the world), and are cunningly arranged to form thematic groups and so present one man's reaction as citizen and writer to a world in crisis. Frisch describes the concept of the diary as essential to his writing; the three major novels of the decade 1954 to 1964 use diary form in some way. Meanwhile he emerged as a political publicist. The Swiss establishment, loving consensus, over-sensitive to frank statements

1. References to Frisch's works are made where possible using his *Gesammelte Werke in zeitlicher Folge* (Frankfurt, 1976) (werkausgabe edition suhrkamp): *Stiller* in vol. 6, *Homo faber* in vol. 7, *Mein Name sei Gantenbein* in vol. 9, *Montauk* in vol. 12. For *Der Mensch erscheint im Holozän and Blaubart* references are to the first editions (Frankfurt, 1979 and 1982 respectively).

of unorthodox views, has often viewed him with distrust; but he likes to tell home-truths to a country he sees as dangerously smug. He learnt much from America, where since the early 1950s he has spent more and more time (and he has lived in Berlin, Rome and the Ticino, but continually returned to Zurich). International affairs (he was a prominent opponent of the Vietnam war) and developments in Switzerland have occupied him equally.

He re-used material from an abortive novel of 1951–2, 'Was macht ihr mit der Liebe', in *Stiller* (1954), his first major novel, a bestseller. Stiller, a mediocre Swiss sculptor, fights on the Republican side in the Spanish Civil War, ineffectually: he cannot shoot at the enemy when he has the chance (later seen as a sign of lack of virility); he marries a ballet dancer, Julika, whose sexual frigidity (unnoticed by him) combined with his problems causes the breakdown of their marriage when she is in a sanatorium and he has an unsatisfying affair with Sibylle, wife of a public prosecutor, Rolf. The finely observed depiction of an unhappy marriage (drawn from Frisch's recent personal experience) fascinated readers: it seemed a topical *Eheroman*. Two sensitive, artistic people live in tension and misunderstanding, and make each other miserable. Both are egocentric: he blames himself for all that is wrong, she trades on her fragility and demands special treatment because she is ill — but she is only (psychosomatically?) ill when he is near. He flees all his complications, stowing away on a boat to America, living there for years, and returning under the name of White, strenuously denying any knowledge of Stiller. He is arrested for various minor offences and prosecuted by Rolf. The court pronounces he is indeed Stiller; his fines paid, he resumes his marriage, living as a potter, till Julika dies. This is the bare plot of a novel whose main fascination is in its themes and its depiction of the inner changes of a personality. Stiller, returning as White, is trying to prove that one can completely escape one's past. White is a type of the modern, dissociated, interchangeable personality; critics compared Frisch to Joyce and Proust.

White's denial of Stiller has a social side too: he is rejecting the fixed image those around him had made of Stiller, the expectations and ambitions they had projected onto him. But his eventual return to Julika shows that he cannot escape the challenge he has once taken up: no less than to deliver her from unhappiness and loneliness — an impossible challenge not from society but from the depth of his own personality. His effort to save her does no good because he makes success here the very touchstone of his life and thus distorts his character: he is morbidly fixated on an insoluble problem at the cost of his own integrity. Put metaphysically, he tries to redeem her; but a man cannot play the role of a god; he rejects himself for not being godlike. *Stiller* can be interpreted by Jung's theories of personality; the novel says much about unconscious adaptation to psychological problems. Stiller develops from an immature personality hoping for public recognition to a man who finds his values within himself. A suicide attempt in America, followed by an experience of his guardian angel telling him to be true to himself, amounts to a mystic rebirth and starts this development. But he misunderstands the message at first, thinking that White, the new start, is his real self, and that he can develop on into the future while disregarding the past. When he does realise that the past must be incorporated into his life, it seems too late for a fresh start. Whether the end gloomily shows a man turning his back on his talent and society, or optimistically shows him self-fulfilled, at last independent of others' opinions, is unclear.

The role of existentialist thought, especially Kierkegaard, in the novel is much discussed. Man's self-realisation cannot be viewed only through depth psychology; Rolf tries to interest Stiller in Kierkegaard's theory of the aesthetic, ethical and religious stages in the individual life, and the wholeness of the personality seen in a religious light. Some think Stiller develops through these stages; but it is unclear whether Stiller, or Rolf, or Frisch himself, actually understood Kierkegaard, beyond recognising his anticipation of Stiller's problem: the personality growing into a false role and unable to escape from it and identify the true potential self.

> Wenn ich beten könnte, so würde ich darum beten müssen, daß ich aller Hoffnung, mir zu entgehen, beraubt werde. Gelegentliche Versuche, zu beten, scheitern aber gerade daran, daß ich hoffe, durch Beten irgendwie verwandelt zu werden. . . . Diese Hoffnung ist mein Gefängnis. Ich weiß es, doch mein Wissen sprengt es nicht, es zeigt mir bloß mein Gefängnis, meine Ohnmacht, meine Nichtigkeit (690).
>
> (If I could pray, I should have to pray to be deprived of all hope of escaping from myself. But occasional attempts at prayer fail precisely because I am hoping to be transformed in some way through praying. . . . This hope is my prison. I know that, but my knowledge does not burst the bars, it merely shows me my prison, my impotence, my nothingness.)

The book's layout is epoch-making. The bulk of it is deemed to be written by White in prison as a self-defence, to prove he is not Stiller by providing the facts on White; but at first White merely tries to bolster his identity by spinning a series of obviously untrue yarns, each of which has a deeper meaning in shedding light on Stiller's unconscious motives; they contain some of Frisch's most celebrated pages. By the act of writing and by confrontations — which he carefully documents — with people from his past, he comes to accept the person of Stiller; he writes both White and the previous, misguided Stiller out of his system. As these meetings do not occur in the order in which the people involved were important for him, the plot events are released only gradually and apparently haphazardly to the reader, who must reconstruct the plot. White's own stories and disordered reminiscences complete the jigsaw puzzle. Themes are developed in different ways in quick succession: thus family relationships are dealt with by an apocryphal New York memory of White's, by a meeting with his half-brother in Zurich, by abstract thought — all within a few pages. A short second section is a postcript written by Rolf, for at the end Stiller, true to his name at last, falls silent. But even before this, as White tries to do justice in his notes to other characters' accounts, we have met different viewpoints (even downright contradictions) which add to the novel's fruitful complexity and irony, making us examine each figure's unstated preconceptions. Frisch makes restrained use of symbolism, and tries to put the themes in action, though the novel does have its pages of conversation and its theoretical discussions; and he anchors events in a living outward reality of brilliant townscape and landscape.

Whereas Stiller's travels end in a struggle with Swiss problems, the hero-narrator of the next novel, *Homo faber* (1957), is a globetrotter with no attachment to home. The novel's subtitle, *Ein Bericht*, suggests factuality. Stiller tried to avoid the clichés of modern life; Faber revels in them until his end nears. *Homo faber* had an immediate success, perhaps because Frisch comes to grips with the world of work, takes technical culture seriously but rejects many aspects of modernity, apparently seeing the proponents of modernity as well-meaning adepts of a quasi-religion of progress, lacking the human dimension. Faber prides himself on practicality, believes in nothing but scientific laws, averages and technological progress, and scorns airy mysticism. Yet he is caught by a series of rare chances (generally machines failing) in a catastrophe that denies the laws of probability; gripped by a subconscious urge, he makes successive irrational decisions about his next move, until he is forced to admit his view of life is inadequate: on a liner he meets Sabeth, a daughter he never knew he had (thinking her mother Hanna had undergone an abortion while he went off to work in Baghdad). He falls in love without recognising her, and they have an incestuous affair (the sharpest example of the unnaturalness of his life), ended by her accidental death on a beach in Greece, home of classical tragedy, myth and vengeance.

Faber has a one-sided view of life (his would-be-modern arguments in favour of abortion do not stand logical examination). But nor does Frisch see belief in Greek myth, eloquently propounded by Hanna, as an alternative salvation. She too is not always right when they argue about the two cultures, nor quite free from blame. Frisch builds up unobtrusively a picture of a woman admirable but flawed: her independent life as a professional person questions Faber's traditional male values without making her unwomanly, but unbridled feminism leads her to have her child without his knowledge and bring her up with no father; it is equally her fault if they are unaware of each other's existence.

Faber's aggressive, flippant, hard-bitten style, ostentatious contempt of sentimentality (and even sentiment), almost neurotic mistrust of women, and tendency to see things in black and white, come gradually to seem only the cover for real sensibility; he can appreciate natural beauty in a way that seems impossible early on. Some believe his belated maturing under the influence of love for Sabeth, a process cut short by his fatal illness, does not take him far towards being a rounded personality. But Frisch does wish to describe the burgeoning of the human being (*Homo*) so far hidden behind the *Faber* (technician); or his discovery of the feminine, sensitive and creative in himself, which he has suppressed so as to be a man in a man's world (which he always inwardly disliked). Thus when late on he sees his films of Sabeth, he realises how his treatment of her reduced her to a body and annulled her personality, how right she was to hate being filmed. His world has consisted of mechanisms and routine, excluding personal experience and the unexpected (and not admitting to ageing, so that he can sleep with a young girl and not see the incongruity). Late in the action he still hides behind routine to avoid facing searching personal questions, but he does so less and less. He is on the way to personal authenticity. His joy at the end of his life, in Cuba, after the moral and physical catastrophe, also suggests that to have really lived, even disastrously, is better than to have existed in mere routine.

The symbolism (women, cars, boats, snakes, ominous meetings with Faber's moribund old professor) is more explicit than *Stiller*'s, but still nicely ambiguous (Faber's dreams of his teeth dropping out mean a change of direction in his life, or fears of illness, or death, or the subconscious fear of being punished by castration for his sexual aberrance). Reminiscences of Greek myth and legend elude clear interpretation and add to the sense of foreboding. The use of landscape, from the pullulating Mexican jungle to the Greek beach, and of townscape, New York and Paris, is immediately attactive, but also symbolic. The jungle strikes Faber only as a repellent mass of fertility and decay, feminine, alien to the tidy, masculine, technical ethos. Towns in Europe have a quality of nature and poetry, their museums and works of art have mythical and depth-psychological overtones; New York is the home of the American way of life, which Faber, staying in Cuba and observing a dark-skinned people with a vitality America lacks, rejects harshly: 'ihre falsche Gesundheit, ihre falsche Jugendlichkeit, ihre Weiber, die nicht zugeben können, daß sie älter werden, ihre Kosmetik noch an der Leiche, überhaupt ihr pornografisches Verhaltnis zum Tod . . .' ('their false health, their false youthfulness, their females who can't admit they are getting older, their make-up even for corpses, in fact their whole pornographic attitude to death . . .') (177). In style, Frisch explores unusual modes of expression which help the reader to take in atmosphere and detail quickly. Niceties of sentence structure bow to the need to put salient ideas in a convincing order. However much Frisch experiments, it is in the larger structures of plot that the reader may lose his way, not in the details of the sentence.

Faber writes down his recent experiences in a sort of diary. But his viewpoint shifts: after writing the first half he expriences more, grows maturer. And at first he skirts round the most traumatic events, so that the reader is confused about the plot and in tension about its outcome until almost the end. Frisch uses techniques of the popular novel to keep the reader's interest, though his intentions are sophisticated. He fascinates us by avoiding direct value judgements, as when Faber in a bar claims he has five children: a story-teller of the mould of White, or just a boastful male?

When living with Ingeborg Bachmann, Frisch wrote his third major novel, *Mein Name sei Gantenbein*, translated as *A Wilderness of Mirrors* (1964), another bestseller, and a more radical formal experiment. The narrator does not claim to tell a real story, but indulges in a series of reminiscences, meditations and inventions introduced by the formula 'Ich stelle mir vor' ('I imagine'); so he is very much an authorial figure. Realistic motivation and verisimilitude are not attempted. Perhaps nothing in the novel at all is real experience of the narrator (immanent reality); certainly fantasy dominates. A few key recurring motifs (falling through a mirror into timeless realms of experience; a man in an empty flat hurriedly abandoned by two people who lived there) allow one to speculate on traumatic events in the narrator's past; but we actually read only his attempts to exorcise them by projecting himself into three imaginary characters, Enderlin, Gantenbein and Svoboda, who react violently to stresses (shooting at chandeliers and so on) in a way he perhaps is too inhibited to do. And sometimes he appears as 'ich' in episodes involving them, adding to the reader's puzzlement.

Gantenbein avoids having to react to the inconsistencies and hypocrisies of human behaviour by feigning blindness, and is accepted as blind by all. He hopes that in his presence people will drop some of their pretences. But in the long run his pretence of blindness vitiates his intentions. However well he acts his part, it is a role, with no access to reality. The truths hoped for do not eventuate; he is as much in the dark about life and love at the end as at the outset. He may stand for Kierkegaard's aesthetic stage of life, remaining an observer, not pressing on to make moral and personal decisions and accept himself and others. For him, all we see of life is our own projections and self-projections, mere images of others and of ourselves.

Enderlin, perhaps a projection of the narrator as he is when drink has loosened his inhibitions, a womaniser, who refuses to play a role or to live for more than the day, has his crisis when at forty he wrongly believes he has only a year to live. Previously he expressed his horror of the idea of repetition, of acquiescing in the passage of time, of being married for ten years. An episode the narrator remembers at the outset, the story of a patient who after a vain attempt to embrace a nurse leaves the hospital naked and runs through the streets, is vaguely connected with Enderlin: nakedness suggests Adam, alone in the world, not yet given a social role or forced to have a consistent persona. The patient is caught, clothed and put in an asylum at last, and Enderlin too succumbs: he embarks on long-term plans, which he has to carry through when he unexpectedly survives. After this he is less open to change, too much like the narrator, who loses interest in him, as he can no longer be used to play through alternative ways of behaving. Svoboda (an architect, a hint at autobiographical elements) is less prominent; his particular experience is an existential crisis when he realises that Lila is unfaithful to him after a long marriage.

All three men, and other shadowy figures, revolve around one woman, Lila, who is Gantenbein's or sometimes Svoboda's wife, Enderlin's mistress, and generally an actress, but sometimes a physiotherapist or an Italian countess. All women seen from the man's view, Frisch implies, are the same. Perhaps she also represents the Jungian *anima*, the female element the male seeks for his self-completion. Another woman is Camilla, a prostitute whom

Gantenbein regales with stories which, like Stiller's, combine surface interest and symbolic intent. The novel's only form is that imposed by the narrator's character; it is a sum of the fictions that occur to this man, and as such a mirror of his real self, more reliable (for Frisch) than any account of his empirical, chance-influenced biography. He comes across as rather paranoid, deeply unhappy, lonely, very jealous. His stories all bear on his situation and underpin his view of himself. 'Ein Mann hat eine Erfahrung gemacht, jetzt sucht er die Geschichte dazu' ('A man has had an experience, now he is looking for the story to go with it') (11). At the end (a tantalising glimpse of immanent reality?) he is seen turning to everyday pleasures, bread, fish and wine (which also have transcendent significance, taking up references in the Enderlin episodes to Jerusalem and Easter), apparently reconciled to life and the approach of death — a theme present throughout in a series of episodes, from the death of a man at the wheel of his car, which sets the novel going, via grave and mummy motifs, to the tale of the corpse floating down the river through Zurich at the end. How well this ending holds together the divergent imaginings, especially late on when Gantenbein's marriage is belatedly blessed with a child, is dubious; but some critics believe every scene in the work has its structural importance.

The novel is socially non-committal. The figures move in an *haut bourgeois* world and can afford problems of identity and interrelations, they scarcely busy themselves with the political and social troubles of the day. In an aside the narrator claims the world's problems will only be solved by starting from the individual; but the novel scarcely gets beyond the individual. It is also a comic work, presenting a rich variety of situations in ironic detail: Enderlin suddenly tongue-tied at a party, Lila rushing in and out of the kitchen in an apron to make the guests think she is taking great pains to cook for them, Gantenbein trying to cope with water flooding from the shower without doing things a blind man could not plausibly do. Such virtuoso passages give pleasure without the embarrassment (as Frisch thinks it) of having to suspend one's disbelief in an invented plot: the novel as such is estranged, a narrative equivalent of Brechtian dramatic technique, and Frisch refuses to comply with our demand for a plot, consistent characters and social commitment; but the fictional imagination flourishes.

For ten years he wrote no novels, though *Tagebuch 1966–1971* like its predecessor has many narrative elements and a tight overall structure, and the short *Wilhelm Tell für die Schule* has a plot, though it only negates the story of the Swiss national hero as usually taught. Since

Gantenbein Frisch has seemed happier with short narrations or contrafactures of existing plots. In a time when current German literature concentrated on personal, subjective experience he launched *Montauk* (1974) an exercise on the boundaries of autobiography and fiction. So far his novels had developed away from the autobiographical, from experience, even from a coherent fictional world, towards introverted fantasy. Now he tries to tell factually, without addition or omission, the story of a weekend spent with a girl by a writer, Max, whose musings and reminiscences on his past prove that here Frisch is baring himself to us; he has never concealed that he in fact experienced that weekend. If the narrator in *Gantenbein* was impossible to pin down, Max is all too identifiable. Yet Frisch mistrusts autobiography: at best it is subjective — the writer remembers selectively and distorts events, knowingly or not. One's present view of one's past is just one interpretation of the facts: all writing is fiction, but sometimes the writer selects, presents, and arranges material which he has not invented. Hitherto Frisch has not believed that a reader who knows the facts about the writer's life knows the writer. Rather, as in *Gantenbein*, it is his imaginings that show his true self. Such an attitude is not easily abandoned, yet *Montauk* shows a major shift of Frisch's approach.

He sees that he cannot spare himself explicit self-exploration. We cannot escape our past: we must recognise that what we have done, and what has been done to us, has shaped what we are now. And the reader has a right to know about the professional writer, who keeps on imposing his views on the world at large. His attempts to assert a public moral authority depend on his frankness about his own character and failings. So he tries to be more honest about bits of his life he has already treated in novels. 'Die jüdische Braut aus Berlin (zur Hitler-Zeit) heißt nicht HANNA, sondern Käte, und sie gleichen sich überhaupt nicht, das Mädchen in seiner Lebensgeschichte und die Figur in einem Roman, den er geschrieben hat. Gemeinsam haben sie nur die historische Situation und in dieser Situation einen jungen Mann, der später über sein Verhalten nicht ins klare kommt; der Rest ist Kunst, Kunst der Diskretion sich selbst gegenüber . . .' ('The Jewish fiancée from Berlin (in the Hitler period) was not called Hanna, but Käte, and they are not at all similar, the girl in his life-story and the figure in a novel he wrote. All they have in common is the historical situation and in this situation a young man who couldn't set his mind at rest about his behaviour afterwards; the rest is art, the art of sparing oneself the worst . . .') (727). Despite this self-irony Frisch later criticised himself for lacking frankness; some critics were disappointed that the long-awaited 'truth' about

Frisch turned out so much like the existing image of a tortured narcissist.

Frisch draws the balance of his life in a fresh variation of his typical diary form. Questions or other outer stimuli continually make him interrupt the story of the weekend with explanations, memories, opinions, strung together by free association, an almost psychoanalytic freeing of the depths of the personality through memory. Unsurprisingly, much runs on the theme of his relations with women: for all his desire to understand them, has he ever done so? Has he treated them as equals, or has he celebrated in his works an unreconstructed male image of woman? The major novels and diaries are often referred to, even quoted without acknowledgement, as part of the objective evidence about his past attitudes. As in other novels, Frisch uses symbols to underline the general import of his personal experiences; he frames them by references to Montaigne's essays, where the author shows his character by his reactions to things around. Perhaps the result is not a novel, but what else is it? A salient feature is the means used to assert a distance from the past. Bent on a weekend's pleasure in America without preconditions or consequences, the author looks at a mesh of personal relationships he had in Europe. Used to thinking in German, he discusses his life in English and it sounds quite different. Used to taking offence at certain criticisms, he accepts them from a stranger in a foreign language: he relaxes — a condition for the dispassionate look at himself.

Frisch had already attempted and shelved another narrative, so short as to be perhaps a novella rather than a novel; after recasting it appeared as *Der Mensch erscheint im Holozän* (1979). Herr Geiser here is an old man living alone in a village cut off by landslides, an isolation symbolising his situation as a widower with no real human contacts left. He acts more and more confusedly, refuses visits, tries to climb out of the valley to go to his daugher but gives up when most of the way to success, and at last apparently suffers a stroke. Though he is seen sympathetically, his disinterest in human things, his preference for book-knowledge about geology, anthropology and so forth, indicate a basic shortcoming. He reaches no insight into the truth of his personal situation, is unprepared for death, and has no more individual life than the salamander he observes in his bath. The superficial preoccupations of his former life, business, family, having faded, he is an empty shell. What he takes for the impending end of the world, because of the spell of bad weather, is only his personal end; life will go on without him. The same snippets of knowledge which he copies or cuts out and tapes to his walls when alive (a masterly use of montage) are repeated after his death or incapacitation: they are still valid and had nothing to do with any personal reality. Unlike Faber who recognised the hollowness of technocentricity before he died, Geiser dies unfulfilled, unaware. A pagoda of crispbread he keeps trying to build stands for the transience and uselessness of his achievements. Frisch uses unemotional language to reflect this desiccated man; so the reader feels called upon to supply the emotion, to be sorry for one who does not know what is happening to him. The accumulated papers which do not fit together, 'ein Wirrwarr, das keinen Sinn gibt' ('a jumble that makes no sense') (137), symbolise Geiser's way of building up knowledge without interpretation or understanding of life.

The next novel is *Blaubart* (1982), a very short, densely written work (again more of a novella), based on a real court case, a kind of detective novel: clues introduced in disguised form only come to fit in at the end. An outer reality, and one from which the novelist can easily keep his distance, is the work's basis. But Frisch tends to identify with the accused, Schaad, a doctor suspected of killing Rosalinde, one of his several ex-wives, out of jealousy — the vice of Gantenbein and Frisch himself. As far as Schaad is concerned (he was drunk at the time) he may have done the deed, but he has been acquitted for lack of evidence. The action is all internal, though one takes some time to realise it: his reconstructions of questionings at the trial, reminiscences, imaginings of further cross-examination. The form is that of interior monologue, or possibly a journal where Schaad notes his thoughts (some of which have a symbolic or leitmotivic nature, such as a description of how to pay billiards with no opponent). His self-examination unearths evidence of potential for violence. Eventually he decides — 'Ich bin nicht unschuldig' ('I am not guiltless') (73) — to admit to the murder. The police do not listen, as he has no new evidence; he crashes his car into a tree, a clumsy attempt (conscious or not) at self-execution, only to hear afterwards that the actual murderer has been found. Schaad shares with Frisch a mother-fixation that invites Freudian interpretation, and the nagging doubt that however many women he has been intimate with he does not understand them. He is a perfectionist, an idealist who lets his wives drift away from him rather than asserting himself or imposing his ideals on them, and who thus suffers (one can only guess at the moral suffering he causes them in the process). He is a neurotic, suffering from amnesia, delusions, and disorientation brought on by his feeling of responsibility, an egocentricity which makes him feel personally in charge even of what he cannot in fact influence. If 'Gantenbein' was fleeing from a past which he could not name, and vainly seeking a future that would avoid further occupation with the past — in this being as misguided as Stiller — Schaad busies himself with the real events of his past, with a real or potential judicial and moral guilt. Whilst individual pieces of outer reality may say nothing about the inner self, the totality of our deeds adds up to a fated life-story of objective significance within a social, even metaphysical reality. The theme of identity has been laid to rest.

Frisch with his major novels led the way in German literature; having overthrown conventions of space and time and espoused Brechtian ideas of *Verfremdung* in drama, he showed that an equal revolution in the novel was possible. The short late works have their peculiar quality in the exploration of new narrative stances, the development of ethical sense, the enhanced awareness of the individual's function within a wider totality, but his reputation as a novelist will continue to rest on the intense observation and descriptive power, perceptiveness about character, formal modernity and playful brilliance, stylistic quality and uncompromising search for self-fulfilment in *Stiller*, *Homo faber* and *Mein Name sei Gantenbein*. Here he moves largely in the sphere of the well-off bourgeoisie, but avoids kitsch, cliché and banality by exactitude of eye, scrupulousness of pen and originality of perspective.

Stiller was a landmark in the history of the novel that does not demand the reader's suspension of disbelief, since its structure depended on the clash of differing accounts of the same set of events — not because one of the characters is lying, but in that all experience is subject to doubt and distortion. We live subjectively, even solipsistically, in a strange world that forces us to put on masks to survive, to waste our true potential, unless we are willing to make a totally unsecured leap into the unknown and fulfil ourselves by insisting on what we alone can see: an application of existentialism in the novel. Ironically, the very vigour with which *Stiller* puts its themes — the loss of the true self or identity, the impossibility of marriage as a bond of two insecure individuals, the need for openness and mobility of personality and opinions, suspicion of the prevalence of second-hand experience and received ideas, dislike of the tendency to make stereotypes of others or to play roles to the detriment of our own inner truth — allowed Frisch to be typecast as the chronicler of the identity crisis; critics undervalued his other themes and disregarded his later development.

But he never writes the same story twice. Each of his outsider-heroes (Geiser expected) is imprisoned in a different way, is seeking a new kind of freedom: freedom from the social demands he has internalised and sexual problems he cannot cope with (Stiller), from the reduction of self and world to mechanical entities (Faber), from the wounds of the past and over-sensitivity ('Gantenbein'), from the hypocrisy of a public persona (Max), from guilt (Schaad); freedom to be insignificant (Stiller), to die in peace (Faber, Max), to take up the threads of life (Schaad, 'Gantenbein'). Themes and motifs recur, but in a spiral: author and reader can again and again stand on a higher level and look down on the lower. Self-quotation serves as a marker of how the same words can express fresh levels of truth. Schaad like Stiller never grows up, but retains the moral fire of an adolescent who has not come to a compromise with the world. But one does not reach middle age without doing things in life and therefore incurring some guilt along the way; Frisch between the two novels has developed an ethical commitment which sees not only that nobody can work at the reconstruction of their lives — the protagonists' task in the major novels — without having faced the past frankly and explicitly, but also that he must not give up there. Having reached their crisis of self-awareness, his early characters are often left to their own devices; we do not see them put their insights into practice. Some suspect that they spend so long finding themselves that they will never do anything decisive. Though equally tormented, the late heroes are more satisfying in this respect.

Frisch's chosen literary material is not society and politics, not the state and capitalism (to him only two of several strands in the web of alienation), but the grinding forces between two individuals who come together and then grow apart, the search for a reconciliation between continuation of self-development and fidelity to a partner, the study of how those who have torn themselves free from a partner suffer from loss of contact, the struggle against being reduced to a two-dimensional cut-out. Any agreement with others, personal or social, is temporary; a crisis, a decision whether to do violence to oneself or risk destroying a relationship, is inevitable; what is unforgivable is compromise or lukewarmness. His heroes break the rules: what happens, they ask, if I start life afresh, if I pretend to be blind and refuse to play society's games, to understand what is demanded of me? The conclusion is always complex, ambiguous. Stiller returns to the marriage he fled from, and no external success attends his surrender to his bourgeois identity and his picking up the threads, but is his inner serenity not enviable? Faber gains some insights into what was wrong with his life so far, but are they not one-sided, and is his joy just the euphoria of a dying man? How well do the Protean disguises of 'Gantenbein' help him to deal with the aspects of his own character that have made him so unhappy? The answers are not easy; there is no room for facile identification, but we are encouraged to think about our own situation and not to eschew radical solutions.

NOEL L. THOMAS

Günter Grass

Born in Danzig in 1927, Grass was subject to the onslaught of Nazi propaganda and served as a soldier on the Russian front in the Second World War. As a result of his experiences during this time his works of fiction are both backward- and forward-looking: backward-looking in the sense that they denounce the modes of thinking, feeling and behaving on which National Socialism was founded, and forward-looking in that they seek to ward off the resurgence of such attitudes of mind and thereby prevent the resort to violence and war as a means of resolving political problems. It is readily understandable that guilt is a major theme in his fiction. Because of the wounds left by Nazi wrong-doing he is firmly, though not fanatically, committed to democratic socialism as a means of making social and political progress. He believes in evolution rather than revolution. This is not to say, however, that Grass pursues a heavy-handed didactic line in his novels, and this is especially so in those works which we shall later classify as the outstanding examples of his art.

Grass's first major work of fiction *Die Blechtrommel* (*The Tin Drum*) hit the literary world in 1959 like a bombshell and was accorded immediate and well-deserved acclaim. This novel is justly regarded as his masterpiece and it is certainly this work on which the fame of Grass rests. The unfortunate result is that all his subsequent narrative works — eight in all — are measured by the ultimate yardstick of *Die Blechtrommel*. The first question a critic poses when a new work of Grass appears is whether it compares favourably or unfavourably with Grass's first brain-child. This first child dominates its brothers and sisters in no uncertain manner. Of the four major novels (*Die Blechtrommel*, *Hundejahre* (*Dog Years*), *Der Butt* (*The Flounder*) and *Die Rättin* (*The Rats*) — major in terms of length and impact — only *Der Butt* competes on equal terms with his big brother. *Örtlich betäubt* (*Local Anaesthetic*), a shorter and less satisfactory novel, occupies a lowly position in the esteem of the public and the critics. Two works, however have side-stepped the head-on clash with *Die Blechtrommel* by achieving excellence in a different category of narrative fiction: the one, *Katz und Maus* (*Cat and Mouse*), is classified as a 'novella' and the other, *Das Treffen in Telgte* (*The Meeting in Telgte*), as an '*Erzählung*' (a story). The other two remaining works are not fully-fledged novels: *Aus dem Tagebuch einer Schnecke* (*From the Diary of a Snail*), labelled as a novel, is a cross between novel, diary and narrative essay, though it makes for very satisfying and worthwhile reading; *Kopfgeburten oder die Deutschen sterben aus* (*Headbirths or the Germans are dying out*) has been described as a narrative essay and may readily be regarded as the least stimulating of Grass's prose works.

Let us now look in turn at each individual work and assess its content and impact. In *Die Blechtrommel* the author surveys the happpenings within a *petit bourgeois* environment in the years between 1899 and 1954, set in Danzig until the end of the Second World War and then in Düsseldorf. He describes this catalogue of events not directly, but through the medium of a narrator, Oskar Matzerath. The latter views the outside world in an eccentric and at the same time egocentric manner. Born in the year 1924 Oskar, so he tells us, interrupts his physical growth at the age of three by throwing himself down the cellar steps in his father's shop and thus retains the stature of a child. Hence the narrator whom Grass employs can be considered to be intelligent, obviously immature and also freed from the need to act in accordance with an adult concept of responsibility. In addition, Oskar is regarded officially as a lunatic, whilst being suspected of murder. A child and a madman writes his memoirs from within the confines of a mental asylum in the years between 1952 and 1954. This is the unique narrative perspective which Grass employs in his survey of a Danzig family. Clearly Oskar cannot and does not sit in judgement upon the events and characters of his age. He merely views them from below, from the vantage point of a child, who, as the narrator says in *Die Rättin*, is involved without actively participating. Oskar does not provide the reader with the set of criteria by which assessment of situation or character can be carried out — nor does the author intervene in order to supply any measuring device. This is one of the main interpretative problems within the novel.

What attracts us to the novel in the first instance, however, is the author's highly developed capacity for story-telling which supplies the novel with its momentum. From the first chapter onwards we are fascinated by the series of episodes which are connected directly or indirectly with the central figure of the novel. The first chapter sets the tone: Oskar's grandfather, Joseph Koljaiczek, is attempting to escape from the clutches of the German police and takes refuge from his pursuers under the voluminous Kashubian skirts of Anna Bronski, who is conveniently sitting by the side of a fire in a potato field. Having entered the sanctuary formed by Anna's four skirts, he puts his time to good use by founding a dynasty. Within hours the two of them are united in marriage. The episode is not untypical: the narrative concentrates upon the actions and the observable behaviour of the characters concerned. There is no sense in which the author concerns himself with the inward world of man. Rather does the converse seem to be true: feelings and thoughts are objectivised, i.e. they are reflected in the objects and situations which comprise the external world. Rarely does the tension created by the story-telling slacken. Frequently the unusual perspective of the narrative adds a special flavour to the episodes. The absurd and the grotesque both heighten the narrative *élan.* And it must be admitted that a pinch of blasphemy or obscenity adds spice to the literary recipe, though it would be wrong to think that Grass indulges in gratuitous blasphemy or obscenity. Oskar's amorous adventures are especially intriguing and grip the reader's attention whilst at the same time being rich in comic effect. Such episodes — and probably the majority in the novel — can be enjoyed for their own sake without reference to previous events. Nor is there any need to occupy oneself with the background political happenings or to be aware of the significance, or even presence, of the imagery. One can be entertained by the anecdotes without being unduly troubled by Oskar's unreliability as a narrator, such is the gusto with which the stories are told. One enters into Oskar's world of fantasy and is delighted by the imaginative inventiveness which gives shape to the series of incidents within the narrative. In this way we frequently find that our disbelief is suspended and our doubt made to look superfluous. It could be maintained that Grass has the capacity of a first-class writer of detective novels for gripping the attention of the reader and keeping him in suspense. Grass's stories — or those of his narrator — are above everything else exciting.

As the reader proceeds through the novel, he inevitably looks for the thread which links the various episodes, that is, apart from their revolving round the central character of Oskar. One of the interlinking elements within the novel is the imagery which has a cohesive and an argumentative quality. It is not coincidental that many of the titles of the chapters refer, not to people or actions, but to objects. The latter take on the role of Eliot's objective correlative and constitute allusive though sometimes elusive pointers to underlying meanings. They form trails of associations throughout the novel and Grass through his narrator is frequently at pains to make evident the links between objects which perform a similar evocative function.

Both the title of the book and the illustration on the dust-cover force the reader to consider the significance of the tin drum itself. The drum has at least two associations, even before we start reading the novel: it is emblematic of war and yet it also conjures up an atmosphere of lamentation and of mourning. At the funeral of his mother, for instance, Oskar feels compelled to express his grief by drumming on her coffin. And in Schlöndorff's film Oskar beats out a doleful rhythm on his drum which takes on almost the quality of a funeral march. In the novel Oskar makes use of the drum as a means by which he can preserve his status as a three-year-old. The drum allows Oskar to indulge in pretence, which is the precondition for his viewing the outside world in ironic and grotesque terms. By means of the drum he can beat the retreat from reality and avoid having to follow in his father's footsteps as a shopkeeper: he can turn to art rather than to business, and thus he parodies the dilemma with which many of Thomas Mann's characters are confronted. He is a grotesque distortion of Adrian Leverkühn, the musician whose life is compared obliquely with Germany's headlong plunge into destruction in Thomas Mann's *Doktor Faustus*.

The imagery of 'Kopf' ('head') and 'Schwanz' ('tail') is another example of metaphorical language which assumes an argumentative quality by its wide-ranging associations. Such imagery adumbrates the triumph of passion and lust over reason and moderation, which has implications on the personal and on the political level. Its net of associations can be seen lightly sketched throughout the novel but it is especially in evidence in the chapter entitled 'Karfreitagskost' ('Good Friday Fare') in which Oskar's parents and his uncle, Jan Bronski, watch eels devouring a horse's head, and in the chapter 'Rasputin und das ABC' in which the forces of unreason as exemplified by Rasputin emerge victorious over Goethe. The imagery in the novel is not obtrusive and does not impede the narrative in any way whatsoever. Nevertheless it fulfils a prefigurative, configurative and recapitulatory function within the novel, whilst contributing substantially to the novel's stimulatory appeal.

By now it will be obvious that Grass in this novel does not deal with the events of monumental history. When they are mentioned this is performed in a cursory, offhand manner. The number of chapters which have as their content a major political happening is very small: two in particular spring to mind, the 'Kristallnacht' ('Crystal Night') and the defence of the Polish Post Office. Nevertheless, events on the personal plane are linked with occurrences on the political or military plane, and the activities in the sphere of politics or war are thereby belittled and deprived of their grandeur. The grotesque relationships between man and woman are sometimes used to emphasise the extent to which real love is absent from their lives but they are also employed as a means of reducing political and military events to the level of the ridiculous and of making them appear sordid. The unfolding of Maria's and Oskar's liaison, for instance, comes to mirror the explosion of feeling which on the national level was a characteristic feature of German irrationality during the Nazi period. Parallels abound between the two realms: for example, the way Oskar's father meets his death — he chokes on his own party badge — comes to symbolise the collapse of Nazi Germany, and Greff's suicide on the gigantic, elaborately constructed drumming machine occurs in October 1942, shortly after the German occupation of Stalingrad. In short, Grass places the decline of a family in the midst of a *petit bourgeois* environment side by side with the disintegration of a national community.

By now it will be clear that irony and the grotesque are constant features of Grass's first novel. Accordingly the juxtaposition of the tragic and the comic, the serious and the amusing is constantly being emphasised. The reader is called upon to respond with a combination of laughter and tears, mirth and indignation. The merriment almost invariably heightens the upsurge of revulsion. True to the nature of irony and the grotesque the reader reacts, for example, to the viciousness of the Nazi treatment of the Jews with a gut feeling of horror and revulsion. No reasoning or criteria are necessary, for our emotional rebellion is immediate. The irony proceeds naturally from Oskar's elevation of pretence to the primary motivation within his life, and the open-endedness, along with the absence of any yardstick, also constitutes an interpretative problem within the novel.

Another source of uncertainty within the novel concerns the narrator himself. Some critics regard Oskar almost exclusively as a narrative device, a means by which the German development and the continuity of German political and social phenomena may be exposed to ridicule. Others would claim, however, that Oskar has a representative function to fulfil, as does Adrian Leverkühn in *Doktor Faustus*, and that he is an oblique and ironic expression of the trends of his time. Oskar indulges in a carnival of amorality and infantilism which is paralleled by the grim saturnalian eruption of National Socialism and by the hedonism of the post-war economic miracle. Oskar's prose is motivated by a desire for psychological facelessness and political irresponsibility. Whatever conclusion one comes to — and it is possible to regard Oskar both as a narrative device and the representative of the climate of his time — *Die Blechtrommel* does emerge as a grotesque lament for the grievous wrongs perpetrated against the Poles and the Jews and an expression of Grass's sense of guilt.

Katz und Maus which was published in 1961 reaches the same degree of expressiveness and quality as *Die Blechtrommel*, though on a much more restricted scale, given the fact that it conforms to all the standard rules of the *Novelle*. The story concentrates on Joachim Mahlke in the four years before his disappearance in 1944 at the age of eighteen. The schoolboy hero and clown Mahlke is described as making every possible effort to compensate for his own feelings of inadequacy as externalised by his oversized, mouse-like Adam's apple. These attempts to prove himself and to gain public acclaim reach their climax in the award of the Knight's Cross which he is awarded for his feats as a tank commander on the Russian front. He regards such a distinction as being the ultimate means of diverting attention from his Adam's apple and of bringing peace and harmony to his tormented mind. Because of a previous misdemeanour he is refused permission to address the pupils in his former school. Denied social acceptance and denied access to the paradise of his aspirations, he finds his life deprived of all meaning, dives into the hold of a sunken Polish mine-sweeper, where many of his previous acts of daring had been accomplished, and does not resurface. The story, however, acquires a second dimension by the fact that it is told by a narrator, Pilenz by name, whose object in writing is to free himself from a troubled conscience. His sense of guilt stems from his original act of placing a cat upon the mouse-like protruberance in Mahlke's neck and thus making his hero hypersensitively aware of his otherness, by lying to him and encouraging him finally to take refuge in the mine-sweeper. It is not unlikely that Pilenz's attitude to his hero may be tinged with homosexuality. Pilenz furthermore relates his story not in the immediate period after Mahlke's death but after the lapse of fifteen years.

Grass has stated that the story of Mahlke implies criticism of 'church, school, heroism and indeed the whole of society'. And it is not difficult to see the validity of this conclusion. Mahlke engages in war solely as a means of self-gratification. He is not inspired by a sense of allegiance to the ideology of the political movement and the state which he is serving; nor is there any indication that he has an understanding of the political realities of the time. In his mindlessness he is exploited and corrupted by a criminal regime which awards the Knight's Cross to those who achieve military distinction in the pursuit of its aims. Pilenz on the other hand still regards the past in exclusively subjective terms. His preoccupation with his own personal problems ensures that he is unable to establish a relationship between the private and the public spheres. Like Mahlke he is amoral and apolitical. Pilenz's attitude is obliquely condemnatory of the post-war German mentality. Grass leaves the reader to come to his own conclusions about the two characters and their predicament. Nor does he force the reader to accept any particular interpretation of the symbolism of cat and mouse. In this sense the *Novelle* remains tantalisingly shrouded in ambiguity and ambivalence. In a manner characteristic of Grass he provokes the reader to sort out the issues for himself.

Hundejahre, which was published in 1963, has much in common with the other two members of the Danzig Trilogy. It possesses the same physical dimensions as *Die Blechtrommel*. It spans the same period of time as Grass's first novel and the action is situated also, at least until 1945, in Danzig. Like *Die Blechtrommel* it is divided into three books — the first two dealing with the period up to 1945 and the third one with the post-war era. Like its companion it consists of a series of anecdotes which describe what happened in Danzig, when, to use the imagery of the novel, it went to the dogs. It shares with its predecessors a preoccupation with the theme of guilt. In this instance Grass is concerned to show the history of a personal relationship between a German, Walter Matern, and a Jew, Eddi Amsel. Their friendship is crisis-ridden, though Amsel never gives up the hope of re-establishing it in a meaningful way. Two events are decisive elements in their relationship: the one occurs in the first few pages of the book — Matern's act of throwing a knife, the token of their blood-brothership, into the river Vistula; and the other is the assault which Matern and his comrades launch against Amsel with their fists. Matern unconsciously suppresses any recollection of his involvement in the vicious attack on his friend, whilst Amsel relentlessly pursues the objective of jolting his friend's sluggish powers of memory and of mobilising his awareness of himself.

Grass continues in *Hundejahre* to experiment with the narrative perspective. In this instance he allocates each of the three books to a different narrator — the first one to Amsel, the victim, the second to Harry Liebenau, ostensibly the unbiased witness and observer, and the third to Matern, the man of action and former SA man. Given the main theme of the novel, this division of narrative labour does not seem to be inappropriate, though some critics have found fault with it. Like *Die Blechtrommel*, *Hundejahre* has its central image, the associations of which Grass effectively integrates into the course of the novel.

However, Grass's second novel differs from the first in that it is not as blackly pessimistic as is *Die Blechtrommel*. Though Amsel does not achieve his objective of re-educating his blood-brother, the possibility that he might realise this aim is left open. Furthermore, Amsel, the editor of the three diaries, provides the reader with a set of criteria by which he may assess the reliability of Liebenau's and Matern's statements. Thus the orientation of the reader is much more secure than is the case in *Die Blechtrommel*. *Hundejahre* differs from its companion novel in the Danzig Trilogy in that there are aspects against which criticism could legitimately be levelled. It seems to me that a discrepancy exists between artistic intention and effect, for example, in the use of Heidegger terminology to satirise not only the philosophy itself but also to denounce the sheer massive wrong-headedness which led to the slaughter of the Jews in concentration camps such as Stutthof near Danzig. Even some of the imagery lacks the power to convince, eg. the idea that the miller, Matern's father, can predict economic developments by listening to the worms in his sack of flour. It appears to be an inadequate imaginative construction — and this is not the only example in the novel. Suffice to say that *Hundejahre*, despite its many positive features, has not met with the universal acclaim which has been so readily accorded to the two other works in the Danzig Trilogy.

Grass' next novel *Örtlich betäubt* was published in 1969, an election year, in the same way that the appearance of *Aus dem Tagebuch einer Schnecke* also coincided with the holding of federal elections in 1972. Of the novels this is the book which has fared worst at the hands of the critics. Its publication in an election year is clearly not the cause of its failure to find favour, but it at least provides a symbolical indication of one of its flaws, for its central preoccupation is overtly political. Furthermore the novel concentrates on a discussion which does not lend itself to treatment in an exciting narrative form, a discussion of the classical question: reform or revolution. A teacher, Eberhard Starusch, a now middle-aged version of a former anarchist who appeared in *Die Blechtrommel* under the name of Störtebeker, is the advocate of evolution and moderation and succeeds in diverting Philipp Scherbaum, a fairly moderate revolutionary, from the use of violence in the defence of his principles. The teacher's objective is to use discussion as a means of preventing action. In short, the theme of this novel diminishes in advance its narrative impact.

The narrator in the novel is the teacher himself who is ably abetted by a dentist in his efforts to dissuade his pupil from burning his dog in public as a protest against the war in Vietnam. The active involvement of the dentist in the teacher's campaign allows the dentist's chair, as though it were a psychiatrist's couch, to be the location of the narrative and permits the introduction of dental imagery, supplying, of course, the title of the book. Though the narrator is closer to the author than his counterparts in the previous three prose works, he is presented as an enigmatic and unreliable narrator (and individual) who is sorely troubled by his own sense of inadequacy, and, irony of ironies, by his own innate disposition to indulge in violence. By the end of the novel he has not managed to resolve any of his own personal problems even with the assistance of the dentist. Thus Starusch does emerge as a many-sided and not uninteresting character but this does not, in my view, compensate for the over-insistence on a political viewpoint and the lack of vitality in the story itself. Fortunately — as some critics feared — *Örtlich betäubt* was not to mark a deterioration in the narrative and imaginative powers of its author. Such a fear was soon to be dispelled by the publication of *Der Butt* in 1977 and *Das Treffen in Telgte* in 1979.

In the meantime a further 'election' novel was produced in the shape of *Aus dem Tagebuch einer Schnecke*, this time in 1972. It constitutes a further step on the road to the closing of the gap between author and narrator, for in this book Grass talks directly to his children about matters political — author and narrator have merged together. The novel consists of three frames of reference: firstly, Grass describes his involvement in the election campaign of 1972 in support of the SPD; secondly, he tells the story of the Danzig Jews from 1933 onwards, in the course of which he introduces a fictitious character, Zweifel by name, who tries to alleviate the suffering of his Jewish compatriots; and thirdly, Grass introduces us to a lecture on Dürer's etching *Melencolia I* which he gave in 1971 on the occasion of the five-hundredth anniversary of the birth of Dürer. The three frames of reference co-exist in juxtaposition with common themes and images interlinking them: the image of the snail which is meant to be the metaphorical representation of the democratic principle, edging its slow pace between utopianism and melancholy, is the foremost example, whilst the horse stands for the ideas associated with Hegel's political thinking, the implications of which Grass is at pains to denounce in the course of the novel. *Aus dem Tagebuch einer Schnecke* makes for worthwhile and stimulating reading simply because it gives us insight into Günter Grass's motivation as a man of politics. It impresses above all by its sincerity.

In 1977 Günter Grass astounded and confounded all his critics by producing a novel which in terms of length, impact, narrative and imaginative intensity came close to equalling or indeed equalled *Die*

Blechtrommel which in the year 1959 had first drawn the attention of the literary world to the name of Günter Grass. In *Der Butt* Grass produces a wide-sweeping survey ranging to and fro from the Early Stone Age to the present day. In so doing Grass provides a history which could be regarded as being complementary to *Die Blechtrommel* and could be said to contain more exact facts than the so-called authentic, standardised version of history. As in *Aus dem Tagebuch einer Schnecke* there are three interweaving themes: cooks and their contribution to history, the fish and its trial, and the birth of a daughter. And as in the previous novel, each theme has its own particular narrative location: the history of the cooks mainly in Danzig, apart from the Father's Day episode, the trial in Berlin and the birth in Wewelsfleth. The birth of the child determines the structure of the novel, which is divided up in accordance with the nine months of the pregnancy. The flounder — along with the implications of Grimm's fairy tale — interlinks the various episodes in the novel, constitutes a central image to which many stimulating associations are attached and makes its contribution to the unfolding of the cooks' history. The history of cooks and cooking provides the chronological sequence in the novel, is at the same time a history of the sexes, of the emancipation of man from woman and of woman from man, and allows a survey of history to take place, which is the counterpart to the official version as presented in the text books. In the course of this version of history the narrator highlights the fact that violence has been a dominant factor in many of the lives and deaths of the cooks. The latter provide an additional cohesive element within the book in that food and recipes are constant ingredients within the novel and that each of the nine parts contains one chapter, or at least the conclusion of a chapter, in which a meal is described. As in *Aus dem Tagebuch einer Schnecke* Grass continues the identity of author and narrator with, however, the significant difference that the narrator projects a fictional narrative ego into the past and dons the mantle of a succession of representative individuals who are related, not by consanguinity, but by the similarity of their attitudes and behaviour. In each stage of reincarnation he is associated with the cook belonging to the relevant period of history. Ilsebill, his wife in the present, is also projected into the past to act as the narrator's companion. In accordance with this narrative scheme Grass includes detailed descriptions of events in which he himself has participated, e.g. visits to Poland, India, and a congress in Bièvres and, of course, the birth of his daughter. Thus the narrator may be equated with the author himself and yet may on other occasions correspond to a fictional ego — yet another example of Grass experimenting with the narrative perspective.

That the flounder is a central image in the novel is obvious from the dust-cover, on which a fish is depicted speaking into the ear of a human being. The reader is thus reminded of the head and tail imagery which can be found in *Die Blechtrommel* or even of the juxtaposition of drum-stick and drum. The fish and head have their counterpart in the snail and the head on the dust-cover of *Aus dem Tagebuch einer Schnecke*, the difference being, of course, that the fish is the advocate of inordinate desire rather than the vindicator of moderation. There is no doubt that Grimm's fairy tale is a unifying factor, spanning as it does the whole novel. Accordingly the reader is reminded early in the narrative of the content of Grimm's fairy tale and learns how the narrator catches the fish back in the Stone Age. In line with Grimm's fairy tale the fish possesses the power of speech — as does the 'she-rat' in Grass's most recent novel — and proceeds to encourage man to shake off the yoke of female bondage and to assert his paternity. In so doing it promotes the triumph of the masculine principle, the victory of the phallic symbol. In a later episode we are told that an unofficial version of Grimm's fairy tale — one in which the fisher is unable to satisfy his monstrous appetites — is suppressed. Yet the novel reveals, as one might expect, that the fisher's example dominates history and leads to those acts of violence which have been characteristic features of man's development. Then towards the end of the novel three lesbians catch the flounder a few months before the oil crisis. This allows the fish to be put on trial by a tribunal of Ilsebills for having aided and abetted man throughout the course of history, though the fish in return is equally inclined, like its counterpart in *Die Rättin*, to indulge in a condemnation of man. The tribunal is an occasion for the women to take revenge on the flounder — and man — since world history has been a history of their suffering. The novel returns to its beginnings in the final episode when Maria Kuczorra catches the fish off the Baltic coast, allowing the possibility that the flounder might become the consultant to a woman.

The conclusion of the novel is open-ended: a child is born, thus bringing with it new hope, and the fish is transferred to Maria as her potential adviser. Thus the possibility exists that woman could follow man's example and set in motion in cyclical manner similar acts of boundless irrationality, a satirical foretaste of what could happen being provided by the chapter entitled 'Fathers' Day', or the women could succeed in discovering an alternative mode of behaviour, a third way which would be a middle course between male and similarly orientated female extremism and absolutism. Narrative and imagery suggest that men and women have throughout the course of history aspired to the possession of such a third entity.

All elements within the novel — narrative perspective, the story itself, the fairy tale, the imaginative *élan*, the imagery and the view of history — all combine to produce a novel which is exceptionally appealing and may be regarded as a close rival, if not the equal of, *Die Blechtrommel*. *Der Butt* provides the opportunity for meditating upon the relationship between the psychology of the individual and the historical process. Like the Danzig Trilogy it is an unofficial, personalised account of history, which, though softened by humour, takes the form of a lament upon the fairy tale which became reality.

Das Treffen in Telgte which was published in 1979 was a side product of *Der Butt* in much the same way that *Katz und Maus* proceeded naturally from *Hundejahre* and produced its own declaration of independence. The ostensible objective of *Das Treffen in Telgte*, which Grass classifies as an 'Erzählung', is to celebrate the seventieth birthday of Hans Werner Richter, one of the co-founders of Gruppe 47. However, Grass does not describe the meetings of Gruppe 47 which took place in the years between 1947 and 1967. Instead he transposes the action three centuries back and has the literary get-together take place in Telgte, a small town on the Ems. The reader is quietly made aware of the similarity of the two historical situations, in that in both cases Germany is suffering from the consequences of a full-scale military and political catastrophe. The readings which the men of literature provide from their works make this poignantly clear and thereby, as in *Der Butt*, the continuity of German history is highlighted. In the course of the description of the three-day conference Grass compares Hans Werner Richter with Simon Dach, who acts as convener and chairman and whose poem forms the climax of the series of readings. Grass also has two other personalities attend the meeting in Telgte, Heinrich Schütz and Christoffel Gelnhausen who is better known by the name of Grimmelshausen. These two characters in their several ways enliven the conference and introduce an element of action into what might otherwise have been a rather static situation. Furthermore, Heinrich Schütz, the composer, and Christoffel Gelnhausen, a commander of a detachment of soldiers at the time and not yet a literary figure, also introduce new perspectives into the literary environment. Those approaching *Das Treffen in Telgte* for the first time will enjoy its artistry, its lightness of touch and its humour and will be saddened by the poignant reminders of the continuity of German history. At the same time they will find this celebratory 'novel' to be an instructive and enlightening introduction to German Baroque literature.

Kopfgeburten oder die Deutschen sterben aus which was published in 1980 is not a fully-fledged narrative work and those who compare it with Grass's earlier fiction will be disappointed. It has been described as a narrative essay and could be regarded as a fairly natural, though much less successful progression from *Aus dem Tagebuch einer Schnecke*. Like its predecessor, it is also the product of an election year, i.e. 1980. The main content of the narrative — though the story-telling scarcely grips the reader's attention — concerns two teachers, Dörte and Harm Peters by name. Like Günter Grass they intend to engage in the election campaign of 1980 and whilst they travel abroad, Harm practises his election addresses, pronouncing on many of the issues which affect modern society and the world as a whole: nuclear energy, disarmament, the poverty and over-population of the Third World. The book thus becomes an election manifesto, a guide for the good citizen, an attempt at political education. All kinds of worthy statements are made but Grass has pushed didacticism too far. They are not enough to titivate our jaded palates. Even the inclusion of 'Kopfgeburten' ('headbirths'), an umbrella term for the scurrilous ideas and fancies which Grass introduces to stimulate our thinking, is not sufficient to dispel our impression of the *déjà vu*.

During the course of Grass's literary career, critics have frequently voiced the opinion that the attempt to marry literature and politics would inevitably lead to the qualitative deterioration of Grass's artistic creations. In 1986, with the publication of *Die Rättin*, Günter Grass decisively proved them wrong and convincingly proved that art can serve the cause of politics. However, the objective that our author pursues is destructive and not in any way constructive. This is the fundamental distinction between this work of fiction — Grass does not label it as a novel — and his previous politically orientated works. A comparison with *Gulliver's Travels* immediately springs to mind. Both Jonathan Swift and Günter Grass emerge in these two works as satirists. In *Die Rättin* Grass satirises the monstrous inhumanity of the nuclear bomb and in so doing he employs many of those methods and devices worthy of Swift. He creates, for example, an all-embracing myth, the make-believe that the narrator can orbit the world in a satellite, whilst he remains in communication with a she-rat on earth capable of describing the before and after of nuclear war. Like the Master Houyhnhnm or the King of Brobdingnag the rat produces an indictment of man and his viciousness and comes to the conclusion that only by imitating the rat and its many good qualities will man manage to reform himself. The satire is, as one might expect, double-edged; the rat denounces man and yet is unmasked by the events in which 'she' is involved. The story itself is told by the narrator who, unlike Oskar, views the world, and Danzig in particular, from above. Given the fact that the book is based upon a dialogue between narrator and rat — and given the fact also that there are five narrative strands — the viewpoint is constantly shifting and the satiric attack proceeds unpredictably from a number of different sources — a technique with which we are well acquainted in *Gulliver's Travels*.

As has been indicated the book consists of five narrative elements: the rat tells the story of the nuclear explosion, and the narrator entertains the rat with the voyage of a group of women across the Baltic, with Oskar Matzerath's visit to Danzig, Malskat's forged paintings in Lübeck and with the story of how characters from Grimm's fairy tales unsuccessfully attempt to prevent the destruction of the German forests. In a superficial sense the narrator is as addicted to travelling as is Gulliver. He orbits the world imaginatively, and ranges to and fro both geographically and historically. In the process the narrator is the (space) vehicle by which the nuclear bomb, pollution and — in the Malskat episode — the false policies of the 1950s as exemplified in Adenauer and Ulbricht are pilloried. The variety of the story-telling coupled with the shifting narrative perspective enhances the effectiveness of the satire. As is the case in *Die Blechtrommel* Grass's fascinated attachment to detail also reinforces the indictment. The narrator, for example, provides a meticulous account of the effects of the nuclear bombing of Danzig and he supplies a description of the presents Oskar's grandmother receives on her birthday. In short, once the reader has swallowed the gigantic myth of man and rat in dialogue, he is then supplied with the dispassionate description of the environment concerned. There is a constant interplay between the real and the unreal. Fantasy is embedded in realistic detail, thereby enhancing the virulence of the condemnation. In line with previous works Grass skilfully exploits the allusive and narrative associations of certain imagery, in this case, obviously, in connection with the rat. As in *Die Blechtrommel* and as in Lilliput the reader is partially dependent upon a knowledge of events external to the book in order to appreciate fully the satirical thrust. Provocative parallels between stated internal events and unstated external events are constantly part and parcel of the satirical intent, though the reader can never be absolutely sure that he is drawing the kind of comparisons which the author himself had in mind.

It could be claimed — justifiably I think — that Günter Grass has established himself as one of the foremost novelists — if not the foremost novelist — in post-war Germany. He has achieved this by narrative zest, inventiveness in his use of narrative perspective, the copiousness of his images, an ironic style which can contain militant and/or grotesque elements and by a view of history and politics which seeks both to redefine the attitude to the past and also to provide a reorientation for the future. Grass initiates the reader into a world which is exciting, bewildering and nauseating. It is a world which is never totally explicable and remains mysteriously ambiguous and ambivalent. Throughout he is obsessed by a sense of guilt and feels the need to prevent future generations being burdened in the same way. The most outstanding works of Grass's fiction possess a unique dynamism and exhibit an intensity of feeling, an outburst of revulsion and negativism against what should never have been and should never be allowed to recur.

MICHAEL LINSTEAD

Peter Handke

Peter Handke burst upon the West German literary scene in 1966, not with a novel or a play, although *Die Hornissen* (1966) and *Publikumsbeschimpfung* (1966) had already been accepted for publication, but with a tirade. At the meeting of the Group 47 in Princeton (USA) that year, Handke stood up and vehemently attacked the literature he had heard read. This caused a sensation and was widely reported in the arts sections of all the major West German papers as well as in the weeklies *Die Zeit* and *Der Spiegel*. Rapidly, however, the criticisms Handke gave voice to were lost under the tumult surrounding what was seen as a media event, a kind of 'happening'. It wasn't then long before Handke was accused of only being concerned with his own image-building at the Princeton meeting — as if he had somehow calculated the reaction to his intervention! When Handke's first novel duly appeared later in 1966 it was of course scrutinised very closely — and found lacking. Hence, the opinion that Handke was all show and no substance became even more rigid. It is an opinion which Handke has had to contend with in various forms right up to the present. He is a writer who seems to attract either unqualified admiration or outright condemnation: he can be mentioned as a possible candidate for the Nobel Prize for Literature or he can be angrily dismissed as a sham, delivering endless variations on the same trivial themes.

A short time after the Princeton meeting Handke attempted to counter this impression of himself as a media creation by setting out in more detail the substance of his intervention. His criticism of the works he had heard read centred on what he called their 'Beschreibungsimpotenz'[1] ('descriptive impotence'). The authors of these works — Manfred Durzak names them as Walter Höllerer and Hermann Peter Piwitt,[2] Handke calls them the authors of the 'Neuer Realismus' ('New Realism') and speaks at one point of Günter Herburger — were operating, according to Handke, with a method of description which merely *added* to the number of objects described in

1. Peter Handke, *Ich bin ein Bewohner des Elfenbeinturms* (Frankfurt, 1972), p. 29.
2. Manfred Durzak, *Peter Handke und die deutsche Gegenwartsliteratur* (Stuttgart, 1982), p. 9.

literature without reflecting on the basic element of description, indeed of all literature, the language used. Handke maintains that for these authors language is merely like glass or a lens, a means of seeing through to the objects in the world. But this is not enough for him: 'Es wird nämlich verkannt, daß die Literatur mit der Sprache gemacht wird, und nicht mit den Dingen, die mit der Sprache beschrieben werden' ('It is in fact not recognised that literature is made out of language and not out of the objects that are described with the language').[3] This kind of writing produces a realism in which language is reduced to the secondary function of merely naming these objects: 'Die Sprache wird nur benützt. Sie wird benützt, um zu beschreiben, ohne daß aber in der Sprache selber sich etwas rührt. Die Sprache bleibt tot, ohne Bewegung, dient nur als Namensschild für die Dinge. Die Dinge werden reportiert, nicht bewegt' ('Language is only used. It is used to describe without anything happening in the language itself. The language remains dead, without movement, it only serves as a nameplate for the objects. The objects are reported but not moved').[4] Such a use of language merely reproduces the world in its already established meaning: it does nothing to help us 'see' the world, it only helps us to 'recognise' it as something we know already.

This juxtaposition of 'seeing' and 'recognising' lies behind another programmatic statement in the 1967 essay 'Ich bin ein Bewohner des Elfenbeinturms' ('I am an inhabitant of the ivory tower'): 'Ich erwarte von der Literatur ein Zerbrechen aller endgültig scheinenden Weltbilder' ('I expect from literature a destruction of all images of the world which appear final').[5] An inattentive use of language can clearly contribute to the reproduction of such final images where the world is presented for recognition by the reader. The reflection upon *how* literature mediates between writer and reader extends in this later essay to the problem of form as well or, as Handke puts it, 'die Methode' (the method). The *way* literature provides the reader with information about the world is then just as important as that information itself. The 'methods' of literature, the means of structuring and presenting reality, are just as prone to petrification and 'deadness' as language. Hence, Handke's own literature must constantly reflect upon these two elements if it is to maintain its enlightening function, to enable the reader to 'see' the world anew. Taken to its extreme this means that for Handke a method of representation can only be used once before it runs the risk of

3. Handke, *Bewohner*, p. 29.
4. Ibid., p. 30.
5. Ibid., p. 20.

becoming 'natural', of producing final images of the world, and thereby of being unrealistic: 'Eine Möglichkeit besteht für mich jeweils nur einmal. Die Nachahmung dieser Möglichkeit ist dann schon unmöglich. Ein Modell der Darstellung, ein zweites Mal angewendet, ergibt keine Neuigkeit mehr, höchstens eine Variation. Ein Darstellungsmodell, beim ersten Mal auf die Wirklichkeit angewendet, kann realistisch sein, beim zweiten Mal schon ist es eine Manier, ist irreal' ('A possibility only exists once for me in each case. The imitation of this possibility is then impossible. A model of representation, applied a second time, does not produce an innovation any more, at most a variation. A model of representation, applied for the first time to reality, can be realistic, by the second time it's a mannerism, unreal').[6]

This understanding of realism means that Handke's literary endeavour in the early period takes on two basic forms. Firstly, he searches for new methods of representation — his early *Sprechstücke* (1966) are examples of this — or, secondly, he tries to make 'unnatural' again those methods which have become so petrified through use that they can only reproduce a conformist view of reality — a good example of this is his second novel *Der Hausierer* (1967) which deals with the 'method' of the detective story. Both strands of his writing aim to disrupt the automatic structures of coherence we apply to the world: literature can defamiliarise reality. This aesthetic undertaking is complementary to the main thematic thrust of much of Handke's fiction: the investigation and disruption of the prescriptive systems of language, perception patterns and social roles, which restrict and model the consciousness of his main figures, robbing each of freedom of individual action and thought. So the following equation applies: literature which uses fixed models of the representation of reality can only produce 'model realities' which in turn can only ever be 'recognised' by the reader: in this act of recognition a 'model', conformist consciousness is reproduced and strengthened: hence the enlightening, defamiliarising function of literature is denied and the 'final images of the world' remain in place.

The idea of literature estranging or making 'unnatural' both our perception of reality and literature's own devices and methods of representation stretches back at least to the Russian Formalists (1915/16). The Formalists believed that literature can displace our habitual modes of perceiving the real world and thus make us more open and attentive of it. It can also make us aware of the mechanics of our perception, just as it makes us aware of its own mechanics.

6. Ibid., p. 20.

Literature works at disrupting the easy process of assimilating information about the world into established structures of coherence, it attempts to subvert fixed hierarchies of meaning and value, the 'seemingly final images of the world' Handke mentions in his essay.

This brief account of the similarities between Handke's aesthetic project and that of the Formalists is necessary in order to delineate the kind of wider European context Handke fits into. Although associated with the West German literary scene, Handke's Austrian origins and background, and his membership of a generation uninvolved in the war, must always be called to mind. The kind of contextualisation associated with major West German writers such as Martin Walser, Günter Grass, Heinrich Böll or Siegfried Lenz, clearly does not apply in this case. Rather, a much longer tradition of scepticism towards language — as found in such forerunners as Hugo von Hofmannsthal's *Ein Brief* (1902), Robert Musil's *Die Verwirrungen des Zöglings Törleß* (1906) or the linguistic philosophy of Ludwig Wittgenstein — and formal experimentation — concrete poetry, the 'Wiener Gruppe', the 'Grazer Gruppe', and the *nouveau roman* — are operative here.

Peter Handke was born in the village of Altenmarkt in the province of Kärnten on 6 December 1942. His natural father was a German soldier, but his mother married another German soldier, Bruno Handke, before her son was born. In 1944 the family moved to Berlin, returning to Austria in 1948. Handke's stepfather was a heavy drinker and their living conditions were cramped and spartan: add to this the monotony, everyday brutality and narrow-mindedness of the rural environment, and the source of many of Handke's own anxieties, feelings of restriction and dependency, which are to find expression time and again in his writing, is clear. A period of time in a highly religious boys' boarding school only served to contribute to this complex. From 1961 until 1965 Handke studied law in Graz, breaking off his studies once the Suhrkamp Verlag had agreed to publish *Die Hornissen.* During the time in Graz Handke became involved with the 'Grazer Gruppe', a literary circle around the magazine *manuskripte* and its editor Alfred Kolleritsch. Many of the concerns of the magazine are to re-appear in later works by Handke. Manfred Mixner characterises the magazine as working to break up 'die politisch-ideologische Bestimmtheit der Sprache . . . sie sichtbar zu machen' ('the political and ideological determination of language, to make it visible').[7] Handke's writing fits snugly into

7. Manfred Mixner, 'Ausbruch aus der Provinz' in Peter Laemmle and Jörg Drews (eds.), *Wie die Grazer auszogen, die Literatur zu erobern* (Munich, 1979), p. 21.

Mixner's description of the general direction of the work published in the journal: 'In den *manuskripten* wurde . . . jene Literatur veröffentlicht, die . . . eine Art anarchische Gegenwehr gegen die Verfügbarmachung des Bewußtseins signalisiert, die . . *gegen die Erstarrung von Bildern* sich richtet' ('In *manuskripte* that literature was published which signals a kind of anarchic resistance to the manipulation of consciousness, which directs itself *against the petrification of images*').[8]

Handke's first novel *Die Hornissen* shows strong influences from the *nouveau roman* and its foremost practitioner and theorist Alain Robbe-Grillet. The emphasis in the *nouveau roman* is on the 'objectification of objects', that is, robbing them of their fixed anthropocentric meaning, making them concrete, definable again, and not merely referents of a human emotion or situation. This subversion of pre-established meanings is approached through the method of description, something which Handke also emphasises in *Die Hornissen*. Through careful, exact description there arises, according to Robbe-Grillet, a creation of distance. This is then the true intent of a recapture of reality. It is not an assimilation of it, but rather exactly the opposite: 'To describe things, in fact, is deliberately to place oneself outside them, facing them. It is not, any longer, to appropriate them to oneself nor to transfer anything to them'.[9] This creation of distance between the reader and the world blocks the automatic process of 'recognition' which Handke found generated by the descriptive impotence of the work he heard read at Princeton. Hence, Handke is by no means against description as such, but rather against this particular kind of description. This was not always appreciated by reviewers of *Die Hornissen*.

The novel is heavily autobiographical, conjuring up through minute description an atmosphere of monotony, repetition, hidden danger, brutality and restriction within a rural setting. At times the notion of formal experimentation is excessively foregrounded as Handke tries out different narrative points of view and different types of narrator. There is no plot structure as such, although the descriptions centre on a main figure who may (or may not) be remembering a book which he may (or may not) have read: 'Aus den zerbrochenen Stücken, an die er sich zu erinnern glaubt, aus Worten, aus Sätzen, aus halbverlorenen Bildern denkt der Mann den Roman aus, und zwar derart, daß unentscheidbar bleibt, ob das Geschehen in dem "neuen" Roman nur den "Helden" des alten

8. Ibid., p. 26.
9. Alain Robbe-Grillet, *Towards a New Novel* (London, 1965), p. 91.

Romans betrifft, oder auch ihn, der ihn ausdenkt' ('The man constructs the novel out of the shattered pieces, which he believes he is remembering, out of words, sentences, partially lost images, and in such a way that it remains inconclusive whether the events in the "new" novel only affect the "hero" of the old novel, or whether they affect the man who is constructing it as well').[10]

Die Hornissen was attacked for being dull, repetitive and full of descriptions, as if Handke's intervention at Princeton had been to condemn *all* types of description. Certainly the novel is not without its *longueurs*, but it is also a testimony to Handke's skill, even at this early stage, in creating atmospheres of tension and anxiety, dislocation and alienation, out of the narration of seemingly everyday events. This is a skill which he is to refine and employ to great effect in many of his later novels.

Handke's second novel *Der Hausierer* is similarly concerned with formal experimentation, with breaking down final images of the representation of the world, in this case the detective story. For Handke, the detective story, once a realistic method of writing, showing 'real fear' and 'real pain', had became sterile, cliché-ridden and automatic. The work of estrangement and renewal involves a division of each chapter of *Der Hausierer* into a theoretical and an expositional section. Within each theoretical section Handke attempts to make the mechanics of this type of writing clear: the detective story is analysed from the point of view of order, disruptions of order (the murder), and restorations of order (the unmasking of the murderer and the confinement of the deed to history). Handke comments: 'Würde ich also nur mir diese Schemata des Sterbens, des Schreckens, des Schmerzes usw. bewußt machen, so könnte ich mit Hilfe der reflektierten Schemata den wirklichen Schrecken, den wirklichen Schmerz zeigen' ('If I would only make myself aware of these patterns of dying, horror, pain etc., then I could show, with the help of the exposed patterns, real horror and real pain').[11] This then is the task of the second section of each chapter, where possible sentences from possible detective stories are listed, which the reader then has to reconstruct as far as possible into some kind of coherent whole. The horror and pain result as much from the reader's difficulties in attempting to order an alogical sequence of sentences as from the content of the sentences themselves.

Handke was later (1975) to describe *Der Hausierer* as a book 'wo

10. Peter Handke, *Die Hornissen* (Frankfurt, 1978), p. 2.
11. Handke, *Bewohner*, p. 28.

ein formales Modell eben als formales Modell erscheint und als nichts anderes' ('where a formal model appears just as a formal model and as nothing else').[12] Certainly Handke's renown during this early period is based almost exclusively on his *Sprechstücke* and on his full-length play *Kaspar* (1968). Whilst still incorporating a measure of abstraction and formal experimentation this play deals with the much more concrete issue of the manipulation of consciousness through language. It becomes clear however that Handke sees this danger inherent in language itself, regardless of who actually *uses* it. He is not concerned in *Kaspar* with showing how, for example, the media use language to influence people. What turns the figure of Kaspar into a 'model', conformist citizen, incapable of an original thought, is rather the model structure of language itself, its rigid grammar, syntax, model phrases. Although language provides Kaspar with a means of expression, Handke wishes to show that it also sets its own limits on that expression, in that it mediates, according to its own rules, like a filter between the self and the world. This situation is to become, in various forms, the main theme of Handke's writing, and as he investigates this theme so the degree of formal experimentation diminishes. Handke's novels (and plays) now begin to examine particular types of mediation between outer and inner world, reality and consciousness: more explicitly they investigate and attempt to disrupt the normative forces of language (*Die Angst des Tormanns beim Elfmeter*, 1970), perception patterns (*Der kurze Brief zum langen Abschied*, 1972), and social roles (*Wunschloses Unglück*, 1972; *Die Stunde der wahren Empfindung*, 1975; *Die linkshändige Frau*, 1976). The disruption or emancipation from these forces which some of these novels propose only takes place however through the straight denial of such mediating forces, via a 'magical' or 'mystical' 'directness' of experience and expression: there is no attempt to confront these forces within their social context.

In *Die Angst des Tormanns beim Elfmeter* the particular state of Josef Bloch's inner world, his consciousness, mediates between and moulds his perception of the outer world. This state is one of fear, of anxiety, of unease. Hence, the outer world appears threatening, encroaching, closing in on him. The reader may initially be tempted to think that this is because Bloch has committed a murder and is 'on the run'. But, in fact, these symptoms were clearly present before the murder was committed: this was itself just another symptom of his feelings of persecution. Believing he has lost his job as a fitter, Bloch, a former

12. H.L. Arnold, 'Gespräch mit Peter Handke', in H.L. Arnold (ed.), *Peter Handke*, Text+Kritik, vol. 24/24a (Munich, 1978), p. 25.

goalkeeper, wanders around the town before spending the night with the box office cashier of a local cinema. In the morning she asks him if he has to go to work, whereupon he strangles her. He flees to a village near the border, becomes involved in various aspects of village life, including the search for a missing boy, whose body he finds but does not report. At the end of the novel he watches a football match and sees a goalkeeper save a penalty. The story of Handke's novel is easily and quickly told. What is far more important is Bloch's inner life, his perceptions. He perceives his environment constantly encroaching upon him, forcing itself into his inner world, giving him guidelines, instructions and rules as to his behaviour: 'Überall sah er eine Aufforderung: das eine zu tun, das andere nicht zu tun. Alles war ihm vorformuliert' ('Everywhere he saw a demand: to do one thing, not to do another. Everything was preformulated for him').[13] The world becomes a system of signs imparting meanings, signs which *have* to be interpreted: the world becomes 'linguistified' ('versprachlicht'). This coercion to interpret is present from the very beginning of the novel. Bloch has not in fact lost his job as a fitter: that is his interpretation of the fact that only the foreman looked up at him when he entered the site hut.

Bloch's particular perspective on reality can be explained in conjunction with his former professions. They are both mentioned in the opening sentence of the novel: 'Dem Monteur Josef Bloch, der früher ein bekannter Tormann gewesen war, wurde, als er sich am Vormittag zur Arbeit meldete, mitgeteilt, daß er entlassen sei' ('The fitter Josef Bloch, who had once been a renowned goalkeeper, was informed, when he clocked in for work one morning, that he had been dismissed') (7). But even before this first sentence there is a reference to his former profession as a goalkeeper in the motto: '"Der Tormann sah zu, wie der Ball über die Linie rollte . . ."' ('"The goalkeeper watched as the ball rolled over the line . . ."') (5). This is an image of failure, an image of the fear of the goalkeeper at the penalty kick. As a goalkeeper in a football match Bloch is dependent on interpreting the movements and feints of the attacking players correctly, on divining their 'meaning'. The complete action of the game is directed towards the goalkeeper, he is at the centre of its world, and yet his is the most passive role. He stands between the posts, able to react but with very little possibility of intervention. His fear is that he will not function well enough, that he will not interpret the shooter's intentions correctly, that he cannot rely upon a system of coherence to order the world, and yet all the time he is

13. Peter Handke, *Die Angst des Tormanns beim Elfmeter* (Frankfurt, 1974), p. 99.

aware that it is the only possibility open to him. This attitude of the goalkeeper in the game is carried on by Bloch through his life and is allied with the 'loss' of his job as a fitter, whose task it also is to manufacture coherence out of isolated, separate units. For Bloch there is now no coherence at all, but merely a constant stream of isolated and false interpretations, and yet he is still tied to the compulsion to interpret: he cannot escape from this system of mediation between outer and inner world. In fact, *all* the characters in the novel are seen at various points to operate with similar systems, causing them to perceive reality in a particular way: what distinguishes Bloch from them is that his compulsion to interpret is much more intense.

A possible liberation from this conventional functioning of experience and perception is then postulated very tentatively by Handke at the end of the novel. Such an 'emancipation' from the mediation between inner and outer world cannot however involve Bloch himself, as the perspective of the goalkeeper is far too established within him. It does however involve another goalkeeper and the central image of the novel's title, a penalty kick. While talking to a company representative at the football match Bloch explains how the goalkeeper will try to interpret the penalty taker's actions before he actually kicks the ball, and how he will use these interpretations in his attempt to save the penalty. Bloch maintains however that ultimately the goalkeeper has no chance because the penalty taker is always 'one thought' ahead of him. But when the penalty is taken, the goalkeeper remains motionless and the penalty taker shoots the ball straight into his arms. It would seem that the goalkeeper rejects the interpretation of signs, feints and dodges, which has become the perspective on life for Bloch. He rejects the memory of former penalty kicks, he rejects his previous experience, he rejects the traditional, 'natural' behaviour on such occasions, indeed he rejects his own historical dimension, and 'magically' saves the kick. Freed from the mediating system between inner and outer world the goalkeeper reverses the motto of the novel.

Clearly, in practical terms this is not a course of action to be recommended to goalkeepers. Rather it functions as a metaphor for a 'direct' (yet ahistorical) relationship to the world. It is a metaphor for an attempt to avoid the normative perception patterns which have led to a stagnation and mechanical functioning of that perception. But to avoid them by simply rejecting them — the goalkeeper does not even attempt to move — is to transcend rather than to confront and change these patterns of experience, perception and living.

1972 marked an important year for Handke's work with the publication of two novels — *Der kurze Brief zum langen Abschied* and *Wunschloses Unglück* — which many critics believe to be his best. The former, set in America, took up a number of aspects of *Die Angst des Tormanns beim Elfmeter* but with the extra dimensions of an autobiographical base — the break-up of Handke's own marriage is mirrored in the first-person narrator's problems with his estranged wife — and an attempt to understand how patterns of perception and resulting alienation are established in the cultural and socio-political environment of early childhood. The novel disappoints however in its ending, which has the narrator and his wife meet the film director John Ford at his home in California. During the meeting the alienation between inner and outer world is overcome in a 'magical' moment when history stops and a state of 'pure nature' is reached. It is a weakness of the novel that it presents an analysis of the disruption of the narrator's perception of the world and of his increasing distance from his wife in terms which link the specific constitution of this gap between inner and outer world to the conditions of the narrator's childhood and his position within the social and property relations in Austria, only then to avoid a similarly concrete coming to terms with this alienation of perception by raising the action in the final instance into a 'magical' moment of unalienated 'directness' of experience. In the end it would seem that Handke has not finally abandoned the hope of a 'direct' unmediated relationship between reality and consciousness, of a 'magical' coincidence of the two as a means of overcoming normative socialising forces, as he had tentatively mooted on the final page of *Die Angst des Tormanns beim Elfmeter*. This pattern is certainly to appear in subsequent novels, which are very close thematically. On the one hand, an historically sited account of the pressures on people to live a socialised existence; on the other hand, the presentation of any liberation from such forces within the terms of an irrational, quasi-mystical withdrawal into purportedly autonomous inner spaces.

Wunschloses Unglück is not only a book about the life of Handke's mother, who committed suicide in 1971; it is also a book about the writing of such a biography. As such, Handke explicitly thematises the reflection upon 'method' which informed the essay 'Ich bin ein Bewohner des Elfenbeinturms'. In the novel he reflects upon the already available models of the literary representation of his subject matter, and realises that he cannot simply reproduce these when writing of his own mother. This is particularly so as his mother is seen to have been the victim of a 'model of existence'. From birth her biography is seen to have been determined, according to a pre-set notion of what women can and cannot do, by the male-dominated society in which she lived. The portrayal of her life, the public form it takes, must not then be such that it again, in its turn, only fits that life into an established representation of it. The problem is how to fit her biography into public, yet individual sentences.

This problem of the tension between public and private, between role-determined behaviour and autonomy, runs throughout the subject matter of the novel as well. Handke's mother is presented as having no sphere of autonomy within her formative years, no possibility of a private life: her life is public and delineated by forces outside her control. Social mobility or the possibility of change would seem to be blocked, for the all-encompassing rigidity of her ascribed position — according to class and gender — within the particular, almost feudal set of social relations dominant in rural Austria at the time denies any notion of an achieved position through personal action. Women's biographies under such conditions are easily mapped: 'Müde/Matt/Krank/Schwerkrank/Tot' ('Tired/Weary/Ill/Seriously Ill/Dead').[14] Women had no individual futures — girls never had their palms read, only boys. Happiness was sometimes present in some form or another, but wishing, the projection of an imagined future on an expected future, the construction of a personal and private reality, was non-existent: 'Selten wunschlos und irgendwie glücklich, meistens wunschlos und ein bißchen unglücklich' ('Seldom: without desires and somehow happy; mostly: without desires and a little unhappy') (19). Personal, private desire was eclipsed by the demands of the specific public existence for women.

Handke takes his mother's life through the Anschluss and the attraction of fascism for the *Kleinbürger* into the post-war period. It is only towards the end of her life that some flickerings of an emancipatory drive announce themselves: she takes more care over her appearance, she goes out more, she begins to read the books that her son has lent her. But these flickerings clash with the comfort she still derives from being typical: she is afraid of 'standing out', of being noticed if she does anything out of the ordinary: 'Spontan zu leben . . . das hieß schon, eine Art von Unwesen treiben' ('living spontaneously, that meant causing some sort of trouble') (52). In the end her internalisation of the social pressures she has had to endure for most of her life is strong enough not to allow her to throw herself whole-heartedly into a new life. She remains trapped in a 'no man's land' between hatred of her former life and fear of any

14. Peter Handke, *Wunschloses Unglück* (Frankfurt, 1975), p. 17.

different one. Her suicide is a refusal to compromise — '"Ich will mich nicht mehr zusammennehmen"' ('"I don't want to compose myself any more"') — but it is also a capitulation — '"an ein Weiterleben ist nicht zu denken"' ('"to live any longer is unthinkable'") (91). It is only Handke's literary undertaking — the novel *Wunschloses Unglück* — which saves her from total oblivion. Although most of Handke's novels contain autobiographical elements, the acuteness, sensitivity and intensity of the involvement in this book and the extremely skilful handling of the narration, which never slips into sentimentality, make it his most accomplished piece of work.

Handke picks up the theme of women and social roles again in *Die linkshändige Frau.* Marianne suddenly asks her husband Bruno to leave her: '"Ich hatte auf einmal die Erleuchtung" — sie mußte auch über dieses Wort lachen — "daß du von mir weggehst; daß du mich allein läßt. Ja, das ist es: Geh weg, Bruno. Laß mich allein"' ('"All at once I had the illumination — she had to laugh at this word as well — that you were going away from me; that you were leaving me alone. Yes, that's it: Go away, Bruno. Leave me alone"').[15] It is clear that the fear of becoming the object of an action — his leaving her — moves her to transform herself into an active subject: she breaks up a relationship which had been characterised by his dominance and her subservience, and by his brutality whenever this dominance was in any way challenged. The rest of the novel charts her attempts to live with her child, to support herself financially, to gain and consolidate her independence. She has rejected the *social* determination of her life and now shuns a society which no longer appears as a medium within which the individual can develop a meaningful identity: rather this society is the place for loss of identity, and relationships between people are reduced to struggles for power.

Marianne declares at one point: '"Wenn mir in Zukunft jemand erklärt, wie ich bin — auch wenn er mir schmeicheln oder mich bestärken will — werde ich mir diese Frechheit verbitten"' ('"If anyone explains to me in future what I'm like — even if he wants to flatter or support me — I'll refuse to tolerate this impudence"') (37–8). Her drive for emancipation is supported then by the narrative organisation of the novel. Handke only ever narrates from without, with the sober, objective eye of the camera — indeed the novel resembles rather a screenplay for the film Handke was later to direct. Descriptions of physical movement abound — e.g., 'Sie

15. Peter Handke, *Die linkshändige Frau* (Frankfurt, 1977), p. 23.

reckte die Arme: ein Loch zeigte sich im Pullover unter einer Achsel; sie schob einen Finger hinein' ('She stretched her arms: a hole appeared in her pullover under an armpit: she pushed a finger into it') (38) — but these actions are never interpreted or explained for the reader by the author, they are merely reported in a detached manner. The narration does not intrude upon her inner world but remains distant and respectful of her isolated individuality.

Marianne is partially reintegrated into society in the final long scene of the novel, a party she throws at her house. It is a scene however which has an unreal quality about it. The party becomes an event where all social hierarchies, individual gaps and personal distances are 'magically' overcome. Strangers embrace each other, arguments are laid aside, and social and economic differences between people are miraculously forgotten — the publisher, having left his chauffeur outside for hours when he visited Marianne previously, now offers to drive him home! Thus the left-handed woman's assertion at the end of the novel — '"Du hast dich nicht verraten. Und niemand wird dich mehr demütigen!"' ('"You haven't betrayed yourself. And no-one will humiliate you anymore"') (130) — remains largely untested by this gathering. Her 'emancipation' is not incorporated into any kind of recognisable social reality, but without such incorporation it becomes instead 'the transcendence of fixed and rigid definitions of social roles'.[16] Inner world merely deems or asserts itself free of the pressures of outer world, and the latter 'magically' disappear.

After the publication of *Die linkshändige Frau* Handke was to wait three years before the appearance of his next novel *Langsame Heimkehr* in 1979 — an unusually long gap for such a prolific writer. This period could well be seen as a time of 'gathering breath'. *Langsame Heimkehr* was to turn out to be not only the title of an individual novel but also of a 'tetralogy' incorporating *Die Lehre der Sainte-Victoire* (1980), *Kindergeschichte* (1981), and the 'dramatic poem' *Über die Dörfer* (1981). If the theme of Handke's previous work can roughly be summarised under the headings of an examination of the forces which attempt to determine the individual from without and possible emancipatory strategies in the face of 'die vorausbestimmte Biographie' ('the predetermined biography'),[17] then the tetralogy, *Langsame Heimkehr*, portrays various attempts to find eternal 'laws'

16. Richard Critchfield, 'From Abuse to Liberation: On Images of Women in Peter Handke's Writing of the Seventies', *Jahrbuch für internationale Germanistik*, 14 (1982), part 1, p. 34.

17. 'Und plötzlich wird das Paar wieder denkbar', *Der Spiegel*, 32 (1978), no. 28, p. 140.

and 'secrets,' a new order which will 'heal' the disharmony, the 'ontological split' between the self and the world, consciousness and reality.

'"Somewhere I lost connection . . ."' was the motto of the volume of poems and essays *Als das Wünschen noch geholfen hat* (1974).[18] The idea of a re-established 'connection' between the self and the world to overcome the individual's alienated state is present in each of the separate works in the tetralogy. In *Langsame Heimkehr* the geologist Valentin Sorger journeys on his quest from the frozen wastes of Alaska via America to Europe with the notion that '"Der Zusammenhang ist möglich"' ('"The connection is possible"').[19] He eventually experiences the 'gesetzgebender Augenblick' ('law-giving moment') in a coffee shop in New York where he leaves his self-imposed isolation behind him and 'heals' his friend Esch of his anxiety in a scene which has strong religious overtones: 'Sorger wurde sein Vorsprecher: befahl und verbot ihm . . . ; sprach ihn frei von Schmerz; weissagte ihm Gutes und gab ihm schließlich den Segen' ('Sorger became his prompter: ordered and forbade him; released him from pain; prophesied good things for him and gave him finally his blessing').[20]

The 'connection' between Sorger and the world is re-established here in a mystical moment of caring for others. In *Die Lehre der Sainte-Victoire* it happens via art. Through the study of Cézanne's paintings of the Mont Sainte-Victoire and a personal pilgrimage to the area, Handke hopes, in his own writing and landscape descriptions, to bridge the gap between man and nature: 'Der Zusammenhang ist möglich', Handke writes again, 'Es existiert eine unmittelbare Verbindung; ich muß sie nur freiphantasieren' ('The connection is possible. There exists a direct link; I only have to free it through imagination').[21]

Handke turns away from nature at the end of *Die Lehre der Sainte-Victoire* towards the figure of his own child: 'Dann einatmen und weg vom Wald. Zurück zu den heutigen Menschen . . . Zu Hause das Augenpaar? ('Then breathe in and away from the wood. Back to the people of today. At home the pair of eyes?').[22] The child's perspective on the world as one that is innocent, 'pure', unsullied by experience and as yet oblivious to social determination, is presented in *Kindergeschichte* as something to be learnt from in the

18. Peter Handke, *Als das Wünschen noch geholfen hat* (Frankfurt, 1980), p. 121.
19. Peter Handke, *Langsame Heimkehr* (Frankfurt, 1980), p. 112.
20. Ibid., pp. 177–8.
21. Peter Handke, *Die Lehre der Sainte-Victoire* (Frankfurt, 1980), p. 100.
22. Ibid., p. 139.

search for the lost 'connection'. It had in fact had a similar function in *Die Stunde der wahren Empfindung*, where the main figure Gregor Keuschnig breaks out of his humdrum, restrictive existence as an embassy official and observes, amongst other things, his own child's attitude to the world, admiring its 'Für Sich Sein' ('Being For Itself'), its refusal of outside control over its life. In *Kindergeschichte* the child embodies 'ein großes Gesetz . . . welches er selber entweder vergessen oder nie gehabt hatte' ('a great law . . . which he himself had either forgotten or never had') and is presented by the narrator as 'sein persönlicher Lehrherr' ('his personal master').[23] The point of view on the child in the novel is however extremely limited. It is never referred to by name and is shown as existing outside human society. It is never given its own voice, but only functions in relation to the narrator. Where, on a few isolated occasions, it is presented with a life of its own — playing with other children, going to school, making irritating demands on the narrator — then the tone of the narration changes from the triumph of the majority of the book to one of sadness, annoyance and disappointment. Any kind of social interaction or experience is immediately seen in a negative light. It becomes clear that the child's identity is understood by the narrator to be complete at birth: 'Als dem Erwachsenen durch die Trennglasscheibe das Kind gezeigt wurde, erblickte er da kein Neugeborenes, sondern einen vollkommenen Menschen' ('When the child was shown to the adult through the dividing pane of glass he caught sight of a complete person, not a new born baby').[24] The child's individuality would seem to pre-exist historical and social forces. The meeting with society does not then become a formative and developmental process, but rather a process of antagonism and destruction of this individuality: any resistance to the wholly negative concept of socialisation must necessitate a turn inwards to those areas of the inner world which are still 'childlike', which still retain traces of a potential for autonomy.

Within the context of West German literature of the 1970s and 1980s and the notions of *neue Subjektivität* and *neue Innerlichkeit* Handke is clearly a central figure. His espousal of the ability of the individual to withdraw into 'free' inner spaces as a bulwark against normative pressures is indicative of the basic antagonism between society and the individual, public and private, outer and inner worlds, running throughout his writing, whereby both are presented as conflicting blocks in a static, hostile relationship. This antagon-

23. Peter Handke, *Kindergeschichte* (Frankfurt, 1981), p. 63.
24. Ibid., p. 9.

ism extends also to the sphere of interpersonal relations, which are almost always presented as power games, where love is yet another means of controlling others and sex is only conceivable as a spontaneous act between strangers on an office floor (*Die Stunde der wahren Empfindung*).

Handke's later novel, *Der Chinese des Schmerzes* (1983), deals with the by now familiar themes of the outsider, power, alienation, violence, the emptiness of human relationships, the attempt to attain different ways of 'seeing' the world. The basic problem of Handke's writing to date still remains then. His total faith in the power of the individual to withdraw into the security of free inner spaces within the inner world contrasts with the portrayal of his mother's life in its social and historical context, where this inner world itself was also completely dominated and defined by social demands: his mother had no such private, autonomous sphere to inhabit. In an interview Handke pleads for the kind of literature he writes to be accepted as 'ein Modell von Möglichkeit, Leben darzustellen' ('a model of the possibility of representing life').[25] This may hold as long as 'life' is perceived as some existential category: as soon as one thinks however of individual *lives* within their respective social and historical contexts, then Handke's writing since 1972 only provides false, passive notions of emancipation, ignoring the active, political ways in which people can effect change in their lives. The final sentence of *Wunschloses Unglück* — 'Später werde ich über das alles Genaueres schreiben' ('Later I will write more accurately about all that')[26] — will never be realised if the present direction of Handke's writing holds.

25. Arnold, 'Gespräch mit Peter Handke', p. 39.
26. *Wunschloses Unglück*, p. 105.

WILFRIED VAN DER WILL

Approaches to Reality Through Narrative Perspectives in Johnson's Prose

In *Vorschläge zur Prüfung eines Romans* Uwe Johnson — having disabused himself of the notion that the novelist's task might be to shore up a particular political or ideological framework of reality — went on to ask the question what the novel might be good for. Addressing the reader directly he gave this answer: 'It [the novel] is an offer. You [the readers] receive a version of reality. It is not a society in miniature, and it is not a scale model. It is also not a mirror of the world and further it is not its reflection; it is a world to be held up against the world'.[1] This definition reverberated with polemical allusions to Georg Lukács's aesthetic theory which, for a while in the 1950s, had virtually become holy writ in the GDR. It had certainly helped to cement a dogmatised notion of Socialist Realism, with which Johnson — as is evident already from the structure and content of his earliest novel, *Ingrid Babendererde. Reifeprüfung 1953*, published posthumously in 1985 — clearly felt ill at ease. This aesthetic prescription, often narrowly interpreted by the newly created State Commission for the Arts[2] and sealed with the stamp of approval by the makers of official cultural policy in the GDR, cramped individual creativity and haunted Johnson all his life. In the fourth volume of *Jahrestage* (1983) there are still references to a certain 'Großdialektiker' ('grand dialectician') and to the 'amtierende Fachmann für sozialistische Theorie in der Literatur' ('expert in the socialist theory of literature'),[3] easily identifiable as Lukács, whose critical views nearly rob a sixth form and its teacher of all enthusiasm for an extended study of Theodor Fontane's *Schach von Wuthenow*. But it is not for the polemical echoes twenty years or so

1. Uwe Johnson, 'Vorschläge zur Prüfung eines Romans', E. Lämmert (ed.), *Romantheorie: Dokumentation ihrer Geschichte in Deutschland seit 1880* (Cologne, 1975), pp. 402–3.

2. Cf. Haase, Geerdts et al., *Geschichte der Deutschen Literatur. Literatur der Deutschen Demokratischen Republik* (Berlin, 1976) p. 210.

3. *Jahrestage 4* (June 1968–August 1968) (Frankfurt, 1983), p. 1706 (= *JT*, IV).

later that Johnson's attempt at defining his conception of the novel is cited here. Rather, I wish to stress from the outset his idea both of 'realism' and of 'narration' as an exploration of possibilities and as an invitation to the reader firstly to allow himself to be guided by a given narrative to engage in a method of searching for truth and, secondly, to consider approaching reality in the same manner; that is to say, not within the blinkered constraints of ideological fixations. Needless to say this is no explicitly didactic aim, loudly announced by the author, but a practice of narrated perception which might be adopted after reading his prose circumscribing a fictional world that is to be held up against the real one.

Like many other German writers after 1945 in both East and West, Johnson's formative critical experience was the distortion of reality by political powers that imposed biased interpretations on the world and that were able, through modern and traditional media, to mould public awareness in line with hegemonic interests. The observation of the propaganda practices employed by National Socialism, the defeat of that system and the 're-education' of Germans by the victorious Allies clearly sensitised the generation to which Johnson belonged in a special way to the dangers of taking at face value official pronouncements of the truth. When he later referred to the GDR as a fatherland in which the young received a truly deep moulding of their character formation[4] and when in the same context he stressed that the state demanded an almost personal pledge of friendship from every citizen while at the same time regarding certain classes of citizen as prima facie suspect, Johnson was talking about his own experiences. His motives for leaving the GDR and for settling in West Berlin were influenced by the consideration that, having arranged for *Mutmaßungen über Jakob* (1959) to be published by Suhrkamp in Frankfurt am Main, he feared that 'the East German authorities would misunderstand as an attack and an accusation what in fact was just a story, an explanation'. He had tried and failed to get his first novel, *Ingrid Babendererde*, published in the GDR and now he naturally wished to avoid the consequences of any further misunderstandings between him and the party and state authorities which might have led to 'criminal proceedings against me'.[5]

In coming to 'the West' he did not 'choose freedom' in the emphatic sense of Western media-speak. He had, as he sometimes

4. Johnson, 'Versuch, eine Mentalität zu erklären' in Johnson, *Berliner Sachen* (=*BS*) (Frankfurt, 1975), p. 55.
5. Johnson in Horst Bienek, *Werkstattgespräche mit Schriftstellern* (Munich, 1962), p. 88.

put it, merely 'moved house' from one part of Germany to another, exchanging one form of German citizenship for another: '1959: Return of my nationality to the GDR authorities after only ten years' use and move to West Berlin with the permission of a local government office there'.[6] Interestingly, Johnson held that East and West Germany were not logical alternatives but had come about as a result of pragmatic arrangements between two power blocs, between two ideological systems with each trying to demonstrate its superiority over the other on its respective portions of the old Reich. The citizens, Johnson held, must retain the right to choose between passports and nationalities foisted on them by accident and without their consent. It is instructive in this context to see how Johnson in an occasional lecture on *Jahrestage* describes the two stages in the first of three changes of nationality which Gesine Cresspahl undergoes (the two later ones are her adoption of Federal Republic citizenship and later her acquisition of a US passport): 'She was born in 1933 in a rather small town on the Baltic . . . so that after the war she became a native of the Soviet Zone of Occupation and a few years later a citizen of the German Democratic Republic, and both these things happened to her without her having been asked'.[7] Her creator had experienced the same and retained a similarly non-committal attitude to the nationality which happened to be entered in his passport. Imitating the diplomatic language in which basic human rights are expressed Johnson once noted: 'If a state is free to impose a nationality on people whom it found to be on its territory at the time of coming to power these people must be given the right to renounce such nationality out of their own free will'.[8]

If Johnson's attitude to nationality was provisional his commitment to the region whence he came was marked by total loyalty. There is an intensely regional, if not to say provincial, flavour to much of his prose, a persistent reminiscence of peculiarities of locality. It is perhaps not surprising then, that a critic like Helmut Heißenbüttel laid the charge against Johnson that, far from being an avant-garde novelist, he was in fact steeped in the mystique of *Blut und Boden.* True, heavily nostalgic reminiscences are in fact frequent in Johnson's writing, particularly in his massive four-volume novel *Jahrestage* (1970–83). Perhaps Johnson did suffer from being homesick after moving first to West Berlin, then to New York, then back

6. Johnson, 'Vita' in R. Baumgart (ed.), *Über Uwe Johnson* (Frankfurt, 1970), p. 175.
7. Johnson, 'Einführung in die *Jahrestage*' in M. Bengel (ed.), *Johnsons Jahrestage* (Frankfurt, 1985), p. 21.
8. Johnson, 'Versuch, eine Mentalität zu erklären', *BS*, p. 63.

to West Berlin and finally to Sheerness in the Thames Estuary, where he died, aged 49, on 23/4 February, 1984. But this homesickness was not of a simple kind. It was more than a yearning to go back to the place of birth, to the land of childhood and youth and to kith and kin. Or was it? Towards the concluding part of *Jahrestage* we find the following passage: 'auf dem Kamm des Heidberges, wo ein Abhang sich öffnet . . . auch dem Auge freien Weg öffnend über die Insel im See und das hinter dem Wasser sanft ansteigende Land, besetzt mit sparsamen Kulissen aus Bäumen und Dächern, leuchtend, da die Sonne gerade düstere Regenwolken hat verdrängen können; welch Anblick mir möge gegenwärtig sein in der Stunde meines [. . .] Sterbens' ('on the ridge of the Heidberg where a slope opens out . . . giving free rein to the eye viewing the isle in the lake and the gently rising land behind, dotted with sparse sets of trees and roofs, shining, since the sun has just been able to shift dark rain clouds; which aspect may present itself to me in the hour of my [. . .] death').[9] The evocation of an obviously exactly remembered landscape, the unsurpassable emphasis it receives as a vision desired in the hour of death, the touches of archaic, prayer-like style in which this wish is couched and finally the normally close relationship between author and narrator, often merging into indistinguishable identity, might allow the reader to assume that an autobiographical mood of nostalgia is becoming transparent here. Yet it is precisely at this point, indicated above by square brackets, that the narrator figure, Gesine Cresspahl, voicing this longing, experiences objections by the author whom she then addresses in a cantankerous, fiercely reprimanding fashion (textually italicised): 'Es ist uns schnuppe, ob dir das zu deftig beladen ist, Genosse Schriftsteller! Du schreibst das hin! wir können auch heute noch aufhören mit deinem Buch. Dir sollte erfindlich sein, wie wir uns etwas vorgenommen haben für den Tod' ('We do not give a toss if this is too heavy for you, comrade writer! You are going to take this down! We are quite capable of terminating your book today. You ought to be able to imagine how we have arrived at certain ideas concerning our own death'). It is therefore hardly warranted to use this quote as evidence of the author's feelings. Gesine and her author may be born in the same landscape, have lived there at the same time and received the same schooling, but they remain discrete beings. In any case, Johnson, when asked what 'Heimat' meant to him, answered decisively: 'Something that is lost. Once you have left it you're debarred from going back. Even if with a tourist visa or following an invitation

9. *JT*, IV, pp. 1821–2.

you were able to walk about there, it no longer belongs to you'.[10] Heißenbüttel was by no means the first and the only eminent critic to level the wholly misplaced and defamatory charge of 'blood-and-soil' literature against Johnson. Reich-Ranicki, Peter Demetz and Manfred Durzak had preceded him with various degrees of insistence. We shall have to return to this question later in an overall assessment of Johnson's work.[11]

In his Frankfurt lectures of 1979, entitled *Begleitumstände* (1980), Johnson, in a remarkably frank account of how he came to write and what problems, difficulties and perils he encountered in the process, revealed that it was in fact Siegfried Unseld, after reading the manuscript of *Ingrid Babendererde* in 1957, who had first mooted the suspicion of the author being an adherent of the 'blood-and-soil' variety of German literature: 'He had himself been a victim of this ideology of blood and soil; it annoyed him that in my manuscript so many people liked to sail so often and so persistently — "Fair wind", they would shout from one boat to the other and "well, well" they said in their very peculiar North German manner to the one who held the tiller and the sailing winch. There were many trees there — Siegfried Unseld wished that this should not become a book in Peter Suhrkamp's publishing house'.[12] Embedment in German provincial idiosyncrasy, even communion with the home idyll, is certainly a feature which in connection with some of Johnson's characters is occasionally in evidence, complete with some of the stylistic devices and images that one associates with the genre. From *Mutmaßungen über Jakob* one might cite the following sentences as examples: ' . . . und Cresspahl stand mächtig vor seinem Haus und ragte mit seiner Tabakspfeife vor in die Gegend und brachte das Wetter des jeweiligen Tages in seine Erfahrung' (' . . . and Cresspahl stood powerfully in front of his house and with his tobacco pipe he protruded into the landscape and took cognisance of the weather obtaining on any given day')[13] or: ' . . . und Jakob zog mit den Pferden ebenmäßig wie die Ewigkeit über die frischen Stoppeln' (' . . . and as regular as eternity Jakob moved with his horses over the fresh stubble') (127). The huge, ponderous, taciturn character formations of the North German plain are sketched in such lan-

10. Interview with Hans Daiber, 'Cooperation mit Gesine', Bengel, *Johnsons Jahrestage*, p. 131.

11. Cf. Heißenbüttel, *Frankfurter Rundschau*, 14.1.1984, Beilage, p. 2; Reich-Ranicki, *Die Zeit*, 2.10.1970, p. 20; Demetz, *Die süße Anarchie* (Frankfurt, 1970), p. 269; Durzak, *Der deutsche Roman der Gegenwart* (Stuttgart, 1971), p. 230.

12. Johnson, *Begleitumstände*, Frankfurter Vorlesungen (Frankfurt, 1980), p. 97.

13. Johnson, *Mutmaßungen über Jakob* (Frankfurt & Hamburg, 1963), p. 10. All quotations from this edn.

guage. These figures must certainly at an early stage in their lives have experienced the bliss of being at one with the locality of their youth. Was not Jakob a boy, it is suggested in pastiche-like fashion, '. . . der glücklich gewesen war in dem weiten Land am Wasser auf dem großen Hof, wo unzählig nebeneinander die Leiterwagen standen in der Sonne und die Luft der blühenden Linden gewichtig vor den kühlen Zimmern stand, über dem klaren Spiegel des frühen Flusses, in dem fügsamen Knistern des Schilfs an der schweren Bewegung des Kahns?' ('. . . who had been happy in this extensive land by the water on this large farm, where a countless number of hand-carts stood side by side in the sun and where the air from the blossoming linden trees hung heavily outside the cool rooms, over the clear mirror of the early stream, in the crackle of the reeds yielding to the ponderous movement of the barge?') (63). But such stylistic moments capturing the harmony of man and landscape are rare and invariably fulfil a purpose within a larger narrative design that shows irrevocable ruptures between individual and nature, community and society. This is mirrored in a narrative structure which is full of breaks, is open-ended and appears to be a straightforward denial of the possibility of a rounded artistic totality, which Lukács had demanded as the hallmark of all great works of art.

Rather than establishing an altogether erroneous link with the typical novels of Nazism one might suggest that at least Johnson's first published novel, *Mutmaßungen über Jakob* (1959) has elements in common with the novels of East German Socialist Realism. Jakob — by no means an ace labourer like Hans Aehre in Eduard Claudius's then much discussed novel *Menschen an unserer Seite* (1951) who more or less single-handedly reclads a furnace while it is in use — would nevertheless fit the pattern of the conscientious working man, aware of the dignity of labour; Herr Rohlfs, serving in the security police, is at the same time a sympathetic party member always ready to help people who run into difficulties; Dr Jonas Blach is the vacillating intellectual, and Gesine Cresspahl might be seen as the person seduced to the West by the lures of capitalist society (she actually leaves because she is frightened by the events during the mass protests of workers in Berlin in June 1953). Jakob himself goes to the West, but he soon comes back to his place of work as a 'dispatcher' with the GDR railways — a key operative position overseeing the efficient dispatch of trains within a defined geographical area. The novel begins with the last episode in his life, when on his return he is killed walking across the tracks. Trying in a fog to avoid one train, he is killed by another, the one presumably from the East, the other from the West — and the possibility is not excluded that he committed suicide. This ending of his life, which gives rise to many 'speculations' about him and determines the multiplicity of perspectives in the narrative structure, distinguishes the novel from the early versions of East German Socialist Realist prose which demanded a more unambiguously positive hero opening up vistas of human progress.

Jakob remains enigmatic. Rohlfs, commissioned to keep him under surveillance and trying to use him to recruit Gesine Cresspahl for East German intelligence, cannot find any disloyalty to socialist principles in him. But he becomes aware of distinct indications of Jakob's ironic distance from the misery of everyday failures in the East German social system and from its friendly guarantor, the Soviet Union, whose dismantling of seizeable portions of railway track ruins the timetable and whose friendship does not extend to supplying the GDR with urgently needed coal. The reason why Jakob is under observation becomes clear only slowly and indirectly: his fiancée, Gesine Cresspahl, has suddenly decided to leave for the West and has found employment with the NATO forces, acting as a translator and broadcaster in language lessons. Only where concrete aspects of Jakob's daily life and technical matters of his job are concerned is the focus sharp and clear. 'Where reality is only known very approximately', Johnson held, 'I would not wish to try to portray it as if it were better known than it is.'[14] The implied answer to the question about Jakob's identity is in the negative, if only because in modern society, and not merely in totalitarian systems, social, political, and ideological pressures will tempt the individual to hide something of himself from the public gaze. Disguising himself in one form or another, the individual hopes to hold on to his identity, provided he can achieve a certain distance from social relations that constantly threaten to invade his integrity of judgement and action. Additionally, there is the general difficulty for the Western reader in evaluating in their proper proportion the meaning and weight of references and actions that make sense only within this society of transition from fascist capitalism to a socialist people's democracy.

The distinctive language and style of *Mutmaßungen über Jakob*, constituting its essential narrative value, absorb the problems of uncertainty, of the wariness of individuals in their interpersonal relations and of the historical and ideological transition. The language employed by the author, usually in the service of a number of narrator figures, persistently tests possibilities of arriving at the

14. In an interview with *konkret*, January 1962, p. 19.

truth. Far from being portrayed as a set of given facts. reality is shown as a matter for enquiry. The first two sentences begin with the word 'aber', and words like 'hingegen', 'vielleicht', 'sozusagen' and the unconventional 'sozudenken', extensive use of the subjunctive, of indirect speech and interior monologue are among the devices sustaining and insisting upon the tone of reservation and doubt. Unexpected punctuation (or the lack of it), unfinished sentences, uncertainty as to who is talking to whom, serve to make it hard for the reader to find his bearings. They either provoke his impatience or involve him with the author and his characters in probing the elusive features of human communication. Johnson once made the characteristic remark that he hoped the reader would go through his novels as slowly as they were written. More than most originally creative writers Johnson demands of the reader a slow, circumspect reception in stark contradistinction to the speed of everyday perception and the superficiality of media consumption. He uses narrative fiction to set his reader wondering and thinking not only about the little imaginary town of Jerichow in Mecklenburg and a number of people who have known Jakob Abs, but also about the reader's own socio-political environment and its historical position. The early GDR is a society in which nothing is settled, however immutable may seem the rule of those in positions of power, like the Russian Commandant, the secret police and, in the not too distant background, the politicians in East Berlin. Indeed, no-one is more sensitive than the powers that be ('die Staatsmacht') to the question of legitimation, of having to win over to their ways of thinking large sections of the population. At one stage, for example, Jakob receives an education in historical materialist dialectics on the instigation of the ruling party. Jonas Blach, the university lecturer, and Jöche, the train driver, in conversation with each other are later readily able to imagine what the gist of such instruction might have been: 'Na was werden sie ihm schon gesagt haben. Sie werden ihm gegeben haben den kleinen historischen Überblick von der Mehrwerttheorie bis zur Verschärfung des Klassenkampfes durch die Avantgarde' ('Well, what will they have told him, after all. They will have given him the concise historical survey, from the theory of surplus value to the intensification of the class struggle by the avant-garde') (29). The contents of this tutorial, including a rather facile explanation of German fascism as merely the hiring of certain criminal politicians by profit-greedy owners of private capital, was a routine ingredient of political education in the GDR. It met with apathy and opportunist consent on the part of many: Jonas and Jöche simply concede: 'sie haben recht, solange sie reden' ('they [i.e. the authorities] are right, as long as they are talking') (29).

Despite the enigmatic character of Jakob and despite the narrative being an epistemological exercise in fictional terms, the novel's structure is neither labyrinthine nor chaotic, as was alleged by some critics. It is quite possible with a little patience to unravel the sequence of events, culminating in October/November 1956, from the disjointed presentation of the narrative.[15] The intricacy of the narrative furthermore reveals a strict parallelism between personal and political occurrences. Jakob, who departs for West Germany on 31 October 1956, meets Gesine and they temporarily find deep fulfilment in love, only to realise that the fissures of the political landscape, the 'political physics', as the book has it, have irrevocably placed them on different sides of the power divide. Individual fate is shown to be bound up with the great secular events of the day. Jakob is in the West at the same time as Hungary suddenly appears to be close to a realisation of democratic socialism under Imre Nagy; i.e. to the possibility of establishing a meeting ground between east and West, only then to be forced back into the Warsaw Pact fold by Russian tanks.[16] Jakob, himself a figure who by his actions wants to keep open communication, at least on a personal level, between East and West, is killed symbolically between trains from these opposing directions: life at the cross-roads between East and West is impossible. The individual is forced by overwhelming historical forces either to stay here or go there; a compromise area in between, a 'third way' between capitalism and Communism, does not appear to exist. The same is true of the fate of Jonas Blach: he is passionately, though not uncritically, involved with a circle of dissident intellectuals in which, after a copy of Khrushchev's secret speech before the XXth Congress of the Soviet Communist Party in 1956 has been obtained via the West Berlin press, possibilities for a 'humane socialism' are discussed. In November that year he is arrested by the state security officer Rohlfs. Historical and biographical parallelisms also occur in the later *Jahrestage* between Gesine Cresspahl's life and the Czech experiment in democratic socialism in 1968.

Apart from such entanglement of individual life with world historical events the major structural elements of the narrative technique in *Mutmaßungen über Jakob* are monologue, dialogue and what

15. This has, in fact, been done by various critics: cf. here H. Popp, 'Einführung in *Mutmaßungen über Jakob* in R. Gerlach & M. Richter (eds.), *Uwe Johnson* (Frankfurt, 1985), pp. 65–6; E. Fahlke, *Die 'Wirklichkeit' der Mutmaßungen* (Frankfurt & Bern, 1982), pp. 114–31.

16. At the same time, beginning 31 October 1956, British and French troops invaded Egypt.

Johnson calls 'recitation'. The first, according to the author's own testimony, comprises 'the memories and imaginings of Rohlfs, Blach and Gesine', printed in italics. The second is organised in paragraphs and with the use of a special speech mark — thus in the first and second chapters the conversation between the train driver Jöche and Mr Blach, in the third chapter between Mr Blach and Gesine, in the fourth chapter between Gesine and Mr Rohlfs. The five sections of the fifth chapter describe how these conversations came about and what the circumstances were. The third element which one might call recitation, consists of information given by the narrator who is never identified in the book.[17] There is indeed no omniscient narrator and an authoritative authorial voice is never heard. The author withdraws behind his characters and it is on them that the reader has to rely for whatever information he can glean about Jakob. This as it were democratic relationship between the author and his narrator figures is of profound importance for the composition of the novel: 'the author cannot know everything about Jakob. There are other things that Gesine knows, and Rohlfs and Cresspahl, etc.'.[18] The author functions as a fictional editor, collecting and arranging the views that people have of Jakob, providing occasional additonal information of a contextualising nature. This makes for an overall structure whose parts relativise each other, teasing the reader into further speculation.

Must we therefore conclude that Johnson's purpose, though recognisably modernist, is achieved by much reference to an ideological, political and regional environment which is in fact redundant? Could he not have demonstrated on a more neutral terrain his central concern, namely the fundamental uncertainty of identity in an age which appears to give the individual so little say in his own fate? The novel's structure and setting gives rise to an ambiguity: it is not clear whether our ignorance of Jakob's true feelings is due to the situation of life under 'Communism' or quite generally to the human condition in advanced industrial society. If the latter — and the ambiguity is not resolved — Johnson's novel implies a critique equally applicable to all these societies, be they of an Eastern or Western variety, and hence much of the East German background is rendered otiose. Against this it is necessary to insist on the writer's legitimate desire to operate within a realistic setting, capable of carrying wider symbolic meanings but, in the first instance, representative only in its own right. Johnson is no Kafka, and his prose

17. Johnson in a letter to W. van der Will, 3.8.1964.
18. Günther Rühle, 'Notiert nach einem Gespräch', *Neue Presse*, 24.10.1959.

does not encourage allegorical, mythological and metaphysical interpretations,[19] while at the same time it encapsulates typical problems of life in contemporary society determined by the great divide of the world into opposing power blocs. There can be little doubt that within the historical, social, political, ideological and provincial particularity of the East German setting there emerges a narrative that gradually captures much of the terrain of modernist awareness. The general and urgent question as to how a person can be responsible for his/her own actions when an overpowering ideological and political framework absorbs individuals in their thousands, is constantly addressed within the narrative realism of minutely recorded observations by a variety of people in the East Germany of the first five-year plan (1950–5) and the beginning of the second up to November 1956. In conversation with the secret service man, Rohlfs, who is trying to propagate the merits of the new social order, Jakob sticks to his guns by talking about the difficulties he has in dispatching trains in the right order and at the right time. There is more than a suggestion that preoccupation with wider matters would only handicap him: 'Ich habe gewiß einen Überblick. . . . Und eben diese Möglichkeit von Überblick: sagte er: beschwert die Arbeit' ('I certainly have an overall view. . . . But it is just this possibility of taking an overall view, he said, which complicates work'). While Rohlfs had meant to test Jakob on his overall view of society, Jakob obsessively sticks to his neck of the woods: an overall view for him is defined by the timetable that demands every second of his attention while he is on duty. He nonchalantly lets on that the social order affects the causes and circumstances of transport only in an external way. Rohlfs, suspecting that Jakob may be evading an explicit commitment to socialism and that he may be harbouring grudges against the regime, is fascinated by the man all the more when he begins to understand that no global criticism of the East German social system is implied in his remarks. In a society whose ideology makes the working man an object of adulation, the critical detail of Jakob's observation is of captivating interest for the intelligence officer. Rohlfs is astounded to learn of the many lengths of wasted rail that lie rusting beside the track in the GDR and he is equally astounded to hear Jakob profess quite seriously that while all the colleagues he knows are 'doing their best' he is of the opinion that one can never do enough for socialism. While Jakob seems quite prepared to regard capitalist class societies as systems of 'un-

19. Cf. Bernd Neumann, *Utopie und Mimesis: Zum Verhältnis von Ästhetik, Gesellschaftsphilosophie und Politik in den Romanen Uwe Johnsons* (Kronberg/Taunus, 1978), pp. 16–24.

reason' and those of socialism as systems of 'reason', he at the same time indicates to Rohlfs that ideological considerations are irrelevant to his job. Jakob, born in 1928, was old enough to have understood the politics of National Socialism and clearly wishes to keep a reserved distance from politics in order to protect his integrity: 'Er hatte etwas versucht mit seinem Dasein, das so überstand: denn die Zeit ("die Sseitn") war und waren so gefügt daß einer wenig Gewalt hatte über sein eigenes Leben und aufkommen mußte für was er nicht angefangen hatte' ('He had tried something with his being and he had survived: for the times were such that a man had little say over his own life and had to be responsible for what he had not started') (37).

The notion of integrity is further complicated by suggestions throughout *Mutmaßungen über Jakob* that men and women are so influenced by changing sets of extraneous forces as to render the idea of an inherent indentity of personality — so cherished by the German educated bourgeoisie, and, beyond that, accepted as a necessary psychological prop of the ego — almost illusory. In some philosophical reflections, recounted in characteristic style as Jakob's suggested deliberations on a speech by the modern philologist and co-editor of a philosophical journal, Jonas Blach, 'freedom' and 'identity' appear as entirely ficticious concepts:

> 'Freiheit' ist eher ein Mangelbegriff, insofern: sie kommt nicht vor. Wer auf die Welt kommt redet sich an mit Ich, das ist das wichtigste für ihn, aber er findet sich mit mehreren zusammen, und muß sich einrichten mit seiner Wichtigkeit; niemand kann so frei sein etwa aus der Physik auszutreten für seine Person. Als soziales und natürliches Lebewesen (ich bin ein . . .) weitgehend fest. Da ist wohl die Auffassung der Welt von einem Punkt Ich aus gemeint, dies sei aber nicht begriffen als Freiheit, solange man genau wie die Führung des Staates den Menschen (unsere Menschen, die Massen) beeinflußbar denke nach einem sehr schlichten Schema von Kausalität . . . (89).

> ('Freedom' is rather a term of deficiency, in so far as it does not exist. A person born into the world addresses himself as I, this is the most important thing for him, but he finds himself together with a number of others and he has to adjust his self-importance accordingly; nobody has the liberty individually to resign from physics. As a social and biological being (I am a . . .) he is largely fixed. 'Freedom' might mean the perception of the world from the vantage-point of a particular individual, but this cannot really be freedom, since man (our people, the masses), along with the leadership of the state, can be conceived as open to all sorts of influences according to a very simple scheme of causality. . . .)

Because of his awareness of forces at work on him from outside, and in spite of them, Jakob insists on his personal responsibility in his job. He thereby upholds the hope for a measure of detachment and freedom, and it is this, as much as anything else, that associates him with the emancipatory interests of the individual in the face of strong deterministic pressures. If Johnson's style is full of philosophical cadences, biblical images and forms of phrase, this makes us all the more alert to a tale which is more than merely the description of an efficient railway workèr who decided to sample the seductions of the West. It is the tale both of the individual's curtailed self-determination and of antagonistic divisions between ideological systems illustrated within the growing separation of the two Germanies. It is also a tale of the uncertainty of individual being and the limitations of individual perception illustrated by a narrative form in which the many-sidedness of truth is at best composed cumulatively of the knowledge of different points of view (in this case six). Johnson learnt much in this respect from Faulkner (particularly his novel *Absalom, Absalom*, where apart from a point-of-view technique there is a similar method of giving recent national and social history a background of biblically enhanced meanings).[19]

In a similar way the narrative interest in Johnson's third novel *Das dritte Buch über Achim* (1961) is focused on more than just a 'sporting hero of the people'. Achim T., an East German cycling star, corresponds to a certain extent to an actual contemporary person, the cycling star Gustav Adolf Schur. Nicknamed Täve by his fans, he was the subject of two books, one by a certain Adolf Klimanschewsky entitled *Täve*, the other by one Klaus Ullrich entitled *Unser Täve. Ein Buch über Gustav Adolf Schur*, which was published in East Berlin in 1960. It was the revised edition of an earlier work entitled *Unser Weltmeister*,[20] and so in Johnson's novel the book that Karsch, a Hamburg research journalist as its fictional author is trying to write, is the third (apart form this book being Johnson's own third novel).

Having been invited to the GDR by a former girlfriend, Karin, who now lives with Achim T., Karsch develops an interest in him above all as a *mediating figure*, esteemed alike by the state authorities and the people. Through a literary agent, Herr Fleisg, Karsch receives a commission from an East German publishing house to write a biography of Achim. It appears that both the public and the authorities have the same simple image of him as a star sportsman, a respected member of the party, a member of the East German parliament, a model citizen, single-minded, fair, unselfish and without corruption and it is clear from his reluctance to provide detailed

20. Cf. ibid, p. 125.

information about his past that Achim does not want anything to happen which might disturb this façade of the public persona that he has become. The novel is the description of how Karsch, the conscientious Western journalist, willing to blot out every preconception he might have about the GDR, by sticking to ordinary Western journalistic methods is quite unable to deliver the kind of secular hagiography that is expected. Probing into his past Karsch is able to ascertain that Achim's father had been a keen Social Democrat, committed enough to his party to have risked listening illegally in Nazi times to foreign broadcasting stations. This would fit the public image well enough. But, as Karsch also finds out, Achim had been active as a boy in the Hitler Youth, though also he had had a Jewish girlfriend. Achim up to the age of sixteen evidently was so totally enveloped by National Socialist ideology that he was ready to betray his father to the Gestapo (but fortunately the war ended before this could happen). There appears to be some evidence that Achim might have taken part in the 1953 uprising in East Germany against the government. Karsch also discovers that he once contravened GDR currency regulations when he went to West Berlin to buy himself a three-speed gear for his bike. Karsch holds discussions with Achim, goes to race meetings and talks to people who know him in order to establish the biographical truth. By the labour of research and imagination he is able to reconstruct with great probability Achim's life before he becomes famous, thus breaking open the polished poster-image he has been given in the press and in previous biographies in the service of ideologically educational interests of the East German regime. In the course of these investigations Achim turns out to be a figure of such complexity and contradiction that Karsch is denied the certainties and character consistencies necessary to complete his book. Neither the exemplary character of the new type of human being, demanded by socialist biographical theory from Lukács to various of his GDR adepts,[21] nor the integrated personality of bourgeois biography emerges. Stylistically this slide into uncertainty is mirrored by the way the subjunctives of hypothesis and hearsay come to dominate the style, while a simple factual statement will be made only to be quickly rectified, and there is increasing need for the extensive use of parenthesis:

> Viereinhalb (und als ich erzählt habe was der Polier gesagt hat, da ließ ihr Blick los, schwamm so und dann hat sie doch gesagt, daß sie in Ostpreußen wo liegt das überhaupt daß sie da eine Freundin gehabt hat,

21. Cf. ibid, pp. 111ff.

die ist nicht mitgekommen. Oder war das früher. Wie meint sie das, als ich dann stillschwieg, war sie ganz freundlich im Gesicht aber ich hab doch ach ich weiß nicht) Stunden.

(Four and a half (and when I recounted what the site foreman had said, her gaze let go, wandered somewhat and then she said that in East Prussia, where is this, she had had a friend, who did not come with. Or was this earlier on. What does she mean. When finally I was silent she was quite friendly in the face, but I have, well I don't know) hours.)[22]

Here a parenthetical statement, prolonged and gropingly unsure of itself, virtually obliterates the fact that, unusually, it took Achim as long as four-and-a-half hours to make the return journey on his bike from the little village, where one weekend in winter shortly after the war he had visited his then girlfriend, to the town where he lived with his father. This section of the narrative is sprinkled with information that it normally took him only three to three-and-a-half hours to cover the distance. The relationship is increasingly made to look like an excuse for Achim to gain his spurs as a cyclist. The bracket, encapsulating conversational exchanges between Achim and this refugee girlfriend from East Prussia — as reported to Karsch by Achim — sounds like 'eine unentschiedene Zusammensetzung von Ungefährem' ('the indecisive composition of vague things') referred to by the narrator shortly before (the two young people are actually trying to make up after emotional scenes caused by Achim's staying away from his girlfriend for four weeks). As to what Achim represents that is new, the answer given is 'not just victory . . . but the competition of individuals or groups for whatever you like or whatever the stakes' (297). The passage omitted is in parentheses and occupies a full page. The lengthy parenthetical explanation is dictated by the inadequacy of the statement that what Achim represented was 'not just victory', a generalisation evidently felt to be in need of elaboration by filling in the organisational details and conjuring up the spirit of an actual race. This is what the parenthesis provides. The whole statement is then followed by a long list of expressions traded between the competing teams before, during and after the race. All this is obviously some attempt by Karsch to gain narrative precision and to explain the overall socio-political significance of competition, of groups and individuals, in the socialist society of the late 1950s and early 1960s that was desperately trying to match the production levels of the capitalist West.

22. Johnson, *Das dritte Buch über Achim* (Frankfurt, 1964), p. 162. All subsequent quotes from this edition.

Sentences unfinished or with casual endings, a strained and often ungainly syntax, the absence of conventional punctuation, and the use of unfamiliar metaphors, provoked considerable criticism: 'His language is like someone grinding blocks of rubble and fitting the pieces together to make bricks'.[23] But the fact remains that Johnson's style opens up new possibilities of describing the uncertainty of meaning attaching to everyday occurrences in a political landscape shot through with ideological preconceptions. At the same time the narrative framework allows to draw on varieties of speech and diction which pursue the certainties or artisanal and technical detail with relentless accuracy (e.g. the description of a deckchair or of parts of a racing bicycle). The book is an exercise in achieving the approximate as the most exactly true. It is pervaded by a self-conscious style, frequently reflecting upon itself: 'you see how awkwardly this second sentence stands in relation to the first, that shouldn't be said in a relative clause, . . . belong surely in the main sentence?' The implications and ambiguities of a word will sometimes have to be explored in order to test the truth of a statement, as in the section devoted to the meaning of *private* (referring to acts of sabotage by colleagues of Achim's father in the Nazi aircraft industry: 128ff.). More extensively this is illustrated in the case of Achim's reference to the experience of his trip to West Berlin as '*sonntäglich*' ('Sunday-like': 205f.). In the ensuing discussion about this word Karsch and Achim try to agree on its meaning in this context, but without being able to settle it with any precision. The discussion ends in a non-committal exchange of phrases, and a few lines of interior monologue, in which the uncertainty of meaning is accepted as the only certainty: 'Vielleicht so: sagte Karsch. — So eher: sagte Achim. — Vielleicht: sagte er: Irgend wie: Irgend wie (dachte Karsch) war sehr genau. Irgend wie war Irgend wie vielleicht auch zu beschreiben' ('Perhaps like this: Karsch said. — More like this: Achim said. — Perhaps: he said: Somehow: Somehow (Karsch thought) was very accurate. Somehow this somebody might someway perhaps be describable') (209).

To discover that one cannot be sure about meanings, even where everyday words and phrases are concerned, is a step on the way to the discovery that man may be in error in believing that he can form notions of an unbroken identity of himself. In discussion with Karsch, Achim has a picture of himself as clear-cut as the official

23. A reviewer in the *Schwäbische Donauzeitung*. For some perceptive comments on language and sentence structure cf. Karl Migner, *Das dritte Buch über Achim. Interpretation* (Munich, 1966).

and public image, but this conceals, amongst other things, complicating features about his past: '. . . er wollte nicht der sein, der roh und gern war im alten und zerschlagenen Verband der staatlichen Jugend . . . nicht einer, den ängstigte die Rote Armee, der hätte seinen Vater verraten (für eine schlechte Sache verraten), den haben wir ja mit Gewalt hineinbringen müssen ins blaue Hemd und eingesehen hat er es doch nicht' ('. . . he did not want to be the one who gladly had been a raw recruit of the old and disbanded organisation of the state youth . . . not one, who had been afraid of the Red Army, who would have betrayed his father (betrayed him in a bad cause), we have had to press him into the blue shirt (of the socialist youth organisation) with force and he still didn't see the point') (213–14). His inner reluctance to admit to his activities in the Hitler Youth, to his abhorrence of the Red Army, to his readiness to betray his father to the Gestapo and to the difficulty of getting him into the Communist youth organisation — all this is understandably concealed by Achim in favour of a polished character mask, with the help of which he can outface any inner contradictions. Also, it is this mask which gives him a privileged position in society for the state can use it as a pointer to its superiority internationally and internally as proof of the excellence of the ordinary man within the collective. Achim is not necessarily a liar, for the extent to which he is aware of his role-playing is open to question. The position he is interested to adopt is of one who has always been as he is now: 'Er wollte gelebt haben schon wie immer jetzt und seit fünf Jahren Mitglied in der Sachwalterpartei: so endlich unterwiesen und entschieden für eine staatliche Gerechtigkeit, die ihm nicht anders denn angenehm gefiel' ('he purported to have lived in the past as he did now, and that he had been a member of the caretaker party for five years: finally instructed and resolved in favour of state justice, which seemed to him nothing but pleasant') (214). Karsch, uncovering inconsistencies of this kind, is confirmed in his early doubt whether the realities of life correspond to the words conventionally used to describe them. This makes the task of writing a biography of Achim increasingly difficult, if only because a person may without dishonesty adapt himself to people's image of him. In his search for an explanation of people's admiration for Achim Karsch is led to consider that as a projection of their own desires he may embody an image quite contrary to that preferred in official circles. He may represent the ordinary man 'against the government and against the world' and his much admired solidarity with his team could be understood as solidarity with the people against the regime.

In the case of Achim's girlfriend Karin, too, it is hard for the outside observer to be sure whether she is for or against the East German state. Regarding recent measures of the government she declares herself 'of one mind with all people of goodwill', but this can be interpreted either as approval of Ulbricht or opposition to him, and the ensuing words ('our best wishes are with her') preserve the ambiguity. Her attitude to the compulsory collectivisation of farms, at least in the eyes of the narrator, have suggestions of a similar ambivalence: ' . . . manchmal sagte sie so entschieden wie Tapferkeit aussieht: Aber Großraumwirtschaft, wie sie die werden machen können auf den zusammengelegten Feldern in der Genossenschaft, die ist doch im Vorteil, das werden sie gewiß noch einsehen, du, Karsch' (' . . . sometimes she said with a look of resolute boldness: But the economy of large fields, which they will be able to pursue on the combined farmlands of the co-operatives, has the advantage [over smallholdings], people will certainly come to realise that, you too, Karsch') (199). The odd opening phrase could imply that she had merely put on a brave face, struggling to persuade herself that collectivisation was a good thing. Her comparison of East and West Germany is non-committal: 'Westdeutschland ist nicht gerecht. Ostdeutschland ist nicht gerecht: vielleicht werden wir es eher' ('West Germany is unjust, so too is East Germany. Perhaps we shall be the first to see things in a just light') (269–70). In Karin's case support of the regime is so interwoven with critical feelings about it that no single and simple formula could accurately catch her attitude. Like Achim, she leads an existence in full view of the public and, as an actress, enjoys the applause of the crowds and, with reservations, the approval of the authorities; again, what she is at present cannot properly be understood in isolation from what she was in the past.

Unlike the question in the earlier novel about the identity of Jakob, the question, 'Who is Achim?' appears capable of a simple answer: 'He was a racing cyclist, for he went cycling with others and tried to go faster than they did' (43). But while the limited knowledge of the different narrators in *Mutmaßungen über Jakob* leads cumulatively to a clearer knowledge of an individual's identity, the more details that emerge in the course of Karsch's investigations the more blurred the image of Achim becomes. It has been argued that this is because of Karsch's attempt to explore the possibilities of a genuinely materialist biography across the socio-political divide of East and West. In other words, Karsch, the West German journalist, is bound to fail in his biographical endeavours and thus confuse the object of his description because he proceeds on the erroneous assumption that reliable facts can be established despite the divisions of ideology and politics. Karsch is indeed a man who comes to write the biography of a prominent figure in East Germany because he is very ready to leave, at least for a while, a West Germany whose capitalist rat race and unpurged Nazism have left him alienated and withdrawn. While his stay in East Germany proves increasingly uncomfortable because of his critical attitude to the lack of democratic openness, he at the same time feels ill at ease in West Germany. By engaging in this biographical project about Achim T. Karsch is searching for a possibility to circumvent the compulsions imposed by the ideological hiatus between East and West. But he, like Jakob Abs, though without fatal consequences, has to learn that there is no third reality between the power blocs and hence Johnson's novel is centrally preoccupied with the description of Karsch's failure as a biographer. It would be wrong, however, to suggest that the radius of meaning encompassed by the novel ends in the no man's land of the critical Western journalist's alienated position between the ideologies and between the two Germanies. Johnson's narrative links up with concerns about the possibility or rather the impossibility of identity which are articulated elsewhere in the twentieth-century German novel, from Rilke's *Die Aufzeichnungen des Malte Laurids Brigge* to Frisch's *Stiller*. Without wishing to press comparisons with the French *nouveau roman* connections with the contemporary French novel clearly do exist. The title of Natalie Sarraute's *Portrait d'un Inconnu* could serve as a subtitle to Johnson's novel and Sartre's remark about Sarraute's text that it is an anti-novel in which 'what happens is the process of challenging the novel as such by the practice of a particular novel'[24] has equal validity for Johnson's book. Clearly, *Das dritte Buch über Achim*, however historically and geographically specific in its setting, is not merely an inner-German story but one which raises, almost in the persistent manner of a detective story, the question of a hidden or disguised or lost or denied identity. If the task of the detective story, according to the philosopher Ernst Bloch, is to ask questions about someone who is hidden and if murder need not necessarily be the driving motive of the investigation then Johnson's narrative thematises the question of identity on the background of the ideological shifts in the history of contemporary German society and its division into a constellation of opposed forces.

In terms of narrative techniques, too, Johnson's novel fits into and expands on patterns of narration practiced since Faulkner. Their

24. J.-P. Sartre, introduction to *Portrait d'un inconnu* (Paris, 1956), p. 8.

further elaboration by Johnson owes much to Brecht's aesthetic theory.[25] The novel is robbed of both its sequential narrative progression and of the guiding hand of an omniscient narrator in order to make it a quest for truth. 'Attitudes of omniscience', Johnson held, 'are suspect'. The author 'ought to admit that he invented what he tells, that his information is incomplete and imprecise', and that he can do this 'by stressing the difficult quest for truth, by comparing or relating his own view of what has happened to that of one of his characters, by omitting what he cannot know'.[26] The reader is not allowed to forget this quest-for-truth quality of the narrative since this is structured as a series of conversational exchanges, stressing the relativity of the point of view of whoever is talking. Karsch as the chief narrator figure is relating his story to friends back in Hamburg. Their questions and interjections appear as italicised subheadings in the text. Within this conversational framework Karsch relates his talks, discussions and meetings with people in the GDR, with Achim, Karin, Fleisg and others. Karsch's own views are also relativised by the anonymous narrator or by Karsch himself looking back critically at what he did. In brief, the traditional function of the narrator is divided between Karsch, his contacts in East Germany, his friends in Hamburg, and an anonymous narrator. This means constant changes in narrative perspective, ambiguities as to who is speaking to whom, the intermingling of past and present tenses and a narrative diction able to exploit a wide range of stylistic levels: informal conversation, formal report, interior monologue, reported speech, and interview. The reasons why Johnson resorts to these methods have to do with matters he discussed in a lecture in America, when he referred to the problems of divided Berlin and what difficulties are involved in merely making a description of how the facts relating to a passenger getting on a train in East Berlin and leaving it in West Berlin may be distorted. The writer, unlike the less independent reporters involved, must seek to do justice to the subject by showing how the various individual and systemic distortions of the truth might be explained if the historical preconditions and the reasons for the personal, technical and ideological refractions became clear. Without necessarily possessing the truth the writer must show how it might be arrived at by becoming aware of all the possible traps for errors. The writer, therefore, is in the business of 'Wahrheitsfindung' ('truth-finding')

25. Cf. Neumann, *Utopie*, pp. 77ff.
26. Johnson in an address at Wayne State University, published in *Evergreen Review*, XXI, Nov.–Dec. 1960, pp. 29–30.

and the structure of the narrative as well as the manner in which it employs the language must at all times be seen to be subject to this supreme task:

> So long as a literary text . . . is concerned with truth, its subject must be checked against two contradictory tendencies of truth-finding. We know some of the sources of error in the collecting and transmitting of news: eye-witnesses who didn't look too closely, who can't say what they didn't see. They make up something that seems to round off the incident. Or they quietly arrange the situation according to their habitual points of reference, which may be private or of sectarian morality or party politics. Press, radio, television, and city gossip make additional changes in the material that has already been prepared for them. To some extent they depend on the interpretation which the first reporter gave to the incident with an adjective. They all damage reality (provided this word still applies), according to their special technical bias, by one or two dimensions. These personally or technically induced errors grow in complexity and become a rigid pattern the moment they are combined with the even more prolific source of error which political bias provides. Each side of the border has its own pattern. Obviously the criteria which operate in the one system of information cannot be applied to the other.[27]

The repercussions of this statement for the position of the author are manifold. He can obviously neither act as a reporter in the pay of a particular medium, partisan to a particular ideology, nor can he act as a neutral demigod, suspended above the quarrelling sides in Olympian distance, nor can he act as a pure artist whose first concern is to create perfect form: '(er kann) nicht für reine Kunst ausgeben, was noch eine Art der Wahrheitsfindung ist' ('he cannot present as pure art something that is still but a quest for truth').[28]

It is for this reason that Johnson's main works are built on a structure of accounts and exchanges that pass between the figures within the narrative. The reader is listening in, as it were, having to submit to the different rationales of changing points of view and challenged all the time to weigh up the validity of what is said. Within this process of judgement the author is at pains not only to present the subjective force of given individual perspectives (Achim's, Karin's, Karsch's; Blach's, Rohlfs's, Jöche's, Gesine's) he also tries to avoid triggering the reader's own ideological prejudices or predilections by translating everyday political references into a reflected, precise, at times disconcertingly hard-hitting, idiosyncratic vocabulary of Johnson's narrative diction. The state security police, for

27. Ibid., pp. 21–2; cf. also *BS*, p. 11.
28. *BS*, p. 21.

example, is referred to as 'der Einblick' ('the insight'), the countries of the Eastern bloc appear as 'die östlich benachbarten Staaten' ('the eastern neighbouring countries'), West Germany as 'der kapitalistisch arbeitende Teilstaat' ('the capitalist part-state'), Hitler as 'der Hausanzünder' ('the arsonist' or the 'the Austrian'), the Nazi party as 'der Verein für große Verschlechterung des Lebens' ('association for the great deterioration of life'), Ulbricht as 'der Sachwalter' ('the trustee'), the GDR as the 'ostdeutsche Militärbasis' ('East German military base') and the Federal Republic as the 'westdeutscher militärischer Stützpunkt' ('West German military base'), Chancellor Kiesinger as 'ehemals Angehöriger und Beamter der Nazis' ('one-time member and official of the Nazis'). These examples are taken from the two novels discussed so far and from *Jahrestage*. The list could be considerably enlarged. They reveal a desire by the author to distance the reader from the pat reactions of established prejudice and the passions of everyday propaganda and to provoke him into fresh thought. It is obvious that a further intention is to reveal the negative congruence between East and West, whatever their considerable and important differences may be. Overall the narrative consciousness, though limited at any given moment to a particular person, is spread over several and thus provides a body of information which does not oblige the reader to one all-knowing source but leaves him free to arrive at his own conclusions.

Jahrestage, a mammoth undertaking of four volumes and 1,900 pages, retains these narrative devices and lexical idiosyncrasies.[29] The chief narrator is Gesine Cresspahl, her fictional audience and questioner is her daughter Marie and the narrative context and scope of the work leave room for nearly all the characters of the previous novels to appear, briefly or at length. The novel serves as an ample balance sheet for the best part of the writer's fictional estate, a colossal exercise in synchronic timekeeping and diachronic memory. Within the mêlée of names quick orientation is possible only if one uses the *Kleines Adreßbuch für Jerichow und New York. Ein Register zu Uwe Johnsons Roman* prepared by Rolf Michaelis.[30] There are two principal levels of narration: Jerichow from the 1920s to the 1950s and New York 1967/8. The author Johnson is part of the fictional structure in that he acts as writer who keeps Gesine's diary and electronic notebook and, as is evident by the persistent 'Ich stelle mir vor . . .' ('I imagine . . .') of the first diary entry (21

29. Subsequent quotations in the text are from *Jahrestage 1* (Frankfurt, 1970) (=I) and *Jahrestage 2*, (Frankfurt, 1971) (=II).
30. Frankfurt, 1983.

August 1967), he is responsible for providing the general contextual setting within which his narrated and narrating figures live. Occasionally tensions are allowed to arise between the various narrator figures and internal addressees (Gesine, Marie, Mr Erichson, etc.) and, more significantly, between the author and the narrator and it is at such moments that the reader is made aware of the complex narrative arrangement that is involved in the final presentation of the text. The reader is therefore listening in, as it were, to conversations, exchanges, notes, Gesine's dialogues with the voices of her former selves, of her conscience and consciousness and her self reflections, all of which are, on the face of it, meant for particular individuals identified in the context of the novel. The author is her medium: 'Ich bin der Aufzeichnende und komme weiter nicht in Betracht' ('I am the note-taker and have no importance other than this'),[31] Johnson has remarked. It is the full range of Gesine's articulate awareness that decides the scope of the narrative. The author, who shares with her the same geographical and ideological background refers to her as 'Genosse Schriftsteller' ('comrade writer') in order to conjure up this common past. He acts on her behalf, at her command, not in his own right, providing a detached perspective of her personal views. By employing an author as her scribe the narrator can refer to herself in the third person, reverting to the first person plural only when Marie, her daughter, is implicitly included in the angle of narration and reserving the first person singular for moments of extremely private and personally involved aspects of her life. Although the author obviously generates the text, he does so in the service of fictional constraints laid on him by the chief narrator figure (Johnson rejected the term 'Figur' for her because it suggested somebody who could be manipulated at will; he preferred instead the term 'Person', to indicate that she had an integrity of her own). In so doing, the author renounces any possibility of acting like an ominiscient narrator and hence stays within the confines of Gesine's sensitivities, her memory, her interests in and witnesses of a contemporary world suspended between Mecklenburg and New York and further enlarged by her regular and critical study of *the New York Times*, which is referred to as 'the most knowledgeable person in the world'.

Given the very private nature of the speaker/hearer circuits which determine the narrative presentation, one might expect a rather esoteric text with little more relevance than the interest of the questioning listener, usually Gesine's twelve-year-old precocious

31. Johnson, interview with Hans Daiber in Bengel, *Johnsons Jahrestage*, p. 129.

daughter, Marie. But this is not the case. Gesine's (and, of course, the author's) historical-materialist schooling are fully brought to bear within the narrative so that it is informed at once by an unusual precision of local and historical detail and a sharp sociological clarity in matters relating to the class and power positions of individuals. This applies to the entire fictional population of the novel, but, of course, first and foremost to Gesine Cresspahl who is described as a white-collar worker in a trusted secretarial position of a large bank. Her white-collar status seems to have been one of the prime motivating forces for the narrative undertaking: 'Sie war eine, die geeignet war, etwas zu beschreiben, das sich anfangs anließ als Erfahrung aus der Welt der Angestellten' ('She was someone who was suited to describing something that at first appeared as experience from the world of the white-collar workers').[32] She considers herself rather lucky to have found a flat in Riverside Drive, a road where 'die Leute mittleren Einkommens, die angestellte Klasse' ('people of the middle income groups, the white-collar class') (*I*, 53) live. Having returned to her work from holiday she re-adopts suitable behavioural attitudes: '. . . die Verhaltensweisen der Angestellten sitzen ihr wiederum dicht auf der Haut' ('. . . the behavioural patterns of the white-collar workers again cling tightly to her skin) (*I*, 82). She earns $8,000 per annum. Her savings amount to something like $3,500. When there is reference to de Rosney, the vice-president of the bank who takes a special interest in her for a financial venture he wishes to launch in Dubček's Czechoslovakia, it is always with the implication that Gesine has little choice but to obey. De Rosney is described as the character mask of money talking, as someone who uses polite manners even to a lowly worker in his bank only for calculated strategic gains. He certainly expects full compliance from subordinates. In any case, Gesine's financial obligations, severely taxed by her rent and by the school fees for Marie, force her to execute her job conscientiously so as to preserve her income and her material independence from D.E., her would-be lover, who acts like a rich 'sugar daddy' to Marie and would without doubt do so to Gesine, if she let him. D.E., a kind of *homo faber*, is also a refugee from the GDR who has risen to a science professorship and to that of a trusted high-tech adviser to the US military. Possibilities for Gesine's upward social mobility exist (she is designated to become an important representative for the bank in Prague) but they come to nothing. In other words, Johnson decided to hang his narrative project on a socially average, ordinary sort of person. But

32. Ibid., p. 131.

she does have exceptional qualities: her memory and her moral conscience in political matters.

While the former makes it possible for the narrative to delve deep into the history of the Weimar Republic, the Third Reich, the Soviet Zone of Occupation and the GDR — always focused on the village of her birth, Jerichow in Mecklenburg, the latter explains her continued preoccupation with the Vietnam war and with crime in New York. The narrative project is nothing less than an account of twentieth-century social and political history on the basis of the lived experience, the collected family memories, and the reading of the informative press by an intellectually alert, ideologically and socially alienated, powerless person without any political influence. This position of powerlessness, akin to that of Johnson himself and perhaps not untypical of a critical stratum of grammar-school products in the Germany of the post-war generations, is half desired and half regretted. It stands in inverse proportion to the extraordinary political interest that Gesine displays. Disgusted with the violence generated by Western imperialist society at home and abroad, unable to accept a type of socialist society in which the state is at all times in the right against the individual and against any law, Gesine harbours the utopian hope for a 'third way', a genuinely democratic socialism. This is why on 7 February 1968 she writes a letter, to be handed to her daughter at age twenty, in which in tones heavy with sincere sentimentality she explains why she wishes to go to the reformed socialism of the Prague Spring republic: 'Dorogaja Marija, es könnte dennoch ein Anfang sein. Für den würde ich arbeiten aus freien Stücken' ('Dear Maria, it could, after all, be a beginning. I would work for it of my own free will') (*II*, 690).

Against the cemented positions of the ideological power blocs Johnson upheld a vision, however fragile, that the historical advances of bourgeois society might be married to those of a socially just society. At the same time he, like his protagonist Gesine, is accutely aware that there is no 'moralische Schweiz' ('morally neutral terrain') (*I*, 382) within the given societies. Johnson's entire narrative achievement, both in terms of narrative structure and of the use of language, is to wrench from the historical and contemporary contexts of violence the portrayal of ordinary people clinging to life at the cost of conformism with prevalent ideologies and of some individuals in whom the utopia of the 'third way' between actually existing socialism and contemporary capitalism stays alive.

GORDON BURGESS

Wolfgang Koeppen

> Ich bin, glaube ich nun, nicht zuletzt deshalb Schriftsteller geworden, weil ich kein Handelnder sein mag. . . . Ich bin ein Zuschauer, ein stiller Wahrnehmer, ein Schweiger, ein Beobachter . . . [1]
>
> (I think I became a writer not least because I don't like taking action. . . . I watch, perceive quietly, remain silent, observe . . .).

Unlike some of his contemporaries (Böll, Grass, Lenz, for example), Koeppen has made few public statements on his view of the position and task of the writer in society, so that his observation quoted above is all the more significant. Rather than get embroiled in political activity, he has preferred to retreat into the world of fiction, he is a chronicler of the world through the filter of the imagination. This is true not only of his pre-war and post-war novels, but also of his essays into the travelogue genre and his last published work to date, a semi-fictional autobiography. It is this process of fictionalising reality, together with a constant desire for formal experimentation, which has made Koeppen a unique figure in modern West German writing.

Koeppen has always been very reticent about his own personal life. An 'Autobiographische Skizze' ('Autobiographical sketch'), published in 1961 and running to over three pages, for example, mentions not a single date, and an 'autobiography' published in 1982 simply reads: 'Wolfgang Koeppen wurde 23.6.1906 in Greifswald geboren. Er lebt in München' ('Wolfgang Koeppen was born in Greifswald on 23.6.1906. He lives in Munich').[2] Our attention, then, must be focused on his published works, and these may be

1. Wolfgang Koeppen, *Rede zur Verleihung des Georg-Büchner-Preises*, p. 103. All translations are my own, except for passages from *Der Tod in Rom*, which are taken from *Death in Rome*, translated by Mervyn Savill (London, 1956).

2. *Begleitheft zur Wolfgang-Koeppen-Ausstellung*, Stadt- und Universitätsbibliothek Frankfurt a.M., p. 7. Cf. also a letter of 26.10.1953, reproduced in ibid., p. 9: 'was geht die Leute meine Biographie an' ('what concern is my biography to other people').

neatly — too neatly, perhaps — characterised chronologically and thematically. After two pre-war novels, Koeppen made his name as a writer with three novels which took issue with the ethical and political reality of post-war West Germany: it is on these three novels that his fame largely rests to this day. His next published venture was in the realm of the semi-fictional travelogue, three volumes appearing between 1958 and 1961. Koeppen has since published only two works in book form: a collection of short stories, and a semi-fictional autobiography of his childhood and adolescent years. Thus, his published output has been punctuated by periods of 'silence', the reasons for which have given rise to much speculation amongst critics, although, as Alfred Andersch pointed out in 1976, 'Er schweigt aber gar nicht, er schreibt. . . . Er *veröffentlicht* nur nichts' ('But he's not keeping quiet: . . . it's just that he's not *publishing* anything').[3] In the following discussion, it will be suggested that Koeppen's lapses into publishing 'silence' have been at least partly due to his desire for experimentation, his search for a medium appropriate to his particular form of fictionalising observation.

For all his rigid insistence on his own autobiographical privacy, Koeppen has indicated that at the heart of his first novel *Eine unglückliche Liebe* (1934) lay a genuine experience of his own.[4] A young man, Friedrich, has met and fallen in love with a young actress, Sibylle, who apparently does not reciprocate his affection for her. The novel charts the progress of their relationship. The work pays only lip-service to this seemingly hackneyed story line however: it is raised from the level of the banal by two things: the way in which Friedrich and Sybille in the end resolve their problematic situation, and the vigour and controlled experimentation of the narrative.

Despite the implication of the title (itself a cliché which Koeppen turns on its head), this is not a love story with a sad ending. The problem at the heart of their relationship is that Friedrich's passion is all-enveloping: he demands total possession of Sibylle. Sibylle, on the other hand, is not willing to give up her individuality, indeed she is fearful that the force of her love for Friedrich would cause her to do so if she were in any way to return his affection physically. Through this relationship which is never consummated, both figures become more mature, until, finally, they attain a *modus vivendi* in

3. Alfred Andersch, 'Die Geheimschreiber', *Merkur*, 30 (1976), p. 555.
4. Cf. Wolfgang Koeppen, 'Eine schöne Zeit der Not', *Jahresring*, 1974/75, p. 39.

which each is able both to receive and to give emotionally, whilst respecting the other's individuality.

The central image of the novel is that of the wall that divides but may also connect, and it changes as Friedrich and Sibylle move closer towards their final realisation. Three examples may suffice to illustrate this. First: Friedrich thinks of Sibylle in terms of an impenetrable fortress that casts him back time and again.[5] Later, it is suggested that this 'wall' between them may be a necessary concomitant of their relationship: 'Die unsichtbare Wand türmte sich auf . . . Wenn sie diese Grenze respektierten . . . , konnten sie ein Herz und eine Seele sein' ('The invisible wall towered up . . . If they respected this barrier, they could be the best of friends') (72). In the end, this is what Sibylle and, above all, Friedrich achieve. The barrier between them has now become a 'wall of the thinnest glass' (198). Their mutual respect for the other's individuality permits them to be acutely sensitive of and towards each other, and so their love can flourish, albeit, indeed due to, this self-imposed limitation. The former conditional has disappeared; now, we read: 'Es war dies eine Grenze, die sie nun respektierten' ('This was a barrier which they now respected') (198).

The novel concentrates almost entirely on the inner lives of the main characters, and a large array of authorial and narratorial devices is utilised to convey the complexity of these emotional processes. Koeppen's self-professed indebtedness to James Joyce, for example, is evident in the first-person, stream of consciousness style in which Friedrich's memories of his first meeting with Sibylle are conveyed (23–39), as well as in the presentation of Sibylle's thoughts later, as they roam over her past life, especially with regard to Friedrich (165–70). Throughout the novel, too, the characters' own interpretation of events is called into question or relativised. On occasion, this may merely take the form of a narratorial comment, but often Koeppen's technique is more subtle, undermining one figure's view only much later in the narrative. For example, at one point in their relationship, Friedrich regularly waits by the telephone for Sibylle to call him in the early hours of the morning, and then immediately runs to her flat. These acts of loving servitude are presented at the time positively; only later does it transpire that this is Friedrich's own interpretation of his behaviour towards

5. References to Koeppen's works will be made to the following editions, all published in Frankfurt by Suhrkamp: *Eine unglückliche Liebe* (1977) (here p. 55); *Die Mauer schwankt* (1983); *Drei Romane* (*Tauben im Gras*, *Das Treibhaus*, *Der Tod in Rom*) (1972); *Nach Rußland und anderswohin* (1973); *Amerikafahrt* (1982); *Reisen nach Frankreich* (1979); *Romanisches Café* (1972); *Jugend* (1976).

Sibylle. In fact, he is doing his cause no good, for in Sibylle's eyes he had been merely making himself 'die elendigste Gestalt, wenn er atemlos nach langem Lauf vor ihrem Bett angelangt war' ('the most wretched of figures, when he had arrived at her bed breathless after his long run') (169). Techniques such as these, together with various clusters of repeated and varied images and phrases, demand an attentiveness on the part of the reader that Koeppen was to tax further in some of his post-war works, notably *Tauben im Gras*.

Although the setting of *Eine unglückliche Liebe* is contemporary, the political unrest of the time scarcely intrudes. In his second novel, *Die Mauer schwankt* (1935) Koeppen concerned himself with the political terrorism of the Nazi dictatorship to a greater degree, but this theme was cloaked to such an extent that the Nazis even allowed the book to be reissued in 1939, albeit under the new title *Die Pflicht*. In a preface to the 1983 reissue of *Die Mauer schwankt*, Koeppen described the book as a 'Horrortrip' (ix) into a fascist Balkan country, in which he was able to camouflage his views of Nazi Germany. The central symbol of the tottering wall, adds Koeppen, is both the Austro-Hungarian Empire, shortly before its collapse, and the sensibility, surroundings and fears of Johannes von Süde, its central character. On a visit to the Balkans, where his brother-in-law has been fatally wounded in mysterious circumstances, Süde meets the exotic Orloga, but their relationship, such as it is, is short-lived: he is witness to her assassination, and she dies in his arms. Together with Orloga, Süde has witnessed the brutal treatment meted out by the state security forces to a man suspected of underground activities. Süde has been filled with 'Mitleid mit dem Mißhandelten, mit dem Verfolgten, Wut gegen die, die ihn geschlagen und verfolgt hatten' ('sympathy with the man who had been mishandled and persecuted, anger with those who had beaten and persecuted him') (47). But, although he protests (and thereby lands himself briefly in prison), he does nothing to prevent further occurrences of this kind. Significantly, it is his sudden passion for Orloga, not the police mistreatment of suspects to which he has been a witness, that is to inform the rest of his life. He withdraws from the political reality of the situation into a subjective idyll of what might have been. Süde returns to Germany, to find himself transferred to a small town in Masuren in the eastern provinces, apparently for three years at most. But the First World War intervenes, and Süde is given the task of building anew this now partially destroyed town. This time, his idealistic vision is destroyed by reality: he hopes to design a new, integrated townscape from the rubble of the old, but is prevented from doing this by the demands of the local inhabitants who want the town rebuilt as it had been before the war. As such, his professional life has been a failure, due to his rigid adherence to what he has regarded as his duty in the service of the state.

By far the greater part of the novel is concerned to chronicle Süde's gradual disillusionment in Masuren and the result of his conception of duty. Within the narrative, for example, the war functions as nothing more than a pretext for Süde to follow orders to return to the distant town in order to supervise its rebuilding. As such, the camouflaged political statement is unfocused, but also the figure of Süde himself is ultimately unconvincing as a symbol of a disintegrating society. Furthermore, the novel as a whole is uneven in both subject-matter and narrative texture, with only the figure of Süde himself providing coherence and cohesion. With the exception of parts of Chapter 1 (Süde's Balkan experiences), the sometimes bold experimentation of Koeppen's earlier novel is here lacking: the narration is linear and at times indulgently descriptive. In many ways, as Reich-Ranicki has pointed out, the novel is a backward step from the tightly controlled experimentation with modern techniques that distinguished *Eine unglückliche Liebe*.[6] It was not until the 1950s that Koeppen was again to explore these techniques, in novels which overtly took issue with the political realities of contemporary Germany.

In 1951, Koeppen published the first of three novels which were innovatory both in their radical unmasking of the reality on and below the surface of contemporary West German society, and in their experimentation with narrative techniques. In *Tauben im Gras* (1951) Koeppen particularly explores the technique of fragmentation and montage, commonly associated in the critical literature on the novel with the work of Dos Passos; in *Das Treibhaus* (1953) he explores, to a greater extent than in the pre-war novels, the possibilities of stream of consciousness and inner monologue; finally, he attempts in *Der Tod in Rom* to combine the two contrasting approaches. Of the three novels, it is *Der Tod in Rom* (1954) which has met with the most favourable critical acclaim on an aesthetic level, and it is, perhaps, significant that it was only after the publication of this novel, and not after *Das Treibhaus*, that Koeppen apparently abandoned the genre of the novel in favour of the semi-fictional travelogue.

The events of *Tauben im Gras* take place within the span of one day,

6. Cf. Marcel Reich-Ranicki, 'Der Zeuge Koeppen', in U. Greiner (ed.), *Über Wolfgang Koeppen* (Frankfurt, 1976), p. 136.

and within one unspecified city in Bavaria, generally assumed to be Munich. Newspaper headlines scattered throughout the text help to pinpoint the temporal setting (one, if it is to be taken at face value, reads 'André Gide gestern verschieden', ('André Gide died yesterday') (93), which would date the action as 20 February 1951) and to relativise the narrated action: 'Atomversuche in Neu-Mexiko, Atomfabriken im Ural' ('atom tests in New Mexico, atom factories in the Urals') (12). The strictly defined geographical and temporal setting, however, is used paradoxically to open out the perspective to that of the global village of the atomic age: 'Deutschland lebt im Spannungsfeld, östliche Welt, westliche Welt, zebrochene Welt . . .' ('Germany lives in an area of conflict, eastern world, western world, broken world') (212). Within the brief timespan of the narrative, the reader is introduced to episodes in the lives of a multiplicity of major and minor characters whose paths cross more or less arbitrarily as the fictional day progresses. There is no central figure, and there is no central, single-stranded narrative: the narrative flow is often interrupted, begun, or continued abruptly and seemingly capriciously. The reader's task is not made any easier by the fact that there are no chapter divisions. Whilst the novel is typographically divided into sections of unequal length (albeit without headings), different editions divide the sections differently, with several passages unaccountably run together: this has caused some arithmetical confusion amongst the critics. And, finally, there is no intrusive narrator to provide links or explanations: the reader is left to find his own way through the maze of figures and events. Although the various narrative strands gradually become more transparent and the characters resolve themselves into one or more of several constellations, the abiding impression is still one of fragmentation, of arbitrariness and chance.

The lack of an ordering principle, the lack of an overall 'sense' of the narrative form of the novel mirrors the predicament of the individual characters in their personal and social lives: their isolation, their lack of a meaningful goal or informed ideal. They are the true 'pigeons on the grass' of the title, as expanded on by Edwin, an American novelist, during a public lecture at the Amerikahaus: 'wie Tauben im Gras betrachteten gewisse Zivilisationsgeister die Menschen, indem sie sich bemühten, das Sinnlose und scheinbar Zufällige der menschlichen Existenz bloßzustellen, . . . sinnlos, wertlos, frei und von Schlingen bedroht, dem Metzger preisgegeben' ('certain pundits on civilisation viewed people as pigeons on the grass, endeavouring to unmask the senselessness and seemingly chance quality of human existence, . . . senseless, worthless, free and threatened by snares, abandoned to the butchers') (200). Edwin and his lecture have already been the subject of ironic treatment by the narrator, and his view of 'das *scheinbar* Zufällige' ('what is only seemingly by chance') is not borne out by the events of the novel. The characters' lives are deeply fragmented, discontinuous, and godless. None of the main characters seems to deserve his or her fate at the end of the novel: Edwin is attacked and possibly killed; Josef, a railway porter and war veteran, is killed by a stone thrown perhaps by chance, perhaps deliberately; an American boy is injured in an anti-Negro riot; and Odysseus, a Negro American soldier, is robbed by Susanne, his German girlfriend. The fates of the individual characters, with their fortuitous twists and turns, coalesce into a microcosm of the global political context within which the events of this one day are played out, lending a sense of immediacy to the final warning of the novel that there may be only 'eine Sekunde zum Atemholen, Atempause auf einem verdammten Schlachtfeld' ('one second to catch your breath, a pause for breath on a damned battlefield') (202).

Many critics reacted positively to Koeppen's depiction of contemporary West German society in *Tauben im Gras*. *Das Treibhaus*, on the other hand, attracted much vituperative comment for what was considered to be an attack by Koeppen on the political inadequacies of the young democracy. The novel appeared just a few weeks after the general election for the second West German parliament had taken place on 6 September 1953 and the preceding debate on the subject of rearmament. Koeppen's novel, set in Bonn and centred on the figure of Keetenheuve, a disenchanted member of the Bundestag, led critics either to treat the work as a *roman-à-clef*, or to censure Koeppen for his generally negative portrayal of West German parliamentary democracy. It was doubtless for its political statement that the first edition of the novel sold out within a matter of days.

Koeppen, however, states in a preface that the political reality of the day merely acted as a catalyst for his own imagination, that events, figures and places are not identical with those of the real world, and that the novel has its own poetic truth (214). The narrative structure and the narrative perspective would certainly seem to support this claim. The multi-stranded narrative of *Tauben im Gras*, with its wide range of major characters, is here abandoned in favour of concentration on the life and thoughts of one individual, and the constantly shifting perspective of the previous novel here gives way to the limited range of vision of its central figure. By comparison with Keetenheuve, the other figures are one-sided: they are presented as he sees them, i.e. in the context of their existence as political allies or opponents. Keetenheuve represents on a personal level the rotting state of the 'hothouse' West Germany of the title (cf. p. 243). He is a failure in both his private and his public life. Politically, Keetenheuve has failed because he is an idealist, a romantic dreamer, without the power or competence to achieve his ideals in practical terms.

The novel opens with Keetenheuve returning to Bonn after attending the funeral of his wife Elke who has died, rumour has it, under mysterious circumstances. It ends with his suicide. After a casual sexual acquaintance with Lena, a young Salvation Army girl, in which he is forcibly reminded of his failure on a personal level — it is 'ein Akt vollkommener Beziehungslosigkeit' ('an act devoid of contact') (376) — he is overcome by the realisation of his own political impotence, and in a final act of despair 'liberates' himself from the oppressions of a world which cannot but fail to match up to his own idealism. Significantly, he is here referred to in his political capacity: 'Der Abgeordnete war gänzlich unnütz, er war sich selbst eine Last, und ein Sprung von dieser Brücke machte ihn frei' ('The member of parliament was totally useless, he was a burden to himself, and one leap from this bridge made him free') (376).

In spite of its title and setting, *Der Tod in Rom* was Koeppen's third statement in novel form on the political and social reality of contemporary West Germany, and a further censure on the restorative processes at work both on the surface and behind the scenes. The novel relates the gathering in Rome, for various reasons, of members of two branches of one family, the Pfaffraths and the Judejahns. Friedrich Wilhelm Pfaffrath, formerly an administrator under the Nazis and now active in the present regime, is in Rome with his wife Anna and son Dietrich to discuss with Judejahn, his brother-in-law, the possibility of Judejahn's return to West Germany: Judejahn is a former SS general, sentenced to death in his absence at Nürnberg, now continuing his warmongering in the service of an Arab state. Also in Rome, unconnected with this mission, are Pfaffrath's son Siegfried, a composer of twelve-tone music, and Judejahn's son Adolf.

By placing the action of the novel in Rome rather than in Germany, Koeppen achieves three things in particular. First: he is able to depict at first hand, as it were, the figure of Judejahn: his lust for power, obsession with Nazi ideals, brutality, limited intelligence, and inferiority complex. He is death personified: 'Dieser Mann war ein Henker. Er kam aus dem Totenreich, . . . er selber war ein Tod, ein brutaler, ein gemeiner, ein plumper und einfallsloser Tod' ('This man was an executioner. He came from the Kingdom of the Dead.

. . . he himself was a brutal, abject, clumsy, purposeless Death') (387); and we are given ample opportunity to witness Judejahn's own thoughts and actions. Second: the setting of Rome provides an ironic background to the Germans visiting the city. The novel is divided into two chapters, roughly equal in length. The first opens with a section outlining Rome's cultural past, the second with a section describing the Pope at prayer. Rome as a cradle of classical culture and also of modern Christianity thus functions here, as Koch has noted, 'als Kontrast zu den Repräsentanten eines nationalistisch beschränkten, barbarischen Deutschland' ('as a contrast to the representatives of a nationalistically limited, barbaric Germany').[7] But, more than this, each of the initial sections undermines its own allusion: the gods of the past are no longer, and the Catholic church is shown to be unsure of its very foundation: 'Sankt Petrus hatte sich wohl von der Erde in die Wolken erhoben, aber ein Zweifel blieb, ob er den Himmel erreicht hatte' ('St Peter had risen from earth into the clouds, but there was some doubt as to whether he had reached heaven') (462). Third: the title of the novel immediately calls to mind Thomas Mann's *Der Tod in Venedig*, and Koeppen reinforces this allusion by quoting the last sentence of Mann's novelle as a prologue to the novel. The world of Koeppen's Germans, and their reasons for being in Rome, contrast sharply with those of Gustav von Aschenbach.

The narrative techniques of *Der Tod in Rom* combine and refine the episodic fragmentation of *Tauben im Gras* with the inner monologue and stream of consciousness of *Das Treibhaus*. Instead of the vast range of main figures on the one hand, and one central character on the other, the novel depicts the interactions of a limited group of figures, all of whom, moreover, are already related to each other before the onset of the narrated action. Furthermore, Siegfried is given added status as the only character to use the first-person narrative form (as opposed to Judejahn, for example, whose thoughts are only given in the third-person form). The reader's task, therefore, is made somewhat easier than it had been in *Tauben im Gras*, and the lack of concentration on the thoughts of one individual endows the issues presented in *Der Tod in Rom* with a less one-sided, more forceful and convincing quality than in *Das Treibhaus*.

As with Koeppen's two previous novels, *Der Tod in Rom* ends with a death, in this case that of Judejahn from a heart attack. But Judejahn's death in no way implies the demise of the militarism he

7. Manfred Koch, *Wolfgang Koeppen. Literatur zwischen Nonkonformismus und Resignation* (Stuttgart, 1973), p. 64.

represents. Pfaffrath will return to the West Germany of military restoration and the economic miracle, and Siegfried looks for fresh cultural impetus and inspiration outside Europe. This was Koeppen's last published statement in novel form on the emergent West German society. Indeed, it was to be over twenty years before he again published anything resembling a novel, and then he shifted the focus of his attention to the early years of this century.

Between 1958 and 1961 there appeared three volumes of essays on Koeppen's travels, originally rising out of a radio commission. The various essays have much in common with each other, and may be conveniently discussed together. Common to all is first and foremost their subjectivity, indeed, on occasion their lack of authenticity. Koeppen reported in one interview, for example, that some tourists had got lost when trying to follow one of his 'travelogues' in France. The subtitle of the first collection sets the tone for all three volumes: *Empfindsame Reisen*, i.e. 'Sentimental journeys', in which the author — one might almost call him the narrator — is more concerned to give an account of the impressions awakened in him than of the scenery and events themselves. Koeppen himself acknowledged this obliquely in an interview he gave in 1961: 'ich will Romane schreiben; die Reisebücher waren für mich Umwege zum Roman. Kulissenbeschreibungen . . . Ich will *meine* Welt' ('I want to write novels; the travelogues were for me detours on the way to a novel, descriptions of scenery . . . I want *my* world').[8] Examples of this process, of the travelogue giving way to the novelistic, are to be found on almost every page, particularly of the first two collections.

The most prevalent feature of the travelogues is Koeppen's constant 'literarisation' and 'culturalisation' of the scene before him. This may, at its most banal, take the form of a string of names — 'Lenin, Joyce, Hemingway, Henry Miller, der die Anarchie preisende Blaise Cendras, der junge Cocteau, Strawinsky, Picasso' (*Reisen nach Frankreich*, 138) — or it may shape Koeppen's whole interpretation of what he is witnessing: 'Es war Dornröschens Reich, durch das ich ging, . . . Urwaldgerank um die Terassen, verwitterte Palmen, und durch die verwunschene Straße ratterte, mit einem einzigen Fahrgast, einem alten Neger, auf den gelben Bänken, Tennessee Williams' Streetcar "Desire" zur Endstation "Sehnsucht"' ('I was walking through Sleeping Beauty's territory, . . . jungle vegetation around the terraces, weather-beaten palms, and through the en-

8. Interview with Horst Bienek, in Greiner, *Koeppen*, p. 254. Koeppen's emphasis.

chanted street there rattled, with just one passenger, an old Negro, on its yellow seats, Tennessee Williams' Streetcar "Desire" on its way to the terminus of Desire') (*Amerikafahrt*, 72). In *Reisen nach Frankreich*, by contrast, Koeppen's imagination is not fired by what he finds and, as a result, this volume is by far the weakest and most lack-lustre of the three. Time and again, we are invited only to share in Koeppen's disappointment at the food he is served, or at the ugliness of provincial France. In this volume, the imaginative tourist seems to have run out of steam: he has explored the possibilities of this semi-fictional genre to their full, just as, in *Der Tod in Rom*, he had attained a level of narrative experimentation which he found himself unable to develop further. With *Reisen nach Frankreich*, Koeppen put the genre of 'sentimental journeys' behind him.

The problem with such an allusory approach in the travelogues, of course, is that the references may all too easily become all too recondite. This is a danger which Koeppen does not always avoid in the travelogues, and it is one to which he falls prey on a number of occasions in the volume *Romanisches Café*. The most blatant example, perhaps, is to be found in 'Der Sarkophag der Phädra', written in 1950, which attempts (unsuccessfully) to transport the figures of Phaedra, Hippolytos, Theseus and others, together with their associated legends, into the modern world of motor-racing. The collection is uneven, as one might expect of a selection of texts written between 1936 and 1971. The most successful, perhaps, is the title piece, a stylistic *tour de force* in which one sentence running to over four-and-a-half pages traces the history and background, from Charles the Great to the Nazi period, of the 'Romanisches Café' in Berlin, where Koeppen had spent formative years in the early 1930s.

Jugend, Koeppen's latest published work in book form, was generally well received by critics, even if they were unsure how to classify it. This is in itself indicative of the experimental nature of the work, which covers roughly the first two decades of the narrator's life, and in which Koeppen's statement 'Ich bin auf der Suche nach einer Romanfigur, die ich selbst bin' ('I am searching for a fictional character that I myself am') found one solution. Koeppen does not supply the reader with a factual account of his own youth;[9] more-

9. The most blatant example of autobiographical fictionalisation is that the narrator in *Jugend* is brought up by his mother in Greifswald, whereas Koeppen had been brought up by an uncle in Ortelsberg, Masuren, present-day Szczynto.

over, historically dateable events are presented and arranged in such a way as to undermine the veneer of authenticity they lend the account. According to the text, for example, the Kapp Putsch (13.3.1920) took place after Lenin's death (21.1.1924), and the boy learns of the latter from a newspaper in a shop that is 'weihnachtsglänzend' ('full of Christmas decorations') (121, 76). Historical accuracy is secondary to the authenticity of the subjective impression, the fiction of the text which Koeppen prefaces with a quotation from Goethe: 'Das Gedichtete behauptet sein Recht, wie das Geschehene' ('Fiction has its own rights, as does fact'). The same process is here taking place as in the fictionalised travelogues: the reader's attention is drawn away from the factual elements, to focus on the inner workings of the individual, and on the processes beneath the social reality.

Once again, Koeppen is experimenting with form. Although the narration is linear overall, it varies between the 'ich', 'du' and 'er' forms, and the text is fragmented to the extent of sections beginning and ending without punctuation, sometimes not even in the form of complete sentences. As before, Koeppen makes use of mythical allusions and allegory to widen the perspective and relativise the individual account, but his use is more muted than in some of his earlier works. And there is a complex web of allusions which serve to place this one, albeit composite, 'Jugend' in the context of the 'youth' of mankind itself, the fall of Adam and Eve and their expulsion from Paradise. The first sentence reads: 'Meine Mutter fürchetete die Schlangen' ('My mother was afraid of snakes'), a motif then taken up and varied throughout the text. Indeed, the social circumstances of the narrator and his mother are themselves a reflection of the original fall from Paradise: his mother, of a rich family, has been disinherited because of the birth of her illegitimate son and now lives outside the family estate, banished and impoverished.

Jugend remains Koeppen's final published work to date. In many ways, it highlights the fact that, for all the different directions it has taken, Koeppen's *oeuvre* is fundamentally unified. Throughout, Koeppen has displayed a readiness, a need almost (which would help explain his 'silences') to experiment with both form and subject-matter. And throughout, he has remained an acute observer on the personal, social, and political levels. It is these two elements which have characterised his published work from *Eine unglückliche Liebe* to *Jugend*, combined with the urge to relativise and fictionalise, through the medium of the imagination, the individual event, which have endowed his work with its literary vigour and uniqueness, but thereby also robbed it of any direct political effectiveness: 'Ich will unsere Geschichte erzählen, meine Geschichte, deine Geschichte, sie geht dich nichts an, ich erzähle sie nur mir' ('I want to tell our story, my story, your story, it doesn't concern you, I am only telling it to myself') (*Jugend*, 67).

RHYS WILLIAMS

Siegfried Lenz

Siegfried Lenz is a problematic novelist. This is not because his novels are difficult in the sense that they employ a range of stylistic or formal devices taxing the reader's powers of comprehension or analysis. On the contrary, the presence of so many of his works on the prescribed book-lists of schools in the Federal Republic and abroad suggests a wide and immediate appeal, an impression borne out by his enormous sales and intensely loyal public. Yet, despite the fact that he enjoys the approbation of Marcel Reich-Ranicki, who is arguably West Germany's most powerful critic and scarcely noted for his generosity of spirit, some academic criticism is grudging, even denigratory.[1] Lenz tends to be admired as a 'story-teller in the traditional mode', as a 'conventional' stylist, yet even his staunchest supporters concede that his plots are too artificially constructed, too obviously symbolic; he is frequently extolled as a profound moralist, yet even his admirers are hard pressed to pin-point the precise nature of that moral commitment. His texts prove curiously resistant to the very readings which they appear to invite, for there seems to be, at the heart of his writing, a crisis, be it personal, political or historical, which the novels purport to confront but about which they are tantalisingly silent. It is this fascinating contradiction in Lenz's work which this essay will tentatively seek to explore.

In an interview with Manès Sperber in March 1979 Lenz was inspired by a remark made by Sperber about his own early life to make the following interjection: 'Aber ist das nicht ein außerordentlicher, ja fast ein musterhafter kritischer oder sagen wir mal, ein krisenhafter Augenblick, wo man Geborgenheit, Glaubenssicherheit aufgeben muß, sie nicht mehr mit den anderen teilt, sondern sich

1. From among the more critical assessments of Lenz's achievement I am particularly indebted to the following: Kurt Batt, 'Geschichten contra Geschichte. Über die Erzählungen und Romane von Siegfried Lenz', *Sinn und Form*, 26 (1974), pp. 847–59; Manfred Bosch, 'Der Sitzplatz des Autors Lenz oder Schwierigkeiten beim Schreiben der Wahrheit', *Text + Kritik*, 52 (1976), pp. 16–23; Theo Elm, 'Siegfried Lenz. Zeitgeschichte als moralisches Lehrstück', H. Wagener (ed.), *Gegenwartsliteratur und Drittes Reich: Deutsche Autoren in der Auseinandersetzung mit der Vergangenheit* (Stuttgart, 1977), pp. 222–40; Rudolf Wolff (ed.), *Siegfried Lenz: Werk und Wirkung*, Sammlung Profile 15 (Bonn, 1985).

zum ersten Mal als *Ich* den anderen gegenüber empfindet. . . . Auf einmal ist man herausgefallen aus der Gemeinschaft' ('But isn't it an extraordinary moment, you could almost call it an exemplary critical, even crisis moment, when one has to give up the comforting security of belief, and can no longer share it with others, when one first experiences one's individuality in relation to others. . . . Suddenly one finds that one has dropped out of the community').[2] Here, within the safe confines of someone else's reminiscences and sheltering behind the impersonal 'one', Lenz touches on a personal experience which must have been traumatic. Characteristically, he presents it as a moment of existential insight, a crisis of self-knowledge which comes to all men when they forsake the securities of childhood for the moral ambiguities and uncertainties of adult life. But from an autobiographical sketch *Ich zum Beispiel. Kennzeichen eines Jahrgangs* (1966) we know that, for Lenz, this experience was located in a specific historical context: the young Lenz's realisation that the values of the National Socialist *Gemeinschaft* were flawed, that obedience to the totalitarian collective did not absolve him from individual responsibility. Lenz's flight from history, his abnegation of social involvement, is itself socially and historically conditioned. This tendency is frequently observed among writers of Lenz's generation who embarked on literary careers in the 1950s, an understandable reaction in a generation which believed that the National Socialist collective had let it down. The wholesale repudiation of history, politics and ideology is a hallmark of West German writing in the 1950s. But what is interesting about Lenz's novels is that for all his avoidance of history, for all his insistence that the great themes of literature in general and his own in particular are 'die Motive von Fall, Flucht und Verfolgung, von Gleichgültigkeit, Auflehnung und verfehlter Lebensgründung' ('the motifs of man's fall, flight, persecution, of indifference, rebellion and lives founded on false values'),[3] he is himself always drawn back to project these universal, existential conflicts into specific historical contexts which do not so much exemplify the universal as call it into question. Existential theme and historical context diverge in Lenz's fictional world and it is this divergence which accounts for the unease of some of his critics.

Lenz's all too brief autobiographical document *Ich zum Beispiel* may serve as a convenient starting-point for an investigation of this problem. It was written over twenty years after the experiences

2. Alfred Mensak (ed.), *Siegfried Lenz. Gespräche mit Manès Sperber und Leszek Kolakowski* (Hamburg, 1980), p. 25.

3. S. Lenz, *Beziehungen. Ansichten und Bekenntnisse zur Literatur* (Hamburg, 1970), p. 41.

which it describes and embodies his first tentative approach to the experience of National Socialism in a non-fictional mode. Significantly, it immediately predates Lenz's first literary treatment of the experience in *Deutschstunde* (1968), the first of Lenz's novels to be set unambiguously in the recognisable historical context of National Socialism in Germany. In his autobiographical essay Lenz briefly recalls his East Prussian childhood among the lakes of what is now Polish Masuria. He describes his progression through the various Nazi youth organisations, his call-up to the navy at the age of seventeen, his war experiences, his desertion, internment and release, and finally his progression via journalism to a literary career. What is striking about Lenz's evocation of his childhood is what he opts to leave out. There are three cursory references to a grandmother, as a source of Masurian folklore and fairytale, but not a single reference to a mother and only one oblique reference to a father, relegated to a subordinate clause: 'die Beamten, zu denen auch mein Vater gehörte, waren gedankenlos in ihren Rollen ergraut' ('the civil servants, of which my father was one, had grown unthinkingly old and grey in their roles').[4] Family warmth, affection, love are conspicuously absent. If we turn to Lenz's novels and short stories we may note that this complex of family relationships, particularly the role of the father, becomes a central concern. His father figures, from *Duell mit dem Schatten* (1953) to *Exerzierplatz* (1985) are stern, remote, frequently authoritarian and curiously imbued with a patriarchal power which brooks no contradiction. Father–son relationships are invariably problematic: fathers fail to offer the example which sons may emulate; sons fail to live up to their fathers' expectations. There is often a desperate need for love and trust, but it usually remains unspoken. The last lines of the novel *Der Mann im Strom* (1957) offer a characteristic illustration:

> Ich habe auf dich gewartet, Vater, sagte Timm.
> Ja, Junge, sagte der Mann.
> Ich möchte dich immer abholen, Vater.
> Ja, mein Junge, sagte der Mann, ja'.
>
> ('I waited for you, father,' said Timm.
> 'Yes, my boy,' said the man.
> 'I'd like to meet you from work always, father.'
> 'Yes, my boy,' said the man, 'yes'.)[5]

4. Ibid., p. 12.
5. *Der Mann im Strom* (Hamburg, 1957), p. 222.

The archetypal, existential figures of 'the father' and 'the boy' appear to share a simple affection, yet what the father cannot say is that he has just been sacked for falsifying his age to obtain work, for making himself younger than he really is. Hence the boy will never again be able to meet him from work. The complex social and economic realities underlying the situation are passed over in silence, for they must not be allowed to intrude into the childlike world of simple trust. Even in this portrayal of a reasonably successful father–son relationship — and this is the exception rather than the rule in Lenz's *oeuvre* — the social reality and the existential pattern fail to coincide.

Relations between the sexes in Lenz's work are also illuminated by a passage in *Ich zum Beispiel*, in which he recalls his first love, a relationship cemented by a common interest in sport and set against the background of the National Socialist youth movement. This relationship taught him 'daß es eine Zuneigung aus Pflicht geben kann' ('that there is such a thing as affection from a sense of duty').[6] Lenz has drawn his own conclusions about the significance of that early experience, explaining his reluctance to deal with his own youth as a reaction to that first love. One of the consequences for Lenz's fictional world is that love, where it exists at all, survives only in conflict with duty or social pressure. This is the reverse side of a rigorous Kantian morality: for Kant duty is recognisable only where it is in conflict with inclination; a moral act is moral only to the extent that all inclination is precluded. For Lenz, reversing the emphasis while retaining the scheme, inclination can only be recognised as such where it is in conflict with duty. Marriage, by this radical definition, practically precludes love, for love can only be recognised as such if it exists outside the rigid, restrictive framework of social responsibility. Although he traces his uncertainty back to a personal experience, Lenz shares his profound suspicion of society, and with it of all socially sanctioned relationships, with other post-war writers, in particular Heinrich Böll. Love is located in an absolute realm of childlike simplicity, uncontaminated by the dubious complexity of social life. The pattern is illustrated amply in Lenz's early short stories, but it survives into his later novels. In *Der Verlust* (1981) Nora begins to commit herself to Uli only after he has been deprived of speech after a stroke, when he has been rejected by his family and by society. Significantly, Uli's regression, through illness, to a childlike state in which he is incapable of communicating complex responses is accompanied by a new-found emotional

6. *Beziehungen*, p. 26.

richness.

Given that Lenz associates the world of childhood with innocence and adulthood with a Rousseauistic growing away from innocence, then it is no surprise to find him particularly concerned with the period of transition between childhood and adulthood. His account, in *Ich zum Beispiel* of his own transition is particularly informative. His early experience of life in the navy was, we are given to understand, still charged with youthful enthusiasm, with total commitment to the values of the society in which he lived, with unquestioning belief in the justness of the cause. Retrospectively, at least, it was the Stauffenberg plot of 20 July 1944 which sounded the first jarring note in this previously harmonious world: 'Ich erfuhr zum ersten Mal, daß man ihm [Hitler] widersprach — also gab es nicht das Wunder eines kollektiven Gehorsams. Man hatte ihm hier und da das Vertrauen entzogen; das schien mir sehr bedeutungsvoll' ('I learned for the first time that Hitler had been contradicted — and hence that there was no such thing as the miracle of collective obedience. Some people somewhere had withdrawn their trust; all that seemed to me most significant').[7] This is at once an astonishing and an honest reaction. Its implications, if we unravel them, are revealing. For the young Lenz, the mere fact that one person does not participate in the Führer-myth shatters the illusion and breaks the spell. The corollary is equally clear: if everyone had continued to accept Hitler's authority, then the stability of Lenz's world would have been maintained. The Stauffenberg plot hurled the young sailor — Lenz was just over eighteen in July 1944 — out of his childhood, out of his childlike, indeed childish, belief in a world devoid of conflict, a world in which all shared the same values and assumptions, into an adult world of moral choice, of individual responsibility. Lenz never questioned at that stage the right or wrong of National Socialist policies; he never contemplated opposition to them; he never, indeed, expressed even the vaguest misgivings, despite his active participation in naval operations. All he recalls is his shocking realisation that we do not live in a fairy-tale world of absolutes but in a world of moral ambiguity and political choice. He did not, he recalls, make any choice himself at that point, but from that moment on he knew that choice was possible, even inevitable.

Naturally, there is a problem here which applies to all autobiographical statements: there can be no guarantee that Lenz's reactions in 1944 actually took this precise form, except in his

7. Ibid., p. 30.

recollection. What is beyond dispute is that in 1966 he elected to describe his experiences in this form and that in so doing he articulated a pattern of response which is implicitly present in his fictional work from its earliest beginnings. That pattern is an ahistorical, existential one, predicated upon the assumption of childhood innocence and subsequent adult guilt. Such guilt is not, for Lenz, associated with a specific crime; it is built into the very order of existence itself. It must be sharply distinguished from historical responsibility for the crimes of National Socialism. Indeed, the existential pattern and the historical situation into which it is projected are disturbingly at variance. The world of childhood innocence coincides with the historical experience of National Socialism, while the acquisition of adult guilt is equated with an awareness of the opposition to National Socialism. Puzzling as this antinomy may appear, it possesses a certain historical and psychological verisimilitude for that generation of which Lenz saw himself as being representative. For many of this generation (which in turn no doubt constitutes at least a part of Lenz's readership) the acquisition of guilt, the awareness of guilt, was indeed retrospective: the full enormity of the crimes of National Socialism became apparent only after the defeat of Germany. Nevertheless, Lenz's nostalgia for a childhood world, his evident hankering after rootedness in a community of shared values, runs counter to the social and historical realities of his own experience. It is difficult to present the innocence of a National Socialist childhood, dangerous to associate opposition to totalitarianism with guilt. But this is precisely Lenz's dilemma and it is that which makes his attempted solutions so intriguing. For that generation of German writers who were born in the late 1920s and consequently spent all their conscious childhood and adolescence under National Socialism, a Proustian lost time of childhood proves particularly difficult to evoke.

In his first novel *Es waren Habichte in der Luft* (1951) Lenz's reflections on guilt, responsibility and oppression are located in that part of Finland which was ceded to the Soviet Union after the First World War and set immediately after a Communist take-over. While it seemed to promise consideration of the totalitarian past in Germany, the novel could also readily be interpreted as a contribution to the cold war politics of the early 1950s. *Duell mit dem Schatten* (1953), the only one of Lenz's novels no longer in print, is set in Libya, where a former German colonel attempts to come to terms with his wartime crime of changing identities with another man and thereby condemning him to certain death. This historical burden (which proves impossible to redeem) is matched by an existential dilemma (which is resolved). The colonel's daughter, Biggi — a name to be echoed later in *Deutschstunde* in the name Siggi, the diminutive of Lenz's own name — escapes from her father's authoritarian control and finds refuge with two sympathetic Englishmen. When, in the 1960s, Lenz moved to a more explicit confrontation with the German past, it was on moral and existential choice that the emphasis lay. Significantly, neither the play *Zeit der Schuldlosen* (1961) nor the novel *Stadtgespräch* (1963) are clearly located in a recognisable social and historical context: the former takes place outside a specific time under a nameless totalitarian regime, while the latter, although moving closer to a historical setting, is located in an unnamed Scandinavian country under German occupation. It is revealing that Lenz preferred to approach the problems of moral choice under a dictatorship in a highly parabolic dramatic form rather than in the novel, which potentially offers the greater scope for a differentiated historical and social setting. *Stadtgespräch*, despite its narrative form, has much in common with the kind of dramatised parable which Lenz favoured in the 1960s under Sartre's influence.

In *Stadtgespräch* the central character, Tobias must, if he is to continue to support the resistance, countenance the sacrifice of a large group of hostages (including his own father) rather than betray his leader, Daniel. To act politically Tobias must jeopardise personal and family ties. Under a dictatorship Lenz opts to present political opposition as involving personal guilt, with the disquieting corollary that innocence may only be preserved at the price of political acquiescence. Tobias's father is a remote, severe character, in keeping with Lenz's father figures; he fully accepts the political necessity of his own death and thus effectively absolves Tobias, despite his agonising, from responsibility. It is striking that the only member of the resistance who enjoys a close relationship with his father, even to the extent that they share the same mistress, should turn out to be a traitor to the resistance. What Tobias learns, for he finds himself characteristically on the borderline between childhood and adulthood, is that innocence does not exist. But his guilt does not emerge as the result of a specific choice; it is given by the situation itself, imposed by an outside agency. It is less the nature of totalitarianism or the scope for political choice which is central to *Stadtgespräch* than the relationship between a son and various competing authority figures.

The enormous success which Lenz achieved in 1968 with *Deutschstunde* in which he examined for the first time specific issues of National Socialism in a recognisable, if somewhat isolated, social setting, was not unconnected with the way in which an existential pattern was superimposed on a historical framework with which it was not congruent. But Lenz's predilection for childhood innocence struck a chord in the experience of a post-war generation of readers which seemed intent on confronting the image of Germany represented by its fathers. Indeed, it is tempting to speculate whether *Deutschstunde* could have been so successful if it had appeared any earlier than 1968. The combination of a generation problem and the Nazi past proved irresistible to a generation who felt little or no personal responsibility for the German past. The hero, Siggi, is torn between two father figures: the natural father Jepson, the policeman and local instrument of totalitarian authority on the one hand, and the surrogate father, the artist Max Ludwig Nansen, on the other. Nansen is loosely modelled on the Expressionist painter Emil Nolde, born Emil Hansen, but his name is a conflation of the name Hansen with those of other Expressionists, Max Beckmann (or Max Pechstein) and Ernst Ludwig Kirchner. The choice for Siggi is not between one kind of politics and another but between duty and inclination, between a Nazi disciplinarian and a humane artist. Siggi's opposition to his father involves the acquisition of guilt on two separate and unrelated counts: opposition to the father suggests existential or Oedipal guilt; but by making Siggi's father the instrument of Nazi control, Lenz finds himself implying that opposition to National Socialism involves criminality. There is no hint of recognition that to oppose a criminal system might be morally less culpable. So successfully has Siggi internalised the values of National Socialism that for him existential and moral guilt seem indistinguishable.

By locating the alternative to National Socialism in a humane artist Lenz oversimplifies the issues. The humane values represented by Nansen in the novel are shown to be proof against the blandishments and bullying of the regime. The doubtful claim that the artist is somehow more humane, more worthy of emulation, than ordinary mortals is a beguiling one, and one moreover which is rooted in the German tradition of *Humanität*. Art represents a realm in which social, political, even moral, concerns are transcended. It is not difficult to see why Lenz should present the conflict in such a way: the Nazis condemned Expressionist art as 'degenerate', and therefore the Expressionist artist, irrespective of his political views, can become a convenient symbol of opposition to National Socialism. Siggi is faced with a dilemma which is too neatly circumscribed. One is tempted to speculate what moral complexities might have emerged if Lenz had portrayed a son who genuinely loved a National Socialist father, or a son who hated a father who was opposed to the regime.

The German lesson which Lenz himself appears to want to pass on to his readers is twofold: that the adult world is a complex moral world in which awkward problems have to be confronted; and that man can rely only upon himself for such decisions. All models, all ideologies become suspect, the individual is alone. Deprived of comforting ideologies man must make his own way in the world, silent and uncomplaining, discovering as he goes along the code which will govern his conduct. This severe code of self-reliance is an understandable response to the fallible ideologies of National Socialism and both explains and is shaped by the Hemingway cult of the immediate post-war period. Because submission to the national collective has proved so disastrous, its opposite, a rugged individualism tempered by vaguely humanistic values, seems to commend itself. The quest for a suitable father figure, one worthy of emulation, underlies Siggi's choice in *Deutschstunde*, but it is taken a step further in *Das Vorbild* (1973), in which three fallible educationalists try in vain to find a story for a school textbook depicting a model life. The hard lesson which they (and the readers) learn is that there are no reliable models. Neither the various suggestions made by the experts, nor their own personal lives, offer a solution: neither the conservative Valentin Pundt nor the radical Janpeter Heller can supply a recipe. Turning in this novel to a recognisable setting in contemporary West Germany, with its student protest and its rock concerts, Lenz restates the lessons arrived at in his earlier fiction.

It is not only the underlying thematic complex of Lenz's work in the 1950s and 1960s but also his style which reflects the unresolved tension between the existential and the historical. His reception of Hemingway may serve as a useful barometer of his changing views. In his essay 'Mein Vorbild Hemingway: Modell oder Provokation' (1966), Lenz himself drew attention both to his early dependence on Hemingway and to his decision to embark on a new mode, of which *Deutschstunde* was to be the first example. In his essay Lenz concedes that he was dependent on Hemingway for his central characters: the hunter, the anarchist, the runner. Hemingway adopts the persona of an uncomplicated narrator who records impressions successively in time, without submitting them to a process of selection, without subordinating the less significant to the more significant. Such a narrative perspective corresponds to his choice of hero: simple men, who work out their values successively, as they go along; men who take nothing for granted, who make no moral judgements, who do not reflect on their perceptions but accept them as given. In his writing up to the mid-1960s Lenz not only adopts the type of hero, but also the parataxis which corresponds to that mode of perception. Lenz's description of Hemingway's style could stand perfectly well as an analysis of his own intentions: 'Alle Wahrnehmungen des Schriftstellers werden unmittelbar, unverändert, ungefiltert mitgeteilt; Hemingway gibt streng darauf acht, jederzeit aus dem Spiel zu bleiben . . .' ('All the writer's perceptions are passed on directly, unchanged, unfiltered; Hemingway takes great pains never to become involved').[8] But by the mid-1960s Lenz appeared ready to discard his model; he no longer found Hemingway's medium suitable to express conflicts and problems which were becoming more pressing for him. He noted Hemingway's lack of historical perspective, his concentration on moments of existential crisis, but his neglect of less powerful experiences; above all, he felt that he should close his account with Hemingway because Hemingway's style had 'zu wenig Raum für Reflexion' ('too little space for reflection').[9] What emerges from Lenz's ambivalence about Hemingway is the uneasy co-existence within his own writing of two conflicting tendencies: the desire to present in a non-discursive, pared-down medium certain existential truths about life, and the need to reflect on the moral complexities of the past and to offer at least the appearance of a moral framework within which they can be viewed. While the former concern predominates in Lenz's work up to the mid-1960s, the latter has tended to become more pronounced since. In keeping with his growing concern to present the problems of the German past and their legacy in a recognisable social setting, Lenz has sought to renounce the spare, paratactic style in favour of a more reflective, differentiated treatment of complex human responses. Nevertheless, even Lenz's early prose exhibits moralising features which accord ill with the style into which they are pressed, and even in his novels of the late 1970s and 1980s echoes of Hemingway persist.

Lenz's nostalgia for the world of childhood and its attendant problems is the impetus behind the novel which followed *Das Vorbild*: *Heimatmuseum* (1978). Its narrator, Zygmunt Rogalla, helped to establish and administer a folk-museum in his Masurian home town of Lucknow; he first considers destroying the museum when the Nazis attempt to exploit it as a symbol of German culture; then after the war he salvages remnants of the museum and rebuilds it in Schleswig-Holstein, only to find that it is once again exploited as a political symbol of the lost territories. Rogalla's destruction of the

8. Ibid., p. 62.
9. Ibid., p. 63.

museum to preserve it from political misuse signals Lenz's own awareness of the dangers and delights of 'Heimat'. The Masurian world of his childhood belongs to an ahistorical order of experience; his nostalgia for that childhood, his projection of its innocence into a timeless Masurian idyll, evoked in the earlier collection of short stories *So zärtlich war Suleyken* (1955), stands in sharp contrast to the political and historical reality of the so-called lost territories. Like Rogalla, Lenz has himself adopted what could be termed a surrogate 'Heimat', a second home which he has evoked, equally indulgently, in a collection of short stories entitled *Der Geist der Mirabelle* (1975). But *Heimatmuseum*, perhaps even more than *Deutschstunde*, indicates that Lenz is highly sensitive to the questionable associations with which the term 'Heimat' (only inadequately rendered in English as 'homeland') has become burdened. The novel itself is a balancing act, for even as Lenz is asserting the political impossibility of regaining that lost Masurian world, even as the museum is burned down to prevent its misuse as a symbol, he permits Rogalla, in his narration of events, to conjure it up in loving detail, to regain it, as it were, within the safe confines of fiction. The novel is not merely *about* a 'Heimatmuseum'; with its evocative recreation of the customs and values of the past, it *becomes* a 'Heimatmuseum' in its own right.

The notion of transplanting a 'Heimat' from the lost territories to within the present boundaries of the Federal Republic is given physical reality in Lenz's latest novel: *Exerzierplatz* (1985): the seeds for the plantation established after the war on a disused military training camp by the Zellers, a refugee family from East Prussia, are transported with them from their former homeland. The East Prussian seeds take root in the soil of their adopted home and the family's fortunes flourish along with them, despite the trials and tribulations which beset them over the years. Much of the plot — tensions between outsiders and the local community, family quarrels and reconciliations, celebrations and set-backs — is the stuff of the conventional family saga. But, as if in tacit answer to this charge, Lenz introduces an element of formal sophistication by locating the narrative perspective in the consciousness of Bruno Messmer, a simpleton who was cruelly and irrevocably separated from his parents during the desperate flight westward in the last months of the war, was saved from drowning by the patriarchal head of the family and was given a home. Bruno's unquestioning allegiance to his surrogate father, his involvement in, yet detachment from, the life of the family, his hypersensitivity to detail, yet his inability to grasp intellectually the implications of what he sees so clearly, all these help to shape and colour his narrative. Bruno's traumatic childhood experience also enables Lenz to suggest that the spirits of the past are never entirely exorcised, that the pain of the refugee experience is never entirely forgotten. A recurrent motif, which links Bruno's relationship with the family to the broader issue of the family's fortunes, is that of property or ownership. The experience of displacement has given the 'Boss', Bruno's saviour, a profound awareness of the provisional nature of ownership, while the influx of refugees has forced the local community to adjust to new pressures. The neighbour Lauritzen is explicit: 'Bevor ihr gekommen seid, die Landplage aus dem Osten, da war es still hier, jeder wußte, was ihm gehörte, nie hatte sich einer vergriffen an fremdem Eigentum' ('Before you lot came, the plague from the east, it was a quiet spot here, everybody knew what belonged to him, nobody touched anyone else's property').[10] Zeller's son Max, who is the author of an academic treatise on the theory of property, seems, by contrast to his father, to have a highly developed sense of what belongs to him. It is Max who tells Bruno: 'Du gehörst doch zu uns, Bruno' ('But you belong to us, Bruno').[11] The estate itself formerly belonged to the army and there is a constant threat that it might be requisitioned anew to fulfil the requirements of a new military expansion, which permits Lenz the gentlest of hints of the threat posed to the natural environment by the war machine. The situation in which the narrative both opens and closes is one of a crisis in ownership: Zeller has decided to split up the estate and give a third to Bruno, prompting the family to unite in opposition and to have Zeller legally certified as incapable of managing his affairs. For Zeller, property should, it seems, be entrusted to those who are best able to care for it, a doctrine which clearly gives preference to plantations over training camps but which threatens to create mayhem with the accepted traditions of family inheritance. Once again, the political and the private spheres are at variance: what is a tolerant and humane justification of a highly provisional, custodial notion of property from a political point of view, becomes arbitrary, even destructive, when it is transposed to a personal plane. The novel does not offer a solution. Bruno, to preserve the unity of the family, is willing to forgo his inheritance, but the patriarch will have none of it. All that is left for Bruno is to flee an intolerable situation. The circumscribed world of a single family proves too restricted a framework for Lenz to explore adequately the complexity, social, political and historical, of the

10. *Exerzierplatz* (Hamburg, 1985), p. 267.
11. Ibid., p. 75.

refugee problem.

In a collection of literary essays and reflections entitled *Elfenbeinturm und Barrikade* (1983), Lenz chooses, as his title suggests, to operate with a series of contrasting word-pairs in an effort to define the nature and function of literature. He locates literature in a no man's land between commitment and detachment, between political and moral effectiveness and aesthetic ineffectualness, between concrete historical situations and timeless, archetypal experiences. Unexceptional as these views are, they help to define that problem which Lenz's narratives pose. For Lenz, art is the concrete universal, corresponding in his own fictional world to the specificity of the German historical experience and the existential truths which, in his view, transcend it. As we have seen, both these aspects are indeed found in Lenz's novels, but it is less their presence than their presentation which is at issue. The theory of the concrete universal assumes congruence, the universal embodied within the concrete, the concrete symbolising the universal. It is precisely this congruence which Lenz's work lacks. Concrete and universal, historical and existential, are merely co-present; not infrequently the implications of the one run counter to those of the other. This dissonance in Lenz's writing may be conveniently illustrated by one of his recurrent symbols, that of the wreck. From the short story *Das Wrack* onwards, the wreck acquires a universal meaning. In *Die Wracks von Hamburg*, a group of radio features written in the 1950s and published in 1978, Lenz is explicit about that universality: the wrecks which litter the port of Hamburg after the war remind man of 'die Verluste der Werke . . ., einst kühn konzipiert und dazu ausersehen unsere Hoffnungen übers Meer zu tragen' ('the loss of his works, once boldly conceived and destined to bear our hopes over the seas').[12] However, these particular symbols of man's hopes come to grief have a second meaning; they are tangible reminders of a specific historical experience. These wrecks, the same ones which figure in *Der Mann im Strom*, are simultaneously reminders of the dubious, but no less grandiose dreams of National Socialism. The universal symbol has a concrete, historical meaning with which it is disturbingly incompatible.

The co-presence of the universal and the historical in Lenz's work has undoubtedly conditioned its reception and contributed in no small measure to its enormous popularity. The fact that the dual aspects of his work might fail to coalesce may well be a literary

12. *Die Wracks von Hamburg* (Munich, 1982), p. 7. This is the paperback edition of he original volume published by Stalling (Oldenburg and Hamburg, 1978).

shortcoming, but it is one which has seldom proved an impediment to his readers. On the contrary, it goes some way towards explaining his appeal to readers of radically different temperaments and persuasions: those whose taste inclines to the political may, at least superficially, find their expectations gratified by the invitation to reflect on the dark side of the German past; while those who prefer their literature uncontaminated by politics may equally find solace in the implicit assumption of the universality of human experience.

ANTHONY PHELAN

Text of Neurosis: Neurosis of the Text. Towards the Later Work of Arno Schmidt

> Ich werde mich weiterhin bemühen, die über alle Maaßen befremdliche Ausdrucksweise meines Interlocuteurs fonetisch getreu wiederzugeben.
> (*Dr Mac Intosh*: 'PIPORAKEMES!')
>
> (I shall make every effort to give a fonetically faithful representation of my interlocutor's immeasurably alien mode of expression.)

Arno Schmidt's[1] mixed collection of short fiction and critical writing, *Trommler beim Zaren* (1966), includes a tiny account of his working conditions, and rather less of his methods, which ends with these remarks:

> Aus der Beschaffenheit solcher Neuigkeiten auf den hohen Grad der Unschuld & Einfalt meines pastoralen Wortmetz-Daseins-hier zu schließen, wäre jedoch voreilig. Unser Schicksal heißt Turbulenz; heißt 'kompliziert leben'; (und das, im Bewußtsein jedes gebildeten Lesers prompt erscheinende 'Einfach-leben' ist nur eine wehmütig-unrealistische Formel, über die man schon im späten Rom resigniert gelächelt haben dürfte.) Nach meinem Arbeitsplatz fragen Sie mich? Was ich will? Was ich bin? : Warten Sie, bis ich *nicht* mehr bin.
> ('Der Platz, an dem ich schreibe', *AjT*, 205)

> (To infer a high degree of innocence and simplicity in my pastoral existence here as a wordsmith from the character of such novelties would nevertheless be to anticipate. Our fate is turbulency; it is 'to live complicatedly'; (and the 'living simply' which appears promptly in the consciousness of every educated reader is no more than a melancholy unrealistic formula that people may well have smiled at with resignation in the late days of Rome). You ask about where I work? What I mean? What I am?
> : Wait until I no longer am.)

1. *The following editions and abbreviations are used in the text: *SH* = *Das steinerne Herz* (1956), Fischer Bücherei (fibü) 802, 1967; *Die Gelehrtenrepublik* (1957),

Schmidt clearly felt the enquiries of the literary *feuilletoniste* to be a considerable impertinence. But he did die, on 3 June 1979 at the age of sixty-five; and the fragment of his last work of fiction, of which one hundred pages had been completed when he had a stroke, *Julia, oder die Gemälde, Scenen aus dem Novecento*, was published by Schmidt's widow Frau Alice and Jan Peter Reemtsma in 1983. Perhaps it is no longer inappropriate to ask the impertinent questions 'Was ich will?' 'Was ich bin?' — what Arno Schmidt wanted, intended, *meant*; and who he was. But it may even now be overhasty to attempt to describe — in any larger sense — the 'place where he worked', let alone the place *of* his work in German writing since the war.

Possible answers to these last two questions will inevitably converge. When asked to describe where he wrote, Schmidt himself provided a punctilious description, both topographical and mathematical, of the room in which and the desk at which he worked. Coquettishly, but far from irrelevantly, he goes on to list the main constituents of his working library, some seventy volumes in all of which about one half is permanent. In a very important sense, the 1854 edition of *Webster's Dictionary*, *Britannica*, *Muret-Sanders*, the *Thesaurus logarithmorum*, the Hanoverian state handbook for 1839 (used as a source of names), and many other volumes to which reference is constantly — if obliquely — made in Schmidt's writing ('Cooper, Wieland, Jean Paul: Moritzcervantestieckundsoweiter. Schopenhauerlogarithmentafeln', as Schmidt confesses in 'Die Umsiedler' (*R&P* 113)) all constitute the place where he worked; a bibliomaniacal realm of hopelessly catholic textuality. The journal devoted to the study of Schmidt's fictions, the *Bargfelder Bote* (Bargfeld Courier), has set out to reconstruct this field of reference through collective labour in a manner reminiscent of the work on Joyce undertaken by the *Newslitter*, or on Ezra Pound by *Paideuma*. This specialised research, set on foot by the publication of Schmidt's monstrous novel *Zettels Traum* (=Bottom's/Jottings' Dream) (1970)

---

fibü 685, 1965; *R & P* = *Rosen & Porree* (1959), which includes the texts published as *Seelandschaft mit Pocahontas*, fibü 719, 1966; *NDK* = *Nobodaddy's Kinder*, Rowohlt Paperback (23), 1963; *KAFF* = *KAFF, auch mare crisium* (1960), fibü 1080, 1970; pagination is identical; *Orpheus*, fibü 1133, 1970 = texts from *Kühe in Halbtrauer* (1964); *AjT* = *Aus julianischen Tagen* (an anthology of Schmidt's criticism), fibü 1926, 1977; *zettel* = *Zettels Traum*, 1970; *SdA* = *Die Schule der Atheisten*, 1972; *AmG* = *Abend mit Goldrand*, 1975; *Julia, oder die Gemälde*, 1983. These are all cited in the standard editions of the Fischer Verlag, with the exception of the last which was published by the Haffmanns Verlag for the Arno-Schmidt-Stiftung.

I use the slash (/) to give some indication of Schmidt's double meanings, *double entendres*, and ambiguities, often represented by the simultaneous presence of distinct phonemes in the same position in a word — usually above and below each other.

in the early 1970s, is fascinating, immensely detailed, and in a curious way ultimately irrelevant. When Schmidt's narrator in the story 'Seelandschaft mit Pocahontas' of 1959 remarks 'also iss scholarship wenigstens zu etwas gut; Gundling' ('at least it's good for something') he merely and wryly acknowledges the exploitation of his astronomical knowledge ('nuntius sidereus') in a suggestive remark about an eclipse of Venus. (For instance, somewhere in the course of my own recent reading of *Die Schule der Atheisten* the phrase 'ni vu ni connu' was recognisable as a quotation from Valéry's collection *Charmes*, but that detail[2] *in itself* does not throw much light on the connotations of voyeurism and anagrammatic/engrammatic sexuality ('con nu' — geddit?) for which the fragment of Valéry's poem about a bee was quoted in the first place.) It will not finally be possible to place Schmidt's writing without the knowledge of his sources which the *Bargfelder Bote* is gradually accumulating,[3] but in the last resort his scholasticism, his recourse to original texts of great obscurity, his reliance on allusion, and the almost infinite interference by prior texts in his own writing, will remain part of the problem that it presents and not its solution.

The question which can be answered — in one way, at least — more easily after Schmidt's death, as he seems to have predicted in *Trommler beim Zaren*, is 'who am I?' In the time since his death Schmidt has emerged, however uncertainly and contestedly, as a classic. Even after the completion of his longest and most complex novel before *Zettels Traum*, *KAFF, auch mare crisium* (1960), otherwise far-sighted and distinguished surveys of the novel in the Federal Republic made no reference to his work[4] and it was only very recently that the Haffmanns Verlag published for the Arno Schmidt Foundation (AS-Stiftung) a collection of reviews of his work (*Über Arno Schmidt*)[5] of the kind which many obviously lesser authors had acquired, particularly in the *edition suhrkamp* series, long before. It is the uncertainty of Schmidt's status that is suggested by Jörg Drews, one of his most brilliant and resourceful exponents, in a 1968 article which described Schmidt and *KAFF, auch mare crisium* as 'erratic blocks' in contemporary literature.[6] This phrase serves to suggest both Schmidt's eccentricity and even isolationism in the landscape of Ger-

2. See Michael Minden's excellent study *Arno Schmidt* (Cambridge, 1982) in which 'detail' becomes a technical term (pp. 131ff.).

3. Cf. Minden, *Schmidt* p. 251.

4. E.g. R.H. Thomas and W. van der Will, *The German Novel and the Affluent Society* (Manchester, 1968).

5. Hans-Michael Bock (ed.), *Über Arno Schmidt* (Zürich, 1984).

6. 'Thesen und Notizen zu "KAFF"', *Text + Kritik*, 20 (1968), p. 28.

man fiction since the war, and the sheer bulk of his work itself. Nevertheless, that work has been distinguished and influential. Schmidt was awarded a number of important literary prizes — though scarcely ever without an atmosphere of controversy surrounding the award; and his earlier work in particular has left its mark on two generations of writers, from Günter Grass and Martin Walser to Uwe Timm.[7] With very few exceptions among twentieth-century authors, this admiration was not mutual; and Schmidt's rare comments on contemporaries merge with his lived role as outsider on the Lüneburger Heide, as when, in a rare interview, he responded to a question about Walser, Grass, and Uwe Johnson with the remark: 'Yes, I know one or two books by each of them. But if I have to make a judgement, then in the *pluralis majestatis* I must say: We are not amused' (the last phrase in English in the original).[8]

The scarcely concealed hostility of this remark does not quite characterise Schmidt's attitudes to all his contemporaries (or predecessors) in the twentieth century. Clues about his preferences, and indeed about the foundational texts of his own writing can be found in the radio essay 'Goethe and one of his admirers' published in the collection *Dya Na Sore* (its title not a creative misspelling of dinosaur, but a reference to a — typically obscure — novel of the late eighteenth century) in 1958. In 'Goethe . . .', the great classic comes back from the dead and the competition to decide who is to interview him during his twenty-four-hour stay is won by none other than Arno Schmidt. At the end of the stipulated period Schmidt gives a press conference, a protocol of which is provided at the end of the essay. This account of Goethe's (i.e. *Schmidt's*) assessment of modern literature is of course polemical — the writers of whom Goethe is said to have approved are given as a list of cyphers: 'D, J, AA, MB (the filosofer), me (general moans and laughter)'. All of these figures are now identifiable, though the guessing-game which Schmidt constructs is characteristic of his self-image as a *poeta doctus* who expects a similar (and perhaps even identical) cultural range of reference in his readers. Further, each of these figures suggests one dimension of Schmidt's writing: Döblin, Joyce, Alfred Andersch, Max Bense.

Of these Andersch, a lifelong friend as their recently published correspondence confirms, clearly stands for a commitment to down-

7. See Günter Grass, *Frankfurter Vorlesungen* (Cologne, 1966), p. 87 and Karl Schumann, 'Dichtung oder Bluff. Arno Schmidt in der deutschen Gegenwartsliteratur', J. Drews & H.M. Bock (eds.) *Der Solipsist in der Heide* (Munich, 1974).

8. *Spiegel* interview with Gunar Ortlepp, 20 April 1970, p. 226.

to-earth narrative, and for the German flirtation with existentialism after 1945. But to clarify that context, it is worth adding one other name to this constellation. The same protocol also lists journals preferred by 'Goethe' and at the top of this list comes the 'Studentenkurier (Hamburg)', which eventually became the leftist/-ish magazine *konkret.* I add this indication because it can serve to establish Schmidt's (not uncontested) position to the left of centre in the 1950s.[9] The admiration expressed here for the *Studentenkurier* was mutual on the part of at least one of its early editors, and of those of one of its journalistic predecessors, the hectographic *Zwischen den Kriegen* (Between the Wars — the title bitterly ironic in the early 1950s). Editorially involved with both publications was the poet Peter Rühmkorf whose 'Variations on a theme of Klopstock' from his first collection *Irdisches Vergnügen in g* offers a specific tribute to Schmidt's role in the construction of an anti-restoration ideology in the 1950s:

> Schulau: der Abend mit silbernem Kamm im Haar,
> wenig Erkenntnis und kaum noch Veränderung
> nur das verdorbene Herz,
> das seine Synkopen hackt;
>
> nur dies Herz, und ein instabiles,
> grobes Gefühl in der Brust, der hochgemöbelte Ursprung:
> und wir sangen hinter dem Segel
> und empfanden wie Schmidt.
> (Schmidt, Arno; Bargfeld, Kreis Celle).[10]

(Schulau: the evening with a silver comb in its hair,/ little knowledge and hardly any change now/ only the ruined heart,/ that hacks out its syncopations;/ only this heart, and an unstable,/ coarse feeling in the breast, the overfurnished origin:/ and we sang behind the sail,/ having feelings like Schmidt's).

The footnote is Rühmkorf's own of course, and it wittily indicates his own *parti pris*: a 'Schmidt' could represent the feelings of any Tom Dick or Harry, but 'Schmidt, Arno' in Bargfeld brings a recognisable precision to such emotions as a *radicalisation* of the everyday. In the larger context of this poem Schmidt's appearance is very striking. Rühmkorf's variations transpose to the environs of Hamburg and into the 1950s Klopstock's 'ode of friendship' on Lake

9. See also Dieter Kuhn, *Das Mißverständnis. Polemische Überlegungen zum politischen Standort Arno Schmidts*, Munich (Bargfelder Bote Sonderhefte) 1982.

10. Peter Rühmkorf, *Wer Lyrik schreibt ist verrückt* (Reinbek, 1976), p. 24.

Zurich, 'Der Zürchersee' of 1750. The result is a systematic substitution of human consciousness and artifice for Klopstock's transcendentally apostrophised 'Mother Nature', who is finally replaced by a celebration of the material, represented in the text by *gravity*. Read against the Klopstock model parodied here, Schmidt replaces another writer in the original line 'Und empfanden, wie Hagedorn'. Schmidt the modern materialist replaces the Anacreontic author of the eighteenth century; but as Rühmkorf's punctuation insists, Schmidt provides not just a similar articulation of a 'structure of feeling', but rather an exemplar for the 'coarse feelings' of the 'ruined heart'. The sympathy Rühmkorf expresses here (and which, as 'Goethe und einer seiner Bewunderer' shows, was evidently reciprocated) is clarified in a very perceptive early assessment of Schmidt's writing published in 1955 by Rühmkorf's close friend (and collaborator on *Zwischen den Kriegen*) Werner Riegel. Towards the end of 'Arno Schmidt. Porträt eines Dichters' he remarks that Schmidt 'feels himself indebted — today! — to minds which have long since been finished off in public opinion, controlled as it is by counter-forces. Schmidt's desperate humour, his scepticism without illusions knows the undiminished value of those condemned doctrines ["verfemte Philosopheme"] and of their ability to change the world; . . .'[11] This summary highlights a sense that Schmidt's writing, in the 1950s at any rate, was resistant to the controlling forces of the restoration in the Federal Republic against which it presented a humour and scepticism which drew on the thought and style of much earlier authors from the eighteenth and early nineteenth centuries — scholarship *is* good for something 'at least'!

Riegel's critical essays of the 1950s were an attempt to constitute the alternative literary canon which had been suppressed or repressed during the Third Reich and which, with the establishment of the Federal Republic within a realigned Europe, would not necessarily see the light of day again. It is important that Schmidt's critical enterprise, especially in his work for radio, had a similar purpose, within the much larger range he allowed himself since the eighteenth century; but Riegel's almost intuitive grasp of Schmidt's work was aided by his own appeal to the typically German variety of the avant-garde which had been Expressionism. (For Riegel and Rühmkorf the leading figure here is Gottfried Benn.)[12] Drews has written of the sympathy for early Expressionist style, and in parti-

11. Werner Riegel, *Gedichte und Prosa* (Wiesbaden, 1961), p. 34.
12. Compare also Rühmkorf's Wagenbach anthology, *131 expressionistische Gedichte*, (Berlin, 1976).

cular for the work of August Stramm, in Schmidt's early work.[13] One of the most celebrated examples of a style derived from Expressionist experimentation is the account of an Allied bombing raid on a German munitions factory ('die Eibia') near the end of the 'short novel' *Aus dem Leben eines Fauns* (1953):

> *Eine glühende Leiche* fiel schmachtend vor mir auf die Knie, und brachte ihr qualmendes Ständchen; ein. Arm flackerte noch und schmorte keck: mitten aus der Luft war sie gekommen, "Vom Himmel hoch", die Marienerscheinung. (Die Welt war überhaupt voll davon: wenn wieder ein Dach hochklappte, schossen sie von den Simsen wie Taucher, gehelmt oder mit nacktem Haar, flogen ein bißchen, und platzten unten wie Tüten. In Gottes Bubenhand!)
>
> *Aus Rubinglas* pulste eine Feueraktinie in döblinener Waldung, schwankte huldvoll mit hundert Armtrossen . . .
>
> (*NDK*, 82)

The Expressionist elements in this style — and in a passage which has been thought inhuman for the enthusiasm with which it registers death and destruction — derive both from the apocalyptic nature of the subject matter which, within the limits of prose, recalls some of the imagery of Georg Heym in the chiaroscuro of flames against the darkness; and from the intense registration of perception through the manipulation of language. The burning corpse flung through the air by successive explosions falls 'on its knees' to offer its 'smokey serenade ('qualmendes Ständchen'), while 'an arm still flickered and cheekily braised: it/she came out of thin air, "From Heaven on high", an appearance of Mary' ('ein Arm flackerte noch und schmorte keck: mitten aus des Luft war sie gekommen, "Vom Himmel hoch", die Marienerscheinung'). Such highly metaphorical writing, with its bizarre imagery and apparently random allusion to the Lutheran chorale, is offered as a direct transcription of the processes of perception and consciousness in the narrating subject. (Ultimately the phrase from the carol is *not* irrelevant, but part of an anti-christian polemic, as the last phrase — something like 'In the rascally hand of God' ('In Gottes Bubenhand') — makes clear.) Each paragraph of this description offers a unit of perception, given in the italicised slogan opening each section, to which further details of memory accrue; and the pattern of offset italics in the lefthand margin typifies the typographical 'look' of Schmidt's fictions up to the time of *KAFF, auch mare crisium*. The Expressionist style can go

13. Jörg Drews in *Text + Kritik*, 20a (1977). *SdA* 221 still puts a premium on Expressionism at the expense of d'Annunzio.

beyond such intense use of metaphor, however, to a direct manipulation of the linguistic material whose most obvious predecessor is Stramm. Thus in the second paragraph quoted here the burning figure is first registered as '[Made] from ruby glass' and pulsing as a 'Feueraktinie'. This last is the kind of usage which might be called, following Schmidt, a word-concentrate. It appears to have three elements in a successively more complicated combination. The first impression is the fire ('Feuer–'), which is next seen as a posed nude figure ('–akt–') in the terminology of painting or photography, before it is finally transformed, through the suffix '–tinie', into a flower which blooms against a specifically 'Döblinesque' woodland. The acknowledgement of the master recalls for the reader Döblin's experiments in montage and collage in the stream of consciousness style of his *Berlin Alexanderplatz*, for instance; but these examples of a technical recourse to Expressionist and high naturalist style scarcely suffice to account for the general ideological enthusiasm expressed by Werner Riegel.

In reality there can never be anything easy or automatic about such 'logopoeia'; the narrative voice of *Das steinerne Herz* (1956) is pleased to note '*Clock in fingerjags* (word distillation working again. Filled with all kinds of twilights)' (*SH*, 13). The appropriately dense registration and transcription of perception is always precarious, and the half-lights of its ambiguities strenuously transcribe the vocal effects that characterise the desperate humour of the ironic pessimist recognised by Riegel. This quality of resistance in Schmidt's writing is inherent in his constant (and increasing) willingness to extend and disrupt conventional orthography, punctuation, and, ultimately, typography, in the interests of a naturalism so obsessively truthful that it must function as a critique of other representations of the human world, and of the controlling language (and language *of* control) in which they are expressed. Speech is itself a break with such conventions, as in this example from the opening of *KAFF, auch mare crisium*: '"*Von was lebst'nn Du?!*" forderte sie brutal . . . auch ich muß lebenslänglich Schtriche ziehen: sogenannte "Grafische Lagerbuchhaltung": ei*ei*eieiei! ('"*Whad'you liv'on, 'enn?!*" she asked brutally . . . I draw lines for a lifetime too: so-called "graphic stock-control": o*dear*odearodear!') (*KAFF*, 9).

The phonetic realisation of 'St' in 'Schtriche' and the marvellously precise registration of the final exclamation here as an ironic commentary on the unspeakable officialese of a job description, both allow the voice of everyday speech to move in on the official forms in which it is normally transcribed. This sensitivity to language — as spoken and as transcribed — is a universal feature of Schmidt's work after the earliest post-war stories, *Leviathan* (1949); it is seen in its simplest form when Schmidt's characters encounter verse writing. Thus in the (post-)catastrophe novel *Schwarze Spiegel* (1963) the narrator celebrates his companion's birthday (after the Third World War) with quotations from Homer (*NDK*, 220). The passage includes a transcription of the Greek of Homer alongside Voß's wonderful version: just this contrast emphasises the importance of linguistic realisation, and so provides an acute example of the critical disjunction between speech and writing which underlies Schmidt's naturalism throughout his *oeuvre* (for the resolution of Germanic stress into — or out of — classical quantity has been a recurrent locus of the discrepancy between speech and writing from Klopstock's theory and practice in the eighteenth century onwards). Elsewhere the distortions imposed by verse can reveal the linguistic bankruptcy of a whole culture when the pleonasm of 'the sound of the played piano' in the line 'denn der Klang des gespielten Klavieres' provokes the response '(Weiß Gott! "gespielten Klavieres"; wir sind gerichtet!)' (*Leviathan*, 54f.).

Schmidt's constant awareness of the deformations to which written language constantly subjects our perceptions and our self-expression makes his most common narrative tone an active critique. The clearest statement of this tendency in his work appears in a footnote attributed to the fictional 'translator' of his novel *Die Gelehrtenrepublik* (The Egg-Head Republic) (1957) into the now (because, once again, post-Third World War) dead German language. At note fifty-two we read: 'Oder gehört [der Verfasser] zu jener unglücklichen Menschenklasse, die sich Objektivität und Freiheit des Urteils durch beständige Schnoddrigkeiten erringen muß (weil sie sonst jedem Einfluß erliegen würde)?'(Or does [the author] belong to that unhappy class of men who can only achieve objectivity and freedom of judgement by constant impudence (because they would otherwise fall prey to any and every influence)?) (*Gelehrtenrepublik* 85). What Schmidt's irritable 'translator' in the *Gelehrtenrepublik* calls 'Schnoddrigkeiten' is glossed in the same note as a constitutional lack of respect ('von Natur aus unehrerbietig'); and it is this bloody-minded downrightness, revelling in its own crass realism, which joins his Expressionist style to generate the coarse and crude feelings of 'the ruined heart' to which Rühmkorf's poem refers. The resistant rhetoric of 'Schnoddrigkeit' can disarm and unmask any dishonest or high-flown use of language. In *Das steinerne Herz* for example the straight talking of '"[einen] Kopf größer als er; Plattfüße; Arme wie Beine; Schultern wie ein Schrank: Ammentitten" (sie sagte das gröbliche Wort so unschuldig wie man eine Nadel einfädelt . . .)' ('"Taller than him by a head; flat feet; arms like legs; shoulders like a wardrobe: tits like a wet nurse" (she uttered the coarse word as innocently as one threads a needle . . .)') (*SH*, 90) almost provokes the utterly implausible East German radio report from Poland that 'anläßlich des Besuches einer Bergarbeiter-Delegation spontane Ausbrüche deutsch-polnischer Freundschaft gemeldet' ('because of the visit of a miners' delegation, reports of spontaneous outbursts of German–Polish friendship'). The false triumphalism of the propaganda announcement is anticipated in parody by the calculated vulgarity of the first quotation. Similarly in *Brand's Haide* (1951) we hear anecdotally of an acquaintance 'who could make the phrase "Parerga and Paralipomena" sound like the filthiest thing you've ever heard' (*NDK* 107). In such ways Schmidt's insubordinate, impudent 'Schnoddrigkeit' offers a resistant and critical version of German as a *plain style* which can bring down the 'haute volée' of intellectual snobbery by making it a heavy-weight '*hoher Flug*' (*literally* a high flight!).

It is this style which is certainly the most memorable aspect of Schmidt's fiction, and in some large-scale way it is related to (and in part derived from) both the linguistic experiments of the Expressionists and the possibilities of shifting focus within the stream of consciousness developed by Döblin. The foundation for this Expressionist style is laid, in Schmidt's own account, by his extended reflections on the theory of prose and prose forms published in the two essays 'Berechnungen I & II' (1955 & 1956). Here the claim is made that the 'classical' prose forms, created at the latest by the end of the eighteenth century, without exceptions reflect 'sociological habits' ('soziologische Gepflogenheiten') of a kind which are not necessarily maintained in our own time. But given that the forms of the diary, of dialogue, or of the epistolary novel no longer correspond to our experience of the world, Schmidt argues that '[it] would be a fateful mistake for the description and illumination of the world through the word (the prime condition for any kind of control!) if we were to stick with these "classical" methods of construction' (*R&P*, 284). His calculations are designed to generate new forms of prose narrative corresponding to those processes in consciousness and varieties of experience which we now have. There are four of these: recollection; present, as it were direct, experience; the doubling of this last mode in the daydream, christened 'das Längere Gedankenspiel' (LG for short) — an extended play of thought over (and above) our immediate experience; and lastly, dreaming itself. Schmidt uses these categories to throw some light on the peculiarities of his own stories and novels — and indeed there was to have been a third essay in the series which was published posthumously in 1980. Michael Minden speculates that 'the material sketched out here was left in abeyance because of the development of Schmidt's thinking in new directions in the early sixties'.[14] It may well be that Schmidt used the models of narrative process developed in these essays to generate the novels of the *Brand's Haide* trilogy — as representations of our lacunary perception of existence — or the disreputable holiday memories of the famous long story 'Seelandschaft mit Pocahontas' — as a representation of our incomplete recollections of any event in the past. On the whole, however, they are eccentric reminders of Arno Schmidt's pedantry and scientism. Once we have recognised that 'Schmidt is always concerned with giving "conformal graphic representation" to internal processes,' in Peter Ott's phrase,[15] we have a sufficient key to his writing already.

Schmidt's methodology gives expression to the single overriding concern of his fiction, however various its form may be, from *Leviathan* to *Julia, oder die Gemälde.* Again and again consciousness and the dialectical relationship between the exterior world and the interiority of human perception provide both the matter and the form of his fiction. Underlying this narrative of consciousness there is a set of quasi-philosophical assumptions which can be summarised as rationalist and materialist; and Schmidt's calculus of narrative possibilities, even though they may have been conceived as a justification of his work, underline his pursuit of a systematic and rational presentation of consciousness in narrative. It is in this context that 'Goethe's' preference for the work of Max Bense can take its proper place. Bense, until fairly recently Professor of Philosophy at the Technical University, Stuttgart, was one of Schmidt's early supporters,[16] and he turns up from time to time in the short stories (in 'Schlüsseltausch' from *Trommler beim Zaren*, for instance; in *Die Gelehrtenrepublik* the island colony boasts a statue in his memory). As a pioneer in the application of information theory to aesthetics, Bense is himself a rationalist and an atheist: 'Ich verteidige also den Atheismus als die notwendige und selbstverständliche Form menschlicher Intelligenz, als menschlichen Sinn der geistigen Arbeit unter der Voraussetzung, daß der Mensch wesentlich Schöpfer seiner erweiterungsfähigen geistigen Welt und Realität ist' ('I there-

14. 'Berechnungen III', *Neue Rundschau*, 91 (1980), pp. 5–20; Minden, *Schmidt*, p. 257f, n3.

15. F. Peter Ott, 'Tradition and Innovation: an Introduction to the Prose Theory and Practice of Arno Schmidt', *Germanic Quarterly*, LI (1978), p. 20f.

16. See the autobiographical interview with Prof. Bense and Prof. Elisabeth Walther, *Bargfelder Bote*, pp. 89–90 (1985).

fore defend atheism as the necessary and unquestionable form of human intelligence, as the human meaning of intellectual labour, on condition that human beings are [understood as] essentially the creators of their extendable spiritual world and reality').[17] Arno Schmidt's atheism is legendary — and, if anything, rather repetitive. His sympathy would also lie, however, with Bense's view that reality — the world of experience and above all the human environment — is not given but *produced*, the result of human 'intellectual labour'. It is through the developing application of reason to this environment that civilisation comes into being, and the locus of this process is language in relation to consciousness. Within the matrix of language as the 'crust of the communicative sphere of our civilisation' the world is subjected to human consciousness.

Bense's rationalism provides an important context for Schmidt's aspiration to the 'illumination of the world through the word', understood as the 'prime condition for any kind of control'. In a very important sense this, as it were, Bensean attempt to understand the world characterises all Schmidt's work. Description seems poised to displace the other more obvious purpose of narrative, to present an action. Hence Helmut Heißenbüttel has drawn attention to the relative unimportance of plot in Schmidt's fiction, and points out that in the immediate post-war period Schmidt found a new way forward by rejecting the exemplary narratives taken up by others, and instead confronting the real, however fragmentary any individual perception of it might be, with his own intuitions and interpretations.[18] Yet the sense of rational control which dominates the theory propounded in Schmidt's narrative calculations is also subject to disruption and resistance.

This occurs in two forms — at the level of action in the later fiction there is an astonishing Romance-like sense of magic and utopian excess, while within the methodological framework the theory of the Etyms appears. While plot breaks down under the weight of 'incidental' detail and allusion, its displacement is also part of Schmidt's calculation. The real organising perspectives of our experience are 'landscape; intellect; eros' (*R&P*, 248);[19] and there are active discouragements to readers who hope for any old-fashioned kind of action: thus the injunction which precedes the first page of *KAFF, auch mare crisium* over the anagrammatic name of

17. Max Bense, *Ungehorsam der Ideen* (Cologne, 1966), p. 86.
18. Helmut Heißenbüttel, 'Annäherung an Arno Schmidt', *Über Literatur* (Olten, 1966) pp. 56–70.
19. Minden draws attention to this 'holy trinity', *Schmidt*, p. 71.

'D. Martin Ochs' warns in its final clause that '[anyone] sniffing around for "plot" and "deeper meaning", or even attempting to see therein a "work of art" will be shot. BARGFELD, 10 March 1960'. This warning is implicit again in the motto to *Abend mit Goldrand* (*Evening Edged in Gold*, 1975), Schmidt's last completed project, where the absence of coherence is taken to be simply consonant with the nature of human existence: '"Then it's as if," Bernard said profoundly, "the whole grand human enterprise had nothing firm and substantial about it? It may perhaps lead to nothing, and might well mean nothing? It would be foolish to search for historical unity or a great poetical harmony . . ."' (*Evening Edged in Gold*, 1).[20] The last phrase represents the German 'eine große poetische Composition', which points more directly to the parallel with the order of fiction. In spite of this insistence on the priority of detail over structure, of the registration of perception over action, the run of Schmidt's novels from *Aus dem Leben eines Fauns* and *Das steinerne Herz* all the way to *Julia, oder die Gemälde* does reveal a surprising conformity. If there is an exception, it is *Die Gelehrtenrepublik* where the visit to an irradiated world of mutants and the constantly moving, mechanical 'propeller-island' (lifted from Jules Verne) provide the framework for a whimsically satirical *jeu d'esprit* which returns in a more characteristic form in *Die Schule der Atheisten*.

What is consistent in the majority of these texts is a set of preoccupations, recurring in quite different contexts, and of which the trinity of landscape, intellect, and Eros gives only a very rough account. Where Schmidt deals with sexual and erotic matters, for instance, the range of experience to which he attends is quite specific. First, there is a recurrent configuration in which an older man in fantasy or in reality seeks a sexual encounter with a much younger woman. *Aus dem Leben eines Fauns* initiates the model, and it already connotes the possibility of voyeurism which becomes dominant in the last texts (from *Zettels Traum* onwards). At the end of *Faun*, when the idyll of Düring's (successful) relationship with Käthe seems doomed, he offers her this advice: '"*Heirat bloß nich, Käthe!: Keinen Alten*, keinen Kriegsversehrten, keinen Frommen, keinen eitlen Anspruchsvollen. — Einen, der gut kann, und bei dem Du Dich nich langweilst." "*Am Ende*" — ich tappte mit der Handfläche auf mich Beleg: "bleibt nur: Kunstwerke; Naturschönheit; Reine Wissenschaften. In dieser heiligen Trinität. — Und gut in Form bleiben.". . .' ('"*Just don' marry, Käthe! Not an old man*, not anyone damaged by the

20. Quoted in the translation by John E. Woods, *Evening Edgedin Gold* (London, 1980).

war, nobody pious, no one with vain big ideas. — Someone who's good at it, who doesn't bore you." "*At the end*" — I tapped myself with my palm in demonstration: "there's only: works of art; natural beauty; pure sciences. In this holy trinity. — And stay in good shape."...') (*NDK*, 88). The advice is not gratuitous, of course; the novel is set during the war and the men against which Käthe is warned represent possible types for a wartime or immediately post-war marriage. For his part, Düring's withdrawal, into a contemplative, voyeuristic sexuality, is announced and anticipated in the sexual gesture which opens the second paragraph quoted here — and perhaps that is why the trinity of 'Kosmas oder Vom Berge des Nordens' ('Of the mountain of the north') loses 'Eros' and differentiates the 'intellect' into art and science.

In this moment the recurrent situation of much of Schmidt's fiction is encapsulated. To read the phrase 'Am Ende' — at the end, or in the end — as a genital reference may seem perverse, but this sense rapidly becomes obvious with any more than a cursory acquaintance with his style.[21] What is striking is that this moment should appear so early in his career. A more celebrated case is offered by the last line of the highly experimental story 'Caliban upon Setebos' from the collection *Kühe in Halbtrauer* of 1964, which is generally acknowledged as the text which decisively inaugurates the later part of Schmidt's work, in anticipation of *Zettels Traum* and its consequences. Escaping from the dangers of his rural retreat, the central figure of the 'Caliban' story, nevertheless still trapped in the trope which identifies him as an Orpheus, in an inevitably unsuccessful search for Eurydice, offers this final remark: '(well so what: in any respectable person the only thing that's alive at the end is the head!).—' [i.e. severed by the maenads!] ('bei einem anständigen Menschen lebt am Ende nur noch der Kopf!'). The ambiguities of this utterance yield: 'ultimately it is reason that dominates over physical need', 'in later life sexual satisfaction can only be sought via the imagination', and (perhaps more remotely) 'cerebral activity is constantly subverted by sexual drives'.

What is adumbrated near the end of *Faun*, and ruefully reflected on in the 'Caliban' story, also informs the advice that William T. Kolderup tries to give his granddaughter Suse in *Die Schule der Atheisten*: Kolderup recognises that though Suse's boyfriend Fritz

21. The point was indeed lost on my own naïve reading of 'Caliban über Setebos' in *Rationalist Narrative in Some Works of Arno Schmidt*, Warwick Occasional Papers in German Studies, 2 (1972); some of the foregoing is nevertheless based on that early effort.

Dümpfelleu may be 'good at it' (partly because of his skills as a herbalist and apothecary), his aesthetic and antiquarian sensibilities leave much to be desired, such that his adequacy as a companion in later life must be in doubt. Indeed, by the time we reach a text like *Die Schule der Atheisten* voyeurism and/or sexual exhaustion no longer depends on age. It is Suse and her friend Nipperchen who observe the laureate Cosmo naked, with this commentary: 'Dér hat villaicht 'n Endchen Ding! :Bloß=fingersdick; ganz=weiß & vorn noch süß=spitz; dafür iss die Länge polizeiwidrig: schätze 3 Finger lang! :wie'n weißer RegnWurm' (*SdA, 86*). Schmidt's late style is scarcely susceptible to translation, but the pun on 'End[e]' is apparent again in the idiomatic 'Cor, he's got no end of a thing!'; and by contrast it is Cosmo's young friend Tim Hackensacker, exhausted favourite boy of the nymphomaniac Isis, who is delighted to find a local in Tellingstedt who, given the probable 'enlargement-fucktor' [*sic*], will be well enough endowed to take his place (*SdA*, 100f.). In these, and in what one is tempted to see as Schmidt's private version of the primal scene, impotence and voyeurism constitute a permanent horizon of human sexuality — even (and recurrently) for someone of the stature of Cosmo Schweighäuser!

The theme of intellect too is given a particular and consistent inflection in Schmidt's novels. His central characters have antiquarian or at any rate obscure literary and cultural interests, from the genealogical and local-historical research conducted variously in the *Brand's Haide* trilogy, to Ekkehard Rauch's readings in the most obscure theological writings ('entlegenste Theologica' ('for fun') as the non-paginated dramatis personae puts it) and Leonhard Jhering's investigations of the aporias in logarithms and calculators, and of sexual symbolism in the works of Bunyan and H. P. Lovecraft (*Julia, oder die Gemälde*). It is the vast range of reading and scholarship dramatised in the novels that returns us to Schmidt's private library as the source for his 'textualised' world. Experience is thus transcribed in these fictions filtered through the network of allusion and scholarship of which the transcription is itself made; narrative dissolves into the recapitulations of cultural debris which is already there. At the extreme this antiquarian *knowledge* invades the smallest phonetic and semantic units of the writing. To take a famous example, which also falls under the previous rubric of impotence and voyeurism, the writing of 'Caliban über Setebos' is loaded — and perhaps loaded down — with allusion. The story's epigraph is constructed as a kind of cultural *bricolage*: 'GEORG DÜSTERHENN entertäind se Mjußes — (tschieper Bey se Lump) — ietsch Wonn of semm re-worded him for hiss hoßpitällittitie wis Sam Bladdi mäd-

Teariels'. This is a transfigured English: Düsterhenn 'entertained the Muses — (cheaper by the lump) — each one of them rewarded him for his hospitality with some bloody materials'. Part of this invasion of language by other elements is sexual and so related to the theory of 'Etyms', but not all is resolvable in this way. The crucial phrase seems to be 'ietsch Wonn of semm re-worded him' which *is* sexual of course ('semm' like 'Sam[en]' (seed) invokes 'semen') but it also claims that a joy (German 'Wonne') of sign and meaning (Greek sema, semasa; of sem-antics, then) re-words, re-writes Düsterhenn. What happens here in little is reproduced on larger and larger scales in the novels, to the point where no 'experience' is possible which is not glossed by a text and only the most extravagant scholarly application can maintain any control in the world we actually already inhabit.

The source of such manipulations of language is of course Joyce and, as we have seen, he has his place in Schmidt's account of 'Goethe's' pantheon. In Schmidt's theory, the practice of *Finnegans Wake* (what Joyce calls 'the proteiform graph') is conjoined with a Freudian theory to produce the doctrine of the 'Etym': 'Also das bw spricht Hoch-Worte. Nun wißt Ihr aber, aus FREUD's "Traumdeutung", wie das ubw ein eigenes Schalks=Esperanto lallt; indem es einerseits Bildersymbolik, andrerseits Wort=Verwandtheiten ausnützt, um mehrere — (immer aber im Gehirn des Wirtstieres engbeieinanderlagernde!) — Bedeutungen gleichzeitig wiederzugeben' ('So the conscious [mind] speaks high words. But now you know from Freud's "Interpretation of Dreams" how the unconscious babbles its own rascal-Esperanto, by exploiting picture symbolism on the one hand, relations between words on the other, to reproduce several meanings (which always lie close together in the brain of the host animal) simultaneously') (*zettel*, 25). As *Zettels Traum* makes clear a couple of pages later (*zettel*, 28) the theory of the 'Etyms' is less a development of the *Interpretation of Dreams* than a creative inversion of Freud's doctrine of parapraxes (in the *Psychopathology of Everyday Life* and *Jokes and the Unconscious*). The whole point of the Freudian slip is that it is fundamentally involuntary; and it may well be that Schmidt developed his theory and practice on the basis of actual typing errors. (The visual presentation of the pan-Freudian works from *Zettel* onwards was only made possible by the printing of the books in facsimile reproduction of Schmidt's typescript.) A lucid understanding of the processes involved in the parapraxis becomes possible, according to *Zettel*, from that point onwards, about the age of forty-five, when a serious interest in Freud can develop, whereupon four distinct parts of the personality are recognised: 'das TriebGeröchel des ubw; den starr=sterilen Tadl des ÜI; das commishaft=überforderte Mit=No/uttieren des Ich; und endlich das HerrlichSDe, das hell-zersprungen klirrende Gelechta der 4. Instanz' ('the drive-rattle of the unconscious; the rigid=sterile crits of the S[uper]E[go]; the officious=overstretched noting-down/knocking-up of the Ego; and lastly the most splendid, the bright and cracked tinkling laufta of the 4th instance' (*zettel*, 916)).

As the biological drives slacken their hold, and within the Freudian economy both libido and super-ego invest less energy in the struggle for the ego, a new and sovereign self is reborn, which is able to rise above the tricks of the unconscious and the strictures of the super-ego to a luminous state of self-knowledge and control. The play of language in this pan-Freudian world should therefore not be thought of as the scene of almost infinite smut (though it is hard to give any sense of the intensity with which Schmidt's later texts pursue sexual innuendo, or how genuinely funny they often are); rather the exercise of 'the 4th instance' restores to language *and to fiction* what had been claimed for it in Schmidt's calculus of narrative forms, namely a power to illuminate the world in the forms in which it is known to us, invested with libido through the fantasy of the LG in the very moment of conscious perception, as a precondition for real human control.

From the advantage of his post-'45imp[otence]' (*zettel* 916) position, Schmidt establishes Freud's authority beyond all question. But his espousal of such a model is itself open to the criticism which a more thoroughgoing materialism than Schmidt's has brought to bear on Freud's doctrines of parapraxis and associativity. There is a zero-sum game involved in such methods of 'interpretation', since both the plausibility *and* the implausibility of the microanalysis implied in each etymic disturbance of language and orthography is taken to validate the method — whether the unconscious breaks cover, so to speak (or, which is more likely in late Schmidt, *wind*), or the 4th instance drags it into the non-repressed light of day. As Sebastiano Timpanaro has written,

> The *lucus a non lucendo* and the *lucus a lucendo* are equally valid in psychoanalysis. The ancient grammarians managed to resolve any etymological problem on the basis of an unconditional admission of either of these types of connexions between word and concept, or by recourse to a practically unlimited manipulation of the words that could be put into an etymological relation.[22]

22. Sebastiano Timpanaro, *The Freudian Slip. Psychoanalysis and Textual Criticism*, translated by Kate Soper (London, 1976) p. 77.

In Schmidt, of course, writing schooled by Freudian parapraxis will inaugurate a unitary, international language in which etymons pass across all traditional language barriers. The notion of a 'Schalks= Esperanto' is more than a joke: the creative misspelling of German compunds with 'Fall' or 'falt' as 'Phall' or, e.g., 'einphälltig', and the importation of Anglo-Saxon material into the Latin loan 'factor', as we have seen, is supposed to give access to the true ground of existence and experience, through the reconstitution of an original language, too fallen to be Adamic, of which natural languages are repressive epiphenomena. In this respect Schmidt follows Freud who also

> . . . paid tribute to an ancient prejudice — one of Greek origin but perpetuated throughout medieval and modern times, and given a final and spasmodic lease of life by Heidegger — that languages (and above all certain languages: Greek and German) are the depositories of a sort of original wisdom, and that etymology . . . discloses the 'true' significance of words which lies beneath a veil of distortion.[23]

Such a pursuit of the founding discourse proliferates widely and strangely in Schmidt's fiction. In these varying instantiations of the quest for a desired object or a lost meaning the last novels can no longer be seen as the documents of a successful (self-)analysis (which is how Siegbert Prawer understands *Zettel* when he writes in a pioneering essay that 'the self-aware twentieth-century writer has done the job of self-exposure consciously and thoroughly and cannot, therefore, be "caught out" in the way that Dän seeks to "catch out" Poe').[24] With a common-sense view, we should rather regard the eccentricity of *Zettels Traum*, *Die Schule der Atheisten*, *Abend mit Goldrand*, and *Julia* — within the metaphor Schmidt himself offers — as *neurotic texts*: as the text of neurosis and as the neurosis of the text.

The symptoms of this neurosis are to be found in the recourse to the miraculous which marks the *action* of the last works. To take a notorious example, it is a speaking teacup ('die Tasseté spricht') in *Die Schule der Atheisten* (250) which helps to identify the father of Isis as Chadband the missionary or (possibly) Butt his convert, but definitely not Kolderup. But the withholding of that final knowledge of origin is a small thing, given the return to a truth about the origin which is granted to all Kolderup's guests in the course of the story of Spenser Island and the visit to Sonderhø. In a different but parallel way the commerce with the world of art, by literal entry into

23. Ibid., p. 23n.
24. S.S. Prawer, 'Bless Thee Bottom, Bless Thee, Thou Art Translated', reprinted in *Über Arno Schmidt*, p. 246.

paintings in *Abend* and in *Julia*, in the sketches for which it is clear that characters were to live on by entering a painting ('Bild 18'), and were to encounter all the characters of Schmidt's previous books ('Bild 16' Die Blumenkrater — Begegnung mit den Gestalten meiner Bücher', non-paginated 'Nachwort'), extends the role of the miraculous in Schmidt's late fiction.

In these cases an object of desire or a secret meaning is attained, such that an idyllic state is achieved at the end of desire. Such events are paralleled in the earlier fiction in less miraculous but in no less surprising ways. *Das steinerne Herz* provides a prime case: not least because its 'hero' Walter Eggers is identified in *Abend mit Goldrand* as an *alter ego* (*AmG*, 132). Eggers shares the kind of antiquarian passion whch is familiar in Schmidt himself, and arrives in a small provincial town (like so many of Schmidt's heroes) in pursuit of his idol, one Conrad Fürchtegott Friedebald Jansen's library, and of the usual Hanoverian state statistics. Through many adventures — including the discovery of a false ceiling — Eggers achieves his desire, with enough money (also in the ceiling) to make a future idyll with Jansen's granddaughter possible. *Aus dem Leben eines Fauns* offers a very close parallel where once again both antiquarian and sexual desires are conjoined and satisfied. Such a desire for the remote and ancient edition, for the obscure text, for the single detail which can make sense of all the others, spreads through the whole of Schmidt's writing — *and through the processes of reading which it demands and which the antiquarianism of the* Bargfelder Bote *promotes*. That is to say, the neurotic desire for precision which finds expression in Schmidt's scientism and in his antiquarianism alike[25] offers his own texts as the space in which this desire can be at once stimulated and denied. Both the obscure — and unattainable — allusions which the reader needs (and so desires) to identify, and the recognisable references whose relevance to the whole text is nevetheless still unclear, draw the reader into the same pursuit of the concealed meaning.

The perfect expression of the unknown truth is ultimately provided by Schmidt himself in the 'Hyperbook' to end all books, *Zettels Traum*. In *Die Schule der Atheisten*, *Zettel* itself becomes one if not *the* object of quest in the journey to Sonderhø, where Kolderup knows there remain a further four signed copies stashed away. Of these one copy each is given to the visiting diplomats from the USA and China, Isis and Sun Wu. Kolderup makes his presentation to the latter with these now famous words: '"Darf ich Mir erlaub'm ?; dem

25. E.g. his obsession with Poe scholarship in 'Der Fall Ascher' (*Aus julianischen Tagen*, p. 129).

geschätzten Herrn Collegen das (gestern erwähnte) irrealencyclopische Buch der Westernwelt zu verehren?-''' (*SdA*, 170). *Zettels Traum*, the 'superbook' ('Überbuch' like Nietzsche's superman (*SdA*, 139)), is presented as the 'irrealencyclopic' book of the western world because it offers an encyclopaedic survey of the permeation of our perceived world by desire, of which every conceivable allusion and reference becomes an expression and trope. The possibility of a world of total significance in which no detail would not take its place in, and reflect in little some systematic whole — a world in short *transformed into a book* — is a Romantic ideal, realised by *Zettels Traum* (and to a lesser extent by its increasingly Romantic successors), just as it realises the dream of Mallarmé's Symbolist *grand'oeuvre*, in the very moment that it destroys it. Instead the great Book disenchants the dream-object to reveal itself as commodity and simultaneously to contest its nature as commodity. Even so, what escapes the typesetter cannot escape reproduction and repetition by offset printing. The hypertrophic sexual investment of the late texts neurotically occludes the fear of commodification which makes all of Schmidt's heroes, from Eggers to Kolderup, 'altmodern' (oldmodern). This is the paradox of Arno Schmidt's extraordinary achievement. As Wolfram Schütte has observed it: 'The late work, rung in with "Caliban über Setebos" . . . polyphonically and polymorphologically, replaces the earlier tartan texture (made up from "realistic" everyday details and utterly subjective additions by the author) with material which more and more abandons "natural" stuff and is increasingly woven from synthetics'.[26]

26. Wolfram Schütte, 'Spätwerkgespi/enst. NovellenComödie und Märchenposse', *Text + Kritik*, 20a, 3rd edn., 1977, p. 76. The notion of the commodity form of the book is given its appropriate context in Frederic Jameson, *The Political Unconscious, Narrative as a Socially Symbolic Act* (London, 1981).

MORAY McGOWAN

Botho Strauß

From *Kursbuch* to the 'Konkursbuchverlag': the self-confident rationality that typified the West German protest movement of the 1960s, a revival of Enlightenment values precisely in its critique of the technocratic rationality into which, it argued, the Enlightenment had been perverted by capitalism, was epitomised by the journal *Kursbuch*, its title borrowed tongue-in-cheek from the sovereign positivism of the West German railway timetable.

The 1970s brought disillusion: the stagnation or reversal of the reforming impulses with which the SPD had entered office and the growing nuclear and environmental threat. In the early 1980s, even the once optimistic Left struggled to defend their Enlightenment humanism against what they saw as 'Eiszeit' and 'Zukunftsangst' ('an ice age' and 'fear of the future': Lattman 1981, 119 & 322). Elsewhere this new crisis of Enlightenment is marked by the rehabilitation of long-spurned cultural pessimists like Nietzsche or Ernst Jünger; by a new irrationalism (see Born *et al.* 1978); by tendencies even in science away from Cartesian–Newtonian logic (e.g. Capra 1982); by the greatly increased reception of the essentially pessimistic, post-Marxist French *nouveaux philosophes*, like Jean Baudrillard, Michel Foucault, André Glucksmann and Jean-François Lyotard; by debates, notably in the journal *Merkur*, on the new crisis of reason and on the asserted demise of modernism in favour of post-modernism.

Post-modernism replaces faith in individual and social progress on the basis of Enlightenment reason or of Marxist historical optimism with a reaffirmation of multivalent or amorphous, irrational and pre-rational modes of thought, drawing on myth, on anthropology, on psychoanalysis (see Huyssen and Scherpe 1986; Raulet 1986). In the mid-1980s, *Kursbuch* soldiered on, but the new spirit was exemplified by the 'Konkursbuchverlag' in Tübingen, devoted explicitly to the new crisis of reason, and whose very name (Bankruptcy publishers) asserted the intellectual bankruptcy of *Kursbuch* and the materialist, progressive era it stood for.

In 1979, the novelist and playwright Botho Strauß (b. 1944) confirmed his abandonment too of Ernst Bloch's Marxist-based 'Prinzip Hoffnung' (optimistic principle) that had inspired him as a student in the mid-1960s, but which now seemed 'ein großes Märchen' and 'ein unglaublicher Betrug' ('a big fairy story' and 'an unbelievable fraud'), in favour of the pessimism of Glucksmann and the *nouveaux philosophes* (Bachmann, 1979). But even in the late 1960s, Strauß's essays in *Theater heute*, while reflecting the materialism and critical theory then dominant in West German intellectual discourse, also quoted Foucault and appealed for a rehabilitation of the irrational (e.g. Strauß 1969).

Thus his first plays, *Die Hypochonder* (1972) and *Bekannte Gesichter, gemischte Gefühle* (1975) and his first prose texts, 'Marlenes Schwester' and 'Theorie der Drohung' (1975), which subverted realistic conventions, explored irrational phenomena and challenged Enlightenment values, were lukewarmly received in a climate still attuned to Social Realism or to autobiographical 'authenticity'. It was not until 1977, with the publication of his novel *Die Widmung* and the first productions of the play *Trilogie des Wiedersehens*, that Strauß's meteoric career really began (see McGowan, 1986). *Die Widmung* went into a third printing in six weeks. *Rumor* (1980), his next prose text, sold 10,000 copies in a fortnight. *Paare, Passanten* (1981), despite its radical eschewal of narrative in favour of a mixed journal form, was reprinted four times in a year. Between 1980 and 1985, his then six plays had 132 German-speaking productions. Massive exposure brought a critical backlash, intensified by controversy over his novel *Der junge Mann* (1984) and his long poem *Diese Erinnerung an einen, der nur einen Tag zu Gast war* (1985), in which he seemed to abandon critical consciousness in favour of a quest for transcendental truth (see Lüdke and Schmidt, 1986).

With fellow author Peter Handke, Strauß was seen as the leading German-speaking literary representative of post-modernism — or, for its critics, of an elitist neo-conservatism or a neo-Romanticism which abandons reality by aestheticising it in search of visionary truths and harmonies realisable only in art (Schneider 1981; Drews 1984; Peter 1986). From the beginning, Strauß's work exhibited post-modernist traits: the abandonment of humanist confidence in the Enlightenment and the self-determining subject, which leads to a fragmentation of linear plot and of character; the rehabilitation of the irrational and the mythic; the constantly shifting range of aesthetic, philosophical and metaphysical themes, out of which the fragmented form creates a mosaic of the poetic and the discursive which consciously subverts genre boundaries, most evidently in

Paare, Passanten; deliberately ambiguous and often misunderstood relationships between author and narrator (see Wefelmeyer 1984); extensive direct, periphrastic or ironically modified quotation. Once the climate of reception progressed — or regressed — sufficiently, Strauß's ability at once to anticipate, to reflect and to satirise the spirit of the age, the open, self-ironising nature of his texts, his richly allusive style, his essayistic speculations, all ensured his work an interpretative attention rarely granted to the straightforward narratives of Social Realist writers.

Not till *Der junge Mann* did Strauß explicitly call any of his prose texts a novel, and even there there is ambiguity. But two other texts at least, *Die Widmung* and *Rumor*, can be read as novels; these three works will be the focus of this chapter.

'Richard Schroubek is a young Berliner who responds to his girlfriend's departure by withdrawing into his apartment and writing a journal of his sorrows. . . . It's hard not to feel that the girlfriend knows exactly what she's doing when, on the penultimate page, she leaves the manuscript, unopened, in a taxi' (Shrimpton 1980). Were *Die Widmung* just another self-indulgent refurbishment of its narrator's and by implication its author's cuckolded ego, one might concur. But despite its conventional theme and minimal plot, it is a many-layered, highly ironic text, though also coolly precise compared with the monomanic raging of *Rumor* or the bombast of *Der junge Mann.* It addresses the state of the subject in an information-saturated society drained of meaning, and the possibility, and the cost, of preserving or creating such meaning in the autonomous world of art.

Schroubek stresses he is not recording a past relationship, but claims to be prolonging his present state of mourning as a bridge across which the lovers may be reunited (*W*, 82). This however sustains the separation and so actually prevents Hannah's return, an irony underlined by the novel's many death and resurrection motifs (e.g. *W*, 12–14, 93, 108). And in fact, despite his protestations (e.g. *W*, 30), it is not the shadowy Hannah, whose whereabouts he makes no real effort to establish, and whose return he in fact excludes from the outset (*W*, 11), but the emotion of love as experienced in the pain of separation which he wishes to nurture.

As in the Romantic reaction to the Enlightenment, love is valued as an area of fateful experience insusceptible to rational planning or social ordering, awakening transcendental longings and sensitivities (*W*, 9–10) and a massive experience of the unknown within oneself

(*W*, 89): a theme to which Strauß returns repeatedly, e.g. in his play *Die Fremdenführerin*, 1986. But in the contemporary world of casually begun relationships, love's real power is often only experienced on separation (*W*, 11). Separation is the ultimate blow to psychosexual process which Strauß, in contradiction to Marx and in common with Georges Bataille and Jean Baudrillard, sees as more fundamental than our superficial social, political or economic motivations (e.g. *W*, 8–9, 50–1). This shock to the subconscious ruptures the seamless flow of normality, an alienation effect, in fact, which jolts Schroubek out of his social identity too (and is reflected in the fragmentary form of his writing) and opens long-closed doors of perception and insight (which the fragmentary form helps to keep open).

So the dedication which gives the novel its title (*W*, 15) is ironic: Hannah has been the catalyst but is not really the goal. He dreads the end of his grief because it would mean a return to the shallowness of normality (*W*, 27). The revolt against this lack of meaning expresses itself as 'das diachrone Verlangen' ('diachronic longing') a central theme in Strauß's work (see Adelson 1984, 60–5) to understand which it is necessary to consider his view of the human subject.

Strauß's work was initially associated with the *neue Subjektivität* ('new subjectivity') of the 1970s: a new *Biedermeier*, another return to private concerns after a failed revolution, or, less simplistically, a rehabilitation of the subject after its neglect or instrumentalisation in the dogmatic politics of the protest movement's later phases (see Ruoff 1983, Adelson 1984).

But Strauß is not, in his work up to and including *Rumor*, concerned with rehabilitating the subject. On the contrary, he shows it in a state of dissolution. In 'Theorie der Drohung' the narrator believes he is preserving his threatened identity by the act of writing, until he discovers that his every word is a plagiarism and experiences complete disintegration into a 'Null-Person' (*TD*, 81). To Schroubek, life appears like a supernatural force at a seance: 'Das Leben hat, nach der Niederwerfung des Subjekts, damit begonnen, seinen Rest selber zu schreiben' ('After the defeat of the subject, life has begun to write the remainder itself') (*W*, 20). The self in history has become history in the self. Strauß's narrative perspective is narcissistic rather than egocentric; his texts abound in *Doppelgänger*, in symbiotic or reflexive relationships between characters, as in 'Marlenes Schwester'. 'To see "I" at the center of the world is a modern feeling. For the self to see itself and become involved with that reflection or doubling as if it were another is a postmodern experience' (Schechner 1982, 99). Like Camus, Strauß shows that studying the self heightens the sensation of its insubstantiality (see

Camus 1975, 22–4; vom Hofe and Pfaff 1980, 1–27. Indeed self-scrutiny destroys the sense of the self as a discrete entity, and in *Die Widmung* he rejects the suggestion that it is escapist: it is a gruesome process of mutilation that robs the self of its last refuge (*W*, 98–9).

Strauß's view of the human subject resembles Adorno's: Enlightenment reason, shrunk to functionalism, is no longer a liberating but an oppressive force, and the individual subject is an involuntary microcosm of social forces. In this light, Adorno argues, to insist, as the Enlightenment tradition does, on the integrity and capacity for self-determination of the individual, is to cement the very conditions which block these aspirations. Control over oneself, the basis of identity, paradoxically furthers the decay of the subject in whose interest it was undertaken (Adorno and Horkheimer 1969, 36–45; Kappner 1977).

Its effects can be seen in the description of Schroubek's charwoman (*W*, 50–4). In contrast to the introspective Schroubek, whose relationship with the everyday is a series of silent-film slapstick disasters (e.g. *W*, 55–8), Frau N. maintains her breezy efficiency by a complete repression of her individuality and her imagination. Language serves not for self-examination, but as an arsenal of ready-made values and desires, out of which she constructs a personality like a suit of armour: invulnerable but empty.

Enlightenment rationality presupposes history as linear progress. But within it, the self-alienated subject, robbed of any personal sense of history, experiences only 'nervöse Synchronität'('nervous synchronicity'), a multiple image without 'Differenz' ('difference' in the sense of distinguishing meaning) (*W*, 12). This engenders what Schroubek calls 'das diachrone Verlangen' (*W*, 64): the longing for meaning, connection, history. But not that of the oppressive domination of abstract systems: he resists the explanatory models of his suffering offered by Freudianism, which, like the reality-impoverishing taxonomy of the 'I-Spy' books of the 1950s, reduce the unique to normative generalisations and confirm the alienation of the subject (*W*, 66–8, 79). Instead, 'diachronic longing' seeks non-linear, non-hierarchic, open-edged relationships between phenomena, events, persons, in accordance with the post-modern rejection of Cartesian–Newtonian logic. Hence the amorphous relationships and boundaries between individuals and the world, and individuals and each other, in Strauß's work (Adelson 1984, 60–5). 'Diachronic longing' has affinities with Yeats's assertion in 'Ideas of Good and Evil' that 'the borders of our mind are ever shifting, and that many minds can flow into one another . . . and that our memories are part of one great memory, the memory of Nature herself': a link with the 'Rede des Ganzen' ('discourse of the whole') in *Rumor* and the pantheism of *Der junge Mann*.

In an interview in 1977, the year *Die Widmung* appeared, Strauß argues that the dissolution of these boundaries is 'zugleich Gefahr und Chance' ('simultaneously a danger and an opportunity') (Zacharias 1977). The oppressive abstractions must be deconstructed, for they prevent real subjective experience. But the need for meaningful connections remains; otherwise the subject, freed from the strait-jacket of linear logic, may disintegrate altogether, as threatens in so many of his texts. In this search for meaning, 'Schrift' ('the written') (*W*, 64) takes on quasi-mystical importance, displacing concrete action in the material world, a neo-Romantic position taken up again in *Diese Erinnerung an einen, der nur einen Tag zu Gast war.*

Moreover, Schroubek shares a problematic inconsistency with his author. His analysis of Frau N. applies exactly the normative social-psychological patterns he resists in his own case, judging her as 'ein durch und durch sozial begründeter Mensch, keine Regung unerklärlich' ('socially explicable through and through, with no unexplainable impulses') (*W*, 50). *Paare, Passanten* abounds in comparable sketches whose Olympian certainty in interpreting the observation produces a one-dimensionality of the human which Strauß then bewails (see McGowan 1984, 60–1). Schroubek does compare Frau N.'s loss of identity with his own (making her another ironic *Doppelgänger* like the comic Fritz) (*W*, 36–48), but really she is a foil for the more interesting sufferings of Schroubek, and as in Goethe's *Werther* we are asked to accept that simple folk live alienated but blissful lives.

It is possible to see most of Strauß's work as 'a covert drama of vain longings for redemption' (Bollmann 1985, 73), longings transferred in *Die Widmung*, as in *Werther*, from the Godhead to the lover, but transferred again by Schroubek in the light of dissillusioning reality to the quest for meaning through literary creation. Unlike television's meaningless flicker, writing promises a redemption from psychic collapse, though, ironically, the introspection that accompanies it may hasten that collapse (*W*, 81), and literature may intensify our alienation from the world by evoking levels of feeling that reality can rarely satisfy (*W*, 62–3). Moreover, the novel's closing image takes back the optimism of the comic but unbowed Schroubek returning to his project of literary resistance to meaninglessness. On television, an ageing crooner tries in vain to mime the forgotten words to a scratched copy of one of his old hits (*W*, 114). Attempts to transcend time and loss, however noble, produce grotesque results. This image of a man whose humanity consists only in his failure to act like a puppet points forward to *Rumor*, in which Strauß probes the depths of anti-Enlightenment pessimism about the human subject.

'Es gibt Stunden des massiven Eisgeistes, in denen Haß die einzige Wärme ist und nur Sprengung Atem schafft' ('There are massive ice ages of the spirit, when hate is the only warmth and only demolition gives space to breathe') (*R*, 74). The city the central character Bekker wanders in *Rumor* is a 'KZ' ('concentration camp'), a 'Tartarien' ('Tartary'), a world of bloody domestic sado-masochism (*R*, 25–8), of cold hatred in the 'dreckige Lügenwelt der Beziehungen' ('dirty lying world of relationships') (*R*, 161), in which Bekker sees 'das Lager in jedem' ('the camp in everyone') (*R*, 28). There is no hope from God. He is slumbering on his palace steps after the gala ball to celebrate the Creation, all the human generations scrabbling over each other in the palm of his hand; on waking he shakes them off and tramples them in petulant disgust (*R*, 66, cf. *R*, 35). Such fatalistic visions, obscuring the real material threats which could destroy humanity as easily and as totally, are characteristic of the novel's perspective.

It is a perspective provided largely by Bekker, alternately apathetic and ragingly energetic, harried by drunkenness, misery, failure and indignity. He is an individualist, yet is dependent on three ambiguous central relationships: with his stepfather (history), with the 'Institut Zachler' (society) and with his daughter Grit (love, human relationships, the future). He wears not only the greatcoat but also the depressive melancholy and the crazed misanthropy of his stepfather, dishonourably discharged from the Wehrmacht, whose hatred of fascism was frustrated into impotent rage (*R*, 21–2). Gifted but stubbornly non-specialist, Bekker has become progressively less useful to the post-industrial information and expertise management functions of the 'Institut Zachler'. He is horrified by its suppression of historical consciousness in favour of vast synchronic systems on the model of the microprocessor (*R*, 39). However, his innermost dreams are to replace Zachler as director or to go under in a fatal 'Kampfesorgasmus' ('orgasm of struggle') (*R*, 73). Bekker repeatedly flees the institute's baleful corporate paternalism, yet this is less independence than the inverted dependence of the supposed adult clinging to a childhood rebellion, behind which, crazed by responsibility for himself in an incomprehensible world, he longs 'einmal vom Ganzen Herzen unterwürfig zu sein an einen Stärkeren' ('just once to subject himself totally to a stronger person') (*R*, 216).

Outside the scientific rationality of the institute, Bekker experiences, and articulates in raging monologues that dominate the novel, the normally suppressed, disorderly discourse of life: 'Risse, Rumor, Gewalt und Unrast, plötzliche Stöße von ungebändigtem Leben unter deinen Sohlen' ('crevasses, tumult, violence and unrest, sudden bursts of untamed life under your feet') (*R*, 52). The 'Rumor' may be positive: unmediated, unsanitised in contrast to the institute's alienated functionality. But its worship may be fascistic, as in Bekker's affirmation of the energising, binding power of hatred or his search for a 'Kampf' ('struggle') that is 'ernst und letztgültig' ('serious and final') (*R*, 56–7).

In any case, the 'Rumor' directly challenges assumptions about the human subject. Bekker echoes Nietzsche's scorn at 'the vanity that man is the great secret objective of animal evolution' (Nietzsche 1968, 124), by arguing that evolution is not a rising progression, but a series of mistakes in the genetic copying process: for the goal of every cell is simply to replicate itself. To undermine the anthropocentric arrogance that has perverted humanism into a lethal destructive potential, Bekker borrows a metaphor from Jacques Monod's *Chance and Necessity*: humanity is 'ein Zigeuner am Rande des Universums . . . das für seine Musik taub ist und gleichgültig gegen seine Hoffnungen, Leiden oder Verbrechen' ('A gypsy on the fringe of the universe, which is deaf to his music and indifferent to his hopes, his sufferings or his crimes') (*R*, 143).

Where Camus' equally radical rejection of false consolations prepares the ground for the truly human dignity of the unblinkered intelligence at grips with an awesome reality (Camus 1975, 54), Bekker is concerned to dethrone every humanist philosophy, indeed humanity itself, a characteristic post-modern view echoed in Richard Schechner's *End of Humanism* (see Schechner 1982, 9). Bekker is inconsistent: if humanity is merely a tiny episode in the space/time totality of the universe, man has less cause to feel lonely than when he stood on a lofty pinnacle; if his existence is a unique chance event, this is a reminder of his profound responsibility. Moreover, mutations depend in fact not only on chance but also on a uni-directional, even purposeful tendency towards organisation (see Eigen and Winkler 1975), contradicting the post-modern replacement of the 'logic of action' by 'indeterminacy' (Schnechner 1982, 98).

Bekker's ontological ravings are especially scornful of the 'teures Subjekt der Weltgeschichte, heiliges Ich' ('precious subject of world history, holy self'). Science shows us to be ruled by systems quite independent of the thinking subject: 'Der Mensch? . . . Schwamm darüber . . . Wenn wir nicht mehr sind, weht noch lang der Wind.

Und die Codes gehen ihren unermeßlichen Gang. Wir aber versanden, wir werden zugeweht wie ein Scheißhaufen am Strand' ('Humanity? . . . Scrub it . . . When we no longer exist, the wind will continue to blow. And the codes will tread their immeasurable paths. But we will be covered with drifting sand, we will be silted over like a heap of shit on the beach') (*R*, 144–5).

Where Adorno, for all his pessimism, sees socio-economic — man-made, therefore mutable — causes for the decay of the subject, Bekker, paraphrasing Foucault's closing words in *The Order of Things*, 'Man disappears, like a face drawn in the sand of the seashore' (Foucault 1977, 387), mixes genetic determinism and the supernatural to echo the dark pessimism of late Romanticism, whose intensity was in proportion to the Enlightenment hopes that had been raised and dashed. Instead of Aeolian harmonies embracing humanity we find terror at the remorselessness of an indifferent nature that begins to live even within man himself as his reason crumbles (*R*, 146–8). Thus one can find parallels to Bekker's world view in — among others — Poe, Thomas Hood (e.g. 'The Sea of Death'), Alfred Kubin's *Die andere Seite* (1909), or Gustav Meyrink's *Der Golem* (1915). Equally, the 'disappointed '68ers' are among the most pessimistic members of 1980s West German society. However, Strauß characteristically deflates his own gloomy pathos by having Bekker choose, as an example of 'die immer noch unterdrüchte Rede des Ganzen' ('the still suppressed discourse of the whole'), a sardonic conversation on humanity's demise between a piece of chewing gum and a garden barbecue (*R*, 145–6).

Strauß of course neither necessarily agrees with Bekker nor argues that the reader should. In view of Strauß's acknowledged debt to Adorno, one might read the novel as an attempt to provoke insight via the purgative process of radical negation. For as Adorno maintains in *Minima Moralia*, there is 'no longer beauty or consolation except in the gaze falling on horror, withstanding it, and in unalleviated consciousness of negativity holding fast to the possibility of what is better' (Adorno 1951, 21). Does *Rumor* demonstrate this possibility?

As in *Die Widmung* love is invested with magic powers of redemption from the unrelieved negativity of social existence (*R*, 95). Caring for his sick daughter Grit enables Bekker briefly to transcend his own self-immersion and to experience moments of elation (e.g. *R*, 109). But it is undermined by incestuous desire and eventually by his own premature senility. Moreover, Bekker experiences tenderness normally when observing Grit from a distance (e.g. *R*, 100); most of their actual interactions are squabbles. Other father–child relationships confirm the pessimistic picture (*R*, 82f., 139), and when two lovers embrace in a still, small act of rebellion, they are torn apart 'wie Laub' ('like leaves') (*R*, 36). Bekker praises love's awakening of elemental experience. Yet, he says, the first glances of love set 'das Liebesfolterwerk' ('the torture machinery of love') in motion and bolt 'die Pforte der Konzentrationskammer' ('the gate of the concentration chamber') from without (*R*, 110). This trivialises the material suffering of millions to justify the real but qualitatively quite different tortures of the emotional life. Social phenomena shrink to props for Bekker's self-dramatisation.

Thus in *Rumor* negation is accompanied by little sense of 'the possibility of what is better'. However, to the extent that the novel provokes the reader to challenge Bekker's position and so to review unreflected humanist assumptions, it may indeed have an enlightening effect only apparently at odds with the death sentence it seems to be pronouncing on the Enlightenment.

Rumor is arguably a warning: negation alone traps the rebel in the structures he negates. Strauß's next prose work, *Paare, Passanten* (1981) contains a much-quoted statement of intent to abandon Adorno's dialectics, critical reason and radical negation (*PP*, 115). Its significance can be overestimated; but it seems confirmed by *Der junge Mann* (1984), whose open-edged form and the citing of a wealth of mythic and cultural motifs have led it to be bracketed with Thomas Pynchon's *Gravity's Rainbow* and Umberto Eco's *The Name of the Rose* as an archetypal post-modern novel (Vester 1985). Like Herbert Marcuse's *Eros and Civilisation*, itself a riposte to the pessimism of Sartre, Adorno and Horkheimer, the novel argues for 'the reconciliation of the individual with the whole', for 'the strange truths which imagination keeps alive in folklore and fairytale, in literature and art', for 'the liberation from time which unites man with god, man with nature' (Marcuse 1966, 143, 160, 162). But irony subverts this and every other position in the novel.

Like *Die Widmung*, *Der junge Mann* has a prologue justifying the main text that follows. The narrator bewails the impoverishing overemphasis on one human dimension, the social, and praises fiction's playfulness as a source of resistance to the 'Zeit-Pfeil' ('arrow of time') (*JM*, 14), the inflexible demand for linear progress. He pleads for an open-edged simultaneity of form, linking past and present, wakeful rationality and dream (*JM*, 11).

The five books that follow are loosely connected by recurrent motifs and a narrator common to four of them, Leon Pracht (another of

Strauß's self-ironising coinages like the colourless, puny Bruno Stöss in *Rumor*). 'Die Straße (Der junge Mann)' gives the novels its title and awakens expectations of a *Bildungsroman*: Pracht's enthusiasm for the theatre echoes Goethe's *Wilhelm Meister*. He longs to give the meaning-impoverished present the richer texture art can provide. But the reality of art is more intransigent than the imagined form: the two tough, experienced actresses whom he directs in a production of Genet's *Maids* inflict humiliation and failure.

That the *Bildungsroman* form dissolves before the novel is one-sixth over, seems in line with the post-modern rejection of cohesive character and linear development. But perhaps the post-modern *Bildungsroman* is one in which the narrator opens him- or herself diachronically and so may virtually disappear (as Pracht does in the second book), and in which 'Werden' ('becoming'), which implies the Enlightenment faith in progress, is replaced by 'Sein' ('being'). Certainly the entire novel is fed by what Swales sees as the life-blood of the *Bildungsroman*: 'the poetry of the heart (inwardness and potentiality) vis-à-vis the unyielding, prosaic temporality of practical social existence' (Swales 1978, 28). The epiphany of liberation from the tyranny of time with which 'Die Straße' ends (*JM*, 61f.) heralds the labyrinthine journey through the timeless structure of the novel's central books.

The final book, 'Der Turm' plays in a VIP-hotel for resigned intellectuals echoing Hofmannsthal's play *Der Turm* and Georg Lukács's attack on the Frankfurt School as 'Grand Hotel Abgrund', and reversing the enlightened goals of the Society of the Tower in *Weilhelm Meister*. Pracht, who has abandoned his lofty ideals, meets Weigert, his theatrical mentor of the first book, again: now calling himself Ossia, the once ebullient celebrant of theatrical pathos has decayed into infantilism, artistic sterility and a confusion of post-modern viewpoints. In turning his back on Ossia, Leon like an archetypal *Bildungsroman* hero gains his independence from his father figure.

The three middle books, approximately two-thirds of the novel's total, have the irrational dream-logic of *Alice in Wonderland* and reflect the rehabilitation of myth and fairy tale in the post-modern crisis of Enlightenment (see Bohrer 1983; McGowan 1986). Myth may support human rationality by converting unlocatable ontological terror into a plain fear of specific named agencies (Blumenberg 1979). Or it may conservatively emphasise the universals in the human, social and natural world (Wetzels 1973, 8) Or it may focus Romantic sufferings at the mechanistic soullessness of Enlightenment rationalism, producing, as in Novalis, the longing for a time when 'man in Märchen und Gedichten/Erkennt die wahren Weltgeschichten' ('one recognises in fairy tales and stories the true histories of the world') (Novalis 1969, 85). Here the firm identity of the ego would dissolve, opening up the individual's boundaries to others, to the natural world and to the infinite: a precursor of 'diachronic longing'. Novalis's dream of making the world into poetry conditions the transition in *Heinrich von Ofterdingen*, whose amorphous characters resemble those of Strauß's early prose, from novel to fairy tale. *Der junge Mann* too loses its subtitle 'Roman' ('novel') between dust-cover and title page, and as one moves into the text, one is drawn like Parsifal or Klingsohr into a labyrinth of fable and fantasy, the irrational and the unconscious. Without myth and metaphor, says one character, we are simply not linked to 'die Ordnung des Lebendigen' ('the vital order'), to 'Ather und Erde, Tier und Strauch' ('ether and earth, animal and plant') (*JM*, 214). But Strauß is too knowing to mirror the dreams of Novalis. Lost innocence once again generates persistent irony and the novel hovers between myth as reactionary transformation of history into labyrinthine nature and myth as reason's necessary pendant.

In the second book 'Der Wald' a woman bank executive plunges like Alice out of her ordered life into a 'Wildnis von Gleicher Zeit' ('wilderness of simultaneity') (*JM*, 96), where she undergoes a seamless sequence of nightmares defying spatial, chronological and biological logic. Escaping, she discovers, in a typical Romantic motif, that the dream persists after waking. Her client wants to build a 'Turm der Stille' ('tower of silence'), an idyllic retreat which points forward to the final book, but is also recognisable as the world she has just fled (*JM*, 105f.).

Leon reappears as narrator in the third book 'Die Siedlung' which seems to retract the Marcusean project of the novel as a whole. Leon observes the 'Syks', who reject the functional, digital 'male' logic of technocratic society in favour of 'female' characteristics and right-hemisphere creative intelligence. Their goal, mixing Buddhist pantheism and Gestalt philosophy, is 'Teilhabe' ('partaking') in the mother-warmth of 'der Große Schmelzfluß' ('the great flux') of all human, natural and metaphysical knowledge (*JM*, 135). This post-industrial community reflects both sides of 'alternative' culture: its utopias of non-aggression, playful creativity, Angst- and taboo-free integration of the irrational (*JM*, 123), but also its facile eclecticism: the 'Syks' are 'kreativ' but only as 'Synthetiker', synthesising elements of existing cultures and philosophies: they are rag-pickers on the rubbish tip of a dying culture, not founders of a new one (*JM*, 144), a flabby, boring, half-childish, half-pietistic community in which individual identity is erased (*JM*, 119–20, 131).

'Die Terrasse' evokes *The Decameron* with its interpolated stories: typically, sexual fantasies (*JM*, 183f. and 215f.: Strauß's problematic portrayal of women needs investigating: despite — or because of — his neo-Romantic praise of the transcendental power of love, women in *Der junge Mann* are mostly *femmes fatales*, liars, sluts, whores or witches; cf. *JM*, 158f.) or novellas on Romantic themes like imprisonment in a timeless world (*JM*, 221f.) or craftsmanship versus vision in art and the psychic costs of creativity (*JM*, 250f.). It evokes Thomas Mann's *Magic Mountain* with its attempt to encapsulate and, this being Botho Strauß, to ironise the spirit of the age. The cultural conservative anti-humanist Reppenfries rejects as a corrupt carnival of decay the post-modernist Haswerner's celebration of synchronicity and variety, and attacks democracy for not providing (suspiciously abstract) values like 'Weisheit' ('wisdom') and 'Geist' ('spirituality') (*JM*, 193f.). He calls for a 'Reinwaschung' ('purification') to make us receptive to the great cultures of the past (*JM*, 213), and a reconciliation of spirit and matter, science and the transcendental to save the world from self-destruction (*JM*, 210). Typically, though, Reppenfries deflates his own arguments by proclaiming them just part of the 'enorme Zunahme an Scheiße' ('enormous increase in shit') that contemporary culture is producing (*JM*, 212).

The guests in 'Die Terrasse' have gathered for the funeral of their king at the 'Ursprung der jüngeren Geschichte' ('the origin of recent history': *JM*, 182). Blinded by reverence for this Belsazar/Hitler so long as he lived, as one man they now reject him and all he stood for: a familiar picture of the hypocrisy of self-denazification. But, the novel argues, just as funeral guests have little in common but the mourning, Hitler's corpse is the only integrative force in West German society (*JM*, 181). The funeral procession of post-war ideological and social archetypes is a *tour de force* of malignant allegory (*JM*, 295f.). The mixture of acute satirical observation, elitist misanthropy, evocation, even if ironised, of the ideal of the *Volk*, transcendental longings for meaning in the face of the mundane social world, intentional bathos and self-irony, is characteristic of Botho Strauß.

Der junge Mann cites and plays with major cultural themes of its time, but never seriously addresses them, decking them instead in a clogging gauze of fictionality and myth. A text need have no yardsticks outside itself, of course, but then it frustrates its own allegorical intentions, and collapses into what Strauß, with his usual ability to anticipate his own commentators, has his character Ossia call 'ein Haufen Zeugs' ('a heap of stuff') (*JM*, 349).

A post-modernism that plays endlessly with ambivalence is ultimately as hollow as a modernism in which critical consciousness has decayed into a hollow pose (see Vester 1985, 28). Strauß's work, with its precise satirical sketches and its addressing of the central philosophical issues of the individual and collective condition and future state of humanity, repays attention. But with its increasing interest in reactionary philosophy and conservative aesthetics, its consumptive or indifferent attitude to material reality, its self-indulgence masked as self-irony, eventually enervation and tedium replace its initially provocative, therefore productive effect on the critical reader.

Author's Note

References to the following editions are by abbreviation and page number in the text. Translations are my own except where stated.

'Theorie der Drohung' (=*TD*), in: *Marlenes Schwester, Zwei Erzählungen*, Munich: Hanser 1975

Die Widmung, Munich: dtv 1979 (=*W*)

Rumor, Munich: Hanser 1980 (=*R*)

Paare, Passanten, Munich: Hanser 1981 (=*PP*)

Der junge Mann, Munich: Hanser 1984 (=*JM*)

Works Cited:

Adelson, Leslie, *Crisis of Subjectivity, Botho Strauß's Challenge to West German Prose of the 1970s* (Amsterdam, 1984)

Bachmann, Dieter, 'Das Ende der Liebe', *Tages-Anzeiger*, 9.6.1979

Adorno, T.W., *Minima Moralia* (Frankfurt, 1951)

—— and Max Horkheimer, *Dialektik der Aufklärung* (Frankfurt, 1969)

Blumenberg, Hans, *Arbeit am Mythos* (Frankfurt, 1979)

Bohrer, Karl-Heinz (ed.), *Mythos und Moderne* (Frankfurt, 1983)

Bollman, Stefan, '"Kaum noch etwas". Zur Poetik von Botho Strauß', Hörisch, Jochen and Hubert Winkels (eds.) *Das schnelle Altern der neuesten Literatur* (Düsseldorf, 1985), pp. 73–96

Born, Nicolas et al., *Literaturmagazin 9: Der neue Irrationalismus* (Reinbek, 1978)

Camus, Albert, *The Myth of Sisyphus* (Harmondsworth, 1975)

Capra, Fritjof, *The Turning Point* (London, 1982)

Drews, Jorg, 'Über einen neuerdings in der deutschen Literatur erhobenen vornehmen Ton', *Merkur*, 38, 1984, pp. 949–54

Eigen, Manfred and Ruth Winkler, *Das Spiel. Naturgesetze steuern den Zufall* (Munich, 1975)

Hofe, Gerhard vom and Peter Pfaff, *Das Elend des Polyphem. Zum Thema der Subjektivität bei Thomas Bernhard, Peter Handke, Wolfgang Koeppen und Botho Strauß* (Königstein, 1980)

Huyssen, Andreas and Klaus R. Scherpe (eds.), *Postmoderne. Zeichen eines kulturellen Wandels* (Reinbek, 1986)

Kappner, Hartmut, 'Adornos Reflexionen über den Verfall des bürgerlichen Individuums', *Text + Kritik. Sonderband T.W. Adorno* 1977, pp. 44–63

Lattmann, Dieter, *Die lieblose Republik* (Munich, 1981)

Lüdke, W.M. and D. Schmidt (eds.), *Literaturmagazin 17: "Wer mir der liebste deutsche Dichter sei?"* (Reinbek, 1986)

Marcuse, Herbert, *Eros and Civilisation* (Boston, 1966)

McGowan, Moray, 'Schlachthof und Labyrinth. Subjektivität und Aufklärungszweifel in der Prosa von Botho Strauß', *Text + Kritik* 81, 1986, pp. 55–71

—— 'Unendliche Geschichte für die Momo-Moderne? Rezeptionskontexte zum märchenhaften Erfolg der Stücke von Botho Strauß', *TheaterZeit-Schrift* 15, 1986, pp. 88–106

Nietzsche, Friedrich, *Twilight of the Idols and The Anti-Christ*, trans. R.J. Hollingdale (Hardmondsworth, 1968)

Novalis, *Werke* (Munich, 1969)

Peter, Klaus, 'Romanticism Today: The "New Irrationalism" in West Germany and Its Historical Context', *Germanic Review* 61, 1986, 1, pp. 19–28

Raulet, Gérard, *Gehemmte Zukunft. Zur gegenwärtigen Krise der Emanzipation* (Darmstadt & Neuwied, 1986)

Ruoff, Karen, 'Rückblick auf die Wende zur "Neuen Subjektivität", *Argument* 142, 1983, pp. 802–20

Schechner, Richard, *The End of Humanism* (New York, 1982)

Schneider, Michael, 'Botho Strauß, das bürgerliche Feuilleton und der Kultus des Verfalls', Schneider, *Den Kopf verkehrt aufgesetzt* (Darmstadt & Neuwied, 1981), pp. 234–59

Shrimpton, Nicholas, 'Flight from death', *New Statesman*, 9.2.1980

Strauß, Botho, 'ANSCHAUUNG oder: Erster Versuch, neue Spielweisen und Darstellungsformen zu rezipieren', *Theater 1969*. Velber, pp. 99–106.

Vester, Heinz-Günter, 'Konjunktur der Konjekturen. Postmodernität bei Pynchon, Eco, Strauß', *L'80*, 34, 1985, pp. 11–28

Wefelmeyer, Fritz, 'Worauf bei Botho Strauß zu blicken wäre. Hinweise zur Rezeption', *Text + Kritik*, 81, 1984, pp. 87–95

Wetzels, Walter D. (ed.), *Myth and Reason* (Austin, 1973)

Zacharias, Carna, 'Jeder Mann ist auch eine Frau', *Münchner Abendzeitung* 11.11.1977

ANTHONY WAINE

Martin Walser

The integrity of post-war literary life in the Federal Republic can be accredited in no small measure to one particular generation of writers, whose years of birth fall approximately between 1925 and 1930. By the time they reached their late teens or early twenties they had witnessed, with growing consciousness, the collapse of no less than two political systems. Although not old enough to take responsibility for the fate of either system they were then, at the end of the war, mature enough to know they had an especial obligation in the building of a new order and, as their literary proclivities unfolded, they were adamant that literature should, amongst other things, also help to construct the invisible foundations of such a new society.

Unlike their colleagues in East Germany, however, their role was not perceived as a political one, at least initially. Their stance was more a moral one and their morality was derived largely from Christian traditions. For a further, though accidentally shared trait in the make-up of this special group of writers, who included Günter Grass (1927) and Hans Magnus Enzensberger (1929), Siegfried Lenz (1926) and Rolf Hochhuth (1931), as well as Walser, was that the majority had grown up exposed to religious influences. When, in the course of the 1950s, their identification with the new republican order became more and more strained, it was not necessarily due to a radicalisation of their political views. It was much more the result of a growing spiritual alienation from the obsessively materialistic mentality of their fellow citizens. Their disillusionment was compounded by the evident support given to the new order by the Church itself. Consequently the writers found themselves out on a limb, unintentionally playing the role apparently abandoned by the Church. As Heinrich Böll, so to speak an elder cousin of this generation, once put it: 'Wie dieser Prozeß vor sich gegangen ist, der völligen Korrumpierung der sogenannten christlichen Werte beziehungsweise ihrer Reduzierung aufs rein Demonstrative, das haben ja sehr viele Literaten darzustellen versucht. Das ist ja der Gegenstand der Literatur gewesen' ('Very many writers have tried to portray how this process of the complete corruption of so-called Christian values, and their reduction to something purely for show, has happened. That was the major issue for literature').[1]

Not only did writers feel estranged from the conformist and secularised ideology of the Church. They also felt deeply mistrustful towards the vying ideologies of American-style capitalism, imported directly into their country via the Allied occupation, and Soviet Communism in whose tenets their Eastern neighbours were being re-educated. After twelve years of incessant National Socialist propaganda during the crucial years of their personal development from childhood to adulthood, this generation of writers had had its fill of all attempts to impose one monolithic view of the world upon their minds, especially since neither of the particular world-views on offer, capitalism or Communism, appeared capable of meeting their moral expectations, let alone satisfying their spiritual needs. Their response was therefore a resolute non-conformism, whereby the individual search for personal integrity and self-realisation was championed against collectivised or institutionalised doctrines of salvation.

One further factor made these writers uncomfortable and even insecure in their early relationship to post-war society. Their class origins lay predominantly in the *petite bourgeoisie*, an amorphous conglomeration of professions and groupings which the homogeneous-sounding English term 'middle classes' covers only approximately. The German *petite bourgeoisie* lacked the political sense of its past or its future which the class struggles had forged for example in the working class. It especially lacked its organisational expression in trade unions and political parties. Beyond the *petite bourgeoisie*, or rather above it, stood the ruling elite with a coherent ideology and firm economic *raison d'être*. Whilst under no illusions about the past failures of their class or its present-day vices and shortcomings these writers have not sought to dissociate themselves from it; if anything they have helped to give it a stronger sense of identity and purpose. As Helmut Halm reflects in *Ein fliehendes Pferd* (*A Runaway Horse*): 'Wenn ich überhaupt etwas bin, dann ein Kleinbürger. Und wenn ich überhaupt auf etwas stolz bin, dann darauf' ('If I am anything at all, I'm a *petit bourgeois*. And if I am proud of anything at all, it's of that').[2]

Helmut Halm's creator, Martin Walser, was born in 1927 in the village of Wasserburg on Lake Constance, seemingly light years away from the industrial heartlands and conurbations of Hessen and Nordrhein-Westfalen. No doubt mindful of this fact, and, more importantly still, of his devoutly Catholic mother, he once remarked

1. A. Eggebrecht (ed.), *Die zornigen alten Männer* (Reinbek, 1979), p. 120.
2. M. Walser, *Ein fliehendes Pferd* (Frankfurt, 1978), p. 96.

in an interview with typical irony: 'Ich weiß nur, daß ich eben durch meine Mutter in einem Bereich mittelalterlich gesicherter Religiosität aufgewachsen bin, daß meine ganze Jugend bis zu meinem sechzehnten Lebensjahr genausogut im Jahre 1220 hätte stattfinden können' ('I only know that it was very much due to my mother that I grew up in a sphere of medievally fortified religiosity and that my whole youth until I was sixteeen could just as easily have taken place in the year 1220').[3] Nevertheless modern socio-economic pressures did intrude quite tangibly on the lives of the Walsers, for their principal source of income was the village inn, and his parents were so afraid of the competition threatened by the other local hostelries that they sent their seven-year-old son out to count the number of guests frequenting the rival institutions. Walser's involvement in the family's small-time commercial activities, which also included a coal distribution business, was deepened after the death of his father in 1938, when he was still only eleven years old. Walser attributes his father's physical decline throughout the 1920s and 1930s not only to ill-health (diabetes) but to his inadequate business acumen in times of chronic economic instability. It is therefore quite likely that such early stressful experiences of business, money and work have made Walser hypersensitive to this area of human existence, even though the environs of Wasserburg are starkly rural and almost pre-industrial. On the other hand this peculiar confluence of rustic beauty and pecuniary dictates helps to imbue particularly his later novels with a characteristically grotesque ambience.

In his earlier novels *Ehen in Philippsburg*, *Halbzeit*, *Das Einhorn* and *Der Sturz* which span approximately the first fifteen years of his career as a prose writer, Walser had explored the urban world with the help of a character, like himself, from a decidedly non-urban South German background. In *Ehen in Philippsburg* (1957) Hans Beumann hails from Kümmertshausen, whilst in the trilogy of works comprising *Halbzeit* (1960), *Das Einhorn* (1966) and *Der Sturz* (1973) Anselm Kristlein's roots are in Ramsegg. But these novels do not reveal Walser to be in the Romantic tradition of German writers who abhor man-made environments and seek more or less permanent refuge in the seclusion of nature. Beumann and Kristlein, at least initially, revel in the opportunities offered by big city life, be they in the form of social advancement, financial self-betterment or simply sexual escapades. They reveal themselves to be gregarious, adaptable and upwardly mobile. Thus Walser's first novel *Ehen in*

3. K.S. Parkes, 'Society and the Individual in the Works of Martin Walser' (unpublished Ph.D. dissertation, University of Bradford, 1971), p. 308.

Philippsburg opens with the greenhorn Hans Beumann on his first day in the big city rising in a crowded lift to the top floor of a Philippsburg skyscraper — symbolically foreshadowing his own smooth rise to the upper echelons of Philippsburg's establishment. Part of Beumann's success in reaching the room at the top is due to his naïve eagerness to learn and adapt to the rules of the social game and to allow himself to be educated by those who have already won their spurs in the contests and battles which Walser reveals social relationships to be mainly about. The imagery of game, competition and confrontation, of losers and victors, of inferiority and superiority is ubiquitous not only in the early works but also in those written after *Der Sturz*. Walser adopts an anthropological and even zoological perspective on social relationships in his first four novels and even introduces key concepts from such disciplines for chapter headings, such as the one entitled 'Mimikry' in *Halbzeit*. In other words, in the works of the 1950s and 1960s Walser's interpretation of the world takes its cue from the ostensibly ideology-free sciences such as anthropology, botany, physics and zoology and eschews the ideologically charged social and political sciences, as befits his particular generation of writer-intellectual. The rat-race atmosphere of 1950s' Germany evidently evoked Darwinian associations in observer-participants like Walser, a fact which is reflected in the prevalence of animal imagery. *Ehen in Philippsburg*, having chartered the success of Hans Beumann, shortly before the novel ends compares him to 'ein Pferd, das den Startschuß nicht mehr erwarten kann' (a horse which cannot wait any longer for the starting gun').[4]

The novel is not just about the social transition of Beumann. It explores states of psychological transition from one phase of life to the next and it is in the sensitive exploration of this theme that Walser was to excel in future works such as *Das Einhorn* and *Ein fliehendes Pferd*. It will not be lost on English readers that the hero's surname phonetically spells 'boy' and 'man'; and the novel seeks to trace the 'Verrat, der den Jüngling zum Mann macht' ('The betrayal which turns the boy into the man').[5] Walser does not view this ageing process as one of maturation, with its positive connotations, but as one of fragmentation and deformation. Towards the end of the novel Beumann is pictured sitting on his bed 'in zwei Hälften zerrissen' ('torn in two halves').[6] He has acquired new values but the author leaves us in no doubt that they are false or corrupted ones: egoism,

4. M. Walser, *Ehen in Philippsburg* (Reinbek, 1963), p. 226.
5. Ibid., p. 42.
6. Ibid., p. 222.

ambition, pride and success. Through the acquisition of such values his personality becomes deformed and in chronicling such a negative development Walser is tacitly rejecting the idealistic legacy of the *Bildungsroman*. If we interpret *Bildung* less in the figurative sense of 'education' and more in the literal meaning of 'formation' we can see how *Ehen in Philippsburg* represents a novel of deformation. But the novel is highly ironic, in that it parades a negative personality development as if it were the natural, socially sanctioned one.

Unfortunately the impact of this depiction is weakened somewhat by the technique of paralleling Beumann's story with that of three other male contemporaries. Though Beumann weaves in and out of their lives too, he is still frequently lost sight of and the overall picture is fragmented. This particular danger was overcome in the following three novels in which Walser chooses to narrate in the first person. The choice of first-person narrator is almost certainly connected with Walser's growing desire to obtain a maximum degree of subjective truth. That is to say, the so-called 'I' narrator enables Walser to project himself very directly into his hero, Anselm Kristlein. Hence realism for Walser was not the reproduction of the objective phenomena constituting one's daily existence, private and public, but their variegated refraction through every nook and cranny of one individual's mind, including dreams, fantasies and memories; reflections on existence and history but also on marriage and sexuality; musings on words, on languages, indigenous and foreign, real and invented (cf. *Das Einhorn*), and on dialects; Proustian inner monologues about the nature of time, and the disparity between experience and recollection (also found in *Das Einhorn*). The structure of the resultant works is therefore determined by the twists and turns of Anselm Kristlein's labyrinthine consciousness rather than by any linear chronology of events.

Yet the author's search for subjective authenticity should not be construed as a purely private exercise in soul-searching. Walser's self-awareness as a socially determined being is translated into his fiction by exposing his central figure to a plethora of changing social situations, from breakfast routines with the family to business discussions with customers, from hospital sojourns to New Year's parties with friends and associates. Furthermore he shows Anselm's changing professional status, from travelling salesman to advertising consultant, followed by his transformation to writer and itinerant intellectual (in *Das Einhorn*) and, completing the odyssey, the journey on foot in *Der Sturz* from Munich to Lake Constance, where he and his wife run a convalescent home and where he continues to write. The ever changing situations and locations enable Walser to demonstrate two basic images of modern man. The individual in modern society is not a free agent. Instead of acting, he reacts. He is not free, but dependent. Second, the modern individual possesses an almost inexhaustible repertoire of roles which he produces in order to conform to the changing dictates of the situation and which enable him not only to survive but also to change.

Regarding the first image of man being, so to speak, in bondage, the terms *abhängig* ('dependent') and *Abhängigkeit* ('dependency') are central ones in Walser's vocabulary. However, Walser is less concerned with states of economic or political dependency, more with states of mental and emotional bondage. These states of mind may well have deeper-lying economic and social causes but it is the non-material effect on the individual's consciousness which fascinates Walser. Furthermore, the sense of dependency may well have been conditioned by more private relationships too, such as those between child and parent, or between husband and wife. Equally one's sexual identity may also impinge on this area. Much of the ironic power of the Anselm Kristlein trilogy is derived from the discrepancy between the salesman-hero's insistence on independence, his frantic pursuit of this particular 'commodity', and his blindness to the web of dependencies in which he is actually caught. Only towards the end of *Der Sturz* does Anselm begin to grasp the reality of his situation, but by then it is tragically and ironically too late. His only escape is an imagined suicidal journey with his wife across the Alps ending with their car sliding off the road and falling into a ravine.

The chronicle of Anselm's fate comprising *Halbzeit*, *Das Einhorn* and *Der Sturz* constitutes a unique achievement in contemporary German literature because if proffers an all-encompassing view of man's illusions, imperfections and inadequacies, which makes it read like some modern religious allegory — not least in view of Walser's pointed choice of surname for his pilgrim Kristlein ('the little Christian')! Indeed Richard Hinton Thomas, discussing the ending of the trilogy, summarised his thoughts thus: 'Like one returned to Eden, he is at peace with himself and the world. If, then, one wants to hear suggestions of a theme of salvation, so be it. The title of *Der Sturz* will then gain in significance, likewise the detail from Michelangelo's "Fall of Man" on the dust-cover of the original edition — and Walser's trilogy will then look less narrowly sociological, less exclusively fixated on the material aspects of the affluent society, than tends sometimes to be assumed'.[7]

7. R.H. Thomas, 'Martin Walser — The Nietzsche Connection', *German Life and*

Hinton Thomas is of course not dismissing the sociological import of the chronicle because he is only too well aware, as he and Wilfried van der Will proved most convincingly, that this trilogy captures with uncanny accuracy the atmosphere of the West German rags-to-riches transformation.[8] It represents a trenchant critique of the consumerist ethic which Walser sees at the heart of present-day capitalism. On his first day back in business after a protracted illness requiring surgery (an illness which Walser, as he so often does elsewhere, give us to understand as a reaction of the body to the stresses and strains of modern life) Anselm fantasises about how he would inculcate this modern *ersatz*-creed in a group of trainee salesmen: 'Sie sollen endlich wissen, daß Verkaufen nichts anderes ist, als Leute zum Konsum zu zwingen' ('They will at last be made to understand that selling is nothing other than compelling people to consume').[9] In selecting a rep as the hero of his novel Walser has not only found an archetypal representative of the *petite bourgeoisie* but in associating selling with this class he has instinctively focused on their *sine qua non* in contrast to the class owning the means of production and the working class whose economic rationale is to produce the goods.

Furthermore, Walser tellingly reveals how this sell-and-consume mentality is all-embracing, extending even to the hero's erotic fantasies and view of the sexes. A good deal of the novel concentrates, as did *Ehen in Philippsburg*, on extra-marital activities. Anselm is shown to be dependent on the affections of a number of female friends, whom he treats less as people, more as products for his own consumption. When Anselm finally alights upon the Jewess Susanne the climax is a seduction scene in which he indulges in his own 'male sale'[10] and operates, using the appropriate English and German jargon, according to the commandments of his professional dogma: 'How to sell myself to Susan? *Führen Sie Ihre Ware glaubwürdig vor!*' ('*Present your product with conviction!*').[11]

Such cynicism on the part of the main male character bears witness to Walser's anti-heroic, anti-idealistic conception of Anselm and his sort. When we next encounter him five years on in *Das Einhorn* (1966) he has graduated to the ranks of the intelligentsia, where different value-systems may be expected to obtain. But, true

Letters, XXXV (1982), p. 323.

8. R.H. Thomas and W. van der Will, *German Literature and the Affluent Society* (Manchester, 1968).

9. M. Walser, *Halbzeit* (Frankfurt, 1973), p. 93–4.

10. Ibid., p. 707.

11. Ibid., p. 698.

to his nature, he is not motivated by moral or political convictions to air his opinions in public, but by money: 'Zuerst reiste er mit Schuhwichse, Modeschmuck, Aussteuerwäsche, dann erfand er stationär Meinungen über Produkte, jetzt reist er mit vier Vorträgen und erfindet stationär Antworten auf Schicksalsfragen. Damals hieß es: die freie Marktwirtschaft, welche unserer Freiheit den Grund legt, braucht Dich. Anselm brauchte Geld . . . Anselm . . . braucht immer noch Geld' ('At first he travelled with shoe polish, jewellery, bottom drawer linen, then he invented on-the-spot opinions about products, now he travels with four lectures and invents on-the-spot answers to questions about our destiny. In those days the saying went: the free market economy, which is the foundation of our democracy, needs you. Anselm, however, needed money . . . Anselm . . . still does need money').[12]

The frank and engaging cynicism with which Anselm, as rep or intellectual con man, tells his readers about his material dependency only thinly disguises the confessional undertone which is strongly audible in the first four works of this Catholic author. In an interview for a BBC radio programme in the late 1970s, Walser, speaking in English, explained frankly:

> The main character of a novel, that's me. At the same time I can always say, that's not me. And I can confess things with the help of such characters which I never would like to mention under my own name, you know? I would be ashamed. In reality I have to defend myself. In fiction I can attack myself, you know? That means, there is freedom. There are operations possible which are not possible in a modern society, in which everybody has to play a certain role. He has to fulfil expectations and so I think in a novel I can live.[13]

Not only does Walser explicitly employ the term 'confess' but his statement also suggests how literature functions as a therapeutic outlet for emotions and thoughts which the author as an ordinary citizen is forced by his society to suppress.

The use of the novel as a therapeutic medium is evident throughout *Die Gallistl'sche Krankheit*, which bears many affinities to *Das Einhorn*, but also reflects significant changes in Walser's own political development since the appearance of *Das Einhorn* in 1966. If, as Beckermann maintains, '*Das Einhorn* ist gerade, weil davon nicht explizit die Rede ist, ein genauer Ausdruck der Situation bundesre-

12. M. Walser, *Das Einhorn* (Frankfurt, 1974), p. 79.
13. Interview with R. Mayne in 'Fire in the Phoenix: The Arts in West Germany since 1945', BBC Radio 3, November 1979.

publikanischer Intellektueller vor der Zeit der außerparlamentarischen Opposition' ('*The Unicorn*, precisely because it is not explicitly stated, expresses exactly the situation of the intellectuals in the Federal Republic prior to the extra-parliamentary opposition')[14] then *Die Gallistl'sche Krankheit* written between 1969 and 1972 is tangible evidence of committed intellectuals like Walser discovering in the student-inspired protest movement of the late 1960s a cause for hope, a reason to believe. The inward-looking and escapist behaviour of Anselm and many other writer-intellectuals in *Das Einhorn* which, in the case of Anselm, culminated in the self-estrangement and self-exile of *Der Sturz*, is now reflected upon critically by Walser's new, more sceptical protagonist Josef Gallistl.

Gallistl's therapy begins with his meticulous and painful examination of his physical and psychological symptoms, many of which he shares with Kristlein, proceeding to an even more important step, namely, the search for their causes. In exemplary fashion Walser illustrates a new dimension to his understanding of the meaning of realism. The critical, realistic novel must not only depict the deformations in the psyche of the individual but must also show the social origins of these deformations. In the case of the sick, *petit bourgeois* intellectual Gallistl, one of the main reasons for his disintegrating personality lies in the *petit bourgeois* clique of friends, known simply as A, B, C, D, E and F (symbolising their lack of real, individual identity). Their interrelationships are clinically dissected by G(allistl) to reveal a core of rivalry, egoism and antagonism. Unlike Kristlein, who willingly subscribed to the post-war achiever and go-getter mentality only to discover at the end the anti-human nature of bourgeois individualism, Gallistl's 'Fall' is halted in time. The Fall of the individualist Gallistl is the precondition for his Rise as he finds in a group of Communist Party activists the fertile soil for a new socialist identity — the first time in his fiction that Walser has sought to espouse an ideology. But the final chapter, in which Gallistl's re-socialisation and re-education commence, is ironically entitled 'Es wird einmal' ('Once there will be'), a deliberate allusion to the fairy-tale convention, informing the reader that this is more a utopian projection, fiction not fact.

As far as Walser was personally concerned, it did unfortunately remain fiction, partly for political reasons and partly for personal ones. Regarding the former the democratic advances made between 1965 and 1970 came under pressure throughout the 1970s as West

14. T. Beckermann, 'Epilog auf eine Romanform', K. Siblewski (ed.) *Martin Walser* (Frankfurt, 1981), p. 102.

Germany's reactionary forces exacerbated and exploited the hysteria over terrorist activities to legitimise their anti-democratic reforms. Intellectuals were frequent recipients of conservative vitriol, as the Böll–*Bild* confrontation tragi-comically evidenced. But the fairly rapid fragmentation of the extra-parliamentary opposition into warring factions was perhaps the single most disillusioning factor for the intellectuals of Walser's generation. Many, like Walser himself, had risked their literary reputation (and therefore their main source of income) by publicly committing themselves to unpopular causes such as the anti-Vietnam campaign, or, as Walser himself did during the first half of the 1970s, associating themselves with extreme political parties like the DKP (the German Communist Party).

His association with this party (which stopped short of actual membership) almost certainly explains the optimism radiating through the final chapter of *Die Gallistl'sche Krankheit*. Equally the rupturing of relations with the Party in 1974, which finally shattered any illusions held about finding a secular substitute for the Catholic faith which had sustained him throughout childhood and youth, can surely be cited as one personal factor behind the bleaker mood permeating Walser's next novel *Jenseits der Liebe*, published in 1976. The novel ends when the central figure Franz Horn, a middle manager with a South German firm manufacturing dentures, attempts, though unsuccessfully, to commit suicide. Horn's problems are a highly explosive mix of the personal, professional and the political. He holds a precarious position in the hierarchical structure of the firm, though he is by no means at the lower end of this hierarchy. Until recently he has been a successful manager, even enjoying a close personal relationship with the firm's boss, Arthur Thiele. This relationship (and hence Horn's own power and status) has changed following the arrival of a younger manager, Horst Liszt.

The arrival of the youthful Liszt has accelerated Horn's sense of ageing — a theme which now begins to come to the fore of Walser's fiction and is especially prominent in the next work *Ein fliehendes Pferd*. Horn has thus been effectively demoted, feels resentful, behaves childishly within the firm and violently in his home, precipitating his separation from the family. Though he feels sympathetically drawn to the Communist works' council delegate Heinz Murg, he is critical towards the Communist Party itself. We learn of all these events and attitudes through Horn's neurotic dwelling upon the various unhappy relationships, private, professional and political, during a week long business trip he is sent on to Coventry, England.

His being sent to Coventry is indeed an ironic expression of his alienation from all and sundry, of his being 'Jenseits der Liebe'. Yet the England trip is a journey of self-discovery in the course of which Horn comes to see the literally unbearable truth about himself and about others, hence his suicide attempt.

The very fact that it has been at all possible to re-narrate the main elements of the story in one and a half paragraphs is itself indicative of a new stage in Walser's fiction, and one which continues through to *Brandung* (1985). Hitherto, even in *Ehen in Philippsburg*, which contains a number of strands of action, Walser had identified with the modernist novel's deliberate vaunting of its own fictitiousness, its artificiality, with its circular and static modes and with its playing with literary conventions and antecedents as well as with the reader's expectations and preconceptions. Walser's writing had also been modernist in its tendency to allow inner action to predominate over external action, inactivity to outweigh activity. Appropriately *Halbzeit*, *Das Einhorn* and *Der Sturz* all begin with Anselm Kristlein in a horizontal position! In the modernist tradition language itself was as much the subject of the novel as it was its mode of expression, and the verbal virtuoso Anselm Kristlein is a fitting heir to this tradition.

Having raided the modernist arsenal (and replenished it) Walser's approach changes, with remarkable results, in terms both of critical acclaim and of popularity with the West German reading public at large, who now buy his hardback novels in far greater numbers than was the case prior to *Jenseits der Liebe*. What then has changed? First, Walser injects a dramatic momentum and a psychological tension into the novel, at last exploiting his experiences of writing dramas such as *Der Abstecher* (1961), *Eiche und Angora* (1962), and *Die Zimmerschlacht* (1967). Second, he delineates clearly and sensitively male–male and male–female relationships so that the central figure is countered, challenged and even changed by an opposing figure possessing his or her own credibility. Third, genuine conflict ensues as a result of these credible relationships especially since the noticeably more vulnerable central figure is often undergoing some profound physiological-psychological transition or even crisis, or is placed under particular pressure by inhospitable social or economic conditions. Fourth, the figures chosen by Walser — Horn, Zürn, Halm — differ in their make-up from their predecessors, Beumann, Kristlein and Gallistl. The latter are more designed and loaded figures responsible for purveying the author's didactic intentions to a public perceived as requiring enlightenment and education — the 1925 to 1930 generation syndrome. In contrast, the new 'monosyllabic' heroes are typical yet also credible as individuals. Furthermore they are more likeable as individuals and evoke more easily our wish to identify with them, as though Walser has resolved to be more benevolent towards his own creations. Fifth, events are telescoped into a much shorter and a much more perceivable span of time — a week during the holiday of Helmut Halm, or three months in the working life of Franz Xaver Zürn — and each day or week brings a new twist or presents an unforeseen problem, sometimes trivial, sometimes momentous. Finally, the essayistic and discursive tendencies, manifest between *Halbzeit* and *Die Gallistl'sche Krankheit* which impeded narrative flow, have been almost eliminated with the advantage that the interaction of central figure and world flows more dynamically and dialectically. In short, Walser now has a tale to tell.

Without any doubt several of these crucial changes are closely bound up with one single factor: the change from a first- to a third-person narrator. Though the narrative perspective stays as close as possible to the consciousness of the central figure, the use of the impersonal voice enables the author to exercise far greater discipline over the content of what is told and, simultaneously, to maintain a distance to his main character. It is as if Walser's first five novels, critically dwelling, as they all do, on the '*I*-centricity' of the male, have given birth to a more mature and less self-centred narrative consciousness, now reflected in the more self-detached *he*-standpoint. Neither Walser nor his protagonist claims to know the definitive solution to the problem, a fact which is axiomatically postulated in the Kierkegaard quotation preceding *Ein fliehendes Pferd*:

> Man trifft zuweilen auf Novellen, in denen bestimmte Personen entgegengesetzte Lebensanschauungen vortragen. Das endet dann gerne damit, daß der eine den andern überzeugt. Anstatt daß also die Anschauung für sich sprechen muß, wird der Leser mit dem historischen Ergebnis bereichert, daß der andere überzeugt worden ist. Ich sehe es für ein Glück an, daß in solcher Hinsicht diese Papiere eine Aufklärung nicht gewähren.[15]

> (Occasionally one comes across novellas in which specific individuals express opposite philosophies. These works invariably end with the one convincing the other. So instead of one point of view being allowed to speak for itself the reader is blessed with the historical revelation that the other has been convinced. I consider it fortunate that these pages do not provide such instruction.)

One might claim with some justification that the two male adver-

15. *Ein fliehendes Pferd*, p. 7.

saries of this story (designated a *Novelle* but almost identical in form to the short dramatic novel *Jenseits der Liebe*) learn from one another in true dialectical fashion. Helmut Halm is portrayed at the outset as introverted, passive and repressed, whilst Klaus is the apparent opposite, loquacious, dynamic and crudely expressive. During the pivotal lake storm scene, involving just the two men, all their deepest instincts and emotions rise dramatically to the surface. Klaus challenges nature, Helmut cowers before it. Believing his life to be in jeopardy Helmut knocks the tiller from Klaus's hands; Klaus falls overboard and is feared drowned. Afterwards Helmut is physically revitalised, at least until Klaus's reappearance, and, on his departure from Lake Constance with his wife Sabine, resolves to tell her all that has happened, i.e. he has become more expressive, as if having learned from Klaus, in fact so much so that when we next meet him as a visiting professor at a Californian campus university in *Brandung* (1985) he bears at times more resemblance to Klaus Buch than he does to his former self. His partial metamorphosis is vividly illustrated when he hurls himself into the surf-capped breakers of the Pacific with the same bravado and passion associated with Klaus Buch in the earlier work. Equally, Buch's manic attempts to escape from his ageing and conform to an age fixated upon the cult of individualism, fitness and potency, are exposed in *Ein fliehendes Pferd* as being, precisely, escapist *vis-à-vis* Helmut's non-conformist philosophy of ironic detachment.

The new pluralism following Walser's change of narrative perspective has brought other advantages. Particularly in respect of the female figures a noticeable and positive shift of emphasis has occurred. In his early works, narrated in the first person, such figures were only superficially drawn. Only through resorting to artificial devices, such as Anselm's illicit reading of his wife's diaries in *Halbzeit* and *Der Sturz* did the reader acquire insights into the deeper levels of the woman's life. Since all his novels from the programmatically entitled first work *Ehen in Philippsburg* have purportedly addressed themselves to the issue of marriage the tenuousness of the female figures constituted a serious flaw. In *Ein fliehendes Pferd* the young wife of Klaus Buch, Helene, fearing he has been drowned is given the opportunity (by the author) to give her version of the marriage in one long uninterrupted monologue. What her account reveals is not her dependency on Klaus, but rather his dependency on her. And this message is broadcast implicitly and explicitly throughout the post-1976 phase, from *Jenseits der Liebe* in which Horn's separation from wife and family almost certainly intensifies his isolation and nihilism, to *Brandung* where Helmut confesses: 'Sabine war ihm alles und alles war ihm Sabine und außer Sabine war nichts'[16] ('Sabine was everything to him and everything to him was Sabine and except Sabine there was nothing').

The wife figure is thereby made synonymous with the well-spring of the man's identity. Even though Helmut's confession may be tinged with characteristic self-irony the essential accuracy cannot be questioned. It is essentially an admission of dependency — the very state of mind Walser's earlier egoists had tried so hard to baulk. But the dependency is a fair price to pay for the measure of security gained. Only within a relationship with a wife of one's own age — a crucial prerequisite as the age imbalance of Klaus and Helene Buch tragi-comically revealed — can friendship, a synonym for solidarity, prosper. Marriage in Walser's work seems to provide the only dependable and stable context in which communication can take place. Hence both *Ein fliehendes Pferd* and *Brandung* close with Helmut girding himself to tell Sabine every detail of the confession we, the readers, have been privy to.

The necessity for communication and the impediments, psychological and social, to this life-saving act are central to the epistolic sequel to *Jenseits der Liebe*, *Brief an Lord Liszt* (1982). Franz Horn, now recovered and reunited with his family, but still insecurely placed in his firm's hierarchy, especially in view of the imminent fusion of Thiele's firm with a multinational concern, feels compelled to write a letter to his former rival Liszt, whose own marital problems, alcoholism and effective demotion (following the arrival of a younger man) within the firm, have made him a potential ally for Horn. Walser demasks this paradox of capitalism, i.e. one's colleague as one's competitor, and demonstrates how (male) friendship is thwarted by rivalry, jealousy, misunderstandings and, above all, communication blockages. Similarly in *Das Schwanenhaus* (1980) Franz Horn's cousin Dr Gottlieb Zürn, a self-employed estate agent, is shown embroiled in the same socially produced paradox, as he is forced to compete with his likewise self-employed colleagues, Schatz and Kaltammer, for the right to sell the glittering prize of the *art nouveau* Swan House. Zürn's fetishistic fascination with this house, itself a symbol of a bygone capitalist era, brings his deeply engrained avarice and ambition to the surface of his consciousness. Only through admitting to his real motives ('Ehrgeiz. Wahnsinniger Ehrgeiz. Sein altes Leiden') ('Ambition. Insane ambition. His old illness')[17] is he able to get his life into perspective and liberate

16. M. Walser, *Brandung* (Frankfurt, 1985), p. 251.
17. M. Walser, *Das Schwanenhaus* (Frankfurt, 1980), p. 220.

himself, at least spiritually, from the draining obsession with his 'Kollegen Konkurrenten' ('colleague competitors').[18]

A spiritual liberation process is also thematised in *Seelenarbeit* (1979). In his portrayal of a master–servant relationship between a chauffeur, Franz Xaver Zürn, and his boss Gleitze, Walser is returning to his central preoccupation with dependency relationships, relationships which should not, but quite manifestly still do belong to modern, democratic societies. Economically, Zürn is relatively secure, even after his demotion to a fork-lift truck operator. But his psychological enslavement to Gleitze, the lack of communication between them even on long car journeys, renders Zürn more and more prone to psychosomatic disorders, especially in his intestinal regions. Furthermore, pressures from the sphere of work engage and entangle themselves with tensions and conflicts smouldering beneath the surface of domestic life — another leitmotif of the later works. And since, as the post-Gallistl characters all do, he had inherited a personality structure with a pronounced tendency both to repress emotion (be it anger or affection) and to crave attention and approval, especially from superiors, the resultant state of soul is one oscillating between destructive and self-destructive urges.

Thus Franz Xaver Zürn develops an uncontrollable urge to collect knives and almost succumbs to fantasies of murdering his boss Gleitze. Halm in *Ein fliehendes Pferd* actually causes his Mephistophelian tormentor Buch to fall overboard during the storm on the lake, whilst in *Brandung* he is sorely tempted to rape his fantasy-object Fran Webb, who has ensnared him so cruelly. But whereas the destinies of Beumann, Kristlein and for a long time Gallistl too, were left to chance, from Horn onwards Walser's protagonists gradually perceive more clearly who they really are through a combination of factors: exhaustive and painful soul-searching ('Seelenarbeit'!); communication and solidarity within the private sphere; and fortuitous encounters with soul-mates and fellow-sufferers such as Keith Heath in *Jenseits der Liebe*, Klaus Buch in *Ein fliehendes Pferd* or Liszt in *Brief an Lord Liszt*. Even confrontations with one's own inner physical being as when Xaver in *Seelenarbeit* undergoes five days of intimate medical examinations in a Tübingen clinic can produce a similar catalytic effect. From Franz Horn to Helmut Halm Walser's suffering males do weather the storm to emerge with their identity a fraction more integrated, whilst so many of their contemporaries are seen disintegrating or dying, the victims of drink, broken marriages,

18. Ibid., p. 15.

societal pressures, incurable illnesses or just untimely accidents.

Furthermore their individual progress, modest as it may appear, has to be set against an era of economic progress, but political and social inertia. This era is characterised by the upper-middle-class owners of wealth and power (personified in these novels by Thiele, Gleitze, Schatz and Kaltammer) continuing to consolidate their positions whilst the *petite bourgeoisie* adapts to economic and social circumstances with mechanical dependability. In highlighting the *petit bourgeois* crises of the trio of cousins, Franz Horn, Gottlieb Zürn and Franz Xaver Zürn, or even of the more private *petit bourgeois* Helmut Halm, and the productive mental processes triggered off by these crises, Walser is implicitly rejecting a mechanistic and static view of history and proferring a dialectical one, as individuals grasp the contradictions of their social situation and age.

The underlying tendency of Walser's *oeuvre* since *Die Gallistl'sche Krankheit* (1972) can therefore, at least with reference to the central figures and their immediate family, be designated as positive. One could even describe these works as novels of (male) emancipation, the term emancipation referring less to a political or ideological process than to a socio-psychological one. His beleaguered and blocked individuals are not, however, released as was Gallistl through the advent of outside forces bearing a doctrinal panacea. Instead they learn, like Gallistl initially, to comprehend the subconscious mechanisms which block them and learn also to perceive the machinery of competition, power and achievement which beleaguers them: 'Gottlieb sah plötzlich die ganze Welt vor sich; ein System, in dem jeder von einem andern zuviel verlangt, weil von ihm ein anderer zuviel verlangt' ('Gottlieb suddenly saw the whole world before him; a system in which each person demanded too much of another person, because another person demanded too much from him').[19] Statements such as this from *Das Schwanenhaus* abound in the works of the years 1976 to 1985. Phrases like 'sah plötzlich' ('suddenly saw'), 'jetzt sah er zum ersten Mal' ('now he saw for the first time'), and, 'sein Fehler all die Jahre' ('his mistake during all these years'), recur frequently in these works and signal the occurrence of a key insight, marking a new phase in a process of becoming conscious or, alternatively, of becoming (self-)critical.

One can maintain, in conclusion, that this quest for individual integrity and individual enlightenment has been basic to all Walser's works from *Ehen in Philippsburg* to *Brandung*, even though his earlier characters were shown failing in their search. He has never

19. Ibid., p. 144.

succumbed to the apocalyptic visions of some of his contemporaries nor to the narcissistic subjectivism of a new generation of younger German-speaking novelists. Moreover, wherever he has indulged in more experimental fiction, it has not been at the expense of social relevance. In fact social relevance has been the keynote of his particular brand of prose writing. Yet the obligation to be socially relevant has not resulted in listless, abstract parables either. Two qualities have constantly coloured and animated all his social analyses. First, the dogged rootedness in the provincial, *petit bourgeois* reality of his native South Germany; and, second, the satirical, ironic and even grotesque transformation of that reality. These qualities, combined with the numerous ones already mentioned, make Walser the critical and comic realist *par excellence* of his generation.

ANTHONY STEPHENS AND JUDITH WILSON

Christa Wolf

Ich verlange in allem — Leben, Möglichkkeit des Daseins . . .

Georg Büchner, *Lenz*[1]

(I demand in everything — life, the possibility of existence.)

In her novel *Nachdenken über Christa T.*, which appeared in 1968, Christa Wolf describes a scene in which the main character and her fiancé, Justus, visit the latter's relatives in West Berlin. Such scenes are invariably charged with tension in East German literature and this is no exception. The narrator comments:

> Drüben, wo die anderen, wo entgegengesetzte Entwürfe von allem — von jedermann und jeder Sache und jedem Gedanken — hergestellt werden; denn das ist der wahre Grund, wenn einem ungeheuer ist, wenn man voll unheimlicher Erwartung um die nächste Ecke biegt: Immer nur derselbe lächelnde Verkehrsschutzmann. Aber ebensogut könnte man von sich selbst überrumpelt werden. Nicht nur das Land, jeden von uns gibt es doppelt: als Möglichkeit, als Un-Möglichkeit. Manchmal löst man sich aus der Verwirrung mit Gewalt. [2]

(On the other side, where the others, where opposing models of every-

1. Georg Büchner, *Lenz, Werke und Briefe* (Wiesbaden, 1958), p. 94. In her 'Büchner-Preis-Rede' of 1980 Christa Wolf says: 'Wenn einer, muß Büchner das Verlangen gekannt haben, das Unmögliche zu leisten: den blinden Fleck dieser Kultur sichtbar werden zu lassen' ('If anyone ever has, then Büchner certainly knew the desire to achieve the impossible: to expose the blind spot of this culture'). Christa Wolf's later writing could be said to attempt much the same.
2. In this essay Christa Wolf's works will be quoted in the text using the following abbreviations and editions: *Der geteilte Himmel* (Munich, 1973) dtv 915 (*GH*); *Nachdenken über Christa T.* (Darmstadt and Neuwied, 1977), Sammlung Luchterhand 31 (*N*); *Lesen und Schreiben: Neue Sammlung, Essays, Aufsätze, Reden* (Darmstadt and Neuwied, 1984), Sammlung Luchterhand 295 (*LS*); *Kindheitsmuster: Roman* (Darmstadt and Neuwied, 1979) Sammlung Luchterhand 277 (*KM*); *Kein Ort. Nirgends* (Darmstadt and Neuwied, 1979) Sammlung Luchterhand 325 (*KN*); *Kassandra: Erzählung* (Darmstadt and Neuwied) (*K*); *Voraussetzung einer Erzählung: Kassandra* (Darmstadt and Neuwied, 1983), Sammlung Luchterhand 456 (*V*); *Gesammelte Erzählungen* (Darmstadt and Neuwied, 1981), Sammlung Luchterhand 361 (*GE*).

thing — of everyone, of every object, of every thought — are produced; for that is the true reason for the uncanny feeling with which one turns the next corner, full of apprehension: but it's always just the same smiling traffic-policeman. One could, in fact, just as well be surprised by oneself. Not only for the country, but for each of us there is a double: we exist as possibility, as impossibility. Sometimes one can only free oneself from the dilemma by force.)

In her previous novel, *Der geteilte Himmel* (1963), the overt attitude of the narrator towards the West is much more unequivocally hostile. There a similar visit to West Berlin elicits the comment: 'Man ist schlimmer als im Ausland, weil man die eigene Sprache hört. Man ist auf schreckliche Weise in der Fremde' ('It is worse than being in a foreign country because you hear your own language. In a terrible way you are in alien territory') (*GH*, 174). It is quite typical of Christa Wolf's work to set up an opposition, such as 'possibility/ impossibility', which at first appears absolute, but then to blur its contours in the final statement which emerges from the text as a whole. Indeed one may see her whole artistic development as a continual experiment, in the sense that it is determined by the need to create fresh possibilities of existence, but always through what Ingeborg Bachman called the 'Widerspiel des Unmöglichen mit dem Möglichen' ('the interaction of impossibility with the possible').[3] Christa Wolf's essays have, since the mid-1960s, played an important role in explaining the models she sets up in her fiction, and in *Tagebuch — Arbetsmittel und Gedächtnis*, written in December 1966 and included in the first edition of *Lesen und Schreiben*, she expounds the model, which in fact underlies *Nachdenken über Christa* T., in terms which highlight the dualism of possibility/impossibility as it applies both to historical reality and to fiction. Before we embark on a survey of her major works in chronological order, it seems advisable to explore further the implications of this model for her work as a whole.

Counterpointing the diary entry of a Jewish boy, written shortly before he was murdered in Treblinka, with an anecdote from the poet Wilhelm Lehmann's *Bukolisches Tagebuch*, she takes offence at Lehmann's sentimentalising the death of an insect: 'Sein süßer Leichnam ruht auf dem Papier, ich sinne ihm nach' ('Its sweet corpse rests on the paper; my thoughts will not leave it').[4] In the face

3. Ingeborg Bachmann, *Werke*, eds. Christine Koschel, Inge von Weidenbaum, Clemens Münster (Munich, 1978), vol. 4, p. 276; cf. Sigrid Weigel, 'Vom Sehen zur Seherin', *Text + Kritik* 46, 3rd edn., 1985, p. 81.

4. Christa Wolf, 'Tagebuch — Arbeitsmittel und Gedächtnis', *Lesen und Schreiben:*

of an historical reality which has reduced the Jewish boy's possibilities in life to a single possibility, death, an apparently innocuous enthusing over nature is transformed for her into inhumanity: 'Ist es unbillig, auszusprechen, daß Dawid Rubinowicz' Tagebuch solche Zeilen in Un-Natur verwandelt?' ('Is it unfair to state that juxtaposing such lines with Dawid Rubinowicz's diary renders them inhuman?').

What determines the possibility or impossibility of an existence, the spuriousness or authenticity of a piece of writing is for Christa Wolf the specific form the play of opposites takes. It may be the political opposition of East and West, the discrepancy between vision and reality in socialist society, the dilemmas posed by censorship and self-censorship, the tension between an authentic inner self and a public personality; increasingly in her later works it is the tension between a patriarchal order of society and its possible alternatives or, as in the above example, the dissonance produced by deliberately confronting writing that is the immediate expression of the self with the posed attitudes of artistic self-consciousness.

In *Nachdenken über Christa T.* the dualism appears in the constant emphasis on dimensions of the main character's life which remain unrealised; in this novel and in *Kindheitsmuster* the possibility of narration itself is repeatedly called into question because of its tendency to fix and thus deform the characters it creates; in the case of the longer narrative works, no longer designated as novels, which follow *Kindheitsmuster*, namely *Kein Ort. Nirgends* (1979) and *Kassandra* (1983), the tension between her determination to push back the limits of what can be said, to recover lost areas of experience or explore new ones, and her scepticism about the adequacy of simple narration, leads to a splitting off of the fictional text from discursive explanations: the essays on Karoline von Günderrode and Bettina von Arnim and the *Voraussetzungen einer Erzählung: Kassandra*. In *Kindheitsmuster* the sheer amount of questioning of the probity of narrative is clearly related to the stresses set up by the enormity of the events it tries to encompass, a childhood and adolescence spent in the Third Reich, but the fabric of the novel ultimately manages to withstand these pressures. With the later works, Christa Wolf has apparently moved away from the novel form, separating off the exposition of ideas in order to articulate a greater range of possible forms of existence and to allow a greater freedom of formal experimentation.

Aufsätze und Betrachtungen (Darmstadt and Neuwied, 1972), p. 65. This essay was not included in later editions.

Her practice of cultivating both a range of possibilities and their opposites within a given context produces in her work a certain lack of fixity, the blurring of contours we spoke of earlier. This may well account for the continued, although uneasy, co-existence of her work with the demands of the regime in East Germany and for the sharp divisions in the critical response to it in both Germanies. On the one hand, the cat-and-mouse game she plays with official disapproval has a proven strategic value in opening up new territory for East German fiction. On the other hand, she generalises specific human difficulties to the point where they become intractable problems of existence and this has resulted in her going over much the same ground several times. It is fair to say that since *Nachdenken über Christa T.* she has shifted much the same set of problems into increasingly distant dimensions of the past: firstly into the recent past of *Kindheitsmuster*; secondly into the early nineteenth-century historical setting of *Kein Ort. Nirgends*; thirdly into the mythic past of *Kassandra*.

As we have shown elsewhere, this process goes hand in hand with a growing detachment from the doctrinaire views of social and historical progress to which the regime in East Germany expects writers to adhere.[5] In *Der Schatten eines Traumes* (1978), the fate of Kleist, Günderrode and their generation is blamed on the perversity of historical processes, the disjunction between exceptional individuals and the confusion of society: 'Die neue bürgerliche Gesellschaft, noch gar nicht ausgebildet und schon verkümmert, benutzt sie als Entwürfe — Vorformen, die hastig verworfen werden' ('The new middle-class society, still inchoate and already debilitated, uses them as drafts, preliminary versions that are all too rapidly rejected') (*LS*, 227). Despite the claims of the present socialist state to be the summation of everything good in history, Kleist and Günderrode have fared no better at the hands of contemporary East German literary orthodoxy. By *Voraussetzungen einer Erzählung: Kassandra*, history in both Germanies seems to have reached a stalemate in the conviction that: 'die jungen Intellektuellen zu beiden Seiten dieser Grenze sich an Unmöglichem abarbeiten . . . Und daß die Älteren, Abgeklärten meiner Generation schon lange erkannt haben: Es gibt keinen Spielraum für Veränderung. Es gibt keine revolutionäre Situation' ('The young intellectuals on both sides of this border are exhausting themselves in the pursuit of the impossible . . . And that the older members of my generation, those

5. Anthony Stephens and Judith Wilson, 'Entwurf einer Poetik der Klage', *Text + Kritik* 46, 3rd. edn., 1985, p. 29.

who no longer have any illusions, have been aware for some time: there is no room for change. There is no revolutionary situation') (*V*, 95f.). Further on in the same text, all the doubts about the morality of fiction, which are familiar from *Nachdenken über Christa T.* and *Kindheitsmuster*, culminate in the formulation of a nexus between linear narrative and male dominance in history and society:

> Erst als Besitz, Hierarchie, Patriarchat entstehn, wird aus dem Gewebe des menschlichen Lebens . . . jener eine blutrote Faden herausgerissen, wird er auf Kosten der Gleichmäßigkeit des Gewebes verstärkt: die Erzählung von der Heroen Kampf und Sieg oder Untergang. Die Fabel wird geboren. Das Epos, aus den Kämpfen um das Patriarchat entstanden, wird *durch seine Struktur* auch ein Instrument zu seiner Herausbildung und Befestigung. (*V*, 147).

> (Not until private property, the rule of priests and the patriarchy arise, is that one blood-red thread torn out of the fabric of human existence, is it reinforced at the expense of the wholeness of the fabric: the story of the heroes' combat and victory or of their defeat and death. Fiction is born. The epic, a product of the struggle to establish the patriarchy, becomes *by virtue of its very structure* as well an instrument to use in its development and consolidation.)

A programmatic statement such as this seems to confront the reader with various inconsistencies. Not only has Christa Wolf in the same work defined narrative as 'making meaningful' (*V*, 37) what is narrated, but the story she finally tells of Kassandra is itself linear in the extreme. Moreover, its purpose is clearly to make Kassandra's life and convictions significant despite the inevitability of her violent death. It is in fact the narrative process itself which produces this meaning, whereas the bare facts of the myth, to which Christa Wolf adheres, would ultimately deny it.[6] The possibility of existence which *Kassandra* makes tangible can only emerge — because of the way in which Christa Wolf has chosen to tell the story — both in opposition to the myth itself and to the author's own programmatic condemnation of linear narrative.

In all of Christa Wolf's work there is a problematic mixing of such contradictions as are clearly strategic with others that have every appearance of being unintentional. It is in a sense the conceptual intransigence of the 'either/or', which she develops as a response to a given historical, political or personal situation, that rebounds on both her theoretical statements and her fictional characters. The criticism which Habermas makes of Horkheimer's and Adorno's

6. Sigrid Weigel, 'Vom Sehen', pp. 74–5.

view of history in their book *Die Dialektik der Aufklärung*, namely that by presenting the negativity of history in such absolute terms they place themselves in a position where it becomes virtually impossible to conceive of resistance as a reality, could also apply to Christa Wolf.[7] By placing increasing emphasis on history as something which can only reduce individuals to objects, she apparently leaves herself little alternative to the descent into myth as pre-rationality, which duly takes place in *Kassandra*. But there is little point in criticism's forcing still further the contradictions which Christa Wolf exercises, for there is a sense in which she herself is really most interested in the possibilities of free play that lie between their terms. This is what she propounds in a commentary on a poem by Ingeborg Bachmann in the third of the lectures on *Kassandra*. The poem is a reflection on the cost of invulnerability; it suggests that one must leave no opening if one is to remain unscathed, yet it is itself an example of what Wolf calls 'the most precise indeterminacy, the most unequivocal ambiguity. This way and no other, it says, but at the same time — which is logically unthinkable —: this way/the other' (*V*, 129). Ultimately, and perhaps paradoxically, the lasting value of her work resides in those figures she creates whose contradictory thinking is a form of opposition to a system that is perceived as preventing far too many contradictions from being articulated.

Christa Wolf's first publications in the 1950s and 1960s, mainly critical reviews in *Neue Deutsche Literatur*, the periodical of the East German Writers' Union, present a position which is as far away as can readily be imagined from the stance she has taken today. Indeed there is a certain amount of competition among writers on her work to fix the moment when the 'real' Christa Wolf begins to emerge. She has herself variously defended and repudiated her beginnings.[8] What they do have in common with all the positions she has put forward since is the seriousness and strength of conviction with which she advocates her current concept of literature. In an article in *Neue Deutsche Literatur* of 1956 she confronts squarely the issue of what literature in East Germany is meant to be: 'Worin besteht denn die Funktion unserer Literatur, as Ganzes betrachtet? Sie müßte klarmachen, wie bei uns das gesellschaftlich Notwendige sich in Übereinstimmung befindet mit der tiefen Sehnsucht der Men-

7. Peter Uwe Hohendahl, 'The Dialectic of Enlightment Revisited: Habermas' Critique of the Frankfurt School', *new german critique* 35, 1985, p. 8.

8. Documentation: Christa Wolf (Interviews), in: *German Quarterly* 57/1, 1984, p. 97; Christa Wolf, 'Über Sinn and Unsinn von Naivität', *LS*, pp. 56–68.

schen nach Vervollkommnung, nach allseitiger Ausbildung ihrer Persönlichkeit. . . . Hier, in dem Bewußtsein von der historischen Notwendigkeit, von der echten Menschlichkeit unseres Kampfes, liegen die Quellen unserer Siegeszuversicht' ('What is the essential function of our literature viewed as a whole? It should ideally make clear the manner in which, in our kind of writing, social necessity is consonant with humanity's deep longing for perfection, for an all-encompassing development of the personality. . . . Here, in our awareness of historical necessity, of the true humanity of our struggle, are to be found the sources of our confidence in victory').[9] The constant factor in all her poetic development is her adherence to an ideal of humanity which is as strong in *Kassandra* as it is here. In the process of maintaining this, however, most of her other early convictions about literature have gone by the board, the desirability of presenting a 'closed world-view' and the belief in 'historical necessity' prominent among them.

Her first published fiction, *Moskauer Novelle* (1961), was written in 1959. Described by the East German critic Peter Gugisch as 'an exemplary gesture towards maintaining German–Soviet friendship', the story endeavours to come to terms with German guilt for the past by working through the complications of an abortive love affair between Vera, an East German pediatrician visiting Moscow, and Pawel, a former officer in the Soviet occupation forces and now an interpreter.[10] In addition to the guilt she bears as a German, Vera also bears some responsibility for the accident which has prevented Pawel from realising himself as a doctor. Its modest scope and marked sentimentality makes the *Moskauer Novelle* fall far short of Christa Wolf's own vision of East German literature at the time and it resembles instead some of the works of others she criticised harshly in print.[11] Looking back on the story in 1973, she castigates her own timidity in dealing with potentially explosive issues and her unwillingness to explore emotional ambiguities.[12] She also deplores the 'closedness' of the structure and the 'clockwork' quality of the plot (*LS*, 62 & 60).

When her first novel, *Der geteilte Himmel*, appeared in 1963, the initial East German reviews were in the main hostile. Heinrich

9. Christa Wolf, 'Popularität oder Volkstümlichkeit?', *Neue Deutsche Literatur* 4/1, 1956, p. 121f.; cf. Heinrich Mohr, 'Die zeitgemäße Autorin — Christa Wolf in der DDR', in Wolfram Mauser (ed.), *Erinnerte Zukunft* (Würzburg, 1985), p. 19ff.

10. Peter Gugisch, 'Christa Wolf', Hans Jürgen Geerts (ed.), *Literatur der DDR in Einzeldarstellungen* (Stuttgart, 1972), p. 402.

11. Heinrich Mohr, 'Die zeitgemäße Autorin', p. 25.

12. Ibid., p. 29.

Mohr has summarised the criticisms as: not portraying the 'national question' in terms of the class struggle; understating the role of the Party in the development of socialism; lacking direction for want of a positive hero; using narrative techniques likely to confuse the reader. But these negative voices soon gave way to official approval, as such prominent establishment critics as Alfred Kurella, Dieter Schlenstedt and Hans Koch, First Secretary of the Writers' Union, found it quite ideologically acceptable. Christa Wolf received the Heinrich Mann Prize the same year and also became a candidate for the Central Committee of the SED (Socialist Unity Party). This, in fact, marked a high point of approval of her and her writing by the regime; for by 1967 she was no longer on the list of candidates and, in the controversies which have surrounded each of her major works since, the attitudes of official literary circles have been equivocal or negative. She has, however, not lacked defenders from the East German literary establishment and even *Kassandra* received a long and sympathetic review from the eminent critic Hans Kaufmann in *Sinn und Form* (1984).

The success of *Der geteilte Himmel* with official circles can be attributed in large part to its seeming to fulfil the requirements of the programme enunciated at the Bitterfeld conference of 1959: that writers and artists should participate in the building of the socialist state by, in particular, experiencing the life of the workforce and reflecting workers' concerns directly in their artistic production. Moreover, it appeared to fit exactly the criteria of *Ankunftsliteratur* (the phase of writing in East Germany, so named in retrospect after the novel by Brigitte Reimann of 1961, *Ankunft im Alltag*) which succeeded *Aufbauliteratur.*[13] In the 1950s, the primary task of literature was seen as promoting the construction of the new social order; in the 1960s, there was a call to reflect a socialist society which had come of age. The ghosts of the past could be taken as exorcised, and instead the focus was to be on the everyday reality of the worker, in which conflicts were no longer taboo. While the solutions themselves remained unquestioned, it was open to portray more difficulties in achieving them than in the previous phase.

As in *Moskauer Novelle*, an abortive love affair occupies the centre of the stage. According to Christa Wolf's own testimony, the novel began as a story based on her own observations of life in a factory, but in this form lacked an 'Überidee' (or 'guiding principle') (*GE*, 33). This she clearly found in the issues surrounding the building of

13. Cf. Dieter Schlenstedt, 'Ankunft und Anspruch', Klaus Jarmatz *et al.* (eds.), *Kritik in der Zeit, Zweiter Band 1966–1975* (Halle/Leipzig, 1978), p. 57.

the Berlin Wall in 1961, to which her stated attitude was entirely positive. The plot takes the form of the main character's reflections on the events which have led to the end of her relationship with Manfred, a chemist who has fled to the West, and to what appears to be her own attempted suicide. The critical moment occurs in West Berlin when she renounces Manfred in favour of a return to socialism, but subsequent events show the cost of her decision in emotional terms.

There is little disagreement in academic criticism on the novel that its positive socialist character is more apparent than real. While Rita does her best to affirm the sacrifice she has made, her own interactions with figures representative of socialism are on the whole less convincing than Manfred's disaffection with the system. John Milfull has suggested that Manfred is basically no more than a projection of Rita's difficulties in coming to grips with reality and other critics have argued that her process of reflection still leaves her strangely passive and dependent on external influences.[14] In terms of the model of possibility/impossibility we have proposed, it is certainly made clear what values are meant to represent which of the polarities, but what is lacking is any convincing mediation of them. In a way that anticipates all Christa Wolf's later works, self-realisation is shown to be a problem that resists all the pragmatic solutions available, whether these be joining Manfred in the West or reintegration into socialist society. Prophetic also is the mythicising of nature in the novel which tends to create epiphanies of feeling that short-circuit the reflective process. Furthermore, by standing in opposition to the drabness of contemporary urban existence, nature in *Der geteilte Himmel* becomes the prototype of those later idyllic settings which are at once escapist and oppositional, such as the utopian community of women on the banks of the Scamander in *Kassandra*.

In the twentieth-century German novel, there appears to be a strong correlation between complication of the narrative perspective and emotional rejection of the narrative present, beginning with Rilke's *Die Aufzeichnungen des Malte Laurids Brigge* (1910). There it is the mistrust of the present as a basis from which one can meaningfully progress that makes the difficulties of narrating even the most recent past seem insuperable: 'Daß man erzählte, wirklich erzählte, das muß vor meiner Zeit gewesen sein' ('The days when stories

14. John Milfull, 'Die Literatur der DDR', Viktor Žmegač (ed.), *Geschichte der Deutschen Literatur vom 18. Jahrhundert bis zur Gegenwart*, vol. III/2 (Königstein/Ts., 1984), p. 625.

could be told, could really be told, must have been before my time').[15] If one may see in *Der geteilte Himmel* some correlation between the complication, in East German terms, of narrative technique and the ambivalences which undermine the dogmatic socialist perspective, then her next work, *Nachdenken über Christa T.* (1968), makes the connection quite explicit. For the novel is full of agonising over the dangers of fiction's manipulating and falsifying human reality, and it singularly fails to reconcile either the main character or the reader with the present dimension of the plot.

The novel sets out to explore a life that is not so much impossible as unfulfilled, but does so in a way which raises wider questions as to the possibility or impossibility of existence — largely because of the extremely problematical relationship of the unnamed narrator to the main character Christa T. Critics continue to disagree as to the extent to which the narrator can be identified with Christa Wolf and the author has deliberately blurred the issue. The issue is, in fact, of minor importance for an understanding of the novel itself; it only becomes significant once one tries to analyse the concept of personal authenticity, which from *Nachdenken über Christa T.* onwards becomes dominant in all her theoretical statements, replacing the orthodox concept of 'Parteilichkeit' ('partisanship').[16] What is important for understanding the novel, as the author herself has said, is to grasp the relationship between the narrator and Christa T. as two characters within a fiction (*LS*, 51f.).

The narrator, who has known Christa T. since their schooldays, sets out to reconstruct, with frequent intervals of reflection, her friend's life up to her death from leukaemia at the age of thirty-five in the year 1963. Her task is described as problematical in various ways: firstly, 'die Farbe der Erinnerung trügt' ('the colour of memory is deceptive') (*N*, 79), the net which the narrator has fashioned and cast to capture the figure of her dead friend may be of no use (*N*, 114); secondly, Christa T. is at the mercy of the narrator — 'Ich verfüge über sie' ('I have power over her') (*N*, 7) — who can arbitrarily determine what is spoken of and what is suppressed (*N*, 46); thirdly, there are the ambivalent feelings which Christa T. arouses, in life and in death, among those who know her, making Gertrud Dölling insecure (*N*, 49) and the narrator at times strongly resentful: 'Das ist mein Grund, über sie zu sprechen. Erbitterung aus Leidenschaft' ('That is my reason for speaking about her.

15. Rainer Maria Rilke, *Sämtliche Werke*, ed. Ernst Zinn, vol. 6 (Frankfurt, 1966), p. 844.

16. Cf. Edward Mozejko, *Der sozialistische Realismus* (Bonn, 1977), pp. 86–92.

Resentment arising from a passionate involvement') (*N*, 128); fourthly, the hiatus of her untimely, senseless death tempts the narrator to invest her life with a meaningfulness of which the reader may well remain unconvinced ('but as there is no ending, just this senseless misfortune, it seems one can only attempt to extend the lines of the life she has abandoned') (*N*, 120); finally, both Christa T. and the narrator experience moments of illumination or discovery — 'Christa T. hat . . . eine große Entdeckung gemacht, . . . doch ohne zu wissen, daß sie groß war' ('Christa T. made a great discovery, but without realising that it was great') (*N*, 87) — which place a good deal of strain on the pretence that they are separate persons.

With such a degree of complication in the narrative perspective, it is little wonder that there has been no consensus in the reception of the work in East and West Germany as to what message, in terms of social criticism, it was intended to convey. The lack of a clear, socialist solution to the dilemmas posed by Christa T. and the narrator drew from Max Walter Schulz, Director of the 'Johannes R. Becher' Literary Institute, at the sixth Writers' Congress (1969), the charge that the book was conducive to resignation: 'So wie die Geschichte nun einmal erzählt ist, ist sie angetan, unser Lebensbewußtsein zu bezweifeln . . . , ein gebrochenes Verhältnis zum Hier und Heute und Morgen zu erzeugen. — Wem nützt das?' ('As it is told, the story is likely to call our positive attitude to life into question . . . , to undermine our ability to relate to the here and now, and the future. — What good does that do anyone?').[17] Certainly the present is consistently devalued in the novel and there are some unflattering observations on life in socialist society. When Christa T. and the narrator meet again at university in the early 1950s, they share an awareness of the lack of alternatives this society offers (*N*, 29); later there is some ironic comment on the supposed perfection of the social apparatus, for the sake of which no sacrifice is too great, even the extinction of the individuality (*N*, 57); Christa T.'s last project, the building of her own house, is made in one passage close to the end of the book into a symbol of her alienation from society (*N*, 149).

But the problem is really more complex than this. Such concrete demands as Christa T. actually makes of her society are in the main met: she can exchange life as a village school-teacher for a relatively untrammeled life as a student; her marriage to Justus is initially a source of great happiness — 'Sie schuf sich noch mal neu . . ., das war

17. Max Walter Schulz, 'Das Neue und das Bleibende in unserer Literatur', quoted in Mohr, 'Die zeitgemäße Autorin', p. 34.

beileibe keine Mühe, sondern das größte irdische Vergnügen' ('She created herself anew . . ., that was by no means an effort but the greatest of earthly delights') — and the marriage seems to have a renewed validity in her last years (*N*, 120); before her death, she has created, in her house, her own private sphere and she seems on the verge of becoming a writer. None the less, there is a certain amorphousness about such positive social values as the text endorses, but this does not mean they are located by implication in the West either. In fact, the problem lies in the way in which self-realisation is defined for Christa T. by the narrator. She is credited with a vision of herself (*N*, 114), with a potential richness and greatness that remains unrealised (*N*, 132), with embodying infinite possibilities for others as well (*N*, 161). But such claims are virtually impossible to verify from the text itself. It is hard to believe, for example, that her inner life has the scope and versatility the narrator claims for it: 'wie sie viele Leben mit sich führte, . . . so führte sie mehrere Zeiten mit sich, in denen sie wie in der "wirklichen" teilweise unerkannt lebte, und was in der einen unmöglich ist, gelingt in der anderen' ('Just as she had many different lives within her, she also had many different times, and in these she partly lived "incognito" as she did in "real" time, and what is impossible in the one works out in the other') (*N*, 170).

The real impossibility in the novel, and one which is not easy to understand, is ultimately that of the narrator's becoming the full character which she is by implication. There seems to be a strange taboo on her talking about herself except in relation to Christa T., and the effect of this is that she projects a good deal onto the figure of her dead friend which sits rather uncomfortably. In fact the narrator seems to want to become the 'other' of herself, as the text strongly implies in the following two passages. The first instance occurs when the impending separation of the narrator from Christa T. is seen as a division of the self: 'Und daß uns kurz bevorstand, uns verlorenzugehen: einander und jeder sich selbst . . ., bis zu einem Augenblick, da dieses fremde Ich zu mir zurückkehren und wieder in mich eingehen wird' ('And that we were shortly to lose contact with each other and ourselves . . ., until a moment comes when this alien self will return and become part of me again') (*N*, 18). The second passage, in which this theme emerges significantly, links the possibility of otherness with the tensions between East and West: 'Den Schnitt machen zwischen "uns" und "den anderen", in voller Schärfe, endgültig: das war die Rettung. Und insgeheim wissen: Viel hat nicht gefehlt, und kein Schnitt hätte "das andere" von uns getrennt, weil wir selbst anders gewesen wären. Wie aber trennt man sich von sich selbst? Darüber sprachen wir nicht. Aber sie wußte es' ('To make the distinction between "us" and "the others", with complete intransigence, irrevocably: that way lay salvation. And yet to know inside: not much more needed to happen and not one step would have separated us from "otherness", because we would ourselves have changed. But how do you divide off from yourself? We never spoke of this. But she knew it') (*N*, 30).

This passage could stand as a motto for her next novel, *Kindheitsmuster* (1976), the main subject of which is a childhood and adolescence in the Third Reich. The novel also includes two dimensions of the narrative present: the one recounts a visit to Poland by the narrator and her family in 1972 and the other mirrors the composition of the novel itself, with many reflections on the problematics of fiction and the relation of present to past. The last segment of the novel is dated 2 May 1975, three days after the end of the war in Vietnam. As in *Nachdenken über Christa T.*, the relation between the narrator and her material is complicated by the question of otherness. In political terms, this is inevitable, since there can be no simple identification with a childhood spent under Nazism. If one of the criticisms made by Max Walter Schulz of her previous novel was that it failed to recognise the past of the Third Reich had been effectively dealt with by the socialist present, *Kindheitsmuster* shows Christa Wolf's determination to contradict this attitude, as summarised by her quoting with approval Freud's maxim: 'Wer sich seiner Vergangenheit nicht erinnert, ist dazu verdammt, sie zu wiederholen' ('He who does not remember his past is condemned to repeat it') (*KM*, 251).

In exploring the childhood of Nelly Jordan, Christa Wolf explicitly rejects the practice of projecting all negativity onto 'the others'. Reconstructing the development of Nelly's identity, she confronts directly the issue of the childhood self's adaptation to a system which the adult personality must reject. She is far from succumbing to the temptation to present this as one brutalisation after another, and maintains the credibility of the character by allowing the childhood talent for dissimulation to go for long stretches uncensured by the ideological strictures of the present. While she frankly declares her projected narration to be a 'Such- und Rettungsaktion' ('a search and rescue operation') (*KM*, 13), she is nevertheless so nervous of evoking the past in too glowing or sombre colours that she hardly succeeds in resurrecting anything of the essential anarchic feelings of childhood. An incident from the autumn of 1943, in which Nelly, to the narrator's own discomfiture, maintains a steady indifference towards the Ukrainian women she is working with in the fields, is typical of her emphasis on the neutrality of which the adolescent self is capable:

> Was sie den Fremden gegenüber empfand, war nicht Mitleid, sondern Scheu, ein starkes Gefühl von Anderssein . . . Wäre ihr die Idee gekommen, aufzustehen, über den Abgrund von dreißig Schritten zu den Ostarbeiterinnen zu gehen, . . . und einer von ihnen den eigenen Essennapf zu geben, in dem Fleisch schwamm? Das schauerliche Geheimnis: Nicht, daß es nicht gewagt, sondern daß es gar nicht gedacht wurde. (*KM*, 232)

> (What she felt towards the foreigners was not pity, but fear, a strong feeling of alienation . . . Would it ever have occurred to her to get up, to walk the thirty paces across the abyss separating her from the workers from the East . . ., and to give one of them her own bowl of soup in which there were pieces of meat? The dreadful secret: not that she didn't dare do it, but that she hadn't even thought of it).

Critical responses to the novel have seen it as out of proportion or deficient in a variety of ways. In East Germany, Annemarie Auer engaged in a long, polemical *Gegenerinnerung* in *Sinn und Form* (1977) in which she deplored the absence of figures representing the anti-Nazi resistance and the consequent implication that Nelly's development, untouched by the spirit of resistance to Hitler, was typical.[18] Other evaluations of the work have seen the issue of self-censorship as avoided rather than solved, questioned the need for the quantity of narrative self-consciousness and its frequent repetitions, castigated the flatness of the characterisation apart from Nelly and her parents and registered a loss of narrative immediacy through the obtrusiveness of the ordering process.

To us the main deficiency in the novel seems to stem from one of the implications of its title. Christa Wolf has emphasised the experimental connotations of the word 'Muster' — 'pattern' in the sense of a model to be tried out (*KM*, 39) —, but the more basic sense of a patterning of the individual through childhood experiences poses problems for a work bent on realising an ideal of authenticity (*KM*, 151, 153, 155, 156, etc.). For there is a real need for the novel to scrutinise the detailed consequences of this patterning for the adult personality, and this is not answered by the endless questionings of the probity of narration itself. When it comes to the further questions of how such patterns may have persisted in German society and been confronted in the post-war decades, the reader is left with

18. Annemarie Auer, 'Gegenerinnerung', *Sinn und Form*, 4, 1977, pp. 847–78.

little to go on but the narrator's intense anxiety. Given that this does nothing to offset the aura of inevitability which surrounds Nelly's apparently normal development, we are left wondering just what alternatives, socialist or otherwise there might be, and this is not helped by the narrator's reticence in pursuing her own relationship with Lenka, her daughter.

Wolfgang Emmerich, in his account of East German fiction of the 1970s, sees a general loss of the belief in a non-antagonistic relationship between the individual and society and a tendency towards constructing self-conscious narratives that must remain incomplete, as *Kindheitsmuster* indeed does.[19] Even before the exclusion of the poet Wolf Biermann in 1976 and the subsequent hardening of attitudes on both sides, the problem of self-realisation tends to be posed in more insistent terms than previously and even the negative resolution of it that an incomplete story represents is cleary preferable to a formula which is too general to impress one as authentic.

While criticism cannot ignore the contradictions in Christa Wolf's works which appear unintentional, they do not constitute grounds for undervaluing her achievement. Both *Nachdenken über Christa T.* and *Kindheitsmuster* are important novels because they give voice to the experience of a particular segment of the post-war generation in both Germanies, and this experience itself cannot help but be contradictory. If the reception of both novels in East and West comes to different conclusions about what message is being conveyed and what aspects are most or least successful, this does not alter the fact that the novels are landmarks, in the sense that they crystallise particular possibilities and impossibilities of coming to terms with present and past which have found a resonance among a wide readership in both Germanies.

In concrete political terms, *Kindheitsmuster* ends, despite everything, on a note of guarded optimism with the conclusion of the war in Vietnam. Christa Wolf's subsequent reaction to events following the exclusion of Wolf Biermann was, in her own words, the conviction that there was no longer any possibility of effecting any changes in the system as a writer, indeed of writing with one's back to the wall, and it was in this climate that she composed her next major work *Kein Ort. Nirgends* in 1977.[20]

19. Wolfgang Emmerich, 'Der verlorene Faden. Probleme des Erzählens in den siebziger Jahren' in P.U. Hohendahl and Patricia Herminghouse (eds.), *Literatur der DDR in den siebziger Jahren* (Frankfurt, 1983), pp. 168 and 171ff.

20. 'Kultur ist was gelebt wird. Gespräch mit Frauke Meyer-Gossau', in Klaus Sauer (ed.), *Christa Wolf. Materialienbuch* (Darmstadt and Neuwied, 1983), pp. 67f.

Kindheitsmuster is in a strict sense Christa Wolf's last novel to date. *Kein Ort. Nirgends*, which tells of a fictional encounter in the year 1804 between Karoline von Günderrode and Heinrich von Kleist, builds its plot around a single significant occurrence in the style of the classical German *Novelle*. Its structure has close affinities with Kleist's two *Novellen, Das Erdbeben in Chili* and *Die Verlobung in St. Domingo*.[21] The key to understanding the author's intentions in the story really has to be found in the essay on Günderrode, *Der Schatten eines Traumes* (1978), rather than in the story itself, as critics were not slow to point out. While *Kein Ort. Nirgends* is very tightly written and coherently structured, it makes even fewer concessions to the expectations of the average reader than *Kindheitsmuster*. Read together with the essay, it makes a satisfactory whole, but the question remains whether Christa Wolf has ceased to find the form of the novel adequate to contain the range of perspectives she now finds essential. This is much the same point as she herself makes in her praise of the advantages of the letter form in her essay on Bettine von Arnim of 1979: 'Die Briefe, die Bettine und Karoline miteinander wechseln, erheben nicht den Anspruch, "Kunst" zu sein, und sind, als Buch, in ihrer Formlosigkeit eben jene Form, in der sie ihre Erfahrungen überliefern können, ohne sie deformieren zu müssen. Keine der schon erfundenen Gattungen — nicht der Briefroman à la Werther, erst recht nicht der bürgerliche Roman hätten dazu ausgereicht' ('The letters which Bettine and Karoline exchange do not claim to be "art", but as a book — for all their lack of form —, they have precisely that form in which they can transmit their experiences without needing to distort them. None of the established genres, neither the epistolary novel *à la* Werther nor the conventional middle-class novel would have been adequate') (*LS*, 310).

Determining what genre *Kassandra* belongs to presents similar problems. When the story was published in East Germany in 1984, it was in a single volume with the four extended lecture-texts, published separately in West Germany in 1983 as *Vorassetzungen einer Erzählung: Kassandra*, preceding it. It is designated as an *Erzählung* rather than a novel. In the *Voraussetzungen*, discursive statements are mixed in with various narrative forms, such as an account of the author's stay in Greece, extracts from a working diary and a long letter to a friend. Here the foundations of a wide range of possible new versions of the myth are laid. Clearly, only some of these can be

21. Cf. Anthony Stephens, '"Die Verführung der Worte" — von *Kindheitsmuster* zu *Kassandra*', in Manfred Jurgensen (ed.), *Wolf, Darstellung — Deutung — Diskussion* (Berne, 1984), p. 137.

realised in the final narrative, whose closed nature contrasts markedly with the openness achieved in the *Voraussetzungen*. While much that Christa Wolf says in them would lead the reader to expect something like the later novels of Virginia Woolf, the story that is told adheres to the tragic ending of the myth and is both linear and convergent in its narrative technique. One explanation for this is that Christa Wolf has, in the *Voraussetzungen*, committed herself to taking the tragic pattern of the myth as a paradigm of the fate of women in history. Whereas much in her own narration, such as the feminist interlude on the banks of the Scamander, seems to demand a different kind of ending, to depart from the tragic conclusion may have seemed tantamount to a falsification of history. Such meaningfulness as there is in the life of Kassandra must therefore be extracted, by a process of reflection, from the impossibility of her final situation. As Sigrid Weigel points out, this makes her very like the type of heroine popular in German Classicism, which hardly coincides with the author's stated intentions (*V*, 89).[22] In our view, the fundamental conflict is between the different demands of the psychological portrait and the myth. Psychological elaboration is unavoidable, if the story is unfolded as a reflection on the past, and is essential for bringing the figure of Kassandra close to the reader.[23] However these improvisations cannot affect the ending of the myth, since this has already been reinforced by assigning it the status of historical inevitability. Trying to meet both sets of demands produces an unevenness in the narrative which has been widely castigated.[24]

It is necessary to conclude our discussion of Christa Wolf's work with some analysis of the concept of authenticity which she introduces in 1966 and which from 1968 onwards, with the publication of *Nachdenken über Christa T.* and the *Selbstinterview* in which she defends her position (*LS*, 51–5), becomes central to all her literary theory and evaluations. As we have shown elsewhere, the main difficulty of

22. Sigrid Weigel, 'Vom Sehen zur Seherin', p. 76.

23. Documentation, 108: 'Zuerst habe ich sechzig Seiten in der dritten Person geschrieben, dann habe ich gemerkt, daß es nicht das bringt, was ich wollte. Ich schrieb dann das ganze als Monolog, was eine größere Intensität und eine stärkere Identifizierung mit der Figur brachte, die sich vielleicht auf den Leser überträgt' ('First I wrote sixty pages in the third person; then I noticed that this did not achieve the effect I wanted. So I wrote the whole thing as a monologue, which resulted in a greater intensity and a stronger identification with the main figure — something that may well carry over to the reader').

24. For example: Werner Ross, *Die Welt*, 23 April 1983, p. 5; Reinhard Baumgart, *Der Spiegel*, 37/14, April 1983, p. 210; Walter Hinck, *Frankfurter Allgemeine Zeitung*, 23 April 1983; Sylvia Adrian, *Stuttgarter Zeitung*, 9 July 1983, p. 50.

using authenticity as a criterion is that it is for Christa Wolf, on the one hand, a distant goal towards which her writing aspires, while on the other it is a kind of essence whose presence or absence can be instantly detected in virtually any piece of writing.[25] As other critics have pointed out, this can lead to the effect that when her fictional characters embark on voyages of self-discovery they seem in very little doubt as to their destination, and this in turn undermines the credibility of the reflective process. Already in *Nachdenken über Christa T.* the narrator seems to know in advance what she will claim for the figure she is reconstructing, and in *Kassandra* the fact that the heroine narrates the story from a point just before her inevitable murder means that all possible developments are stigmatised as leading ultimately to this end.

Part of the difficulty stems from the fact that Christa Wolf has developed the concept in opposition to a number of different things: the increasing alienation of the individual from society; the structures of power, be they political, technocratic or partriarchal, which restrict self-realisation as she has come to define it; and the complicity of literature over the centuries in this process. Contrary to what critics such as Bernhard Greiner have said, authenticity is not simply an aesthetic principle but is rather a set of moral imperatives which extend beyond the sphere of art.[26] In point of fact, it means the importing into the realm of fiction of an ethical norm, requiring a renunciation of the narrator's traditional position of power *vis-à-vis* both the fictional characters and the reader. This leads to the setting up of various models of communication which, as Gerhard Neumann has shown, have in common the abdication of dominance.[27]

Communication of this kind necessarily involves a high degree of empathy, such as Christa Wolf praises in the dialogue between Bettine von Arnim and Karoline von Günderrode, or between Kassandra and Arisbe in her story, but when this is applied to the relation of reader to work, there is a tendency for the reader to have no vision beyond that of the main character, as also happens in *Kassandra*. *Kein Ort. Nirgends* is a more successful work in this respect because it presents a genuine dialogue between Kleist and Günderrode, and includes a third position as well, that of the narrator, thus offering the reader perspectives that are somewhat less convergent than in *Kassandra*. So one is left, in the case of Christa Wolf's last

25. Anthony Stephens and Judith Wilson, 'Entwurf einer Poetik', p. 34.

26. Bernhard Greiner, '"Mit dieser Erzählung gehe ich in den Tod": Kontinuität und Wandel des Erzählens im Schaffen von Christa Wolf' in *Erinnerte Zukunft*, p. 119.

27. Gerhard Neumann, 'Christa Wolf: *Kassandra*. Die Archäologie der weiblichen Stimme' in *Erinnerte Zukunft*, pp. 260f. and *passim*.

work to date, with the uneasy tension between the wide range of strongly critical perspectives offered in the *Voraussetzungen* and the narrowing of perspective in the story itself. While the principle of authenticity has met with a reasonably sympathetic reception in East Germany, Ursula Püschel, writing in *Neue Deutsche Literatur* (1979), has complained about what she sees as a restriction of freedom on the part of the reader by precisely this close-focusing. [28] While her criticism is explicitly aimed at the underdevelopment of the minor characters in *Kein Ort. Nirgends*, it certainly can also be applied to the story of Kassandra. Despite its undoubted good intentions and the successful fiction it has produced, there is some risk that the cult of authenticity, since it ultimately produces its own ideology, ends up by manipulating the reader. The problem of imposing a non-fictional criterion on fiction is in some ways similar to that of writing to ideological recipes, a difficulty that has beset East German literature from the outset. While Christa Wolf's position has become more and more oppositional over the last two decades and while she takes infinite pains to preserve an openness of experience, the danger of ideology is present as soon as any concept is built up, by sheer repetition, to mythical proportions.

If the concept of authenticity has been worked through to the point where it no longer seems susceptible of further development, it none the less remains essential as a guarantee of the value of her literary project in its present form, since it is its integrity which differentiates her own myth-making from that much more questionable sort which the Trojans in her *Kassandra* practise on the figure of Helen of Troy (*V*, 61 and *K*, 97f.). The attitudes expressed in the *Voraussetzungen* have taken her even further out of the mainstream of East German literature than the abnegation of historical progress in *Der Schatten eines Traumes*. What is clear is that the path she has taken has been determined by her sincere resolve to keep certain possibilities of self-realisation alive in her fiction, to guard against their being lost sight of in either of two German societies. The pessimism of *Kassandra* and the *Voraussetzungen* is very obviously a product of the deterioration of the political climate in Europe in the first year of Reagan's presidency, with the corresponding Soviet inflexibility offering no amelioration. It is not clear how the feminist position which she adopted at this time will develop. It may well come to dominate her responses to political and social realities. We began by presenting a model of possibility/impossibility, and it has become

28. Ursula Püschel, 'Zutrauen kein Unding, lieber kein Phantom', *NDL*, Heft 7, pp. 134, 136f.

evident that it is the devaluation both of the present and of the notion of historical progress as well that makes the impossibilities of existence come through more strongly in her fiction and those possibilities dearest to her be projected increasingly into a utopian or mythical dimension. Even so, what Ingeborg Bachmann called the 'Widerspiel des Unmöglichen mit dem Möglichen' ('the interaction of the impossible with the possible') is likely to remain one of the mainsprings of Christa Wolf's writing, for essentially it gives her room to move.

DAVID ROBERTS

Recent Developments in the German Novel

Any attempt to give an account of recent developments in the German-language novel is pulled in two directions. As necessary and desirable as is the interest in keeping abreast of the latest developments, it does tend to carry with it the uncritically 'progressive' implication that the most recent is the most significant. Against this the contrary tendency makes its claims: instead of seeking to trace some progressive and exclusive line of development, the need for an inventory which does justice to the range and multiplicity of contemporary writing asserts itself. Though each approach requires the other, for both are methods of orientation, it is hard to combine the two, the route and the map. While we are not likely to get lost on the well-mapped guides to tradition, it is another matter, however, when we arrive at the uncharted territory of the present. If literary history could be termed the verdict of the collective reader, this process of critical sifting is necessarily partial and provisional when it comes to recent developments. I therefore propose to attempt neither a route nor a survey map, but to complement the contributions on individual novelists by means of a typology, whose purpose is to indicate — however crudely — the basic narrative possibilities of the novel, a generic term which is used here to mean nothing more exact than an almost endlessly variable form, whose adaptability has made it the unchallenged narrative medium of modern society. Given this apparently unlimited variety, a typology represents a drastic reduction of complexity, whose function is to focus on the main options available to the novelist. If we take the individual and society as the subjective and objective poles of the novel, there are three basic possibilities of subject–object relations: (1) the emphasis on the subject as subject; (2) the emphasis on the subject as object; (3) the search for the mediation of subject and object, individual and society.

The individual stands in a double relation to himself and the world. The individual perceives himself as a person in the world, as one among many, as object among objects. At the same time the empirical individual is also the centre of his world, he is the subject *vis-à-vis* the world as a whole, that is, a subjectivity which is the source of meaning and unity to which the world as totality relates. From the perspective of the subject as centre the task is that of arriving at an understanding of the self and the world and thereby achieving autonomy. This is a hermeneutic process of self-reflection and self-consciousness. As empirical individual by contrast the self is the object of scientific investigation and description (sociological, psychological, etc.). How does this double relation relate to the basic possibilities of the novel? On the one side we have the scientific, experimental approach in which the individual is the object of observation. This is essentially a documentary method, its form is that of montage and its strategy is estrangement. Here the emphasis is on all that makes the subject object: the forces of social determination, including language. The document, e.g. preformed material, is both social and linguistic and it is but a further step to see language itself as the experimental object of literature. On the other side we have a literature of self-consciousness, which can range from free associations, diary entries, essayistic reflections, to the narrative history which gives unity and meaning to experience (the biographical and autobiographical form). Both opposed types of narrative naturally have their own subject–object dialectic — the cold, analytic prose of Alexander Kluge, for instance, is designed to provoke the subjectivity of the reader; conversely, the protocols of a unique consciousness can reveal the blind social and psychological determinations of an illusory autonomy. It is clear that each approach privileges the one pole at the expense of the other. The weakness of the objective method lies in its tendency to the behaviouristic reduction of the individual to an object of demonstration. The weakness of the literature of subjectivity is that of a self-consciousness which destroys itself by a process of endless reflection which nihilistically negates autonomy. Social and self-alienation are thus the two aspects of the individual, each points to the other and it is the task of the social and historical novel to find the story, the history and the form which can both objectify and subjectify the relation of individual and society. It must not be assumed, however, that the more ambitious intention of the social and historical novel makes it necessarily superior to the other two tendencies. Each of these three basic tendencies of our typology exists in its own right and requires no justification. Rather they are parallel possibilities which stand in a relation of mutual correction and criticism, a reminder of the complex plurality of empirical truths and subjective meanings, whose totality, the German Novel, is made up of thousands of individual works.

The second possibility — the emphasis on the subject as object — appears unlike the others to be a province particularly characteristic of the twentieth century. Kafka's *Der Prozeß* announces the inhumanity of our age of anxiety and alienation, in which the individual is reduced to impotence as the object of the anonymous forces of the state and the economy. In the face of forces which have become omnipresent and invisible, the realism or naturalism of the nineteenth-century novel has been felt inadequate, since it cannot penetrate beyond the façade of illusion. All the invocations of the crisis of the novel since the 1920s reflect precisely this power of society over the individual. Its complement in the 1920s and again in the 1960s were the proclamations of the end of 'bourgeois' literature, i.e. of a literature centred on the subject. When in 1954 Adorno characterised the situation of the novel by the paradox that narration has become impossible although the form of the novel demands narrative, he was directly relating the permanent crisis of the novel to the disappearance of the subject. For Adorno story-telling presupposes the individual who can give meaning to his experiences, whose identity is the guarantee that the mediation of the inner and outer world is possible.

The great German and Austrian novels of the 1920s and 1930s — from Kafka's posthumously published novels to Döblin's *Berlin Alexanderplatz*, Mann's *Der Zauberberg*, Broch's *Die Schlafwandler*, Canetti's *Die Blendung* and Musil's *Der Mann ohne Eigenschaften* — are all a response to this crisis which was of course grasped as a reflection of the crisis of bourgeois society and the bourgeois individual. And yet after 1945, after the total catastrophe this literature remained in exile. Whether scorned as decadent in the Communist East or honoured as modern classics in the capitalist West no continuity seemed possible across the caesura of total defeat ('Stunde Null'). It was not until the 1960s that a new literary generation emerged in the two Germanies and in Austria, whose presence has still not been decisively challenged. Apart from Weiss, Hochhuth and Heiner Müller for the drama or Enzensberger and Kunert for poetry, the preferred medium remains prose forms, and here major figures are Grass, Walser, Kluge, Lenz, Johnson, Wolf, Bernhard, to whom we must add such older writers as Stefan Heym, Frisch, Böll, Arno Schmidt and Helmut Heißenbüttel. These writers have maintained and reinforced their place over the last twenty-five years and are very much part of the contemporary scence, as witnessed for instance by Grass's new novel *Die Rättin*, Heißenbüttel's ongoing experimental texts, Kluge's latest collection of stories, the appearance of the fourth and final volume of Johnson's *Jahrestage*, Christa

Wolf's *Kassandra* or Bernhard's unfaltering productivity, as evidenced most recently by *Holzfällen* and *Alte Meister*.

The common experience of this 1960s' generation was of course the Third Reich and the war. The relation between individual and society was thus a moral and political question which had to be confronted in the form of coming to terms with the past. For the student revolt of the late 1960s the electoral victory of the SPD under Brandt in 1969 marked, however, the final end of the Adenauer era of restoration and reconstruction. The problems of contemporary industrial society and the accompanying growth of new social movements in the 1970s — ecology, feminism, alternative subcultures and most recently the vigorous revival of the peace movement — signalled a shift from the guilt of the past to the concerns of the present and anxiety about the future. In East Germany the construction of a new socialist society had demanded of the novelist an affirmative presentation of the relations between individual and society in the 1950s and 1960s. Only the end of the Ulbricht era with the advent of Honnecker in 1971 led to the (partial) acknowledgement of the reality of social conflicts, the belated and tentative exploration of continuities between the Nazi past and the 'real existing socialism' of the present and, parallel to developments in the West, a serious engagement with the rights of the individual and the whole problematic of subjectivity in a society regimented by collective pressures to conformity. The much celebrated return to the subject in the 1970s, as opposed to the political engagement of the 1960s, heralded by the slogans of *neue subjektivität* and of *Tendenzwende*, registered not only the reaction to the shocks of the student revolt but more importantly a significant and ongoing revision of ideological positions and values, for which the new social movements as the offspring of the New Left of the 1960s remain the most conspicuous manifestation. The bearers of this change of values were above all the student cohorts of the late 1960s and the early 1970s — a new literary generation in that they represented a mutation of social values and perceptions which fed back into the work of the older writers, but at the same time a generation largely lacking the strong individual profile of a Grass, Böll, Bernhard or Christa Wolf.

Turning now to recent developments: I understand 'recent' in the context of post-'68 developments, one important aspect of which has been the debates in the West on post-industrial society, post-material values, post-avant-garde art and post-modern philosophy and culture. None of these developments impacts directly on the basic possibilities of the novel but the questioning of the paradigms of production and progress in both East and West serves to underline the difficulties of tracing a 'progressive' route through the 1970s and 1980s, just as the post-modernist celebration of pluralism reminds us of the virtues of a typology as provisional compass and grid until the passage of time crystallises into the retrospective consensus of literary histories.

The *objective* tendency, in which the emphasis falls on the individual as object, rejects the autonomy of the subject as a fiction. Often labelled anti-humanist, this position is rather post-humanist in that it stresses the primacy of the system, of social, political and economic structures, of ideology and the all pervasive power of language. These forces determine and define individual consciousness and identity. It is therefore no longer possible to organise a narrative from the viewpoint of the subject. This has led to two very different responses, the sociological and the language experimental, which have both tended to dissolve the traditional narrative forms and structures of the novel into a montage of 'texts'. If we can speak of a common feature here between a documentary literature, whose interest is immediate social issues and which often presents itself as anti-literary, and the often esoteric texts of experimental writing, it lies in a shared perception of language as their common material, whether it takes the form of documents from the administered world or the linguistic repertoire of quotations and clichés which can be endlessly recycled. Two kinds of a post-subjective realism are indicated: one which appeals to the direct evidence of the document which speaks for itself, and one which demonstrates the inescapable prison of language, in which all originals are copies and both 'author' and reader are entrapped in a second-hand world of words. Although the documentary approach largely supports social engagement while experimental writing appears to reside in the ivory tower, both are involved in the critical project of enlightenment: the estrangement and deconstruction of the social and narrative structures which underpin the fictions of the subject.

Thus Reinhart Baumgart could argue in his 1967 Frankfurt Lectures on Poetics that the collapse of the stories of individual consciousness with their creation of a representative world out of experience and imagination has led to a new phase of the novel. The anonymity and abstraction of reality means that individual experience has been replaced by the blind world of information, narrative illusion by language and organic form by documentary montage. He sees this new phase of disenchantment best represented by a documentary literature which registers the reification of social and human relations through a new 'literal' objectivity. Heißenbüttel had likewise argued in his Frankfurt Lectures in 1963 that the history of the novel since Flaubert is that of the journey of the author into the isolation of subjectivity. The unbridgeable gulf between self and world has finally dissolved the ever subtler differentiation of the subject into language. Heißenbüttel and Baumgart both expound the common framework — the disappearance of the subject — underlying the social documentary and language experiments. At one extreme we have the enormously successful social reports of Günter Wallraff, at the other the hermetic universe of Arno Schmidt's idiosyncratic language creations, based on a phonetic etymology (*Zettels Traum*, 1970) and confined to a tiny community of admirers.

The reportages of Wallraff combine investigation and political agitation directed to the uncovering of the hidden practices of government, bureaucracy, industry and the media. Significant here is Wallraff's sustained campaign against the systematic manipulations of the mass circulation *Bildzeitung* in *Der Aufmacher* (1977), *Zeugen der Anklage* (1977) and *Das Bild-Handbuch* (1981). The reports, protocols and documentary montages, represented by such works as Erika Runge's *Bottroper Protokolle* (1981), F.C. Delius's satirical *Unsere Siemens-Welt* (1972) or by Maxie Wander's *Guten Morgen, du Schöne. Frauen in der DDR. Protokolle* (1977) and Rainer Kirsch's *Kopien nach Originalen* (1974) (in which we are given through curriculum vitae, interviews and documents, portraits of managers, planners and professionals functional to the spheres of material and ideological production in the German Democratic Republic) are far removed from the conventional fictional world of the novel. Their 'fictional' counterparts are the novels which present case-studies from the world of work, the office and the research laboratory, as in Walter Richartz's *Büroroman* (1976) and *Reiters Westliche Wissenschaft* (1981), or autobiographically based accounts of the individual's socially typical experience of subjection to his environment, as in the novels of the Austrian Gernot Wolfgruber. *Auf freiem Fuß* (1975) tells of a youth in a working-class milieu, *Herrenjahre* (1976) of a carpenter who is left after the death of his wife as a creature without identity, his consciousness possessed by the clichés of everyday language. *Niemandsland* (1978) shows the fate of an upwardly mobile worker who has become alienated from his background and is left in the no man's land of an 'individuality' in search of a new social mask. Compared with Wolfgruber's or Franz Innerhofer's authentic documents of life, Walter Kempowski, Alexander Kluge or Hans Magnus Enzensberger have sought for authenticity in the form of documentary fictions. Kluge's montage narratives — *Lebensläufe* (1962), *Schlachtbeschreibung* (1964), *Lernprozesse mit tödlichem Ausgang*

(1973) and *Neue Geschichten* (1977) — constitute the most interesting and productive endeavour to come to terms with the abstract reality of a world defined by the deformed functional logics of the division of labour with the concomitant fragmentation of the personality, and the systematic imperatives of, for instance, the military-industrial complex, ruled by the blind perspectives of specialists and experts. Kluge's montage technique involves not only a mosaic of materials but also a multiplicity of viewpoints which demand an active participation on the part of the reader. His 'work in progress' is a puzzle of perspectives and information which defies the possibility of reduction to meaning and form. Similarly, in *Der kurze Sommer der Anarchie* (1972) on the life and death of the Spanish anarchist Durruti, Enzensberger presents history as a collective fiction, an assembly of material open to interpretation by the reader.

The problem of self-consciousness and identity can also be tackled from the side of language. Handke's play *Kaspar* remains the most striking demonstration of the constitution of the world and the subject through the paradigms of language, which he followed up with the study of the disintegration of perception, thought — the relation of words and objects — and personality in *Die Angst des Tormanns* (1970), and refined in his (auto-)biographical study of his mother, *Wunschloses Unglück* (1973), in terms of a constant reflection on the formulas of biography applied to a life deprived of self-articulation. A radical attack on the domination of language and on the novel form itself is given in Oswald Wiener's 'wild' narrative *Die Verbesserungen von Mitteleuropa* (1968). Just as the novel is dissolved into a montage of essays, notes, digressions and appendices so the subject disappears into language. Wiener's scientific, cybernetic perspective serves, however, as the vehicle of anarchic protest, the desire to escape the constraints of language in the name of experience beyond all social and historical norms and predeterminations. This dialectic of (linguistic) predetermination and freedom, repetition and play is integral to the language-experimental texts of such writers as Heißenbüttel, Ror Wolf (*Fortsetzung des Berichts*, 1964, and *Die Gefährlichkeit der großen Ebene*, 1976), Helmut Eisendle (*Jenseits der Vernunft*, 1976) or Herbert Achtenbusch (*Alexanderschlacht*, 1971). With these writers we enter the textual world of parodistic quotation and the surrealism of random combination. Perhaps the most significant example of the substitution of quotation for narration is Heißenbüttel's exhaustive satirical inventory of the false consciousness of the times in his Project Number 1, *D'Alemberts Ende* (1970), in which the techniques of fragmentation and combination are employed to subvert habitual modes of reading (cf. also *Eichendorff's*

Untergang, 1978, and *Das Ende der Alternative*, 1980). The reader is declared sovereign, free to make what use he will of the linguistic montage. The formalisation of this elevation of the reader to co-producer (everyman his own surrealist) is undertaken by Andreas Okopenko in his *Lexikon-Roman* (1970) and *Meteoriten* (1976). As the title indicates, the lexical principle permits endless reading permutations.

The high point of documentary and experimental literature around 1970 echoed the political proclamations of the death of 'bourgeois' literature, but it is itself open to critical objections. At the one extreme the literature of reportage demands too little of the author, at the other extreme the experimental avant-garde texts demand too much of the reader. At its complex best, however, as in the work of Kluge and Heißenbüttel, it represents a challenging alternative to more traditional forms of narrative.

The 'new subjectivity' of the 1970s and beyond must be seen as a reaction to the instrumentalisation and formalisation of literature in the 1960s. The recoil from political engagement and from aesthetic experiment expressed itself in a renewed emphasis on individual experience. The new sufferings of Goethe's Werther (Ulrich Plenzdorf) or of Büchner's Lenz (Peter Schneider) showed that the old models of bourgeois subjectivity and the old existential questions of meaning and identity had not lost their relevance. Handke's formula of the 'inner world of the outer world' reminds us, however, that the inner world and the outer world form the split halves of a lost narrative totality. In this situation personal experience alone appeared to offer many writers the possibility of narration. Autobiography and biography present themselves as 'natural' forms of the search for meaning and identity, as a natural resistance to the disappearance of the subject. And so writing becomes a process of therapy, a means of producing the subject, but this very act of constitution threatens always to reverse into its opposite. The very emphasis on subjectivity can register disintegration as well as integration of the self because identity and alienation are inextricably entangled in the reflections of self-consciousness. Thus the literature of subjectivity tends to circle in the prison of a self-consciousness which consumes itself. The novels and stories of Thomas Bernhard relentlessly unfold this logic of disintegration. As with Werther, suicide becomes for Bernhard the ultimate paradoxical demonstration of the autonomy of the subject. The underlying melancholy, alienation and despair of much West German, Austrian and Swiss prose indeed presents the inner world of the outer world, but it is in the form of a deeply troubled return to the subject. Nevertheless, however much the subject is called into question, narration itself is not. Subjective fiction lives from the crisis of the subject. The quest for meaning and identity, whatever its outcome, is always a meaningful process, which invites empathy and identification from the reader. It would thus be mistaken to regard the resurgence of subjectivity since the early 1970s as a negative phenomenon, as no more than the narcissistic protocols of dissatisfied society in late capitalism, whose constant refrain is alienation. It is also the expression of the awareness that the subject is an end (in both senses of the word) and not means, that the existential cannot be evaded and a reassertion of the necessity of writing for self-discovery. The problematic of this literature lies not so much in its 'negativity' as in its abstraction. The everyday world of work remains the silent background to these journeys into the self or across empty landscapes in search of identity.

The journey can function as a metaphor of existence, as in Peter Rosei's *Von Hier nach Dort* (1978), or of the voyage into the unknown in his 'log-books' of imaginary expeditions in *Der Fluß der Gedanken durch den Kopf* (1976). It can be the break-out from the prison of work and marriage which leads through the dream reality of a Hollywood America to the moment of self-discovery 'in the chaos of an alienated world' in Gerhard Roth's novel *Der große Horizont* (1974), but equally this break-out can lead ever further into the icy isolation of a 'winter journey'. At the end of Roth's *Winterreise* (1978) the hero buys a one-way ticket to Alaska. And it is from Alaska that Handke's hero, a surveyor, sets out on his journey back to civilisation in the story *Langsame Heimkehr* (1979). Above all, the journey inward takes the form of the existential crisis which shatters the false self and its empty socialisation. The crisis can result in a new sense of identity with the familiar as for instance in Martin Walser's *Seelenarbeit* (1979), its outcome can be the relapse into the apathy of defeat, the surrender to the status quo (Otto Marchi's *Rückfälle*, 1978), again and again it sets free the urge to self-destruction, the longing for the end. Uwe Timm portrays 'the progressive loss of the meaning of life which threatens a whole generation' in his novel in diary form *Kerbels Flucht* (1980). Paul Nizon's *Stolz* (1975) traces the process of a 'progressive discontent and paralysis', which takes the hero into the vacuum of total isolation, whose end is death. This sense of living death finds brilliantly grotesque expression in Hermann Burger's *Schilten. Schulbericht zuhanden der Inspektorenkonferenz* (1976). The hero Peter Stirner (!), a teacher in an isolated Swiss village, reports to a higher instance on his failures as a pedagogue. The novel ends with him dictating to an empty classroom his obsessive fear of being buried alive. Widely recognised as representative of the pessimism and despair of the post-'68 generation in West Germany, Nicolas Born's *Die erdabgewandte Seite der Geschichte* (1976) is to be read as an 'annihilation of history', whether individual or collective or narrative (the novel within the novel). The three main figures struggle in vain with an all encompassing sense of meaninglessness which erodes all integrative feelings and values. Given such moods of disintegration and despair, it is easy to understand the fascination exerted by the exemplary figure of the artist for whom life and work fuse. Such an artist figure is the schizophrenic poet of Heinar Kipphardt's *März* (1976), who is brought back to life by a young psychiatrist after many years' incarceration in an asylum. More typical, however, are the tortured and tragic figures from the past who return to authenticate contemporary romantic sensibilities: Peter Härtling's biographical novels of Lenau and Hölderlin, Ludwig Harig's *Rousseau* (1978), Christa Wolf's fictional encounter between Kleist and Caroline Günderode in *Kein Ort. Nirgends* (1977), Jürg Amann's *Verirren oder Das plötzliche Schweigen des Robert Walser* (1978).

The figures in the novels of Roth or Rosei, Marchi or Born can neither live alone nor with others. A recurrent theme of this literature of threatened subjectivity is the failure of human relations. The disappointments of love, the separations, guilt and aggressions of the present — Handke's *Die linkshändige Frau* (1976), Hannelies Taschau's *Landfriede* (1978), Christoph Meckel's *Licht* (1978) or Botho Strauß's *Die Widmung* (1977) — find their retrospective complement in the attempts to understand the failures of relations between parents and children. Here one can point to the particular popularity of father portraits which are at the same time the autobiographical search for the roots of the present in the past, a past overshadowed by the Third Reich. Bernward Vesper's posthumously published *Die Reise* (1977) about his father, the Nazi poet, stands at the beginning of a whole series of (belated) subjective workings through of the past: Peter Henisch's *Die kleine Figur meines Vaters* (1975), Elizabeth Plessen's *Mitteilung an den Adel* (1976), Meckel's *Suchbild* (1980), Brigitte Schwaiger's *Lange Abwesenheit* (1980), Jutta Schutting's *Der Vater* (1980), Härtling's *Nachgetragene Liebe* (1980). By contrast we find in three of the writers of the 1960s' generation a determined effort to bridge the gap between the generations and between past and present by means of a dialogue between parents and children. Grass's *Aus dem Tagebuch einer Schnecke* (1972), Johnson's *Jahrestage* and Christa Wolf's *Kindheitsmuster* (1976) stand out as attempts to write against the obliteration of memory, the annihilation of history which haunted Nicolas Born.

The dialectic of alienation and self-discovery, central to the autobiographical literature of subjectivity, poses itself with particular urgency in feminist writing, one of the most socially significant developments since the early 1970s, for here the insistent question has been the search for a woman's voice, the need to cast off imposed identities and speak for oneself. Two important works of the older generation are Christa Wolf's autobiographical novel *Nachdenken über Christa T.* (1968) and Ingeborg Bachmann's monologic expression of alienation, *Malina* (1971). The real breakthrough came, however, with the radically subjective confessional writing of Karin Struck's, *Klassenliebe* (1973) and *Die Mutter* (1975), and the more consciously stylised programmatic commitment to feminism of Verena Stefan's *Häutungen* (1975). The difficulty of saying 'I', which has lent such an impetus to feminist fiction, has an additional literary-political dimension in the East German context. The struggle against patriarchy involves not only the search for personal identity but also social alternatives. With Irmtraud Morgner's *Leben und Abenteuer der Trobadora Beatriz nach Zeugnissen ihrer Spielfrau Laura* (1974), it takes the form of the vindication of the utopian rights of the imagination. The free associations of fantasy as the anticipation of the free association of individuals are celebrated through the form of her montage novel. In Helga Schubert's stories, *Das verbotene Zimmer* (1982), it takes the form of the defence of the private sphere, the free space of self-identity against the ever intrusive pressures and demands of the system. This search for alternatives has found its most anguished expression in Wolf's parable of war and peace, patriarchy and matriarchy, *Kassandra* (1983). This monologue of emancipation from the fateful logic of patriarchal domination — both East and West — is bitterly ironic: the 'I' which has found its voice is doomed to disbelief.

The tradition of the social novel in Germany, compared with its European counterparts, has been characterised more by its absence than its presence. The closed form and prescriptive fables of 'Socialist Realism', which dominated the East German novel into the 1960s, thus provided a model against which the critical presentations of 'real existing socialism' could articulate themselves. A comparable model was not available in the West. Despite the efforts of Böll, Lenz and Walser or, more recently, F.C. Delius in *Ein Held der inneren Sicherheit* (1981) and *Adenauerplatz* (1984), it seems that a polarised objectivity and subjectivity more adequately reflect the atomised realities of an over-complex functional society. The possibility of objectifying the interactions of the individual and society in typical, representative stories has a greater chance in the closed society of the German Democratic Republic (cf. Volker Braun, *Unvollendete Geschichte*, 1975) than in the West where the typical has become the contingent. The social novel, moreover, presupposes a certain social continuity which has been destroyed by the catastrophes of German history since 1914. Where the social novel in its traditional form could assume this continuity and thereby comprehend at the same time its present historically (*Buddenbrooks*), the social novel since 1945, if it is to have more than immediate reference, has been forced to undertake the task of reconstructing a shattered continuity and identity. The recovery of the past remains the fundamental concern of the founding post-war generation in both parts of Germany (Grass, Lenz, Kluge, Johnson, Wolf), the generation for which all origins and continuities were destroyed. Grass's Danzig trilogy or Horst Bienek's Silesian quartet — *Die erste Polka* (1975), *Septemberlicht* (1977), *Zeit ohne Glocken* (1979), *Erde und Feuer* (1982) — are requiems for the lost German provinces in the East. Wolf's *Kindheitsmuster* is in a double sense a journey, back to the child that she was and to the German town which is now Polish. The discontinuities of exile are compounded in the case of Uwe Johnson, who views the sunken world of childhood in Mecklenburg in the 1930s through the optic of a global consciousness, mediated by the daily reports of the *New York Times*.

In many ways *Kindheitsmuster* occupies a comparable place in East German literature to *Die Blechtrommel* in West German literature. The almost twenty years which separate them are indicative of the power of the official fiction of the *tabula rasa* ratified by the creation of a new socialist state. The new realism of the descriptions of East German society in the 1970s either could be published only in the West or were the products of enforced exile after the repressions in the wake of the expulsion of Wolf Biermann in 1976. Representative examples are: Jürgen Fuchs's *Gedächtnisprotokolle* (1977); Erich Loest's *Es geht seinen Gang* (1978); H.J. Schädlich's *Versuchte Nähe* (1979); Jurek Becker's *Schlaflose Tage* (1980); Thomas Brasch's *Vor den Vätern sterben die Söhne* (1979); and most recently Paul Gratzik's *Kohlenkutte* (1982); Günter de Bruyn's satire on the new class society of the Democratic Republic, *Neue Herrlichkeit* (1984); and Volker Braun's Faust-parody of masters and servants, *Der Hinze-Kunze-Roman* (1985). The new realism has been complemented by the breaking of the taboos on the Nazi past by the socialist present, as in Klaus Schlesinger's *Michael. Roman* (1971) or Hermann Kant's *Der Aufenthalt* (1979). In *Völkerschlachtdenkmal* (1984) Erich Loest traces from a proletarian perspective the dismal continuities of nationalism and militarism in terms of Saxony's history from 1813 to 1983 under Prussian domination.

If *Blechtrommel* and *Kindheitsmuster* remain the representative documents of the divided consciousness of the two Germanies in search of identity, Uwe Johnson is the one novelist who has succeeded in incorporating the consciousness of the division through his refusal to identify with either of the successor states to Hitler's Third Reich. It is precisely this refusal in the form of a double exile which defines the moral, political and historical consciousness of the dissident between East and West. The four volumes of his *Jahrestage* (1970–83) are an impressive attempt to find a form adequate to the demands of his material. The two narrative time levels — German and European history from the 1930s to the 1960s, and New York from December 1967 to August 1968 — are unified and refracted through the life and consciousness of the narrator Gesine Cresspahl. The novel thus provides the pre- and post-history to *Mutmaßungen über Jakob* (1959). There the Hungarian uprising of 1956 was the historical focus, here it is the extinction of the hopes of a reform of socialism through the crushing of the Czech search for a 'socialism with a human face'. But 1968 is also the year of student revolts and of the Vietnam war. German history is thus embedded in the conflicts of a divided Europe and a divided world, just as Gesine's life (born 1933, Johnson 1934) takes her from a village in Mecklenburg through East and West Germany to the metropolis of New York. The objective, documentary and fictional reconstruction of her past and of German history is accompanied by constant reflections on memory, guilt and identity, the knowledge that there is no 'moral Switzerland' to which the inhabitant of the twentieth century can migrate. Johnson's journey through our century into exile and premature death is complemented by the journey through time of the eternal rebel and dissident, the Wandering Jew of Stefan Heyms *Ashasver* (1981). The brutality and dogmatism of the earthly and heavenly authorities in Heym's baroque world theatre serve as the frame for a biting satire on the continuity of the German *Misere* from the theological persecutions of Luther's time to the 'scientific atheism' of the German Democratic Republic.

The typology employed here ignores national boundaries. If the Austrian, Swiss, East and West German novels have one language in common, they are shaped by very different presuppositions and histories. For Swiss writers the tradition of Keller's realism remains strong, for Austrian writers sensitivity to the creative and confining forces of language is particularly characteristic. In the two Germanies the pressing problems of the burden of history, of national identity and of social and political alternatives to the progress of capitalism or state socialist rationalisation form the background to a certain division of labour between the two systems. The political and social dimensions of the relationship between individual and society have been more surely grasped by writers from the GDR, as against the greater emphasis in the West on the isolation and alienation of the individual. It is this division which has made the German novel, especially since the 1960s, a fascinating reflection of the division of Europe. As the unresolved legacy of the Third Reich, the division of Germany continues to determine the parameters of historical consciousness, against which the writing of the 1970s and 1980s must define itself. This accounts in large part for the ongoing significance of the 1960s' generation, but also for the search for alternatives and the diversity of artistic and ideological tendencies of the present scene.

Select Bibliography

It is clearly not possible to give here an exhaustive bibliography of studies on the modern German novel or of analyses of the work of individual writers. The reader of German is in the fortunate position of having available to him or her *Germanistik* and the excellent *Kritisches Lexikon der deutschsprachigen Gegenwartsliteratur*, edited by Heinz Ludwig Arnold, which together provide more or less complete bibliographical information on ongoing work on the contemporary German novel and all of the individual writers examined in this volume, as well as on many more. The Modern Language Association of America's *International Bibliography of Books and Articles in the Modern Languages & Literatures* and the Modern Humanities Research Association's *The Year's Work in Modern Languages* can also be recommended as keeping readers abreast of new publications in these areas. Given these excellent sources of information, such studies of authors as are listed are aimed at those without German; the desperate lack of works in English on leading German novelists is clearly visible in the shortness of this list.

General studies of modern German literature, including the novel

Arnold, H.L., and T. Buck (eds.), *Positionen im deutschen Roman der sechziger Jahre* (Munich, 1974)

Bance, Alan, *The German Novel 1945–1960* (Stuttgart, 1980)

Batt, Kurt, *Die Exekution des Erzählers* (Frankfurt, 1972)

Blamberger, Günter, *Versuch über den deutschen Gegenwartsroman: Krisenbewußtsein und Neubegründung im Zeichen der Melancholie* (Stuttgart, 1985)

Bullivant, Keith, *Realism Today* (Leamington Spa and New York, 1987)

—— (ed.), *German Literature of the Seventies: Writers and Themes* (Leamington Spa and New York, forthcoming)

——, and H.J. Althof (eds.), *Subjektivität — Innerlichkeit — Abkchr von Politischen?* (Bonn, 1986)

Durzak, Manfred, *Der deutsche Roman der Gegenwart: Entwicklungstendenzen und Voraussetzungen*, 3rd. edn. (Stuttgart, 1979)

—— (ed.), *Deutsche Gegenwartsliteratur* (Stuttgart, 1981)

Eisele, Ulf, *Die Struktur des modernen deutschen Romans* (Tübingen, 1984)

Flood, John L. (ed.), *Modern Swiss Literature: Unity and Diversity* (London, 1985)

Hage, Volker, *Die Wiederkehr des Erzählers? Neue deutsche Literatur der siebziger Jahre* (Frankfurt, 1981)

Hamburger, Michael, *After the Second Flood: Essays on Post-war German literature* (Manchester, 1986)

Hermand, Jost, *Literatur nach 1945* (Wiesbaden, 1979)

Hinton Thomas, R., and W. van der Will, *The German Novel and the Affluent Society* (Manchester, 1968)

—— and K. Bullivant, *Literature in Upheaval* (Manchester, 1974)

Jurgensen, Manfred, *Deutsche Frauenautoren der Gegenwart* (Berne, 1983)

Koebner, Thomas (ed.), *Tendenzen der deutschen Literatur seit 1945* (Stuttgart, 1971)

Lützeler, P. M. and E. Schwarz (eds.), *Deutsche Literature in der Bundesrepublik seit 1965* (Königstein, 1980)

Marckwardt, Ulf-Heiner, *Der deutsche Schelmenroman der Gegenwart* (Cologne, 1984)

Ryan, Judith, *The Uncompleted Past: Post-war German Novels and the Third Reich* (Detroit, 1983)

Tate, Dennis, *The East German Novel: Identity, Community, Continuity* (Bath and New York, 1984)

Trommler, Frank (ed.), *Interpretationen zum Roman in der DDR* (Stuttgart, 1980)

Vormweg, Heinrich, 'Prosa in der Bundesrepublik seit 1945', Dieter Lattmann (ed.), *Die Literatur der Bundesrepublik Deutschland* (Munich, 1973), pp. 141–343

Wagener, Hans (ed.), *Gegenwartsliteratur und drittes Reich: Deutsche Autoren in der Auseinandersetzung mit der Vergangenheit* (Stuttgart, 1977)

Wallace, I. (ed.), *The Writer and Society in the GDR* (Tayport, 1984)

Weber, Norbert, *Das gesellschaftlich Vermittelte der Romane österreichischer Autoren seit 1970* (Frankfurt, 1980)

Individual authors

Butler, Michael, *The Novels of Max Frisch* (London, 1976)

Conard, Robert C., *Heinrich Böll* (Boston, 1981)

Ezergailis, I., *Women Writers: the Divided Self. Analysis of Novels by Christa Wolf, Ingeborg Bachmann, Doris Lessing and Others* (Bonn, 1982)

Hayman, Ronald, Günter Grass (London, 1985)

Hollington, Michael, *Günter Grass: The Writer in a Pluralist Society* (London & Boston, 1980)

Lawson, Richard H., *Günter Grass* (New York, 1984)

Leonard, Irène, *Günter Grass* (Edinburgh, 1974)

Minden, M.R., *Arno Schmidt* (Cambridge, 1982)

Murdoch, B., and M. Read, *Siegfried Lenz* (London, 1978)

Pender, Malcolm, *Max Frisch. His Work and its Swiss Background* (Stuttgart,

1979)
Reddick, John, *The 'Danzig' Trilogy of Günter Grass* (London, 1975)
Reid, J.H., *Heinrich Böll* (Leamington Spa and New York, 1987)
Schlueter, June, *The Plays and Novels of Peter Handke* (Pittsburgh, 1981)

About the Contributors

Keith Bullivant: Reader in German Studies, University of Warwick. Publications on German literature and thought in the nineteenth and twentieth centuries, including *Literature in Upheaval* (1974, with R.H. Thomas) and *Realism today* (Berg Publishers, 1987).

Gordon Burgess: Lecturer in German, Aberdeen University. Publications on seventeenth-century and contemporary German literature.

Gerald Fetz: Associate Professor, Department of Foreign Languages & Literatures, University of Montana. Publications on Austrian literature, esp. Thomas Bernhard, and the modern historical drama.

Michael Linstead: sometime Lecturer in German at University College Dublin and Lancaster University. Publications on Peter Handke and on contemporary British literature.

Moray McGowan: Lecturer in German, University of Strathclyde. Numerous articles on German literature of the twentieth century.

Malcolm Pender: Lecturer in German, University of Strathclyde. Publications include *Max Frisch: His Work and its Swiss Background* (1979) and numerous articles on German-Swiss literature.

Anthony Phelan: Lecturer in German Studies, University of Warwick. Publications include *The Weimar Dilemma: Intellectuals in the Weimar Republic* (1984) and numerous articles on German literature from the eighteenth to the twentieth centuries.

J.H. (Hamish) Reid: Reader in German, University of Nottingham, Publications include *Heinrich Böll: Withdrawal and Re-emergence (Oswald Wolff,* 1973); *Heinrich Böll: A German for his Time* (Berg Publishers, 1987); and numerous articles on post-war East and West German literature.

David Roberts: Reader in German, Monash University. Publications include *Artistic Consciousness and Political Consciousness: The Novels of Heinrich Mann 1900-1938* (1971), *Tendenzwenden* (1984) and numerous articles on modern German literature.

Simon Ryan: Lecturer in German, University of Auckland.

Anthony Stephens: Professor of German, University of Adelaide. Publications include *Rainer Maria Rilke's 'Gedichte an die Nacht'* (1972); *Rilke's 'Malte Laurids Brigge'* (1974); *Nacht, Mensch und Engel: Rilke's Gedichte an die Nacht* (1978); and numerous articles on German literature of the nineteenth twentieth centuries.

Dennis Tate: Lecturer in Modern Languages, University of Bath. Publications include *The East German Novel: Identity, Community, Continuity* (1984) and various articles on GDR literature.

Noel Thomas: Professor of Modern Languages. University of Salford. Publications include *The Narrative Works of Günter Grass — a Critical Interpretation* (1983) and numerous articles on contemporary West German literature.

Wilfried van der Will: Senior Lecturer in German, University of Birmingham. Publications include *Pikaro heute* (1967); *The German Novel and the Affluent Society* (1968, with R.H. Thomas); *Arbeiterkulturbewegung in der Weimarer Republik* (1982, with R.A. Burns); and numerous articles on German culture since the eighteenth century.

Anthony Waine: Lecturer in German Studies, Lancaster University. Publications include *Martin Walser: The Development as Dramatist* (1978) and *Martin Walser* (1980, 'Autorenbücher').

Alfred D. White: Senior Lecturer in German, University College Cardiff. Publications include *Bertolt Brecht's Great Plays* (1978) and articles on German literature of the twentieth century.

Juliet Wigmore: Lecturer in Modern Languages, University of Salford.

Rhys Williams: Professor of German, University College Swansea. Publications include *Carl Sternheim: A Critical Study* (1982) and numerous articles on twentieth-century German literature.

Edited by KEITH BULLIVANT

The MODERN GERMAN NOVEL

There is at present no standard work in English on the modern German novel; this carefully composed collection of essays by scholars from Britain, the United States and Australasia has been designed to remedy this situation. The volume includes general analyses of the modern and contemporary novel in the various German-speaking countries (West Germany, the GDR, Switzerland and Austria) and of the individual work of the important novelists in these areas. The period since 1945 has been a most productive one for the German novel, but it is not well known in the English-speaking world. This first up-to-date survey affords an excellent introduction to this subject area for all students of German literature; at the same time, since quotations are given throughout in both German and English, it aims to acquaint a general readership with the richness of the contemporary German novel.